Contemporary African Political Economy

Series Editor

Eunice N. Sahle, University of North Carolina Chapel Hill, Chapel Hill, NC, USA

Series Editor Eunice N. Sahle is Associate Professor with a joint appointment in the Department of African, African American and Diaspora Studies and the Curriculum in Global Studies at the University of North Carolina at Chapel Hill, USA.

Advisory Board: Bertha O. Koda, University of Dar es Salaam, Tanzania, Brij Maharaj, University of KwaZulu-Natal, South Africa, Cassandra Veney, United States International University-Africa, Kenya, Fidelis Edge Kanyongolo, Chancellor College, University of Malawi, Law School, Malawi, John Pickles, the University of North Carolina at Chapel Hill, USA, Rita Kiki Edozie, University of Massachusetts, Boston, USA, Willy Mutunga, Office of Former Chief Justice and President of the Supreme Court, Nairobi, Kenya, and Wisdom J. Tettey, University of Toronto, Canada. Contemporary African Political Economy (CAPE) publishes social science research that examines the intersection of political, social, and economic processes in contemporary Africa. The series is distinguished especially by its focus on the spatial, gendered, and cultural dimensions of these processes, as well as its emphasis on promoting empirically situated research. As consultancy-driven work has emerged in the last two decades as the dominant model of knowledge production about African politics and economy, CAPE offers an alternate intellectual space for scholarship that challenges theoretical and empirical orthodoxies and locates political and economic processes within their structural, historical, global, and local contexts. As an interdisciplinary series, CAPE broadens the field of traditional political economy by welcoming contributions from the fields of Anthropology, Development Studies, Geography, Health, Law, Political Science, Sociology and Women's and Gender Studies. The Series Editor and Advisory Board particularly invite submissions focusing on the following thematic areas: urban processes; democracy and citizenship; agrarian structures, food security, and global commodity chains; health, education, and development; environment and climate change; social movements; immigration and African diaspora formations; natural resources, extractive industries, and global economy; media and socio-political processes; development and globalization; and conflict, displacement, and refugees.

Kennedy Mbeva · Reuben Makomere ·
Joanes Atela · Victoria Chengo · Charles Tonui

Africa's Right to Development in a Climate-Constrained World

palgrave
macmillan

Kennedy Mbeva
Blavatnik School of Government
University of Oxford
Oxford, UK

Reuben Makomere
Africa Research and Impact Network
(ARIN)
Nairobi, Kenya

Joanes Atela
Africa Research and Impact Network
(ARIN)
Nairobi, Kenya

Victoria Chengo
Africa Research and Impact Network
(ARIN)
Nairobi, Kenya

Charles Tonui
Africa Research and Impact Network
(ARIN)
Nairobi, Kenya

ISSN 2945-7351 ISSN 2945-736X (electronic)
Contemporary African Political Economy
ISBN 978-3-031-22886-5 ISBN 978-3-031-22887-2 (eBook)
https://doi.org/10.1007/978-3-031-22887-2

© The Editor(s) (if applicable) and The Author(s), under exclusive license to Springer
Nature Switzerland AG 2023
This work is subject to copyright. All rights are solely and exclusively licensed by the
Publisher, whether the whole or part of the material is concerned, specifically the rights
of translation, reprinting, reuse of illustrations, recitation, broadcasting, reproduction on
microfilms or in any other physical way, and transmission or information storage and
retrieval, electronic adaptation, computer software, or by similar or dissimilar methodology
now known or hereafter developed.
The use of general descriptive names, registered names, trademarks, service marks, etc.
in this publication does not imply, even in the absence of a specific statement, that such
names are exempt from the relevant protective laws and regulations and therefore free for
general use.
The publisher, the authors, and the editors are safe to assume that the advice and information in this book are believed to be true and accurate at the date of publication. Neither
the publisher nor the authors or the editors give a warranty, expressed or implied, with
respect to the material contained herein or for any errors or omissions that may have been
made. The publisher remains neutral with regard to jurisdictional claims in published maps
and institutional affiliations.

Cover illustration: © J. Ruscello/Alamy Stock Photo

This Palgrave Macmillan imprint is published by the registered company Springer Nature
Switzerland AG
The registered company address is: Gewerbestrasse 11, 6330 Cham, Switzerland

We dedicate this book to the memory of the late Prof. Calestous Juma, who planted a seed of thought leadership in Africa and left an indelible mark as one of Africa's greatest scholars and public intellectuals.

Preface

This book is a culmination of several years of research and policy discussions and insights under the Africa Research and Impact Network and partners. Much could be said and written about the connection between climate policy and the right to development in Africa.

We had three main objectives in writing this book. First, we sought to provide a "big picture" overview of the past, present and emerging developments in the international climate policy space, and the subsequent implications for Africa's development interests. Second, we have distilled insights from the rich and growing body of literature related to Africa. And third, we sought to highlight some of the major emerging policy developments that could pose strategic challenges and opportunities to Africa, and highlight and evaluate Africa's response to them.

This book has therefore adopted a "big picture" approach by identifying the key policy and scholarly issues. It highlights specific examples of policy initiatives in Africa and their interplay with the shifting global climate agenda and politics. A rich body of literature on this already exists, and we point to it throughout the book. We have instead revisited the key assumptions that have underpinned much of the scholarly and policy approach to Africa's engagement in international climate policy and politics. In doing so, we hope to reinvigorate the debate on aligning climate and development policy in Africa, by emphasising the need for a more

viii PREFACE

dynamic and creative approach. We hope that this book enriches the relevant debates and policy developments, even though it does not provide all the answers to the questions we pose.

We write this book as African scholars based in Africa and the diaspora. Hence, we engage the world from Africa, allowing us to present a distinctive perspective that also draws from other parts of the world, thanks to our extensive and broad partnerships. The current zeitgeist in Africa is one of optimism, despite numerous challenges, and indeed African countries have proven that they can undertake and successfully develop bold policy objectives, such as the completion of the landmark Africa Continental Free Trade Agreement (AfCFTA). This book underscores the need for such creativity and bold policy development to meet the challenge of securing a just transition for Africa. Overall, our outlook is, therefore, an optimistic one. The book is also written to appeal to a broad audience.

During the lengthy process of writing this book, we have accrued innumerable intellectual debts. We would like to express our gratitude to our various project partners, with whom we have learned much from each other. We would like to especially thank Ian Scoones, Andy Stirling, David Ockwell, and Adrian Ely from the Institute for Development Studies, Sussex University. We would also like to thank members of the following projects and initiatives, from whom we learnt a lot from: ClimateSouth project; tomorrow Cities - Nairobi Risk Hub project; Annual ARIN Conference participants; ARIN Fellows and stakeholders; the UKRU for convening pre-COP adaptation events; the Adaptation Research Alliance project; and the Future of Climate Cooperation project.

We would like to appreciate the following institutions for providing an excellent working environment during the writing process, but also engaging in many discussions with colleagues, many of which found their way into the book: the Africa Research and Impact Network (ARIN); the African Centre for Technology Studies (ACTS); the Blavatnik School of Government, University of Oxford; Faculty of Law, University of Tasmania; and the Climate and Energy College, and the Melbourne Sustainable Society Institute (MSSI), at the University of Melbourne.

Earlier drafts of the book manuscript benefited from incisive review comments. We would like to thank Thomas Hale, Steffen Bauer, Luke Kemp, Nicholas Chan, Sander Chan, Pieter Pauw and Winnie Asiti for their generous review comments. We also acknowledge anonymous review comments on the initial book proposal. Our thanks also go to Elizabeth Obel-Lawson for helping to improve the quality of the manuscript through copyediting.

The publications of this book would not have been possible without the support of several people. Eunice Sahle was kind enough to suggest the book project after a lengthy discussion of the key ideas during a lunch meeting. Alina Yurova and Hemapriya Eswanth were very patient and skilful in helping us to navigate the publication process.

Any errors and shortcoming are solely the responsibility of the authors.

Oxford, UK Kennedy Mbeva
Nairobi, Kenya Reuben Makomere
Nairobi, Kenya Joanes Atela
Nairobi, Kenya Victoria Chengo
Nairobi, Kenya Charles Tonui

Praise for *Africa's Right to Development in a Climate-Constrained World*

"An important contribution to scholarship on International Relations and African Politics, this book offers a solid and well-grounded treatment of how Africa can best achieve sustainable economic development while also taking ambitious action on climate change."

—Professor Chukwumerije Okereke, *Director of the Center for Climate Change and Development, Alex Ekwueme Federal University Nigeria*

"By focusing on the need to balance climate and development goals in Africa, the authors fill a conspicuous knowledge gap on the reality that transition pathways for countries in the Global South will look very different to those in the Global North."

—Dr. Zainab Usman, *Senior Fellow and Director, Africa Program, Carnegie Endowment for International Peace*

"The authors have done a timely and excellent job in articulating a 'just transition' from an African perspective."

—Dr. Bhim Adhikari (Ph.D.), *Senior Environmental Economist, Canada's International Development Research Centre (IDRC)*

CONTENTS

1	**Introduction**	1
	Notes	8
	References	10
2	**The Great Climate Transformation**	13
	2.1 Theorising the Great Climate Transformation	14
	2.1.1 Complexity, Evolution and Novelty	14
	2.1.2 Shift in the Logic of Multilateral Climate Cooperation	16
	2.2 Drivers of the Great Climate Transformation	20
	2.2.1 Shift in Climate Policy Discourse	21
	2.2.2 Evolving Geopolitics of Climate Change	23
	2.2.3 Adoption of Dynamic Differentiation	25
	2.2.4 The Rise of Non-State Actors	27
	2.2.5 Emergent Long-Run Policy Developments	29
	2.3 Implications for Africa	30
	2.4 Conclusion	31
	Notes	32
	References	39
3	**Shift in Climate Discourse**	47
	3.1 Defining the Context of Environmental and Climate Policy	49
	3.2 Africa in the Post-War World Order	50

xiii

3.3	The Global Politics of Sustainable Development	52
3.4	Sustainable Development in the Multilateral Climate Change Regime	57
3.5	The Great Climate Transformation and Continental Economic Integration in Africa	62
3.6	Conclusion	67
	Notes	69
	References	77

4 The Evolving Geopolitics of Climate Change — 85

4.1	Africa in Multilateral Climate Cooperation	86
4.2	The Post-World War Consensus	88
	4.2.1 In the Shadow of the Cold War	89
	4.2.2 Advent of Derived Development	90
	4.2.3 The Emergence of Multilateral Environmental Governance	91
4.3	Establishment of the Multilateral Climate Regime	92
	4.3.1 Hegemonic Leadership and Differentiation	92
4.4	Kyoto and the 'China' Question	94
	4.4.1 An Unsustainable Model	94
4.5	A Universal Approach	96
	4.5.1 In Search of a Universal Approach	96
	4.5.2 The Copenhagen Climate Talks	96
	4.5.3 The Paris Agreement and Catalytic Cooperation	97
	4.5.4 Elusive Solidarity: Paris and Beyond	98
	4.5.5 Continental Climate Coordination in Africa	99
4.6	Emerging Spheres of Climate Influence	100
	4.6.1 South-South Cooperation	101
4.7	Conclusion	105
	Notes	106
	References	117

5 Dynamic Differentiation — 127

5.1	Hegemonic Leadership and Selective Incentives	129
5.2	The Origins of Differentiation in Multilateral Environmental Governance	131
5.3	Common but Differentiated Responsibilities in the Multilateral Climate Change Regime	134
	5.3.1 A Bifurcated Approach	135

	5.3.2	From Limited to Universal Participation	136
5.4		Towards Dynamic Differentiation: The Paris Agreement and Beyond	139
	5.4.1	Subtle and Dynamic Differentiation	139
	5.4.2	Conditionality as an Insurance Policy	140
5.5		Net Zero and Structural Transformation	144
5.6		Implications of Dynamic Differentiation for African Countries	146
5.7		Conclusion	147
Notes			148
References			154

6 The Rise of Non-state Actors — 159

6.1		Non-state and Transnational Climate Governance	160
6.2		Non-state Climate Action in Kenya	162
	6.2.1	National Climate Landscape in Kenya	162
	6.2.2	Mapping Non-state Climate Action in Kenya	163
6.3		Reconceptualising Non-state and Transnational Climate Governance	172
6.4		Conclusion	176
Notes			177
References			182

7 Emergent Climate-Related Policy Issues — 189

7.1		Long-Run Policy Developments	190
7.2		Strategic Challenges	191
	7.2.1	The Tightening Vice of Climate Ambition	191
	7.2.2	Divestment and Fossil Fuel Extraction	192
	7.2.3	Climate-Related Trade Measures	193
	7.2.4	Transformative Structural Climate Targets	195
	7.2.5	Proliferation of Anti-Fossil Fuel Norms	196
	7.2.6	Nexus Policy Issues	197
7.3		Strategic Opportunities	199
	7.3.1	Renewable and Clean Energy Supply Chains	199
	7.3.2	Continental Just Transition	201
	7.3.3	Aligning Regional Integration with Climate Policy	202
	7.3.4	Reconsidering Multilateral Cooperation	204
	7.3.5	South-South Cooperation	205
7.4		Conclusion	205

xvi CONTENTS

	Notes	206
	References	216
8	**Governing Complexity**	227
	8.1 Complexity and Decision-Making	228
	8.1.1 The Regime Complex for Climate Change	228
	8.1.2 Bounded Rationality	229
	8.1.3 Complex Designers	230
	8.2 Climate Policy Landscape in Africa	231
	8.3 Consolidated Lessons	233
	8.3.1 Transformation and Uncertainty	234
	8.3.2 Institutional Innovation	236
	8.3.3 Building and Enhancing Endogenous Capacity	239
	8.3.4 Dynamic Transnational Partnerships	242
	8.3.5 Strategic Geopolitical Engagement	243
	8.3.6 Experimentation and Learning	245
	8.4 Conclusion	245
	Notes	246
	References	252
9	**Conclusion**	259
	Notes	261
	References	261
	References	263
	Index	303

ABBREVIATIONS

ACPC	African Centre for Climate Policy
ADP	Ad Hoc Working Group on the Durban Platform for Enhanced Action
AfCFTA	Africa Continental Free Trade Agreement
AfDB	African Development Bank
AGN	Africa Group of Negotiators
AMCEN	African Ministerial Conference on the Environment
ARIN	Africa Research and Impact Network
AU	African Union
AUC	African Union Commission
B3W	Build Back Better World
BRI	Belt and Road Initiative
BRICS	Brazil, Russia, India, China, and South Africa
CAS	Complex Adaptive System
CBAM	Carbon Border Adjustment Mechanism
CBDR	Common But Differentiated Responsibility
CBDR&RC	Common, But Differentiated, Responsibilities and Respective Capabilities
CDM	Clean Development Mechanism
CoG	Council of Governors
COMESA	Common Market for East and Southern Africa
COP	Conference of Parties
CRIBS	Climate Relevant Innovation Systems-builders
CSR	Corporate Social Responsibility
DFID	Department for International Development
DFIs	Development Finance Institutions

EAC	East African Community
EASD	Equitable Access to Sustainable Development
ECOWAS	Economic Community of West African States
EU	European Union
FOCAC	Forum for China-Africa Cooperation
FSC	Forest Stewardship Council
GCF	Green Climate Fund
IDRC	International Development Research Centre
IEA	International Energy Agency
IMF	International Monetary Fund
INC/FCCC	Intergovernmental Negotiating Committee for a Framework Convention on Climate Change
INDC	Intended Nationally Determined Contributions
IPCC	Intergovernmental Panel on Climate Change
ISA	International Solar Alliance
ISDS	Investor-State Dispute Settlement
KAM	Kenya Association of Manufacturers
KEPSA	Kenya Private Sector Alliance
LDCs	Least Developed Countries
LPAA	Lima-Paris Action Agenda
LTS	Long Term Strategies
MDBs	Multilateral Development Banks
MDGs	Millennium Development Goals
MEAs	Multilateral Environmental Agreements
MoI	Means of Implementation
NAM	Non-Aligned Movement
NAZCA	Non-State Zone for Climate Action
NDCs	Nationally Determined Contribution
NEPAD	New Partnership for Africa's Development
NIEO	New International Economic Order
NSAs	Non-State Actors
NSE	Nairobi Securities Exchange
NZJTF	Net Zero Just Transition Framework
OAU	Organization of African Unity
PPE	Personal Protective Equipment
PTAs	Preferential Trade Agreements
RECs	Regional Economic Communities
SADC	Southern Africa Development Community
SDGs	Sustainable Development Goals
SIDS	Small Island Developing States
SMEs	Small and Medium Enterprises
SSC	South-South Cooperation

ABBREVIATIONS xix

STEPS	Social, Technological and Environmental Pathways to Sustainability
SWFs	Sovereign Wealth Funds
TCG	Transnational Climate Governance
UN	United Nations
UNCED	United Nations Conference on Environment and Development
UNCHE	United Nations Conference on the Human Environment
UNCTAD	United Nations Conference on Trade and Development
UNDP	United Nations Development Programme
UNECA	United Nations Economic Commission for Africa
UNEP	United Nations Environment Programme
UNFCCC	United Nations Framework Convention on Climate Change
USSR	Union of Soviet Socialist Republics
WCED	World Commission on Environment and Development
WTO	World Trade Organization

List of Figures

Fig. 4.1	Annual number of AGN submissions in climate change negotiations under the UNFCCC	99
Fig. 5.1	Overview of the variation in the degree of conditionality of African NDCs	141
Fig. 5.2	Geographical overview of the variation in the degree of conditionality of African NDCs	143
Fig. 6.1	Non-state (companies) climate action in Kenya	168
Fig. 6.2	Sub-national (County government) climate action in Kenya	173
Fig. 8.1	Temporal trend in the adoption of climate policies in African countries	231
Fig. 8.2	Geographical trend in the adoption of climate policies in African countries	232
Fig. 8.3	Adoption of long-term emission reduction targets by African countries	234

LIST OF TABLES

Table 2.1	Conceptualising the drivers of the great climate transformation	30
Table 5.1	Long-term climate neutrality targets indicated by African countries	145
Table 6.1	Non- and sub-state climate action in Africa vis-à-vis the global perspective	162
Table 6.2	Summary of non- and sub-state climate action in Kenya	174

CHAPTER 1

Introduction

In 2015, the adoption of the landmark Paris Agreement on Climate Change marked an important milestone in international climate cooperation, after almost three decades of searching for a broadly acceptable global climate agreement. Globally, only three countries are yet to sign the Paris Agreement, while all African countries have signed it. Two years earlier, in 2013, African countries had adopted the African Union (AU) Agenda 2063, a blueprint for continental transformation in the next fifty years. As part of the implementation of the AU Agenda 2063, African countries adopted in 2018, in record time, the African Continental Free Trade Agreement (AfCFTA) as the foundation for continental economic transformation through industrialisation. This book examines the implications of these three landmark policy developments on Africa's quest to achieve sustainable development. It focuses on the concept of 'Just Transition' as the bridge to simultaneously achieve climate and development policy goals, but within a unique African context.

Africa's unique conditions pose significant, unprecedented questions to African policy makers trying to balance the two relevant policy objectives of development and climate policy, which seem to be pulling in opposite directions. That is, African countries will need to meet

© The Author(s), under exclusive license to Springer Nature
Switzerland AG 2023
K. Mbeva et al., *Africa's Right to Development in a Climate-Constrained World*, Contemporary African Political Economy,
https://doi.org/10.1007/978-3-031-22887-2_1

ambitious climate targets—especially emissions reductions—while also achieving rapid industrialisation goals. Crucially, this policy challenge needs to be viewed in the context of chronic underdevelopment, significant dependence on hydrocarbons and other natural resources, and rapid demographic change with the continent's population expected to double to about 2.5 billion people by 2050.[1] The key question, therefore, is how Africa can conceptualise and reconcile the global drive towards net zero emissions with the urgent need to achieve rapid industrialisation that may lead to rising emissions in the pursuit of the continent's socio-economic development agenda?

This book focuses on this dual dilemma and explores the dynamic forces in Africa that will shape the direction of the continent's response to its climate and developmental needs. It argues that there is a need to conceptualise Africa's engagement with the global climate agenda within the context of its practical short-, mid- and long-term development needs. That African countries would need to undertake increasingly greenhouse gas emission reductions while also promoting development especially through rapid industrialisation recasts the rhetorical challenge of climate-compatible development into a practical one of realising sustainable development. In articulating an alternative approach through a 'Just Transition', we place Africa at the centre of our analysis, and recognise its agency in crafting and implementing its policies as well as some of its unique policy contexts.

Analysis in this book is centred on what we term as the *Great Climate Transformation*, which is premised on the notion that the multilateral climate change regime has transformed in ways that significantly depart from its conception. The establishment of the multilateral climate regime was premised on the Stockholm and Rio bargains, whereby industrialised countries would take the lead in reducing greenhouse gas emission while also offering support to developing countries to address climate change.

Over time, however, this bifurcated approach to multilateral climate cooperation has been infeasible. The United Framework Convention on Climate Change (UNFCCC), which is the foundation of multilateral climate cooperation, embodied the bifurcated approach of differentiating the rights and responsibilities of countries in addressing global climate change. The failure of the Kyoto Protocol, which embodied this approach, is the most salient example.[2] In a departure from the Kyoto

Protocol approach, the Paris Agreement is based on the universal participation of countries, as well as a catalytic model of cooperation where countries make their national climate pledges more ambitious over time.[3]

We further argue in this book that, given the implications of the Great Climate Transformation, predicating Africa's engagement in international climate cooperation on the bifurcated logic of cooperation is becoming untenable. To highlight the challenge of engaging with the Great Climate Transformation, while also pursuing development policy goals, some African countries have expressed a "buyer's remorse". As the realisation of the structural transformation set in motion by the catalytic model of the Paris Agreement is becoming apparent, concerns on how to balance deep emission reductions with the broader development goals remained, especially for least developed countries. As a policy maker and climate change negotiator and policy maker from Chad, which had set an emissions reduction target of 71% by 2030, put it,

> I personally think that the very ambitious INDC [climate plan] like ours is not achievable and it need [sic] to be reviewed...We have been rushed by other countries, and we have elaborated a quick INDC, we did not gather all the data to reflect our national and achievable contribution, which normally [should] take into account sustainable development.[4]

To effectively engage in the dynamic transformations set in motion by the Paris Agreement, an approach that appreciates the dynamics of the Great Climate Transformation, where the international climate regime is rapidly evolving, along with attendant strategic risks and opportunities, is needed. The Paris Agreement, for instance, has weakened differentiation of rights and obligations, despite African countries fighting hard to secure them, but the text of the Agreement represents a balance of pro- and anti- differentiation interests, which continue to be contested in the regime. Such a shift in the conceptual vantage point of engagement in international climate cooperation would position African countries to better realise and secure sustainable development. In articulating our argument, we identify three key and interrelated features of the Great Climate Transformation: increasing *complexity*, *evolution* and *novelty*. A systems approach is therefore needed in appraising and articulating a new paradigm of Africa's engagement in international climate cooperation.

Scholars have noted that international climate cooperation is becoming more complex, leading to the 'regime complex for climate change'.[5]

Increasing complexity means that the international climate regime will continue having more components over time. In its inception, the multilateral climate regime was underpinned by a simple formula: industrialised countries would take lead in reducing their greenhouse emissions and provide developing countries with resources such as technology, finance and capacity building to realise their commitments; developing countries on the other hand would make voluntary commitments on climate action. But as the emergence of the 'regime complex for climate change' has demonstrated, this formula is becoming increasingly multifaceted, since climate change is a cross-cutting issue. Exclusive focus on the multilateral climate regime under the UNFCCC, is thus untenable. The multilateral climate regime should instead be viewed as part of a bigger picture, as the other emergent forums for climate cooperation do not necessarily incorporate the principle of differentiated responsibilities and support for means of implementation. The UNFCCC could thus be seen as more of a coordination forum in the pursuit for a just transition in Africa.

As the international climate change regime is becoming more complex, it is also continuing to *evolve*. Three decades ago, the UNFCCC was the main forum for international climate cooperation. But over time, many other forums based on different policy domains have also become important. Trade policy, through the multilateral World Trade Organization (WTO) and Preferential Trade Agreements (PTAs), for example, has emerged as a crucial piece of the puzzle of addressing global environmental problems. A system that is evolving is far from equilibrium. As noted, the key evolution of international climate cooperation has been from a static bifurcated regime to a dynamic landscape. Moreover, as contemporary trends indicate, international climate cooperation will continue to evolve, especially as more actors and issues are incorporated in addressing the challenge.

Moreover, the international climate regime is becoming more complex, the process also generates *novelty*. Novelty is an important feature as it implies that a system that is evolving also presents novel challenges and opportunities. Thus, if a system is evolving and becoming more complex, and the process generates novelty, then prior assumptions that underpinned earlier phases of the system need to be continuously reappraised. That the shift in logic in multilateral climate cooperation has transformed means that some of its prior assumptions might also need to be reconsidered. For instance, the optional participation of developing countries, and the transfer of resources from industrialised countries in the form of reparative justice and equity are becoming less salient features. As a consequence, concepts such as 'technology acquisition' become more important than 'technology transfer', as the former concept emphasises the domestic capability of recipient countries while the latter emphasises the normative responsibility of disbursing countries. Moreover, the exponential innovation in climate technologies and their cheap and ubiquitous abundance, an irreversible process, also underscore the limits of the concept of technology transfer.[6]

If indeed a Great Climate Transformation characterised by the aforementioned features is underway, then an alternative approach to international climate cooperation, especially for Africa, is necessary. In this book, we argue that an approach based on 'Governing Complexity' is the most suitable for African countries.[7] Governing complexity requires models that are well-suited for such systems. Using the philosopher Isiah Berlin's formulation, we need a 'fox' and not a 'hedgehog' approach to Africa's engagement in international climate policy. After all, a fox knows many things, while a hedgehog only knows one big thing; navigating complexity requires knowledge of many things.[8] We also examine the Great Climate Transformation within a longer time horizon, both its historical antecedents and the prospective policy outlook of the coming decades.

This book is, in general, about how Africa can realise sustainable development in the context of the Great Climate Transformation. While such an approach has been the mainstay of scholarly and policy discourse in Africa and elsewhere, in rhetoric and practice, this book fundamentally recasts the challenge. In doing so, the book is not only meant to contribute to scholarly and policy debates on realising sustainable development in Africa as well as international climate cooperation, but it also draws on the concrete policy and project examples to substantiate the argument. Importantly, our approach is premised on optimism, but without overlooking the challenges posed by the Great Climate Transformation.

To effectively navigate the Great Climate Transformation, African policy makers will have to assume the role of what has been termed as *Complex Designers*.[9] Such actors can deploy flexibility in navigating the complex system. Moreover, the public policy environment in Africa is characterised by complexity, hence the need for complex designers. This book adopts this approach, which was also presciently articulated in the conclusion of an article on public policy in Africa,

In this article an attempt has been made to present an agenda for the policy process applicable to African countries as the twenty-first century approaches. Central to the recommendations is the argument that traditional approaches to policy have been dominated by a mechanistic world view, a view that is out of touch with the complex and dynamic nature of modern [social] systems. On the contrary, the important feature of such systems is that they are experiencing very rapid structural change as a result of contemporary technological and socioeconomic developments. It is no longer possible to manage such change using the old bureaucratic procedures, at least not if the country in question wishes to benefit from economic development. Inevitably there will be a period of experimentation as new ideas and institutional forms are tried out. Sometimes mistakes will be made, but these are a price well worth paying for a better future.[10]

Overall, this book is organised into three key parts. The first part outlines the conceptual and theoretical framework underpinning the book. The present chapter has argued for the need to rethink how Africa can engage with the Great Climate Transformation. Following this theme, Chapter 2 presents a theoretical framework of how to think about the Great Climate Transformation. We begin by conceptualising the international climate regime as a complex and evolutionary system. Drawing on the ideas of the Nobel Laureate scientist Ilya Prigogine and theories of international cooperation, the chapter also lays out a conceptual and theoretical framework based on the analysis of complex adaptive systems such as the Great Climate Transformation. Prigogine examined complex macrosystems, which are characterised by an evolutionary dynamic that is irreversible and operating far from equilibrium. Crucially, Prigogine argued that the evolution of complex systems leads to new structures, which also present opportunities for novelty. Consequently, the chapter draws on theories of international cooperation to articulate the causal mechanisms that are driving the Great Climate Transformation. In particular, the chapter draws on the Catalytic Cooperation theory to explain the Great Climate transformation.[11] This chapter, therefore, articulates the conceptual and theoretical framework against which subsequent analysis is undertaken.

In the second part of the book, the main drivers of the Great Climate Transformation are examined in detail. Chapter 3 shows how the discourse on climate policy has evolved. Specifically, it shows that while African and other developing countries have long favoured the conception of climate policy within the broader context of sustainable development, the contemporary international discourse has emphasised the mitigation component of climate policy over the broader sustainable development issues. This discourse, thus, poses a major challenge for African countries as they try to reconcile their climate and development policy objectives.

Chapter 4 explores how the changing geopolitical environments have reshaped international climate cooperation. The chapter shows how the rise of the prominence of some developing countries, especially the major economies such as China and India, led to the infeasibility of the Kyoto Protocol model; in constrast, their participation led to the ultimate political success of the Paris Agreement model. The chapter also shows how the changing geopolitical environment is leading to a shift in focus from the multilateral climate regime to spheres of influence managed by great and major powers. These geopolitical developments have also opened up opportunities for African countries to engage beyond the multilateral climate system, especially through bilateral engagements with great and major powers.

Chapter 5 builds on this argument to show how dynamic differentiation has replaced bifurcated differentiation, meaning greater obligations for African countries in light of their perceived growing capability. The chapter also shows the diminishing role of traditional multilateral concepts such as technology transfer in favour of endogenous approaches to strengthening domestic capability such as technology acquisition and absorptive capacity. To underscore the argument, the chapter also shows how the interest in and adoption of net zero targets by African countries could lead to a structural transformation through the global harmonisation of climate policies. Chapter 6 examines how the rise of transnational and non- and sub-state actors have also driven the Great Climate Transformation, focusing on a case study of Kenya.

Prospectively, the third part of the book considers long-run international climate cooperation from an African perspective. Chapter 7 presents an overview of the emerging climate and climate-related policy developments that will continue to drive the Great Climate Transformation. These include the tightening vice of climate ambition; divestment from fossil fuels; the adoption of coercive policy instruments such as sanctions; clean energy supply chains; aligning regional integration with climate policy; south-south cooperation; and the dynamics of structural climate targets. Reflecting on projects and initiatives that the authors have worked on, and others they are familiar with, Chapter 8 makes the case for the adoption of 'Governing Complexity' as the main paradigm of climate policy-making in Africa. In 'Governing Complexity', it is argued that policy makers will need to assume the role of Complex Designers, so as to effectively engage with the complex and evolving international climate change regime. Moreover, reconciling climate and development policy goals also requires Complex Designers. We primarily draw on the disciplines of psychology and decision-making to outline the suitable mental models for engaging with complexity. The chapter distils the key lessons and insights from the authors' engagements in climate policy within and outside Africa to elaborate on the Governing Complexity model. Chapter 9 concludes the study and suggests key policy recommendations on how, in the long run, Africa should engage with the Great Climate Transformation.

At a time when African countries are emerging from decades, if not centuries, of domination and underdevelopment, securing sustainable development is an important imperative. Major and rapid developments such as the adoption and operationalisation of the Africa Continental Free Trade Agreement (AfCFTA) are a significant indicator of the political and policy momentum that can be generated to deal with developmental challenges.[12] But such gains will only be realised and preserved by securing a just transition; doing so would require a novel and strategic engagement with the Great Climate Transformation. Scholarly and policy debates, in turn, have to be retrofitted to effectively address this challenge.

Importantly, we write this book as African scholars who have also engaged closely with the policy development within and outside of Africa. As the prominent scholar Ali Mazrui aptly noted, one's mode of reasoning—based on the totality of their education and life experiences—deeply informs their world view.[13] We have sought to draw on Mazrui's dictum in writing this book, as the following chapters will hopefully make evident.

NOTES

1. Economist, 'Africa's Population Will Double by 2050', *The Economist*, 26 March 2020, https://www.economist.com/special-report/2020/03/26/africas-population-will-double-by-2050.
2. Pieter Pauw, Kennedy Mbeva, and Harro van Asselt, 'Subtle Differentiation of Countries' Responsibilities under the Paris Agreement', *Palgrave*

Communications 5, no. 1 (30 July 2019): 1–7, https://doi.org/10.1057/s41599-019-0298-6; Steve Rayner and Gwyn Prins, 'The Wrong Trousers: Radically Rethinking Climate Policy', Other Working Paper (Oxford, UK: James Martin Institute for Science and Civilization, University of Oxford and the MacKinder Centre for the Study of Long-Wave Events, London School of Economics, 2007), http://www.sbs.ox.ac.uk/centres/insis/Documents/TheWrongTrousers.pdf; Gwyn Prins and Steve Rayner, 'Time to Ditch Kyoto', *Nature* 449, no. 7165 (25 October 2007): 973–75, https://doi.org/10.1038/449973a.

3. Robert Falkner, 'The Paris Agreement and the New Logic of International Climate Politics', *International Affairs* 92, no. 5 (1 September 2016): 1107–25, https://doi.org/10.1111/1468-2346.12708; Thomas Hale, 'Catalytic Cooperation', *Global Environmental Politics* 20, no. 4 (1 November 2020): 73–98, https://doi.org/10.1162/glep_a_00561.

4. Edward King, 'Africa's "Buyer's Remorse" over Paris Climate Deal', Climate Home, 3 November 2016, http://www.climatechangenews.com/2016/11/03/africas-buyers-remorse-over-paris-climate-deal/.

5. Robert Keohane and David Victor, 'The Regime Complex for Climate Change', *Perspectives on Politics* 9, no. 1 (March 2011): 7–23, https://doi.org/10.1017/S1537592710004068.

6. Calestous Juma, 'Exponential Innovation and Human Rights: Implications for Science and Technology Diplomacy', SSRN Scholarly Paper (Rochester, NY: Social Science Research Network, 27 February 2018), https://papers.ssrn.com/abstract=3131243; David Ockwell and Rob Byrne, 'Improving Technology Transfer through National Systems of Innovation: Climate Relevant Innovation-System Builders (CRIBs)', *Climate Policy* 16, no. 7 (2 October 2016): 836–54, https://doi.org/10.1080/14693062.2015.1052958.

7. For pioneering and inspiring cognate studies on Africa, see Norman Clark and Calestous Juma, *Long-Run Economics: An Evolutionary Approach to Economic Growth* (London and New York: Pinter Publishers, 1987); Calestous Juma and Norman Clark, 'Policy Research in Sub-Saharan Africa: An Exploration', *Public Administration and Development* 15, no. 2 (1995): 121–37.

8. Isaiah Berlin, *The Hedgehog and The Fox: An Essay on Tolstoy's View of History* (London: Hachette UK, 2011).

9. Anthea Roberts and Taylor St John, 'Complex Designers and Emergent Design: Reforming the Investment Treaty System', *American Journal of International Law* 116, no. 1 (January 2022): 99, https://doi.org/10.1017/ajil.2021.57.

10. Juma and Clark, 'Policy Research in Sub-Saharan Africa', 135.

11. Hale, 'Catalytic Cooperation'.

12. Francis Mangeni and Calestous Juma, *Emergent Africa. Evolution of Regional Economic Integration* (Terra Alta, WV: Headline Books, 2019).
13. Ali Mazrui, 'Tanzaphilia', *Transition*, no. 31 (1967): 21, https://doi.org/10.2307/2934403.

REFERENCES

Berlin, Isaiah. *The Hedgehog and The Fox: An Essay on Tolstoy's View of History*. London: Hachette UK, 2011.

Clark, Norman, and Calestous Juma. *Long-Run Economics: An Evolutionary Approach to Economic Growth*. London and New York: Pinter Publishers, 1987.

Economist. 'Africa's Population Will Double by 2050'. *The Economist*, 26 March 2020. https://www.economist.com/special-report/2020/03/26/africas-population-will-double-by-2050.

Falkner, Robert. 'The Paris Agreement and the New Logic of International Climate Politics'. *International Affairs* 92, no. 5 (1 September 2016): 1107–25. https://doi.org/10.1111/1468-2346.12708.

Hale, Thomas. 'Catalytic Cooperation'. *Global Environmental Politics* 20, no. 4 (1 November 2020): 73–98. https://doi.org/10.1162/glep_a_00561.

Juma, Calestous. 'Exponential Innovation and Human Rights: Implications for Science and Technology Diplomacy'. SSRN Scholarly Paper. Rochester, NY: Social Science Research Network, 27 February 2018. https://papers.ssrn.com/abstract=3131243.

Juma, Calestous, and Norman Clark. 'Policy Research in Sub-Saharan Africa: An Exploration'. *Public Administration and Development* 15, no. 2 (1995): 121–37.

Keohane, Robert, and David Victor. 'The Regime Complex for Climate Change'. *Perspectives on Politics* 9, no. 1 (March 2011): 7–23. https://doi.org/10.1017/S1537592710004068.

King, Edward. 'Africa's "Buyer's Remorse" over Paris Climate Deal'. Climate Home, 3 November 2016. http://www.climatechangenews.com/2016/11/03/africas-buyers-remorse-over-paris-climate-deal/.

Mangeni, Francis, and Calestous Juma. *Emergent Africa. Evolution of Regional Economic Integration*. Terra Alta, WV: Headline Books, 2019.

Mazrui, Ali. 'Tanzaphilia'. *Transition*, no. 31 (1967): 20–26. https://doi.org/10.2307/2934403.

Ockwell, David, and Rob Byrne. 'Improving Technology Transfer through National Systems of Innovation: Climate Relevant Innovation-System Builders (CRIBs)'. *Climate Policy* 16, no. 7 (2 October 2016): 836–54. https://doi.org/10.1080/14693062.2015.1052958.

Pauw, Pieter, Kennedy Mbeva, and Harro van Asselt. 'Subtle Differentiation of Countries' Responsibilities under the Paris Agreement'. *Palgrave Communications* 5, no. 1 (30 July 2019): 1–7. https://doi.org/10.1057/s41599-019-0298-6.

Prins, Gwyn, and Steve Rayner. 'Time to Ditch Kyoto'. *Nature* 449, no. 7165 (25 October 2007): 973–75. https://doi.org/10.1038/449973a.

Rayner, Steve, and Gwyn Prins. 'The Wrong Trousers: Radically Rethinking Climate Policy'. Other Working Paper. Oxford, UK: James Martin Institute for Science and Civilization, University of Oxford and the MacKinder Centre for the Study of Long-Wave Events, London School of Economics, 2007. http://www.sbs.ox.ac.uk/centres/insis/Documents/TheWrongTrousers.pdf.

Roberts, Anthea, and Taylor St John. 'Complex Designers and Emergent Design: Reforming the Investment Treaty System'. *American Journal of International Law* 116, no. 1 (January 2022): 96–149. https://doi.org/10.1017/ajil.2021.57.

CHAPTER 2

The Great Climate Transformation

Africa's position in international politics has often been perceived as that of a 'taker'.[1] Since African states gained independence after the Second World War, they have been engaged in international politics from the periphery.[2] As part of a coalition of developing countries, often under the banner of the Group of 77 (G77), they have often demanded for better engagement in international politics and diplomacy. The pursuit of fairer participation in international politics and diplomacy has underpinned Africa's engagement in global climate governance, especially on climate change.[3] To address this imbalance, a consensus was reached where industrialised countries would support developing countries to address environmental challenges. Therefore, this notion of static equilibrium has been at the heart of Africa's engagement in international climate change policy.

However, recent developments in the multilateral climate change regime have significantly challenged this equilibrium. This chapter argues that these developments have led to the Great Climate Transformation. In this transformation, some of the core pillars on which the establishment of the multilateral climate change regime was founded have been abandoned in favour of a more dynamic approach. Consequently, the Great Climate Transformation necessitates the adoption of a different conceptual and theoretical vantage point in the analysis of Africa's engagement

© The Author(s), under exclusive license to Springer Nature Switzerland AG 2023
K. Mbeva et al., *Africa's Right to Development in a Climate-Constrained World*, Contemporary African Political Economy, https://doi.org/10.1007/978-3-031-22887-2_2

13

in the new dispensation of the multilateral climate regime. This chapter first articulates the concept of the Great Climate Transformation, then outlines its key theoretical drivers, before examining the implications for African countries.

2.1 THEORISING THE GREAT CLIMATE TRANSFORMATION

It is necessary to take a different conceptual and theoretical vantage point in order to understand how the multilateral climate regime has evolved over time. Since its inception, the regime has transformed in many ways. Overall, the regime has shifted from a static to dynamic logic of cooperation.[4] We term this shift as the *Great Climate Transformation*. In the static equilibrium conception of the regime, industrialised countries would take the lead in addressing global climate change, while developing countries would voluntarily participate. Moreover, the industrialised countries would provide support for implementation to developing countries, in the form of climate finance, technology and capacity building.

However, the international climate regime has evolved into a more dynamic system. In this irreversible evolution, the selective approach to participation has been replaced by a more universal participation. In addition, the bifurcated approach to rights and responsibilities of countries has been substituted with a dynamic approach premised on changing national circumstances. Taken together, these two developments have ushered in a transformative shift in global climate governance, with significant implications especially for African countries. The next two sections elaborate the conceptual and theoretical underpinnings of the Great Climate Transformation.

2.1.1 Complexity, Evolution and Novelty

An appropriate worldview is critical to conceptualising the Great Climate Transformation. But to do so, one has to go back to the philosophical underpinnings of the various world views, especially in relation to static and dynamic systems. Dissatisfied with the predominant classical conceptual approaches in natural sciences, that are predicated on static equilibrium, Ilya Prigogine articulated an alternative approach which accounted for dynamic systems that operated far from equilibrium. Prigogine's point

2 THE GREAT CLIMATE TRANSFORMATION   15

of departure was that systems in chaos, i.e. operating far from equilibrium, were not necessarily unstable.[5] Classical approaches in natural science—especially physics—formulated by luminaries such as Newton, Descartes and Einstein, were premised on the notion of static equilibrium. Classical scientists argued that in their natural state, systems were always in static equilibrium.[6] When pushed from their natural state, they would eventually revert to their state of equilibrium. Such systems were therefore reversible, and chaos was considered a form of disorder.

But Prigogine argued, counterintuitively, that chaos is in fact a form of order. For Prigogine, there were three key elements that made "chaotic" macrosystems important: complexity; irreversibility; and novelty.[7] Prigogine argued that it was in fact a law of nature for systems to move far from equilibrium. Irreversibility could create conditions for the emergence of self-organisation in complex systems, triggering creative processes (novelty) that led to new dynamic states of matter identified as *dissipative structures*.[8] The concept of dissipative structures is especially relevant for understanding the Great Climate Transformation, since such structures emerge from the transition of macrosystems from one phase to another. The transition in phases follows the law of thermodynamics, and it is an irreversible process.

Dissipative structures are thus not just products of predetermined conditions but also a consequence of creative choices and processes that produce novelty when complex systems operating far from equilibrium reach a bifurcation point. It is thus difficult if not impossible to predict or preordain the state at which bifurcation and the course of innovation will likely occur.[9] In other words, creativity and choices taken therein within the context of disequilibrium are devoid of destiny which in turn leads to uncertainty. Uncertainty can create conditions for developing alternative pathways from a given point of bifurcation. It can manifest through inter alia institutional experiments when it comes to the political and economic spheres. Dissipative structures, therefore, open up opportunities for novelty through new pathways and possibilities in engaging in a rapidly changing international climate change regime.

Importantly, the concept of dissipative structures offers a more concise and relevant framework for thinking about the dynamic evolution of the Great Climate Transformation, especially when compared with the more widely adopted concept of a complex adaptive system (CAS) that has been applied to the study of international regimes.[10] Indeed, the

Great Climate Transformation is a complex adaptive system. What is interesting about the concept of dissipative structures is the added utility of bifurcation, whereby the irreversible shift from one phase to the next creates new opportunities for novelty and policy creativity. Novelty in this case is however not predetermined. It arises from the non-linear and dynamic structure of the system. Applied to the present study, while the Great Climate Transformation in some ways challenges long-held and even cherished assumptions such as the necessity of significant transfer of resources from industrialised to developing countries making it necessary for developing countries to align their development and climate policies. In Africa's case, this would include harnessing the internal momentum for continental economic integration, such as through infrastructure projects, to realise low-carbon and climate resilient economies, and the broader continental agenda of sustainable development as outlined in the landmark African Union Agenda 2063.[11] Additionally, it would also require shifting the focus from undue reliance on multilateral resource transfers to strengthening domestic capacity of African countries to realise their climate commitments.

In this context, the Great Climate Transformation can be perceived as a transformation from the initial conception of the international climate regime as characterised by static equilibrium, to a catalytic regime operating far from equilibrium and evolving into greater complexity. In other words, the international climate regime is irreversibly evolving as a complex adaptive system. Our conceptual analysis, in effect, departs from the conventional static and reductionist approach of analysing Africa's engagement in the international climate change regime within the narrow context of the UNFCCC. Instead, we adopt a systems approach that recognises the broadening landscape and dynamism of which the international climate change regime is just but a catalytic component. Having conceptualised the Great Climate Transformation, how can we theorise its implications on the collective goal of achieving a stable balance with continental developmental priorities.

2.1.2 Shift in the Logic of Multilateral Climate Cooperation

In its elementary conception, addressing the global climate change challenge is a classic collective action problem. That is, it is necessary for states to cooperate to address global climate change. Various theories on the provision of the global public goods have been developed over the past decades on the design and evolution of the international climate regime.[12] This section weaves together this literature to provide a theoretical account of the Great Climate Transformation. It demonstrates that it has been occasioned by the shift in the logic of international climate cooperation, from the static regulatory logic based on leadership by a small group of states, to the dynamic catalytic logic of cooperation based on universal participation (all hands on deck).[13] In Prigogine terms, the international climate regime had irreversibly evolved from one dissipative structure (static regulatory model) to a new dissipative structure (dynamic catalytic model).

2.1.2.1 Olsonian Logic of Cooperation

At its inception, the multilateral climate regime embodied the classic conceptions of the provision of global public goods. Specifically, the design of the regime was premised on two core assumptions. First, a small group of countries—industrialised countries—would take the lead in addressing global climate change by undertaking bigger greenhouse gas reductions and supporting developing countries. Second, developing countries would voluntarily contribute to addressing global climate change. In addition, the developing countries would receive support for means of implementation—climate finance, technology and capacity building—from industrialised countries. The United Nations Framework Convention on Climate Change (UNFCCC), the foundational legal instrument of the multilateral climate change regime, embodied this logic in its architecture.[14] The Kyoto Protocol, which was adopted to implement the UNFCCC, reflected the logic, and included a regulatory framework that comprised a top-down setting of targets for industrialised countries, and an attendant compliance mechanism.[15]

The UNFCCC and the Kyoto Protocol were representative by the Olsonian logic of international cooperation. In his seminal book *Logic of Collective Action,* Olson advanced a simple, counterintuitive, and profound insight. Olson noted that collective action through groups was not primarily driven by group interest over individual interests. Rather, individual interest was the predominant driver of cooperation. Thus, in cooperation including large enough groups, a few members of the group (the privileged group) undertook a disproportionate responsibility in the provision of collective action, while the rest of the group members barely contributed.[16] That is, only a small number of group members contributed to the attainment of group interests, while the rest of the members engaged in free-riding. Olson's groundbreaking insight was in reformulating free-riding as rational, and not irrational, behaviour. In his famous phrase, Olson concluded that collective action through groups was based on the maxim of "the small exploiting the great".[17]

Applied to the multilateral climate change regime, Olson's logic of cooperation was the foundation of the UNFCCC and the Kyoto Protocol. It reinforced the main theories of the formation of international regimes, especially the neoliberal institutionalist theory as advanced by Robert Keohane. In his famous book *After Hegemony*, Keohane argued that international regimes were crucial in fostering international cooperation. Absolute—and not relative—gains were the most important factor in international cooperation.[18] Industrialised countries could therefore bear a disproportionate share of responsibility in addressing global climate change, and also provide support to developing countries.[19]

A cognate theory, namely the hegemonic stability theory, reinforced the Olsonian logic of cooperation. In its simplest definition, the hegemonic stability theory holds that a hegemon—be it a super power or a small group of powerful countries—was necessary in the establishment and operation of international regimes.[20] This small group of leaders, also known as the "k-group", would provide leadership in the provision of global public goods—climate stability in this case. The US and other major industrialised Western states provided leadership in the establishment of the multilateral climate change regime. A clear illustration of this "division of labour" is evident in the classification of countries into Annex I and non-Annex I in both the UNFCCC and the Kyoto Protocol. The Annex I countries would be the leading "k-group", while the rest of the countries could "free ride" in addressing global climate change.[21]

While the adoption of the Kyoto Protocol marked an important milestone in the multilateral climate cooperation, it also began to expose the limits of the Olsonian approach to cooperation. In particular, the "k-group" of countries that had been identified as the leaders in both the UNFCCC and the Kyoto Protocol was no longer content with taking up the disproportionate responsibility in addressing global climate change.[22] The failure of the US Senate to ratify the Kyoto Protocol, the withdrawal by Canada and the initial failure to ratify the Protocol by Australia underscored the unsustainability of the regulatory model. Of particular concern was that major emerging economies, especially China and India, had been excluded from undertaking binding commitments.[23]

As insightfully noted by Duncan Snidal in his critique of the hegemonic stability theory, cooperation could only be possible so long as the relative gap between the size and capacity of the "k-group" and the rest of the members were large enough. When the gap begins to narrow, the "k-group" of leaders can no longer ignore the perceived free-riding especially by the bigger subordinate members.[24] Concerns over distributional costs become more salient, and the Olsonian logic of cooperation begins to falter.[25] Snidal's insight explains the failure of the Kyoto Protocol's regulatory logic of cooperation in spite of the conditions necessary for hegemonic leadership, and the subsequent search for an alternative model.[26]

2.1.2.2 Catalytic Logic of Cooperation

In the search for a new logic of multilateral climate cooperation, two key features would characterise the new regime. First, the responsibility to address global climate change would be universal—all hands on deck.[27] It would no longer be the primary responsibility of the "k-group" of leaders—Annex I countries—to provide the global public good of a safe climate.[28] Second, the new regime would abandon the bifurcated approach of the "k-group" and subordinate states. Instead, rights and responsibilities would be allocated in the light of changing national circumstances.[29] These two assumptions radically transformed the international climate change regime, and they are thus the basis of the Great Climate Transformation. Put differently, the international climate change regime has shifted from the Olsonian to a Catalytic logic of cooperation.

Re-envisioning the international climate change regime entailed reframing the global climate change problem. In his seminal article, Thomas Hale challenged the Olsonian logic of cooperation focused on free-riding as the chief barrier to cooperation, and characterised the alternative catalytic cooperation logic as follows:

> Important elements of climate mitigation exhibit three key features that depart from the canonical model: joint goods, preference heterogeneity, and increasing returns. The presence of these features creates the possibility for "catalytic cooperation." Under such conditions, the chief barrier to cooperation is not the threat of free riding but the lack of incentive to act in the first place. States and other actors seek to solve this problem by creating "catalytic institutions" that work to shift actors' preferences and strategies toward cooperative outcomes over time.[30]

Hale derived his catalytic cooperation model from the design of the Paris Agreement on Climate Change. In its architecture, the Paris Agreement differs from the UNFCCC and the Kyoto Protocol in that it embraces the two assumptions identified earlier in this section: universal participation; and dynamic differentiation based on national circumstances. Following the catalytic model of cooperation, global climate change is perceived not as the classical "prisoner's dilemma", but as a "tipping point" problem where the focus is to shift actors' preferences towards a common outcome.[31] As per the catalytic logic, therefore, it is expected that the responsibilities of the "k-group" and the subordinate states would converge at a certain preference point over time. For the global climate change problem, the convergent point would be global net zero emissions in the second half of this century, as well as stabilising global temperature rise to below two degrees Celsius.[32]

To operationalise the "tipping point" feature of catalytic cooperation, the Paris Agreement includes an "ambition mechanism" at the core of its architecture. Based on the notion of pledge-review-ratchet notion, the ambition mechanism of the Paris Agreement ensures that states submit and strengthen their national climate change plans over time. The idea is to strengthen collective action over time.[33] Conceptually, the ambition mechanism is the heart of the dynamism of the Paris Agreement, and the Great Climate Transformation that it has ushered in. Crucially, the Paris Agreement lays the foundation for the Great Climate Transformation.

The catalytic logic of the Paris Agreement has spurred climate action outside of the regime. Instead of the Agreement being the main if not only forum to address climate change, it has catalysed climate action in many other regimes. The Paris Agreement can thus be understood as the core framework of the Great Climate Transformations. As a consequence, the Agreement has set in motion other developments that are further driving the Great Climate Transformation, as outlined in the next section.

2.2 Drivers of the Great Climate Transformation

Having outlined Prigogine's ideas as appropriate metaphors for the evolution of the international climate change regime, the present section develops a theoretical explanation of why the international climate change regime evolved from an integrated approach, based on static notions of equilibrium, to the dynamic regime complex for climate change. Crucially, Africa's role in the transformation is underscored. In brief, it identifies five main factors that have driven the transformation of the international climate regime: (1) shift in discourse from legitimacy to effectiveness; (2) shift from unipolarity to multipolarity in world politics; (3) shift from bifurcation to dynamic differentiation; (4) shift from state-centred multilateral action to the proliferation of sub- and non-state actors; and (5) Emergent climate-related policy developments.

2.2.1 Shift in Climate Policy Discourse

Adil Najam aptly captured the evolution of the engagement of developing countries, including African states, in global environmental politics. Using the three major environmental conferences as heuristic markers,— Stockholm 1972, Rio 1992 and Johannesburg 2002—Najam argued that developing countries helped to shift the discourse of global environmental politics from effectiveness to legitimacy.[34] Developing countries were not necessarily *demandeurs* of global environmental governance. Moreover, developing countries, which were initially reluctant to engage, largely agreed to so with the understanding that their economic development concerns would be taken on board. Industrialised countries on the other hand mostly focused on the improvement of the quality of the environment. As Najam put it, developing countries, including African states, did not press for the politics of the environment, but the politics of sustainable development.[35]

Najam's conceptualisation of the tensions between legitimacy and effectiveness underscores the tensions in the multilateral climate change regime. Since the creation of the UNFCCC in 1992, the discourse has focused on enhancing the participation of developing countries in international climate diplomacy. Tensions underlying the lack of universal participation in the international climate regime boiled over with the rejection of the Kyoto Protocol by the US, Canada and Australia. The key reason was that the Protocol did not include large emerging economies, especially China, which would be major future sources of GHG emissions.[36] In essence, any new treaty would have to be universal in nature; the Paris Agreement fulfilled this aspiration.[37]

Once the Paris Agreement had secured legitimacy through universal membership, the focus of discourse has shifted to one of effectiveness. The focus on effectiveness, which was preferred by industrialised countries but de-emphasised by developing countries, was in significant part premised on the push for achieving better environmental outcomes. In the international climate change regime, the discourse on effectiveness is arguably best epitomized by the quest to achieve the Paris Agreement's temperature targets (2 °C, and the aspirational target of 1.5 °C).[38] Moreover, the architecture of the Paris Agreement has adopted a catalytic approach where NDCs submitted by countries must be strengthened every five years, making them stringent in the long run.[39] The discourse represents a shift from the previously held emphasis on legitimacy and additional focus on of developing countries that has been primarily driven by the climate change epistemic community in the north.[40]

African states have however embraced the Paris Agreement's catalytic approach with caution. Even though all African states—with the exception of Libya—have submitted an NDC, almost all the NDCs include a conditional element. The conditional element means that the African states, and other developing countries, commit to a certain level of action, but pledge stronger action upon receiving means of support from industrialised countries.[41] Even though the Paris Agreement includes provisions for support of means of implementation, the inclusion of conditionality in African states' NDCs reveal their reluctant engagement in the regime. Furthermore, since much of the discourse on environmental, and climate change politics, is dominated by the global North, topics such as support for means of implementation have often become secondary to the overall climate governance priorities.[42]

For African states, the topics they care most about have been arguably overshadowed by the call for on 'All Hands on Deck' to reach the temperature targets of the Paris Agreement.[43] Upon realising that their country had submitted an overly ambitious mitigation target in their NDC that they could not meet, a diplomat from Chad expressed 'buyer's remorse' by stating that 'I personally think that the very ambitious INDC [climate plan] like ours is not achievable and it need[sic] to be reviewed...We have been rushed by other countries, and we have elaborated a quick INDC, we did not gather all the data to reflect our national and achievable contribution, which normally [should] take into account sustainable development'.[44] Thus, the discourse has shifted from the perception of climate change within the broader concept of sustainable development, adaptation, means of implementation and how the remaining carbon budget should be shared, to 'taming carbon' above all else.[45]

2.2.2 Evolving Geopolitics of Climate Change

When the UNFCCC was negotiated and adopted, the world had just entered into a unipolar moment. The US had emerged as the winner of the Cold War, and the world had reached 'the end of history'.[46] In its hegemonic position, the US engaged in shaping the world in its image. Under the banner of liberal hegemony, the US took the lead in the development of key multilateral institutions, including on climate change.[47] It is therefore not surprising that the US was instrumental in the development of the international climate change regime, especially the UNFCCC. In addition to diplomatic leadership, the US was also a major contributor to the multilateral finance institutions dealing with climate change. Thus, the US did not put up much of a fight when the UNFCCC obligated the industrialised countries would take the lead in climate change mitigation, and to support developing countries with climate finance, technology development and transfer, and capacity building.

However, the onset of multipolarity in the international system meant that the approach used in the development of the UNFCCC would be untenable. Efforts to develop a legal instrument under the UNFCCC revealed these tensions. When the Kyoto Protocol was adopted in 1997 as the first treaty developed under the UNFCCC, it embraced a regulatory approach that included mitigation targets for industrialised countries, formally known as Annex I, and a timetable to achieve the targets. Moreover, the Annex I countries were also required to enhance their support for means of implementation to developing countries. Even though the adoption of the Kyoto Protocol was a major milestone in international climate diplomacy, there were lingering concerns over its limited membership. The key issue of concern was the exclusion of emerging countries such as China and India from the legally binding aspects of the treaty. It was also argued that the emerging economies would be major future emitters, hence the need to engage them through a legally binding instrument.[48] This trend was consistent with the realities of multipolarity, which had contributed to gridlock, in other areas of global governance.[49]

At the time of the adoption of the Kyoto Protocol, critics of the treaty argued that, China and India would be large emitters and economic powers hence the need to not be simply treated like other developing countries. The equilibrium underpinning the UNFCCC and the Kyoto Protocol had become untenable, and the system became highly unstable.[50] In rejecting the Kyoto Protocol which was signed by his predecessor the Democrat Bill Clinton, the US President, George W. Bush, a Republican, argued that ratifying the Koyo Protocol would significantly damage the US economy, thus allowing other countries comparative advantage. Moreover, President Bush argued that the treaty could not work since it did not include binding commitments for the majority of the world.[51] On cue, Canada withdrew from the Kyoto Protocol, with the Minister for Environment arguing that 'The Kyoto Protocol *does not cover the world's largest two emitters, the United States and China,* and therefore cannot work...It's now clear that Kyoto is not the path forward to a global solution to climate change. If anything it's an impediment.'[52] Ironically, industrialised countries were now using arguments often used by developing countries, predicated on the right to development. China's ascendance in world politics, and its growing economic power, was the canary in the coalmine of international climate diplomacy. The Kyoto approach, premised on static notions of equilibrium, had reached a bifurcation point.

Once it was apparent that the Kyoto Protocol's approach was untenable, efforts shifted towards developing a legal instrument that would be applicable to all.[53] After the spectacular failure of the Copenhagen climate change negotiations on the adoption of a new legally binding instrument to replace the Kyoto Protocol, diplomatic efforts shifted towards engaging emerging powers. Specifically, the newly elected US President Barack Obama, who supported a multilateral response to climate change, worked with China to develop such an instrument. A critical milestone towards such an instrument was the agreement on the Durban Platform in 2011 to develop a 'legal instrument, applicable to all'.[54] African states were in support of the Platform, since they had received assurances of support for means of implementation from industrialised countries, in exchange for their participation. As a penultimate diplomatic step towards agreement on the Paris Agreement on Climate Change, the US and China agreed upon a bilateral climate change agreement. Arguably, the conclusion of the bilateral agreement in 2014 paved the way for the adoption of the Paris Agreement in 2015. India also secured assurances of support for clean technology, among others, from the US and the EU as a condition for its endorsement of the Paris Agreement.

Other geopolitical developments have also contributed to the Great Climate Transformation. Most important has been the rise of China as a great power. While the rise of China and other major emerging economies led to the infeasibility of the Kyoto Protocol approach, it has also opened up other avenues for international climate cooperation. Spheres of influence are emerging as a key feature of the contemporary geopolitical environment. As great and major powers, China, the US and the EU in particular have sought to exert their influence on developing countries. China has developed the Belt and Road Initiative as its main geopolitical vehicle of influence, and the US has established the Build Back Better World (B3W), while the EU has established the Global Gateway Initiative in response. Through these initiatives, the great and major powers have sought to address climate change. Multipolarity has thus led to the resurgence of spheres of influence, further contributing to the Great Climate Transformation.

2.2.3   Adoption of Dynamic Differentiation

A major implication of the changing dynamics of the discourse on global climate governance and multipolarity is on how the burden of climate action, especially mitigation, should be divided amongst countries. At the inception of the UNFCCC in 1992, the status quo was that of bifurcation: industrialised countries would take the bulk of climate change mitigation, and support developing countries through means of implementation; developing countries on the other hand were encouraged to undertake climate action commensurate with their capacity. This delicate balance, based on a static notion of equilibrium, and underpinned by the principle of CBDR, would form the foundation of the multilateral climate change regime.[55] For African states, this balance was ideal, since they would receive support for climate action while having no obligation to reduce their emissions. Importantly, African states could realise their right to development, without stringent ecological constraints.

But as earlier noted, the international climate change regime evolved in ways that sought to move from the equilibrium underpinned by CBDR. The first major change came with the failure of major industrialised countries especially the US to ratify the Kyoto Protocol. The core argument was that the equilibrium notion of bifurcation did not reflect the changing global landscape of emissions, especially the projected future emissions of the major emerging economies. With this in mind, policy makers and scholars from industrialised countries argued that for any future regime to be effective, it had to include all major emitters.[56] While bifurcated differentiation was predicated on the high historical emissions of industrialised countries, attention was shifting towards current and future emissions. Emerging economies argued that, in retrospect, their greenhouse gas emissions were small.[57] For African states in particular, their limited historical emissions and high vulnerability to climate change underpinned a powerful argument for maintaining the bifurcated mode of differentiation.

Rejection of the Kyoto Protocol, however, revealed that any future regime would have to be universal. Thus, the bifurcated approach to differentiation of responsibilities and capabilities would be a key feature of that regime. The question though was whether bifurcation could be maintained in such a regime. The first compromise emerged with the adoption of the Durban Platform, technically known as Ad Hoc Working Group on the Durban Platform for Enhanced Action (ADP), in 2011, involving universal membership in exchange for guaranteed support for means of implementation for developing countries. Moreover, concerns on how differentiation could be undertaken was still a topic of serious disagreement.[58]

A breakthrough compromise was reached with the Paris Agreement on Climate Change. Based on a pledge, review and ratchet mechanism, the Paris Agreement adopted a dynamic form of differentiation[59] that considered the nature of countries' economies and power in the global system. Where there was static differentiation, it was towards specific groups of countries such as least developed countries (LDCs), and small island developing states (SIDS), among others.[60] Interesting, or perhaps disappointing, for Africa was that the region sought to be included as a special vulnerable group deserving of particular attention. But this did not eventually happen, thus delivering a major diplomatic setback for Africa.

While the Paris Agreement's de jure differentiation adopted a dynamic approach, developing countries signalled their dissatisfaction with the differentiation by making their NDCs conditional on receiving support for means of implementation.[61] Developing countries, including almost all African countries, included two types of mitigation targets in their NDCs, as a form of de facto differentiation. The first one was unconditional mitigation targets, which they could undertake with their own resources. The second type was unconditional mitigation targets, which were higher and subject to external support for means of implementation, especially industrialised countries. Inclusion of conditionality therefore served as an insurance policy for African states, and other developing countries, should industrialised countries not honour their obligations for support.[62] Thus, both de jure and de facto differentiation give rise to a 'differentiation-complex', which clearly captures the emergent complexity of the international climate change regime.

At a broader level, the shift away from bifurcated differentiation is evident. The Paris Agreement was part of the broader UN Agenda 2030, which also includes the sustainable development goals (SDGs). The 17 SDGs were adopted in 2015, and they marked a decisive turn from their predecessors, the Millennium Development Goals (MDGs). When the MDGs were developed, they focused on developing countries, with an emphasis on the least developed countries (LDCs). Moreover, the eight MDGs represented issues that were specifically important for African states, hence allowing for targeted intervention. In contrast, the SDGs adopted a universal approach, with a broader range of themes that were not necessarily targeted at developing countries.[63] In effect, the global development agenda had moved from focusing on a subset of countries to a universal approach.

But perhaps a more compelling example is the recent collapse of negotiations towards a Global Compact for the Environment. One of the main reasons for the collapse was the fallout between industrialised and developing countries. The latter demanded support for implementation, while the former rejected the obligation to provide the support.[64] In addition, the proponents of the Global Compact for the Environment sought to open up principles such as CBDR, an objective that was rejected outright by developing countries. Finally, the Compact sought to make environmental litigation easier, while developing countries wanted to limit its scope to identifying gaps in international law. Even though some African states supported the Compact, the majority of African states did not.[65] In sum, it could be argued that the international environmental, and specifically climate, regime has irreversibly moved from the bifurcated differentiation to a new dissipative structure of dynamic, complex differentiation.

2.2.4 The Rise of Non-State Actors

Finally, there has been a major shift from the state-led multilateral climate change regime, to a regime complex with a proliferation of diverse non-state actors. When the UNFCCC was adopted in 1992, the main actors were nation-states. Thus, the rules, norms and obligations during that time reflected the state-centric nature of the regime. But there has been a proliferation of actors, including sub-state (cities and provinces) and non-state actors such as multilateral development banks, financial institutions, Non-Governmental Organisations (NGOs), private companies and others.[66]

While the proliferation of sub- and non-state actors, hereafter non-state actors (NSAs), is apparent, their geographical distribution and objectives vary tremendously. Most of the NSAs are from the global North, which comprises industrialised countries.[67] Thus, while scholars have applauded the proliferation of these actors, their geographical variation reveals that a very limited number of these NSAs are from Africa.[68] Efforts to map these actors by geographical region have revealed that Africa is one of the least represented regions. As scholarship has demonstrated, NSAs are not neutral; for instance, NSAs are critical to shaping the discourse on climate change, and global North NSAs have often shaped the discourse on global environmental politics, including climate change, to focus on ecological targets, while eschewing the broader context of sustainable development.[69] Such discourse is also at odds with the interests of African states, especially the exclusion of the development dimension in the ecological targets.

Some scholars have noted that the rise of NSAs has been partly due to the recalcitrance of key states in multilateral climate change diplomacy.[70] A key concern has been that the multilateral process has been too slow, especially when viewed against the backdrop of rapidly increasing greenhouse gas emissions. The recent withdrawal of the US from the Paris Agreement on Climate Change perhaps best illustrates the point. When newly elected President Donald Trump fulfilled his promise of withdrawing from the Paris Agreement, observers were divided between those who claimed that the Paris regime was better off with US participation, and those who welcomed the withdrawal of the US and it would have otherwise undermined the Paris Agreement from within.[71] Moreover, there was hope that the NSAs in the US, especially cities and states, would fill the void left by the federal government.[72] As a follow-up, the US withdrew funding from the UNFCCC Secretariat, and reneged on fulfilling its remaining US$ 2 billion pledge to the Green Climate Fund (GCF).[73]

More generally, however, the rise of non-state actors has also opened up new opportunities for fostering global climate action. Transnational, sub- and non-state actors are engaging in climate action. While the initial engagement of these actors was nominal, it is also transforming in tandem with the Great Climate Transformation. Perhaps the most salient example of the growing salience and contribution of these actors is captured in the global portals that aggregate such climate actions. Consider the Global Climate Action portal of the UNFCCC, which has registered tens of thousands of climate actors across the world. These include companies, inventors, organisations, regions and cities.[74] Moreover, governments have recognised the importance of non-state climate action; they launched the Lima-Paris Action Agenda (LPAA) under the UNFCCC, which seeks to support transformational climate action. The establishment of the LPAA in many ways underscored non-state climate action as a key pillar of international climate cooperation. Moreover, the rise of transnational, non- and sub-state climate actors is in tandem with the broader rise of these actors in global environmental politics.[75]

Non-state climate action has also gained momentum and begun to mature. A remarkable initiative is the Race to Zero Campaign, which is also convened in partnership with the UNFCCC. The Race to Zero 'is a global campaign to rally leadership and support from businesses, cities, regions, investors for a healthy, resilient, zero carbon recovery that prevents future threats, creates decent jobs, and unlocks inclusive, sustainable growth. It mobilises a coalition of leading net zero initiatives, representing 1,049 cities, 67 regions, 5,227 businesses, 441 of the biggest investors and 1,039 Higher Education Institutions. These 'real economy' actors join 120 countries in the largest ever alliance committed to achieving net zero carbon emissions by 2050 at the latest. Collectively these actors now cover nearly 25% global CO_2 emissions and over 50% GDP.'[76] It is thus apparent that the Race to Zero Campaign symbolises the rising importance of non-state actors in driving the Great Climate Transformation.

2.2.5   Emergent Long-Run Policy Developments

In addition to the aforementioned four drivers, there are other emergent policy developments that will continue to drive the Great Climate Transformation. In this book, we examine these emerging policy developments and argue that policy makers and other actors should consider them in their analysis and engagement with the Great Climate Transformation. In particular, we examine the following emergent long-run policy developments: the tightening vice of climate ambition; divestment from fossil fuels; the adoption of coercive policy instruments such as sanctions; clean energy supply chains; aligning regional integration with climate

30   K. MBEVA ET AL.

Table 2.1 Conceptualising the drivers of the great climate transformation

Driver	Olsonian logic	Catalytic logic
Shift in climate policy discourse	Participation	Effectiveness
Evolving geopolitical environment	Unipolarity	Multipolarity
Dynamic differentiation	Bifurcation	Dynamic
The rise of non-state actors	Nation-states	States, trans-, sub- and non-state actors
Emergent long-run policy developments	Climate policies	Climate and climate-related policies

Irreversible arrow of time

policy; south-south cooperation; and the dynamics of structural climate targets. While still in their emergent stage, the salience of these climate and climate-related policy developments will continue to rise in the long run. Incorporating them into the analysis of the Great Climate Transformation is thus critical. Table 2.1 presents a summary of the key drivers of the Great Climate Transformation.

2.3   Implications for Africa

The Great Climate Transformation will have significant implications on African countries. We explore these implications in detail in subsequent chapters, but a brief overview would suffice. Three main implications for Africa are apparent from the Great Climate Transformation. The first is the expectation of African countries to contribute to the global effort to address climate change. While African countries were part of the initial subgroup of "subordinate states" at the inception of the multilateral climate change regime, the Great Climate Transformation has led to the loss in salience, if not relevance, of the subgroup. Alongside other countries, almost all African countries have made pledges via their nationally determined contributions (NDC), undercutting long-standing efforts to secure recognition as a special vulnerable category.[77]

Second, and related, African countries will have to strengthen their NDCs over time. The catalytic logic of the Paris Agreement, which hinges on the ambition mechanism, means that African countries would have to submit increasingly ambitious NDCs. Developing and implementing more ambitious NDCs over time will be a challenging policy issue for African countries, especially as they try to also realise other development policy objectives such as continental economic integration.[78]

Third, the Great Climate Transformation means that African countries can no longer secure a just transition via primary reliance on the multilateral climate regime. While the initial approach to multilateral climate cooperation included support for implementation in the form of climate finance, technology and capacity building, the dynamics of the Great Climate Transformation imply that African countries will have to increasingly rely on domestic resources to implement their NDCs. International support through means of implementation will continue being part of a bigger picture, and perhaps lose its salience in the long run. Instead, African countries would have to endogenously secure their just transition, especially through creative domestic and regional policies. Ultimately, securing a just transition by African countries should shift from being a primarily normative to strategic imperative.

2.4 Conclusion

In the long run, the Great Climate Transformation has changed the logic of international climate cooperation, with significant implications for African countries. Navigating this new international policy terrain will by no means be an easy task, especially for African countries. This chapter has laid out the conceptual and theoretical framework underpinning the Great Climate Transformation. Adopting a dynamic perspective, as outlined in this chapter, is necessary if African countries are to simultaneously realise their twin objectives of contributing to addressing global climate change and development. To operationalise the framework, the rest of the chapters in the book elaborate on the Great Climate Transformation, how Africa has engaged with the transformation, and the subsequent long-run challenges and opportunities.

Notes

1. William Brown, Sophie Harman, and Sophie Harman, 'African Agency in International Politics', 2013, https://doi.org/10.4324/978020352 6071-6; Christopher Clapham, *Africa and the International System: The Politics of State Survival*, Cambridge Studies in International Relations: 50 (Cambridge: Cambridge University Press, 1996), https://ezp.lib.uni melb.edu.au/login?url=https://search.ebscohost.com/login.aspx?direct= true&db=cat00006a&AN=melb.b2195139&site=eds-live&scope=site.

2. Kevin C. Dunn, 'Introduction: Africa and International Relations Theory', in *Africa's Challenge to International Relations Theory*, ed. Kevin C. Dunn and Timothy M. Shaw, International Political Economy Series (London: Palgrave Macmillan UK, 2001), 1–8, https://doi.org/10.1057/978033 3977538_1; Jonathan Fisher, 'Reproducing Remoteness? States, Internationals and the Co-Constitution of Aid "Bunkerization" in the East African Periphery', Knowledge and Expertise in International Interventions, 2018, https://doi.org/10.4324/9781351241458-6; James M. Goldgeier and Michael McFaul, 'A Tale of Two Worlds: Core and Periphery in the Post-Cold War Era', *International Organization* 46, no. 2 (1992): 467–91, https://doi.org/10.1017/S0020818300027788; Kathryn Lavelle, 'Moving in from the Periphery: Africa and the Study of International Political Economy', *Review of International Political Economy* 12, no. 2 (2005): 364–79, https://doi.org/10.1080/096922 90500105946.

3. Joanes Odiwuor Atela et al., 'Exploring the Agency of Africa in Climate Change Negotiations: The Case of REDD+', *International Environmental Agreements: Politics, Law and Economics* 17, no. 4 (1 August 2017): 463–82, https://doi.org/10.1007/s10784-016-9329-6; Ronald Hope Kempe, 'Climate Change and Poverty in Africa', *International Journal of Sustainable Development & World Ecology* 16, no. 6 (2009): 451–61, https://doi.org/10.1080/13504500903354424; Anthony Nyong, 'Climate Change Impacts in the Developing World: Implications for Sustainable Development', *Climate Change and Global Poverty: A Billion Lives in the Balance*, 2009, 43–64.

4. Robert Falkner, 'The Paris Agreement and the New Logic of International Climate Politics', *International Affairs* 92, no. 5 (1 September 2016): 1107–25, https://doi.org/10.1111/1468-2346.12708; Thomas Hale, 'Catalytic Cooperation', *Global Environmental Politics* 20, no. 4 (1 November 2020): 73–98, https://doi.org/10.1162/glep_a_00561.

5. Ilya Prigogine, 'Order through Fluctuation: Self-Organization and Social System', in *Evolution and Consciousness: Human Systems in Transition*, ed. Erich Jantsch (Reading, MA: Addison-Wesley, 1976), 93–130.

6. Ilya Prigogine, *From Being to Becoming: Time and Complexity in the Physical Sciences /Ilya Prigogine* (New York: W.H. Freeman, 1980); Francis Mangeni and Calestous Juma, *Emergent Africa: Evolution of Regional Economic Integration* (Terra Alta, WV: Headline Books, 2019), 27.
7. Paul Glansdorff and Ilya Prigogine, *Thermodynamic Theory of Structure, Stability and Fluctuations*, vol. 306 (New York: Wiley-Interscience, 1971).
8. Ilya Prigogine, 'Time, Structure, and Fluctuations', *Science* 201, no. 4358 (1978): 777–85; Mangeni and Juma, *Emergent Africa. Evolution of Regional Economic Integration*, 27.
9. Ilya Prigogine and Isabelle Stengers, *The End of Certainty* (New York: Simon and Schuster, 1997).
10. Rakhyun E. Kim and Brendan Mackey, 'International Environmental Law as a Complex Adaptive System', *International Environmental Agreements: Politics, Law and Economics* 14, no. 1 (1 March 2014): 5–24, https://doi.org/10.1007/s10784-013-9225-2.
11. AU, 'Agenda 2063: The Africa We Want (Popular Version)' (Addis Ababa, Ethiopia: African Union Commission, 2015), https://au.int/sites/def ault/files/documents/36204-doc-agenda2063_popular_version_en.pdf.
12. Falkner, 'The Paris Agreement and the New Logic of International Climate Politics'; Jen Iris Allan et al., 'Making the Paris Agreement: Historical Processes and the Drivers of Institutional Design', *Political Studies*, 6 October 2021, https://doi.org/10.1177/003232172 11049294; Hale, 'Catalytic Cooperation'; Daniel Bodansky, 'The Paris Climate Change Agreement: A New Hope?', *American Journal of International Law* 110, no. 2 (April 2016): 288–319, https://doi.org/ 10.5305/amerjintelaw.110.2.0288; Daniel Bodansky, 'The Legal Character of the Paris Agreement', *Review of European, Comparative & International Environmental Law* 25, no. 2 (2016): 142–50, https://doi.org/10.1111/reel.12154; Nicholas Chan, 'The Paris Agreement as Analogy in Global Environmental Politics', *Global Environmental Politics*, 20 September 2021, 1–8, https://doi.org/10.1162/glep_a_00622; Jutta Brunnée and Charlotte Streck, 'The UNFCCC as a Negotiation Forum: Towards Common But More Differentiated Responsibilities', *Climate Policy* 13, no. 5 (1 September 2013): 589–607, https://doi.org/10.1080/14693062.2013.822661.
13. Thomas Hale, '"All Hands on Deck": The Paris Agreement and Nonstate Climate Action', *Global Environmental Politics* 16, no. 3 (15 July 2016): 12–22, https://doi.org/10.1162/GLEP_a_00362.
14. Brunnée and Streck, 'The UNFCCC as a Negotiation Forum'.
15. Christoph Böhringer and Carsten Vogt, 'The Dismantling of a Breakthrough: The Kyoto Protocol as Symbolic Policy', *European Journal of Political Economy* 20, no. 3 (1 September 2004): 597–617, https://doi.org/10.1016/j.ejpoleco.2004.02.004.

16. Mancur Olson, *The Logic of Collective Action. Public Goods and the Theory of Groups* (Cambridge, MA: Harvard University Press, 1965).
17. Olson, 3.
18. Robert Keohane, *After Hegemony: Cooperation and Discord in the World Political Economy* (Princeton: Princeton University Press, 1984), http://www.jstor.org/stable/j.ctt7sq9s.
19. Brunnée and Streck, 'The UNFCCC as a Negotiation Forum'.
20. Russell Hardin, *Collective Action* (New York: Routledge, 1982), chap. 3; Duncan Snidal, 'The Limits of Hegemonic Stability Theory', *International Organization* 39, no. 4 (ed 1985): 599, https://doi.org/10.1017/S002081830002703X.
21. Brunnée and Streck, 'The UNFCCC as a Negotiation Forum'; Jeffrey McGee and Jens Steffek, 'The Copenhagen Turn in Global Climate Governance and the Contentious History of Differentiation in International Law', *Journal of Environmental Law* 28, no. 1 (1 March 2016): 37–63, https://doi.org/10.1093/jel/eqw003.
22. Manjana Milkoreit, 'The Paris Agreement on Climate Change—Made in USA?', *Perspectives on Politics* 17, no. 4 (December 2019): 1019–37, https://doi.org/10.1017/S1537592719000951.
23. McGee and Steffek, 'The Copenhagen Turn in Global Climate Governance and the Contentious History of Differentiation in International Law'; Dieter Helm, 'The Kyoto Approach Has Failed', *Nature* 491, no. 7426 (November 2012): 663–65, https://doi.org/10.1038/491663a; Amanda M. Rosen, 'The Wrong Solution at the Right Time: The Failure of the Kyoto Protocol on Climate Change', *Politics & Policy* 43, no. 1 (2015): 30–58, https://doi.org/10.1111/polp.12105; Gwyn Prins and Steve Rayner, 'Time to Ditch Kyoto', *Nature* 449, no. 7165 (25 October 2007): 973–75, https://doi.org/10.1038/449973a.
24. Snidal, 'The Limits of Hegemonic Stability Theory', 599–600.
25. Thomas C. Schelling, *Micromotives and Macrobehavior* (New York: W. W. Norton & Company, 1978), 221; Hardin, *Collective Action*, chap. 3; Snidal, 'The Limits of Hegemonic Stability Theory', 599.
26. Prins and Rayner, 'Time to Ditch Kyoto'; Helm, 'The Kyoto Approach Has Failed'; McGee and Steffek, 'The Copenhagen Turn in Global Climate Governance and the Contentious History of Differentiation in International Law'.
27. Hale, '"All Hands on Deck"'.
28. Daniel Bodansky, 'A Tale of Two Architectures: The Once and Future U.N. Climate Change Regime', *Climate Change and Environmental Hazards Related to Shipping: An International Legal Framework*, 1 January 2013, 35–51, https://doi.org/10.1163/9789004244955_005.

29. Lavanya Rajamani, 'The Durban Platform for Enhanced Action and the Future of the Climate Regime', *International & Comparative Law Quarterly* 61, no. 2 (April 2012): 501–18, https://doi.org/10.1017/S00 20589312000085; Lavanya Rajamani, 'The Reach and Limits of the Principle of Common But Differentiated Responsibilities and Respective Capabilities in the Climate Change Regime', in *Handbook of Climate Change and India* (London: Routledge, 2011), https://doi. org/10.4324/9780203153284.ch8; Lavanya Rajamani, 'Negotiating the 2015 Climate Agreement: Issues Relating to Legal Form and Nature', Research Paper (Cape Town, South Africa: Mitigation Action Plans & Scenarios, 2015), https://cprindia.org/sites/default/files/Paper_Negoti ating-the-2015-Climate-Agreement_Rajamani.pdf.
30. Hale, 'Catalytic Cooperation', 73.
31. Hale, 83–84.
32. Hale, 89.
33. Hale, 74; Hannah Ritchie and David S. Reay, 'Delivering the Two Degree Global Climate Change Target Using a Flexible Ratchet Framework', *Climate Policy* 17, no. 8 (17 November 2017): 1031–45, https://doi. org/10.1080/14693062.2016.1222260.
34. Adil Najam, 'Developing Countries and Global Environmental Governance: From Contestation to Participation to Engagement', *International Environmental Agreements: Politics, Law and Economics* 5, no. 3 (1 September 2005): 303–21, https://doi.org/10.1007/s10784-005-3807-6.
35. Najam, 312.
36. Rosen, 'The Wrong Solution at the Right Time'; Prins and Rayner, 'Time to Ditch Kyoto'.
37. Falkner, 'The Paris Agreement and the New Logic of International Climate Politics'.
38. Joeri Rogelj et al., 'Paris Agreement Climate Proposals Need a Boost to Keep Warming Well below 2 °C', *Nature* 534, no. 7609 (30 June 2016): 631–39, https://doi.org/10.1038/nature18307; Sander Chan, Paula Ellinger, and Oscar Widerberg, 'Exploring National and Regional Orchestration of Non-State Action for a <1.5 °C World', *International Environmental Agreements: Politics, Law and Economics* 18, no. 1 (1 February 2018): 135–52, https://doi.org/10.1007/s10784-018-9384-2; Pauw et al., 'Beyond Headline Mitigation Numbers: We Need More Transparent and Comparable NDCs to Achieve the Paris Agreement on Climate Change', *Climatic Change* 147, no. 1 (1 March 2018): 23–29, https://doi.org/10.1007/s10584-017-2122-x.
39. Hale, 'Catalytic Cooperation'.

40. Nicole Klenk and Katie Meehan, 'Climate Change and Transdisciplinary Science: Problematizing the Integration Imperative', *Environmental Science & Policy* 54 (1 December 2015): 160–67, https://doi.org/10.1016/j.envsci.2015.05.017; Najam, 'Developing Countries and Global Environmental Governance', 314.
41. Reuben Makomere and Kennedy Liti Mbeva, 'Squaring the Circle: Development Prospects Within the Paris Agreement', *Carbon & Climate Law Review* 12, no. 1 (2018): 31–40, https://doi.org/10.21552/cclr/2018/1/7.
42. Karen O'Brien et al., 'Why Different Interpretations of Vulnerability Matter in Climate Change Discourses', *Climate Policy* 7, no. 1 (1 January 2007): 73–88, https://doi.org/10.1080/14693062.2007.9685639; René Audet, 'Climate Justice and Bargaining Coalitions: A Discourse Analysis', *International Environmental Agreements: Politics, Law and Economics* 13, no. 3 (1 September 2013): 369–86, https://doi.org/10.1007/s10784-012-9195-9; Mary E. Pettenger, *The Social Construction of Climate Change: Power, Knowledge, Norms, Discourses* (Aldershot: Ashgate Publishing, Ltd., 2013).
43. Hale, '"All Hands on Deck"'.
44. Edward King, 'Africa's "Buyer's Remorse" over Paris Climate Deal', Climate Home, 3 November 2016, http://www.climatechangenews.com/2016/11/03/africas-buyers-remorse-over-paris-climate-deal/.
45. Lukas H. Meyer and Dominic Roser, 'Distributive Justice and Climate Change: The Allocation of Emission Rights', *Analyse & Kritik* 28, no. 2 (2016): 223–49, https://doi.org/10.1515/auk-2006-0207; Pauw et al., 'Beyond Headline Mitigation Numbers'; David G. Victor, 'International Agreements and the Struggle to Tame Carbon', in *Global Climate Change*, ed. James N. Griffin, Bush Series in the Economics of Public Policy (Cheltenham, UK and Northampton, MA: Edward Elgar Publishing, 2003), 204–40.
46. Francis Fukuyama, 'The End of History?' *The National Interest*, no. 16 (1989): 3–18.
47. Charles F. Parker and Christer Karlsson, 'The UN Climate Change Negotiations and the Role of the United States: Assessing American Leadership from Copenhagen to Paris', *Environmental Politics* 27, no. 3 (4 May 2018): 519–40, https://doi.org/10.1080/09644016.2018.1442388; John J. Mearsheimer, 'Bound to Fail: The Rise and Fall of the Liberal International Order', *International Security* 43, no. 4 (1 April 2019): 10, https://doi.org/10.1162/isec_a_00342.
48. Rosen, 'The Wrong Solution at the Right Time'; Robyn Eckersley, 'Ambushed: The Kyoto Protocol, the Bush Administration's Climate Policy and the Erosion of Legitimacy', *International Politics* 44, no.

2 (1 March 2007): 306–24, https://doi.org/10.1057/palgrave.ip.880 0190; William Nordhaus and Joseph Boyer, 'Requiem for Kyoto: An Economic Analysis of the Kyoto Protocol', *The Energy Journal* 20 (1999): 93–130; Peter Christoff, 'Post-Kyoto? Post-Bush? Towards an Effective "Climate Coalition of the Willing"', *International Affairs* 82, no. 5 (1 September 2006): 831–60, https://doi.org/10.1111/j.1468-2346.2006.00574.x; Jon Hovi, Tora Skodvin, and Steinar Andresen, 'The Persistence of the Kyoto Protocol: Why Other Annex I Countries Move on Without the United States', *Global Environmental Politics* 3, no. 4 (1 November 2003): 1–23, https://doi.org/10.1162/152638003322757907.

49. Thomas Hale, David Held, and Kevin Young, *Gridlock: Why Global Cooperation Is Failing When We Need It Most* (Cambridge, UK and Malden, USA: Polity Press, 2013), 36.

50. Prins and Rayner, 'Time to Ditch Kyoto'.

51. Michael Lisowski, 'Playing the Two-Level Game: Us President Bush's Decision to Repudiate the Kyoto Protocol', *Environmental Politics* 11, no. 4 (1 December 2002): 101–19, https://doi.org/10.1080/714000641; David E. Sanger, 'Bush Will Continue to Oppose Kyoto Pact on Global Warming', *The New York Times*, 12 June 2001, sec. World, https://www.nytimes.com/2001/06/12/world/bush-will-continue-to-oppose-kyoto-pact-on-global-warming.html.

52. Ingrid Barnsley, 'Dealing with Change: Australia, Canada and the Kyoto Protocol to the Framework Convention on Climate Change', *The Round Table* 95, no. 385 (1 July 2006): 399–410, https://doi.org/10.1080/00358530600748358; Staff, 'Canada Pulls out of Kyoto Protocol', *The Guardian*, 13 December 2011, sec. Environment, https://www.theguardian.com/environment/2011/dec/13/canada-pulls-out-kyoto-protocol.

53. Bodansky, 'The Legal Character of the Paris Agreement'.

54. Bodansky.

55. Kennedy Mbeva and Pieter Pauw, 'Self-Differentiation of Countries' Responsibilities. Addressing Climate Change through Intended Nationally Determined Contributions', Discussion Paper (Bonn, Germany: German Development Institute/Deutsches Institut für Entwicklungspolitik (DIE), 2016), https://www.die-gdi.de/uploads/media/DP_4.2016.pdf; Lavanya Rajamani, 'The Principle of Common but Differentiated Responsibilities and Respective Capabilities in the International Climate Change Regime', in *Research Handbook on Climate Disaster Law*, ed. Rosemary Lyster and Robert Verchick (Cheltenham, UK and Northampton, MA: Edward Elgar, 2018), 46–60, https://www.elgaronline.com/view/edc oll/9781786430021/9781786430021.00009.xml.

56. Prins and Rayner, 'Time to Ditch Kyoto'; Nordhaus and Boyer, 'Requiem for Kyoto'.

57. Aurélie Méjean, Franck Lecocq, and Yacob Mulugetta, 'Equity, Burden Sharing and Development Pathways: Reframing International Climate Negotiations', *International Environmental Agreements: Politics, Law and Economics* 15, no. 4 (1 November 2015): 387–402, https://doi.org/10.1007/s10784-015-9302-9; Harald Winkler et al., 'Reconsidering Development by Reflecting on Climate Change', *International Environmental Agreements: Politics, Law and Economics* 15, no. 4 (1 November 2015): 369–85, https://doi.org/10.1007/s10784-015-9304-7.
58. Bodansky, 'The Legal Character of the Paris Agreement'.
59. Falkner, 'The Paris Agreement and the New Logic of International Climate Politics'.
60. Mbeva and Pauw, 'Self-Differentiation of Countries' Responsibilities. Addressing Climate Change through Intended Nationally Determined Contributions'.
61. Zou Ji and Fu Sha, 'The Challenges of the Post-COP21 Regime: Interpreting CBDR in the INDC Context', *International Environmental Agreements: Politics, Law and Economics* 15, no. 4 (1 November 2015): 421–30, https://doi.org/10.1007/s10784-015-9303-8; Makomere and Mbeva, 'Squaring the Circle'.
62. Makomere and Mbeva, 'Squaring the Circle'.
63. Norichika Kanie and Frank Biermann, *Governing Through Goals: Sustainable Development Goals as Governance Innovation* (Cambridge, MA: MIT Press, 2017).
64. IISD, 'ENB Report | Global Pact for the Environment OEWG-3 | 20–22 May 2019 | Nairobi, Kenya | IISD Reporting Services', *Earth Negotiations Bulletin (ENB)*, 22 May 2019, http://enb.iisd.org/vol35/enb3503e.html.
65. IISD.
66. Karin Bäckstrand et al., 'Non-State Actors in Global Climate Governance: From Copenhagen to Paris and Beyond', *Environmental Politics* 26, no. 4 (4 July 2017): 561–79, https://doi.org/10.1080/09644016.2017.1327485; Sander Chan et al., 'Reinvigorating International Climate Policy: A Comprehensive Framework for Effective Nonstate Action', *Global Policy* 6, no. 4 (2015): 466–73, https://doi.org/10.1111/1758-5899.12294; Hale, '"All Hands on Deck"'.
67. Sander Chan et al., 'Promises and Risks of Nonstate Action in Climate and Sustainability Governance', *Wiley Interdisciplinary Reviews: Climate Change* 10, no. 3 (2019): e572, https://doi.org/10.1002/wcc.572.
68. Thomas N. Hale, 'The Role of Sub-State and Non-State Actors in International Climate Processes', Research Paper (London, UK: The Royal Institute of International Affairs [Chatham House], 2018), 9–10, https://www.chathamhouse.org/sites/default/files/publications/research/2018-11-28-non-state-sctors-climate-synthesis-hale-final.pdf.

69. Najam, 'Developing Countries and Global Environmental Governance', 314; Chan et al., 'Promises and Risks of Nonstate Action in Climate and Sustainability Governance'.
70. Bäckstrand et al., 'Non-State Actors in Global Climate Governance'.
71. Kempe, 'Climate Change and Poverty in Africa'; Luke Kemp, 'US-Proofing the Paris Climate Agreement', *Climate Policy* 17, no. 1 (2 January 2017): 86–101, https://doi.org/10.1080/14693062.2016.117 6007; Luke Kemp, 'Limiting the Climate Impact of the Trump Administration', *Palgrave Communications* 3, no. 1 (31 October 2017): 9, https://doi.org/10.1057/s41599-017-0003-6; Jonathan Pickering et al., 'The Impact of the US Retreat from the Paris Agreement: Kyoto Revisited?', *Climate Policy* 18, no. 7 (18 December 2017): 818–27, https://doi.org/10.1080/14693062.2017.1412934.
72. Hale, '"All Hands on Deck"'.
73. Megan Bowman and Stephen Minas, 'Resilience through Interlinkage: The Green Climate Fund and Climate Finance Governance', *Climate Policy* 19, no. 3 (16 March 2019): 342–53, https://doi.org/10.1080/14693062.2018.1513358.
74. https://climateaction.unfccc.int/.
75. Harriet Bulkeley et al., *Transnational Climate Change Governance* (Cambridge: Cambridge University Press, 2014), https://doi.org/10.1017/CBO9781107706033; Thomas Hale, 'Transnational Actors and Transnational Governance in Global Environmental Politics', *Annual Review of Political Science* 23, no. 1 (2020): null, https://doi.org/10.1146/annurev-polisci-050718-032644.
76. https://unfccc.int/climate-action/race-to-zero-campaign.
77. Nicholas Chan, '"Special Circumstances" and the Politics of Climate Vulnerability: African Agency in the UN Climate Change Negotiations', *Africa Spectrum* 56, no. 3 (1 December 2021): 314–32, https://doi.org/10.1177/0002039721991151.
78. Makomere and Mbeva, 'Squaring the Circle'.

References

Allan, Jen Iris, Charles B. Roger, Thomas N. Hale, Steven Bernstein, Yves Tiberghien, and Richard Balme. 'Making the Paris Agreement: Historical Processes and the Drivers of Institutional Design'. *Political Studies*, 6 October 2021. https://doi.org/10.1177/00323217211049294.

Atela, Joanes Odiwuor, Claire Hellen Quinn, Albert A. Arhin, Lalisa Duguma, and Kennedy Liti Mbeva. 'Exploring the Agency of Africa in Climate Change

Negotiations: The Case of REDD+'. *International Environmental Agreements: Politics, Law and Economics* 17, no. 4 (1 August 2017): 463–82. https://doi.org/10.1007/s10784-016-9329-6.

AU. 'Agenda 2063: The Africa We Want (Popular Version)'. Addis Ababa, Ethiopia: African Union Commission, 2015. https://au.int/sites/default/files/documents/36204-doc-agenda2063_popular_version_en.pdf.

Audet, René. 'Climate Justice and Bargaining Coalitions: A Discourse Analysis'. *International Environmental Agreements: Politics, Law and Economics* 13, no. 3 (1 September 2013): 369–86. https://doi.org/10.1007/s10784-012-9195-9.

Bäckstrand, Karin, Jonathan W. Kuyper, Björn-Ola Linnér, and Eva Lövbrand. 'Non-State Actors in Global Climate Governance: From Copenhagen to Paris and Beyond'. *Environmental Politics* 26, no. 4 (4 July 2017): 561–79. https://doi.org/10.1080/09644016.2017.1327485.

Barnsley, Ingrid. 'Dealing with Change: Australia, Canada and the Kyoto Protocol to the Framework Convention on Climate Change'. *The Round Table* 95, no. 385 (1 July 2006): 399–410. https://doi.org/10.1080/00358530600748358.

Bodansky, Daniel. 'A Tale of Two Architectures: The Once and Future U.N. Climate Change Regime'. *Climate Change and Environmental Hazards Related to Shipping: An International Legal Framework*, 1 January 2013, 35–51. https://doi.org/10.1163/9789004244955_005.

———. 'The Legal Character of the Paris Agreement'. *Review of European, Comparative & International Environmental Law* 25, no. 2 (2016): 142–50. https://doi.org/10.1111/reel.12154.

———. 'The Paris Climate Change Agreement: A New Hope?' *American Journal of International Law* 110, no. 2 (April 2016): 288–319. https://doi.org/10.5305/amerjintelaw.110.2.0288.

Böhringer, Christoph, and Carsten Vogt. 'The Dismantling of a Breakthrough: The Kyoto Protocol as Symbolic Policy'. *European Journal of Political Economy* 20, no. 3 (1 September 2004): 597–617. https://doi.org/10.1016/j.ejpoleco.2004.02.004.

Bowman, Megan, and Stephen Minas. 'Resilience through Interlinkage: The Green Climate Fund and Climate Finance Governance'. *Climate Policy* 19, no. 3 (16 March 2019): 342–53. https://doi.org/10.1080/14693062.2018.1513358.

Brown, William, Sophie Harman, and Sophie Harman. 'African Agency in International Politics'. African Agency in International Politics, 2013. https://doi.org/10.4324/9780203526071-6.

Brunnée, Jutta, and Charlotte Streck. 'The UNFCCC as a Negotiation Forum: Towards Common But More Differentiated Responsibilities'. *Climate Policy*

13, no. 5 (1 September 2013): 589–607. https://doi.org/10.1080/146 93062.2013.822661.

Bulkeley, Harriet, Liliana B. Andonova, Michele M. Betsill, Daniel Compagnon, Thomas Hale, Matthew J. Hoffmann, Peter Newell, Matthew Paterson, Charles Roger, and Stacy D. VanDeveer. *Transnational Climate Change Governance*. Cambridge: Cambridge University Press, 2014. https://doi.org/10.1017/CBO9781107706033.

Chan, Nicholas. 'The Paris Agreement as Analogy in Global Environmental Politics'. *Global Environmental Politics*, 20 September 2021, 1–8. https://doi.org/10.1162/glep_a_00622.

———. '"Special Circumstances" and the Politics of Climate Vulnerability: African Agency in the UN Climate Change Negotiations'. *Africa Spectrum* 56, no. 3 (1 December 2021): 314–32. https://doi.org/10.1177/000203 9721991151.

Chan, Sander, Idil Boran, Harro van Asselt, Gabriela Iacobuta, Navam Niles, Katharine Rietig, Michelle Scobie, et al. 'Promises and Risks of Nonstate Action in Climate and Sustainability Governance'. *Wiley Interdisciplinary Reviews: Climate Change* 10, no. 3 (2019): e572. https://doi.org/10.1002/wcc.572.

Chan, Sander, Paula Ellinger, and Oscar Widerberg. 'Exploring National and Regional Orchestration of Non-State Action for a <1.5 °C World'. *International Environmental Agreements: Politics, Law and Economics* 18, no. 1 (1 February 2018): 135–52. https://doi.org/10.1007/s10784-018-9384-2.

Chan, Sander, Harro van Asselt, Thomas Hale, Kenneth W. Abbott, Marianne Beisheim, Matthew Hoffmann, Brendan Guy, et al. 'Reinvigorating International Climate Policy: A Comprehensive Framework for Effective Nonstate Action'. *Global Policy* 6, no. 4 (2015): 466–73. https://doi.org/10.1111/1758-5899.12294.

Christoff, Peter. 'Post-Kyoto? Post-Bush? Towards an Effective "Climate Coalition of the Willing"'. *International Affairs* 82, no. 5 (1 September 2006): 831–60. https://doi.org/10.1111/j.1468-2346.2006.00574.x.

Clapham, Christopher. *Africa and the International System: The Politics of State Survival*. Cambridge Studies in International Relations: 50. Cambridge University Press, 1996. https://ezp.lib.unimelb.edu.au/login?url=https://search.ebscohost.com/login.aspx?direct=true&db=cat00006a&AN=melb.b21 95139&site=eds-live&scope=site.

Dunn, Kevin C. 'Introduction: Africa and International Relations Theory'. In *Africa's Challenge to International Relations Theory*, edited by Kevin C. Dunn and Timothy M. Shaw, 1–8. International Political Economy Series. London: Palgrave Macmillan UK, 2001. https://doi.org/10.1057/978033 3977538_1.

Eckersley, Robyn. 'Ambushed: The Kyoto Protocol, the Bush Administration's Climate Policy and the Erosion of Legitimacy'. *International Politics* 44, no. 2 (1 March 2007): 306–24. https://doi.org/10.1057/palgrave.ip.8800190.

Falkner, Robert. 'The Paris Agreement and the New Logic of International Climate Politics'. *International Affairs* 92, no. 5 (1 September 2016): 1107–25. https://doi.org/10.1111/1468-2346.12708.

Fisher, Jonathan. 'Reproducing Remoteness? States, Internationals and the Co-Constitution of Aid "Bunkerization" in the East African Periphery'. Knowledge and Expertise in International Interventions, 2018. https://doi.org/10.4324/9781351241458-6.

Fukuyama, Francis. 'The End of History?' *The National Interest*, no. 16 (1989): 3–18.

Glansdorff, Paul, and Ilya Prigogine. *Thermodynamic Theory of Structure, Stability and Fluctuations*. Vol. 306. New York: Wiley-Interscience, 1971.

Goldgeier, James M., and Michael McFaul. 'A Tale of Two Worlds: Core and Periphery in the Post-Cold War Era'. *International Organization* 46, no. 2 (1992): 467–91. https://doi.org/10.1017/S0020818300027788.

Hale, Thomas. '"All Hands on Deck": The Paris Agreement and Nonstate Climate Action'. *Global Environmental Politics* 16, no. 3 (15 July 2016): 12–22. https://doi.org/10.1162/GLEP_a_00362.

———. 'Catalytic Cooperation'. *Global Environmental Politics* 20, no. 4 (1 November 2020): 73–98. https://doi.org/10.1162/glep_a_00561.

———. 'Transnational Actors and Transnational Governance in Global Environmental Politics'. *Annual Review of Political Science* 23, no. 1 (2020): null. https://doi.org/10.1146/annurev-polisci-050718-032644.

Hale, Thomas, David Held, and Kevin Young. *Gridlock: Why Global Cooperation Is Failing When We Need It Most*. Cambridge, UK and Malden, USA: Polity Press, 2013.

Hale, Thomas N. 'The Role of Sub-State and Non-State Actors in International Climate Processes'. Research Paper. London, UK: The Royal Institute of International Affairs (Chatham House), 2018. https://www.chathamhouse.org/sites/default/files/publications/research/2018-11-28-non-state-sctors-climate-synthesis-hale-final.pdf.

Hardin, Russell. *Collective Action*. New York: Routledge, 1982.

Helm, Dieter. 'The Kyoto Approach Has Failed'. *Nature* 491, no. 7426 (November 2012): 663–65. https://doi.org/10.1038/491663a.

Hovi, Jon, Tora Skodvin, and Steinar Andresen. 'The Persistence of the Kyoto Protocol: Why Other Annex I Countries Move on Without the United States'. *Global Environmental Politics* 3, no. 4 (1 November 2003): 1–23. https://doi.org/10.1162/152638003322757907.

IISD. 'ENB Report | Global Pact for the Environment OEWG-3 | 20–22 May 2019 | Nairobi, Kenya | IISD Reporting Services'. *Earth Negotiations Bulletin (ENB)*, 22 May 2019. http://enb.iisd.org/vol35/enb3503e.html.

Ji, Zou, and Fu Sha. 'The Challenges of the Post-COP21 Regime: Interpreting CBDR in the INDC Context'. *International Environmental Agreements: Politics, Law and Economics* 15, no. 4 (1 November 2015): 421–30. https://doi.org/10.1007/s10784-015-9303-8.

Kanie, Norichika, and Frank Biermann. *Governing Through Goals: Sustainable Development Goals as Governance Innovation*. Cambridge, MA: MIT Press, 2017.

Kemp, Luke. 'US-Proofing the Paris Climate Agreement'. *Climate Policy* 17, no. 1 (2 January 2017): 86–101. https://doi.org/10.1080/14693062.2016.1176007.

———. 'Limiting the Climate Impact of the Trump Administration'. *Palgrave Communications* 3, no. 1 (31 October 2017): 9. https://doi.org/10.1057/s41599-017-0003-6.

Kempe, Ronald Hope. 'Climate Change and Poverty in Africa'. *International Journal of Sustainable Development & World Ecology* 16, no. 6 (2009): 451–61. https://doi.org/10.1080/13504500903354424.

Keohane, Robert. *After Hegemony: Cooperation and Discord in the World Political Economy*. Princeton: Princeton University Press, 1984. http://www.jstor.org/stable/j.ctt7sq9s.

Kim, Rakhyun E., and Brendan Mackey. 'International Environmental Law as a Complex Adaptive System'. *International Environmental Agreements: Politics, Law and Economics* 14, no. 1 (1 March 2014): 5–24. https://doi.org/10.1007/s10784-013-9225-2.

King, Edward. 'Africa's "Buyer's Remorse" over Paris Climate Deal'. Climate Home, 3 November 2016. http://www.climatechangenews.com/2016/11/03/africas-buyers-remorse-over-paris-climate-deal/.

Klenk, Nicole, and Katie Meehan. 'Climate Change and Transdisciplinary Science: Problematizing the Integration Imperative'. *Environmental Science & Policy* 54 (1 December 2015): 160–67. https://doi.org/10.1016/j.envsci.2015.05.017.

Lavelle, Kathryn. 'Moving in from the Periphery: Africa and the Study of International Political Economy'. *Review of International Political Economy* 12, no. 2 (2005): 364–79. https://doi.org/10.1080/09692290500105946.

Lisowski, Michael. 'Playing the Two-Level Game: Us President Bush's Decision to Repudiate the Kyoto Protocol'. *Environmental Politics* 11, no. 4 (1 December 2002): 101–19. https://doi.org/10.1080/714000641.

Makomere, Reuben, and Kennedy Liti Mbeva. 'Squaring the Circle: Development Prospects Within the Paris Agreement'. *Carbon & Climate Law Review* 12, no. 1 (2018): 31–40. https://doi.org/10.21552/cclr/2018/1/7.

Mangeni, Francis, and Calestous Juma. *Emergent Africa. Evolution of Regional Economic Integration*. Terra Alta, WV: Headline Books, 2019.

Mbeva, Kennedy, and Pieter Pauw. 'Self-Differentiation of Countries' Responsibilities. Addressing Climate Change through Intended Nationally Determined Contributions'. Discussion Paper. Bonn, Germany: German Development Institute/Deutsches Institut für Entwicklungspolitik (DIE), 2016. https://www.die-gdi.de/uploads/media/DP_4.2016.pdf.

McGee, Jeffrey, and Jens Steffek. 'The Copenhagen Turn in Global Climate Governance and the Contentious History of Differentiation in International Law'. *Journal of Environmental Law* 28, no. 1 (1 March 2016): 37–63. https://doi.org/10.1093/jel/eqw003.

Mearsheimer, John J. 'Bound to Fail: The Rise and Fall of the Liberal International Order'. *International Security* 43, no. 4 (1 April 2019): 7–50. https://doi.org/10.1162/isec_a_00342

Méjean, Aurélie, Franck Lecocq, and Yacob Mulugetta. 'Equity, Burden Sharing and Development Pathways: Reframing International Climate Negotiations'. *International Environmental Agreements: Politics, Law and Economics* 15, no. 4 (1 November 2015): 387–402. https://doi.org/10.1007/s10784-015-9302-9.

Meyer, Lukas H., and Dominic Roser. 'Distributive Justice and Climate Change. The Allocation of Emission Rights'. *Analyse & Kritik* 28, no. 2 (2016): 223–49. https://doi.org/10.1515/auk-2006-0207.

Milkoreit, Manjana. 'The Paris Agreement on Climate Change—Made in USA?' *Perspectives on Politics* 17, no. 4 (December 2019): 1019–37. https://doi.org/10.1017/S1537592719000951.

Najam, Adil. 'Developing Countries and Global Environmental Governance: From Contestation to Participation to Engagement'. *International Environmental Agreements: Politics, Law and Economics* 5, no. 3 (1 September 2005): 303–21. https://doi.org/10.1007/s10784-005-3807-6.

Nordhaus, William, and Joseph Boyer. 'Requiem for Kyoto: An Economic Analysis of the Kyoto Protocol'. *The Energy Journal* 20 (1999): 93–130.

Nyong, Anthony. 'Climate Change Impacts in the Developing World: Implications for Sustainable Development'. *Climate Change and Global Poverty: A Billion Lives in the Balance*, 43–64. Washington, DC: Brookings Institution Press, 2009.

O'Brien, Karen, Siri Eriksen, Lynn Nygaard, and Ane Schjolden. 'Why Different Interpretations of Vulnerability Matter in Climate Change Discourses'. *Climate Policy* 7, no. 1 (1 January 2007): 73–88. https://doi.org/10.1080/14693062.2007.9685639.

Olson, Mancur. *The Logic of Collective Action. Public Goods and the Theory of Groups*. Cambridge, MA: Harvard University Press, 1965.

Parker, Charles F., and Christer Karlsson. 'The UN Climate Change Negotiations and the Role of the United States: Assessing American Leadership from Copenhagen to Paris'. *Environmental Politics* 27, no. 3 (4 May 2018): 519–40. https://doi.org/10.1080/09644016.2018.1442388.

Pauw, P, Richard J. T. Klein, Kennedy Mbeva, Adis Dzebo, Davide Cassanmagnago, and Anna Rudloff. 'Beyond Headline Mitigation Numbers: We Need More Transparent and Comparable NDCs to Achieve the Paris Agreement on Climate Change'. *Climatic Change* 147, no. 1 (1 March 2018): 23–29. https://doi.org/10.1007/s10584-017-2122-x.

Pettenger, Mary E. *The Social Construction of Climate Change: Power, Knowledge, Norms, Discourses.* Aldershot: Ashgate Publishing, Ltd., 2013.

Pickering, Jonathan, Jeffrey S. McGee, Tim Stephens, and Sylvia I. Karlsson-Vinkhuyzen. 'The Impact of the US Retreat from the Paris Agreement: Kyoto Revisited?' *Climate Policy* 18, no. 7 (18 December 2017): 818–827. https://doi.org/10.1080/14693062.2017.1412934.

Prigogine, Ilya. 'Order through Fluctuation: Self-Organization and Social System'. In *Evolution and Consciousness: Human Systems in Transition*, edited by Erich Jantsch, 93–130. Reading, MA: Addison-Wesley, 1976.

———. 'Time, Structure, and Fluctuations'. *Science* 201, no. 4358 (1978): 777–85.

———. *From Being to Becoming Time and Complexity in the Physical Sciences /Ilya Prigogine.* New York: W.H. Freeman, 1980.

Prigogine, Ilya, and Isabelle Stengers. *The End of Certainty.* New York: Simon and Schuster, 1997.

Prins, Gwyn, and Steve Rayner. 'Time to Ditch Kyoto'. *Nature* 449, no. 7165 (25 October 2007): 973–75. https://doi.org/10.1038/449973a.

Rajamani, Lavanya. 'The Reach and Limits of the Principle of Common But Differentiated Responsibilities and Respective Capabilities in the Climate Change Regime'. In *Handbook of Climate Change and India.* London: Routledge, 2011. https://doi.org/10.4324/9780203153284.ch8.

———. 'The Durban Platform for Enhanced Action and the Future of the Climate Regime'. *International & Comparative Law Quarterly* 61, no. 2 (April 2012): 501–18. https://doi.org/10.1017/S0020589312000085.

———. 'Negotiating the 2015 Climate Agreement: Issues Relating to Legal Form and Nature'. Research Paper. Cape Town, South Africa: Mitigation Action Plans & Scenarios, 2015. https://cprindia.org/sites/default/files/Paper_Negotiating-the-2015-Climate-Agreement_Rajamani.pdf.

———. 'The Principle of Common But Differentiated Responsibilities and Respective Capabilities in the International Climate Change Regime'. In *Research Handbook on Climate Disaster Law*, edited by Rosemary Lyster and Robert Verchick, 46–60. Cheltenham, UK and Northampton, MA: Edward

Elgar, 2018. https://www.elgaronline.com/view/edcoll/9781786430021/9781786430021.00009.xml.

Ritchie, Hannah, and David S. Reay. 'Delivering the Two Degree Global Climate Change Target Using a Flexible Ratchet Framework'. *Climate Policy* 17, no. 8 (17 November 2017): 1031–45. https://doi.org/10.1080/14693062.2016.1222260.

Rogelj, Joeri, Michel den Elzen, Niklas Höhne, Taryn Fransen, Hanna Fekete, Harald Winkler, Roberto Schaeffer, Fu Sha, Keywan Riahi, and Malte Meinshausen. 'Paris Agreement Climate Proposals Need a Boost to Keep Warming Well below 2 °C'. *Nature* 534, no. 7609 (30 June 2016): 631–39. https://doi.org/10.1038/nature18307.

Rosen, Amanda M. 'The Wrong Solution at the Right Time: The Failure of the Kyoto Protocol on Climate Change'. *Politics & Policy* 43, no. 1 (2015): 30–58. https://doi.org/10.1111/polp.12105.

Sanger, David E. 'Bush Will Continue to Oppose Kyoto Pact on Global Warming'. *The New York Times*, 12 June 2001, sec. World. https://www.nytimes.com/2001/06/12/world/bush-will-continue-to-oppose-kyoto-pact-on-global-warming.html.

Schelling, Thomas C. *Micromotives and Macrobehavior*. New York: W. W. Norton, 1978.

Snidal, Duncan. 'The Limits of Hegemonic Stability Theory'. *International Organization* 39, no. 4 (ed 1985): 579–614. https://doi.org/10.1017/S002081830002703X.

Staff. 'Canada Pulls out of Kyoto Protocol'. *The Guardian*, 13 December 2011, sec. Environment. https://www.theguardian.com/environment/2011/dec/13/canada-pulls-out-kyoto-protocol.

Victor, David G. 'International Agreements and the Struggle to Tame Carbon'. In *Global Climate Change*, edited by James N. Griffin, 204–40. Bush Series in the Economics of Public Policy. Cheltenham, UK and Northampton, MA: Edward Elgar Publishing, 2003.

Winkler, Harald, Anya Boyd, Marta Torres Gunfaus, and Stefan Raubenheimer. 'Reconsidering Development by Reflecting on Climate Change'. *International Environmental Agreements: Politics, Law and Economics* 15, no. 4 (1 November 2015): 369–85. https://doi.org/10.1007/s10784-015-9304-7.

CHAPTER 3

Shift in Climate Discourse

Reconciling international environmental and development policy has been a longstanding contested issue, especially in treaty and other multilateral negotiations. In tandem, the relationship between climate policy and development has always followed these contours. On the one hand, the view advanced by developing countries has been that underdevelopment—especially poverty—is the main driver of environmental degradation. Hence to effectively address environmental issues, it would be imperative to also address the underlying development challenges. An alternative view, advanced by industrialised countries, has been that environmental problems have been mainly due to the excesses of industrialisation. The concomitant remedy has thus been to curtail industries that pollute the environment. These two alternative conceptions of the climate and economic development nexus have distinguished the approaches to international climate policy in the global North and South. It is within this context that this chapter explores how Africa can realise its right to development, while undertaking ambitious climate actions that may at times constrain this development, under conditions of diminishing international support for implementation.

For African countries, the impetus to shift from dependency on aid to endogenous economic development based on regional economic integration and industrialisation, has been an issue of top priority. But the Great

© The Author(s), under exclusive license to Springer Nature
Switzerland AG 2023
K. Mbeva et al., *Africa's Right to Development in a Climate-Constrained World*, Contemporary African Political Economy,
https://doi.org/10.1007/978-3-031-22887-2_3

47

Climate Transformation, which was articulated in the preceding chapter, has necessitated a reconceptualisation of achieving sustainable development. The discourse on industrial development as the main cause of the climate change problem dominates global climate cooperation, especially the focus on mitigation action. But for African countries, as this chapter argues, reconciling the climate and development policy dimensions would require the continued emphasis on poverty reduction, while also being attentive to emerging policy developments that may upend this balance. A discourse on just transition, we argue, provides a better framing, as it emphasises the strategic element of the transition in addition to the normative dimension of justice. Crucially, a framing of just transition would enable African countries to predicate its realisation on endogenous policy-making and implementation, hence a shift from undue focus on the multilateral climate regime as the exclusive forum for seeking and releasing a just transition. This can be achieved through effectively and creatively engaging with the five drivers of transformation that underpin the Great Climate Transform, as outlined in the previous chapter.

Given this dilemma, this chapter suggests and articulates an alternative approach for Africa's approach to reconciling international climate and development policy. It argues that the discourse on international climate policy has shifted from a strong emphasis on sustainable development to a focus on climate effectiveness, especially on global mitigation. Drawing on literature and analysis of the evolution of multilateral climate and sustainable development cooperation, the chapter traces the debates on the politics of climate and sustainable development and their implications for Africa's quest to secure a just transition. It is concluded that Africa's approach to reconciling international climate and development policy would need to be reconceptualised through the concept of endogenous just transition, a shift from undue reliance on the multilateral regime as the main locus for securing a just transition. Crucially, the challenge is now no longer a rhetorical, but very much a practical one, as almost all African countries have submitted Nationally Determined Contributions (NDCs) under the Paris Agreement, which they are expected to strengthen over time, are framed within the broader context of sustainable development.

3.1 Defining the Context of Environmental and Climate Policy

Connecting and reconciling the environment and development policy dimensions has been of primary interest to African countries, especially as regards climate change. But despite their increased engagement in international climate change diplomacy, African states have often been frustrated with the poor implementation of commitments, especially those meant to support them to address climate change challenges.[1] While Africa, and developing countries in general, succeeded in shaping discourse on environmental governance within the broader context of sustainable development, they are yet to secure its translation into action. A major point of contention has been inadequate support from industrialised countries especially on technology transfer and development.[2] Adil Najam captured this challenge elegantly when he argued that even though developing countries, including African states, had secured legitimacy of global environmental politics through their enhanced participation, they are yet to secure effectiveness through the realisation of the politics of sustainable development.[3]

But perhaps this challenge is most apparent in the climate change regime, where African states are faced with the challenge of realising their development objectives but have committed to undertake climate change actions that may constrain their economic development agenda.[4] Moreover, support for means of implementation, which has been a key condition for Africa's engagement in international climate diplomacy, is declining and taking forms that are different from those preferred by African states.[5] This approach is underpinned by the notion of static equilibrium: Africa will undertake greater commitments on climate change with the expectation of support for means of implementation by industrialised countries. Hence Africa is faced with a dilemma: *how can it realise its right to development, while undertaking climate actions that may at times constrain this development, under conditions of diminishing support for implementation?*

Efforts to rapidly meet Africa's industrialisation goals while at the same time engaging in a global climate agenda that has increasingly shifted towards achieving the 1.5 degree Celsius mitigation target represent a unique juncture in the continent's future. Internally, the continent's pursuit of rapid industrialisation has increasingly departed from the status quo notions which primarily positioned it as a net exporter of raw materials and importer of manufactured goods. It has consequently sought to challenge the equilibrium notions premised on the idea of comparative advantage by seeking pathways to development that are not as reliant on traditional ties that date back to colonial times. But to fully understand these dynamics, one has to step back and take a broader view of Africa's position in the post-world war order, as well as the global politics of sustainable development, a task undertaken by the next two sections.

3.2   AFRICA IN THE POST-WAR WORLD ORDER

Raúl Prebisch in his seminal work showed that the international economic order was marked by countries at the centre which produced manufactured goods and those in the periphery which depended on the export of raw materials.[6] This status quo meant that countries at the periphery, most of which were developing countries, would remain underserved by the trade relationships they had with their more developed counterparts.[7] To address this issue, he argued that it was necessary to improve the economic relationships between countries on the periphery.[8] The Latin American case subsequently demonstrated that peripheral countries that managed to establish meaningful economic relationships operated far beyond the established equilibrium epitomised by unbalanced linkages between countries at the centre and those in the periphery. These studies resonated with African States which under status quo conditions not only relied on exportation of raw materials to industrialised countries but also experienced worsening terms of trade, increasing indebtedness and poverty.[9]

Moreover, African economies were and still are largely dependent on primary economic sectors including mining, agriculture, forestry, fishing and increasingly the extraction of oil and gas with little connectivity between constituent states. This reliance has inevitably generated rapid economic decay due to the closed nature of the continent's economic systems.[10] This prolonged stagnation and decay of already underdeveloped economies continued to manifest as the continent's population increased exponentially with some estimates suggesting that Africa's population will double by 2050.[11] Additionally, most of the continent's economies have also been victims of extensive corruption which is itself indicative of the weak political and extractive dependent economic structure that confined them to a limited role in global value chains and undermined the development of more meaningful regional economic ties.[12]

Post-cold war developments also flung the continent into more socio-economic uncertainty. The west's pivot towards increasing economic ties with Europe together with the creation of multilateral institutions such as the World Trade Organization (WTO) also weakened African economies by inter alia discouraging preferential trade agreements. Coupled with rapid economic globalisation, these developments further undermined Africa's underdeveloped industries' ability to compete with other more established economies.[13] Further, internal shocks including major environmental disasters, and political instability forced African states to look internally for solutions that inevitably involve greater interactions between regional countries. Africa's unique political structures are of particular interest here. Remember, many African countries were formed by stitching together disparate autonomous ethnic groups and separating others. Some colonial powers used systems of indirect rule where select local rulers exercised delegated authority on behalf of the imperial power to administer large swathes of the population in countries like Kenya. This created a dynamic where two systems of power co-existed i.e. one that was customary but ethnicised, and another that was civic but racialised resulting in double division amongst different communities.[14] This dynamic was amplified in the lead up to and during the post-colonial era where political edifices was often structured along ethnic lines.

Additionally, several post-independence governments responded to divergent political views through autocratic rule and suppression of democratic expression in part to advance ethnic interests even where there was multi-party-political activity. This dynamic was exacerbated by instances where a handful of ethnic groups controlled instruments of state and power driving further internal unrest and ethnicising the exercise of authority.[15] At the same time, numerous African countries experienced devastating military coups, civil wars and despotic leaders who were interested in consolidating power and wealth for themselves and their cronies. Untenable, and coupled with the slow but gradual rise of popular movements demanding for democratic change, this situation has slowly begun to challenge and erode the centrality of military and despotic leaders and replacing them with democratically elected leaders, and constitutional reforms. These processes of political innovation, however, are still ongoing and will take years before the full manifestation of these movements is realised across the continent.[16]

3.3 The Global Politics of Sustainable Development

On the global climate discourse front, African countries have always had a tenuous relationship with the global climate regime from its inception. As Adil Najam puts it, African countries, together with other developing countries, did not start off as the agitators for multilateral environmental governance to which climate change has become an integral element.[17] Their role can instead be characterised as reluctant participants in the environmental discourse epitomised by deep epistemological divisions between northern industrialised and African developing states. This relationship precedes the global climate agenda and has shaped multilateral climate cooperation between African countries and the world. Engagement in international climate diplomacy was predicated on the understanding that poverty was the main driver of environmental degradation, and climate change, in African states.[18] This was consistent with the positions of other developing countries.[19]

The story of African engagement and the problematisation of the environment including climate change begins in the early years prior to the 1972 United Nations Conference on the Human Environment (UNCHE) in Stockholm. African states had worked with other developing countries to articulate a conceptual approach that captured the role of economic development as crucial to addressing environmental degradation. This was part of broader efforts to develop a more just international system, underpinned by a New International Economic Order (NIEO).[20] Three basic texts were developed to form the intellectual foundation of the negotiations: the Stockholm Declaration; the Founex Report; and the Cocoyoc Declaration.

The Stockholm Declaration embodied the final compromise from the negotiations. But the Founex Report, by contrast, sought to foreground the negotiations by outlining the relationship between economic development and the objectives of environmental policy. About two years after the Stockholm Conference, the Cocoyoc Declaration of 1974 reinforced the Stockholm compromise as well as the central thesis of the Founex Report.

To fully appreciate the challenge of reconciling environmental and development policy for developing countries in general, and African countries in particular, it would be useful to consider the key message of the

Founex Report. It is worth noting that the Founex report's framing of the environmental problematique, which noted that

> The current concern with the Human Environment has arisen at a time when the energies and efforts of the developing countries are being increasingly devoted to the goal of development. Indeed, the compelling urgency of the development objective has been widely recognized in the last two decades by the international community and has more recently been endorsed in the proposals set out by the United Nations for the Second Development Decade.
>
> To a large extent, the current concern with environmental issues has emerged out of [sic] the problems experienced by the industrially advanced countries. These problems are themselves very largely the outcome of a high level of economic development. The creation of large productive capacities in industry and agriculture, the growth of complex systems of transportation and communication, and the evolution of massive urban conglomerations have all been accompanied in one way or another by damage and disruption to the human environment. Such disruptions have indeed attained such major proportions that in many communities they already constitute serious hazards to human health and well-being. In some ways, in fact, the dangers extend beyond national boundaries and threaten the world as a whole.
>
> Developing countries are not, of course, unconcerned with these problems. They have an obvious and a vital [sic] stake in them to the extent of their impact on the global environment and on their economic relations with the developed countries. They also have [sic] an interest in them to the extent that they are problems that tend to accompany the process of development and are in fact already beginning to emerge, with increasing severity, in their own societies. The developing countries would clearly wish to avoid, as far as is feasible, the mistakes and distortions that have characterised the patterns of development of the industrialised societies.
>
> However, the major environmental problems of developing countries are essentially of a different kind. They are predominantly problems that reflect the poverty and very lack of development of their societies. They are problems, in other words, of both rural and urban poverty. In both the towns and the countryside, not merely the "quality of life", but life itself is endangered by poor water, housing, sanitation, and nutrition, by sickness and disease and by natural disasters. These are problems, no less than those of industrial pollution, that clamour for attention in the context of the concern with human environment. They are problems which affect the greater mass of mankind.[21]

In outlining a suitable paradigm of addressing environmental challenges, the Founex Report made the following recommendation, with a strong connection to the development policy dimension,

> It is evident that, in large measure, the kind of environmental problems that are of importance in developing countries are those that can be overcome by the process of development itself. In advanced countries, it is appropriate to view development as a cause of environmental problems. Badly planned and unregulated development can have a similar result in developing countries as well. But, for the greater part, developing countries must view the relationship between development and environment in a different perspective. In their context, development becomes essentially a cure for their major environmental problems. For these reasons, concern for environment [sic] must not and need not detract from the commitment of the world community -- developing and more industrialized nations alike to the overriding task of development of the developing regions of the world. Indeed it underscores the need not only for a maximum commitment to the goals and targets of the Second Development Decade, but also for their redefinition in order to attack that dire poverty which is the most important aspect of the problems which afflict the environment of the majority of mankind.[22]

Consequently, they were highly reluctant to engage in the mostly northern-led talks driven by suspicions that committing to such an environmental agenda was a threat to their developmental interests.[23] With high levels of poverty and underdevelopment across the continent, their central focus, at least on the international stage, had been correcting the crippling socio-economic inequities that had been perpetuated by the existing international economic and political order. Consequently, a push to establish a new environmental agenda by their former colonisers was not only seen as a distraction from more important concerns but also as an attempt to undermine their developmental ambitions. These sentiments even drove concerns that African and other developing countries would not be keen to engage with the talks.[24] Studies indicate that some of these countries saw the UNCHE conference as an attempt to enhance the existing equilibrium characterised by perpetual poverty, economic and technical dependence.[25]

Other countries went further to assert that industrialised countries preferred to undermine the development of poorer countries by slowing down industrial development to protect and restore the global environment, thus pulling the ladder behind them.[26] This suspicion was best captured by a famous statement from the Côte d'Ivoire (Ivory Coast) delegation which announced that it would prefer more pollution problems as opposed to poverty if it meant that more industrialisation would be achieved.[27]

Perhaps the most notable effort to frame African and other developing country concerns when it came to the global environmental agenda was the 1972 Founex Report created by a group of intellectuals from developing states as part of UNCHE preparations.[28] The report defined the concerns that resonated with African states but also framed global environmental problems within the context of poverty and underdevelopment. It famously asserted that major environmental concerns facing developing countries were of a different nature. They were predominantly issues that reflected lack of development in their respective countries.[29] The report also emphasised that these problems were not inferior to those caused by industrial pollution which have dominated the discourse on environmental governance.

Instead, these developmental problems affected a larger proportion of the global population and thus deserving of attention. Importantly, the report also asserted that while it was appropriate for developed countries to view environmental problems as an outcome of industrialisation and development, the opposite was the case for developing states where development was meant to be a cure for their environmental concerns.[30] Such was the importance of this articulation that it has since remained largely consistent and unchanged, shaping engagement with subsequent multilateral regimes especially climate change governance. It is therefore no surprise that the preamble of the Stockholm Declaration reflected this fundamental difference,

> In the [sic] developing countries most of the environmental problems are caused by under-development. Millions continue to live far below the minimum levels required for a decent human existence, deprived of adequate food and clothing, shelter and education, health, and sanitation. Therefore, the developing countries must direct their efforts to development, bearing in mind their priorities and the need to safeguard and improve the environment. For the same purpose, the industrialized countries should make efforts to reduce the gap themselves [sic]

and the developing countries. In the industrialized countries, environmental problems are generally related to industrialization and technological development.[31]

Two years after the Stockholm Conference and Declaration, the UNEP and UNCTAD organised a follow up event to reconsider the relationship between environmental policy and development. The Cocoyoc Declaration, which resulted from the meeting in Cocoyoc, Mexico in 1974, reinforced both the Founex Report and the Stockholm Declaration. In its contribution to the debate, the Cocoyoc Declaration crystallised the concept of "development without limits", which recognises "the threats to both the 'inner limits' of basic human needs and the 'outer limits' of the planet's physical resources".[32]

African countries were and are not necessarily opposed to addressing environmental problems. They were, however, challenging how the issue was problematised and prioritised.[33] Processes leading to the 1992 United Nations Conference on Environment and Development (UNCED, also known as Rio Earth Summit), which also ushered in the multilateral climate regime represent a crucial juncture in Africa's engagement with the global climate agenda.

The introduction of the concept of sustainable development in global environmental discourse through the World Commission on Environment and Development (WCED also known as the Brundtland report) was key in setting the course of engagement in later environmental governance regimes.[34] It essentially created room for buy-in in the global environmental agenda and slowly shifted the African and developing country approache to the issue, from one based on contestation to one of reluctant participation.

The 1989 Resolution 44/228 of the United Nations Economic and Social Council perhaps best captured the terms of engagement for environmental participation by ensuring that the Rio Earth Summit was not another conference on the human environment but one that also included development as the main agenda.[35] Even though developed countries were principal advocates for the Rio Earth Summit, the Resolution was inspired by developing country concerns around framing the global environmental agenda.[36] Specifically, Resolution 44/228 emphasised the intricate linkage between poverty and environmental degradation and affirmed that enhancing socio-economic growth and development was key to addressing ecological problems. Further, the resolution also asserted developing country rights over exploitation of their natural resources, while maintaining that their industrialised counterparts were more responsible for global environmental degradation. This meant that developed states had primary responsibility towards addressing environmental challenges.[37] In essence, the resolution framed the Rio process in a way that was more in line with their concerns.

Additionally, it captured the desire by African and other countries to obtain assurances and craft principles from the Rio process that reflected their concerns on the evolving global environmental agenda. This included inclusion of key concepts especially the additionality principle, polluter pays principles and the common but differentiated principle.[38] It was the incorporation of these principles into the global environmental discourse that therefore enabled African and other countries to participate in the environmental policy-making in a manner that had not been seen before.

3.4 Sustainable Development in the Multilateral Climate Change Regime

It is in this context that the international climate regime began in the late 1980s, right around the time discussions on the environmental—development nexus were at their peak.[39] To be clear, there had been previous discussions around the need to address climate change. The World Climate Conference for instance was convened as far back as 1979 to draw both scientific and possibly political attention to the issue.[40] However, these early efforts had little participation from African states. Furthermore, international legal mechanisms had also not provided any guidance on how to equitably address climate change.[41] It was not until about 1988 when it finally became a global environmental policy issue for discussion at the UN General Assembly and the Toronto Conference on Changing the Atmosphere.[42] Understanding these dynamics is critical to providing a context for Africa's conception of the relationship between climate and economic/development policy. Moreover, Africa's engagement in multilateral climate change negotiations as a bloc provides a sound basis for viewing the region as an entity.[43]

United Nations Resolution 45/212 was also passed around this time, triggering negotiations for developing a new multilateral agreement on climate change at the end of 1990 while the Intergovernmental Panel on Climate Change (IPCC) was established.[44] States eventually adopted the

United Nations Framework Convention on Climate Change (UNFCCC) at the 1992 UNCED conference after about 3 years of negotiations.[45] Less than two years later, the UNFCCC entered into force on the 21 March 1994.[46] Contained in the UNFCCC were provisions that institutionalised key principles that captured some African concerns including inter alia the provision of new and additional support from developed to developing countries for the implementation of the Convention's objectives, and common but differentiated responsibilities.[47] Under the Berlin Mandate, states discussed the contours of the then new agreement [48] and the Kyoto Protocol which was subsequently adopted in 1997.

The Protocol set overall legally binding greenhouse gas emission reduction targets for developed countries (5% below 1990 levels for developed countries during its first commitment period of 2008–2012), while exempting African and other developing countries from new obligations, only allowing them to engage voluntarily.[49] This bifurcation represented a strict application of the common but differentiated responsibility and would be christened as 'the firewall'.[50]

Limits on the Kyoto Protocol approach, however, began to appear, especially when the world's biggest GHG emitter and economy, the US, did not ratify the Kyoto Protocol. Specifically, the US Senate did not approve of the exclusion of emerging economies such as China and India from the Kyoto Protocol.[51] For the US Senate, the only acceptable treaty would be one that includes all major emitters, especially emerging countries. By implication, this caveat by the US Senate sets the stage and momentum to abandon the exclusive approach, and instead develops a universal treaty. Canada, and eventually Australia's withdrawal from the Kyoto Protocol marked a logical conclusion of the top-down, regulatory, and exclusive approach in international climate diplomacy.[52]

All the while, African states, in collaboration with developing countries, tried to secure their economic growth imperative in the international climate regime by formulating variations of the right to development. The most prominent formulation, perhaps, is equitable access to sustainable development (EASD).[53] EASD articulated the need to 'reserve' space for developing countries, noting that they would inevitably need to increase their GHG emissions in pursuit of economic growth. Moreover, EASD was premised on the notion that industrialised countries had already used up their 'carbon budget', hence their obligation for more drastic GHG emissions. Even though EASD was a persuasive formulation, at least rhetorically, it did not match developments in international climate diplomacy. Additionally, studies point to declining climate finance, both in terms of its adequacy and nature.[54] For instance, Africa only received 3% of the funds under the Kyoto Protocol's Clean Development Mechanism, with the bulk of the 3% going to South Africa.[55] Moreover, African states have often found it challenging to access international climate finance due to complex bureaucratic processes. Much of the climate finance is increasingly being disbursed in the form of loans, raising concerns of a 'climate debt-trap' for the numerous debt-stressed African states.[56]

Consequently, the climate regime began to shift towards the development of a legal instrument applicable to all.[57] The Bush administration sponsored several bilateral and mini-lateral arrangements around themes like enhanced research, mitigation, and technology development, among others. Importantly, these arrangements eschewed the key distributional concerns that fuelled the dominant affirmative multilateral approach to climate governance.[58] For instance, the 2005 Asia Pacific Partnership on Clean Development and Climate brought together seven countries, most importantly including India and China to design a mini-lateral arrangement that was aimed at enhancing cooperation around areas such as economic and technological development, climate change and pollution.[59] Crucially, while it set no joint goals, targets and/or objectives, it encouraged each participating state to set its own domestic targets for mitigating greenhouse gas emissions.[60] This represented one of the first explicit attempts to design an international climate governance regime that expressly took up a voluntary pledge-based framework and focused on self-differentiation and nationally determined contributions as opposed to the bifurcated targets and timetables espoused by the Kyoto Protocol.

It is these efforts that eventually culminated in the first major shift from the affirmative approach through the Copenhagen Accords in the 15th session of the Conference of Parties (COP) to the UNFCCC.[61] The Accord contained a few crucial provisions that would later become critical to the eventual design of a post-Kyoto climate regime. Crucially, it abandoned the bifurcated binding targets approach in the Kyoto Protocol with 1990 as the baseline year, in favour of more universal nationally determined voluntary non-binding pledges, echoing the initiatives sponsored by the US before the talks.[62] This approach was confirmed in the subsequent decision of the 16th session of the UNFCCC's COP in Cancun after failure of the Copenhagen talks to reach a formal COP decision.[63] Consequently, even though the differentiation between countries remained a key feature of the accords, the structure of global cooperation had changed such that the status quo that had previously allowed it to underpin an affirmative multilateral model of climate change cooperation was no longer as tenable as had been earlier designed.

The landmark 2015 Paris Climate Agreement was arguably the culmination of efforts to shift the affirmative approach of multilateral climate cooperation from its original design under the Kyoto Protocol-led regime. The Agreement ushered in a more hybrid (bottom-up and top-down features), pledge and review approach to multilateral climate cooperation as opposed to the regulated, top-down targets and timetables' approach of the Kyoto Protocol.[64] Under the Paris Agreement, states would submit voluntary pledges, officially known as Nationally Determined Contributions (NDCs), which would be strengthened every five years. This approach marked a decisive shift from a 'regulatory' to a 'catalytic' international climate regime.[65] Even though CBDR&RC was to continue to be a key feature of global climate governance, its application had fundamentally changed such that universal self-differentiation would prevail over the Annex I/ Non-Annex model. Crucially, it also enshrined the non-binding nationally determined contributions mechanisms as a medium through which universal action and self-differentiation could be enhanced as opposed to the previous model where developing countries large and small were excluded from mandatory mitigation obligations.

However significant structural changes in the climate regime have translated to a gradual departure from the framing that had been forcefully articulated prior to the Rio Earth Summit. It is these efforts that eventually culminated in the first major shift from the affirmative approach through the Copenhagen Accords in the 15th session of the Conference of Parties (COP) to the UNFCCC.[66] The Accord contained crucial provisions that would later become critical to the eventual design of a post-Kyoto climate regime. Importantly, it abandoned the bifurcated binding targets approach in the Kyoto Protocol, in favour of more universal nationally determined voluntary non-binding pledges, echoing the initiatives sponsored by the US before the talks.[67] This approach was confirmed in the subsequent decision of the 16th session of the UNFCCC's COP in Cancun after failure of the Copenhagen talks to reach a formal COP decision.[68] Consequently, even though the differentiation between countries remained a key feature of the accords, the structure of global cooperation had changed such that the status quo that had previously allowed it to underpin an affirmative multilateral model of climate change cooperation was no longer tenable as had been earlier designed.

While this does not mean that this shift from an affirmative approach happened overnight, it was reflected in subsequent climate change negotiations that followed COPs 15 and 16. For instance, states decided that they would design their own intended nationally determined contributions (INDCs) on key climate change-related issues including emission targets at the 19th COP in Warsaw, departing from the bifurcated differentiated approach that had been a core pillar of the Kyoto-led regime.[69]

Similarly, the 20th COP in Lima culminated in inter alia the tempering of the CBDR Principle through a rider that it should be considered 'in the light of different national circumstances'.[70] This less forceful version of the CBDR principle was once again a reiteration of the push to get rid of the bifurcated differentiation seen in the Kyoto climate regime and perhaps importantly came just one year before the landmark Paris Climate Agreement was adopted in 2015. It did away with the strict, bifurcated categorisation of countries along differentiation lines and applied to all countries. Even though CBDR&RC was to continue to be a key feature of global climate governance, its application had fundamentally changed such that universal self-differentiation would prevail over the Annex I/ Non-Annex model. Crucially, it also enshrined the non-binding nationally determined contributions mechanisms as a medium through which universal action and self-differentiation could be enhanced as opposed to the previous model where developing countries large and small were excluded from mandatory mitigation obligations.

Moreover, having secured the participation of African and other developing countries, climate governance has seen a shift in discourse from one that sought to balance climate and developmental concerns to one that is focused on achieving climate mitigation targets epitomised by the 2-degree Celsius goal. This focus on effectiveness, preferred by industrialised countries, thus de-emphasised concerns of African and other developing countries as articulated by the Founex report of 1972.[71] To be clear, the idea of using targets as a tool of environmental governance is not new.[72] Targets are indeed mechanisms for framing the global environmental agenda and giving salience to associated response actions.[73] The 2-degree target thus represented attempts at reshaping the climate discourse and focusing global actions towards addressing climate change, making it one of the most recognisable avatars for global environmental governance.

Importantly for the purposes of this book is how the target gradually departed from the problematisation of global climate governance captured in the Founex Report. The 2-degree target is not a recent invention. It has featured in several scientific and policy discussions for several decades. In 1991, Vellinga and Swart for instance discussed the 2-degree target as a way of normatively framing global climate policy.[74] However, the European Union was the main driver of northern-led efforts to mainstream this target in the global climate agenda. A 2005 report by the International Climate Change Taskforce recommended the establishment of "a long-term objective of preventing average global surface temperature from rising by more than 2 °C".[75] Additionally, the Council of the European Union stated that achieving the UNFCCC's objective of reducing greenhouse gas emissions will require limiting the global annual mean surface temperature increase to 2 degrees Celsius above pre-industrial levels.[76]

The 2-degree target was eventually captured in the final decisions of the 15th and 16th conferences of the parties to the UNFCCC in Copenhagen (2009) and Cancun (2010) representing the first time it had been included in a multilateral climate negotiation outcome (Decision 2/CP.15, UNFCCC 2009) (Decision 1/CP.16, UNFCCC 2010). Small Island Developing States, however, advocated for the inclusion of a more ambitious 1.5-degree target supported by other like-minded states. The targets were eventually included in the Paris Agreement, with its aim to keep global temperature levels well below 2 degrees Celsius with the further intention of reaching 1.5 degrees reflecting the mainstream framing of the issue.[77]

3.5 THE GREAT CLIMATE TRANSFORMATION AND CONTINENTAL ECONOMIC INTEGRATION IN AFRICA

The far from equilibrium conditions that epitomised both Africa's post-colonial socio-economic dynamics and her engagement with the global climate agenda has created opportunities for innovation, despite the constraints of poor infrastructure, low technical and institutional capacity, and underdeveloped economies. The abundance of innovation in the continent amid significant structural and capacity challenges is arguably a key factor in understanding why African societies continue to thrive under conditions of low socio-economic development. Institutional and policy innovation subsequently has made it possible for African states to harness this new dynamic to both manage the extraordinary challenges the continent faces while also engaging in the fast-changing global climate space.

Understanding the dynamics of Africa's response to these dual states of disequilibrium therefore requires a different conceptual starting point. One example of creativity and experimentation relates to Africa's efforts to harness regional integration and turbocharge continent-wide industrialisation. Conventional understandings of regionalisation processes mirroring the European Union have often taken the shape of a gradual evolution towards shared sovereignty, social cohesion, and trade integration. These features are largely absent from Africa's regional integration efforts and represent attempts to chart a different course towards realising collective goals.[78]

This alternative path was characterised by a pan-African developmental vision pursued primarily through sub-regional innovations. These innovations have been key to facilitating the slow but gradual transition from post-colonial chaos to a situation that would be characterised by socio-economic prosperity. Further, Africa's efforts to integrate its fragmented economies have also been underpinned by the need to create different dissipative states that depart from the colonial relationships and exportation of primary products in exchange for processed goods.[79] To be clear, this does not mean that transformations will happen overnight. Developmental work is indeed an arduous grinding process that proceeds in fits and starts. It is a non-linear process with missed opportunities and sub-optimal governance that can eventually create channels for socio-economic transformation if utilised. Despite the obvious challenges, there have been welcome legal, socio-economic and political changes that have radically transformed the internal governance dynamics in the continent away from colonial dependency.

Studies have identified three key overlapping phases that characterise Africa's efforts to foster regional economic integration.[80] The first of these roughly begins from Ghana's independence in 1957 to the commencement of the African Economic Community treaty in 1994, where the primary focus was emancipation from decolonisation wars and the curation of a long-term socio-economic and political vision. Subsequent institutions were created to give effect to these goals including the founding of the Organization for African Unity in 1963.[81] The decades-long fight to end colonisation was also a significant milestone in this era, culminating in the independence of Namibia in 1990 and the ending of apartheid rule in South Africa in 1994. Other key institutional mechanisms that reflected this early phase include the establishment of the Lagos Plan of Action in 1980 and the African Economic Community through a treaty which entered into force in 1994.[82]

The second phase roughly extending from 1975 to about 2012 saw a noticeable shift in focus on inter alia development of internal socio-economic governance structures, enhancing political stability and fostering economic growth.[83] This period also saw significant policy experimentation through establishment of regional level institutions and programmes across the continent as a response to these priorities. Key landmarks during this phase include the establishment of the Economic Community of West African States (ECOWAS) in 1975 and the Preferential Trade Area of Eastern and Southern Africa in 1981.[84] Further, the Southern African Development Community (SADC) was established in 1992 followed by the Common Market for Eastern and Southern Africa (COMESA) in 1994. and the revival of the East African Community (EAC) in 1999. These developments led to the creation of more than 14 overlapping regional economic organisations in Africa by the year 2000 that emphasised the need for enhanced coordination to optimise the new institutional space created by these institutions. It is therefore understandable that African leaders agreed to issue a moratorium on the formation of new regional entities in 2006 in a bid to stem further fragmentation.[85]

This period also saw significant transformation in the continent's geo-economic landscape as China became a key player in Africa's developmental space. Traditional economic relations between Africa and the world had been predicated on historical links with Europe and the US. These relationships dominated aspects such as trade and foreign direct investment and largely operated on the equilibrium paradigm of comparative advantage discussed above i.e. exportation of raw material in exchange for processed goods. However, China's involvement in the continent dramatically changed this dynamic and introduced multipolarity in Africa's calculus of how it realised its developmental objectives. Conventional understandings of this involvement often attribute it to exogenous factors i.e. the rapid rise of China as a global power and its outward looking foreign policy.[86] While this is certainly key, an important consideration is also the internal political and institutional conditions within the continent that facilitated this dynamic.

It is this combination of both external and internal factors that enabled Africa to operate far out of the status quo that has increasingly seen its stake in global politics rise again. One key consequence of this dynamic is the increased access to capital for development that has provided new opportunities for industrialisation. Chinese foreign direct investment in Africa increased from a meagre US$75 million in 2003 to a massive US$4.2 billion in 2020, representing new and additional capital that had not been available prior to this period.[87] This investment into Africa subsequently exceeded those from the US in 2013 with the latter being in gradual decline since 2010.[88]

The third phase, roughly commencing in 2012 with the negotiations to conclude the Tripartite and Africa Continental Free Trade Agreements' negotiations, epitomises efforts to consolidate regional economic communities and accelerate economic development.[89] Policy experiments were seen across the continent in a bid to harness the new developments. COMESA, EAC and SADC commenced negotiations in 2012 to scale up economic development beyond their individual regional arrangements.[90] The final Tripartite Free Trade Agreement was concluded in 2015 and set the scene for the conclusion of the larger Africa Continental Free Trade Agreement in 2018.[91]

This period has also seen even more intense geo-economic activity in the continent that has thrust Africa in on-going great power competition between China and the Western world.[92] Increased economic activity primarily around developmental sectors including infrastructure, agriculture, energy, transport and mining for instance enabled African economies to increase their focus on creating enabling institutions to scale up industrialisation across the continent.[93] This is not to say that new investment has not had its fair share of challenges. Chinese investment in Africa has stirred significant debate regarding its ecological and socio-economic implications.[94] China has often been accused of sinking African countries into debt distress, exploiting Africa's natural resources, driving ecological destruction among others.[95]

Despite these dynamics, the trajectory of Africa's economic activity points to new opportunities being available and feasible but will require institutional creativity and initiative. Only through greater economic development can the continent hope to realise its full potential as a key international player. Further, Africa's experiments have culminated in the adoption of a different approach to regional integration that places primacy on development and industrialisation instead of solely focusing on trade. In this sense, there has been a recognition that while trade-based integration can have large enough markets to scale up economies and support investment, industrialisation is key to creating products and linkages that bring together different markets.[96] Markets therefore require interconnectivity through inter alia infrastructure and technology to function. This can eventually translate to realising developmental needs including access to reliable and affordable energy, agricultural development, harnessing the continent's natural resources among others. It is therefore no surprise that this approach has been referred to by scholars as developmental integration, which differs from purely trade based agreements.[97]

African states have, however, embraced the Paris Agreement's catalytic approach with caution. Even though all African states—except for Libya—have submitted an NDC, almost all the NDCs had a conditional element. The conditional element meant that the African states, and other developing countries, committed to a certain level of action, but pledged stronger action upon the receipt of means of support from industrialised countries.[98] Even though the Paris Agreement had provisions for support of means of implementation, the inclusion of conditionality in African states' NDCs revealed their reluctant engagement in the regime. Furthermore, since much of the discourse on environmental, and climate change politics, is dominated by the global North, topics such as support for means of implementation have increasingly become peripheral.[99] For African states, the topics they care most about have been overshadowed by the discourse on 'All Hands-on Deck' to reach the temperature targets of the Paris Agreement.[100] Conditionally, therefore, offers an "insurance policy" for African countries as they engage with the multilateral climate change regime.[101]

African and other developing countries have included two types of mitigation goals in their NDCs, as a form of de facto differentiation: unconditional mitigation targets, which they could undertake with their own resources; and conditional mitigation targets, which were higher and subject to external support for means of implementation, from industrialised countries. Inclusion of conditionality therefore served as an insurance policy for African states, and other developing countries, should industrialised countries fail to meet their obligations for support.[102] Thus, both *de jure* and *de facto* differentiation give rise to a 'differentiation-complex', which clearly captures the emergent complexity of the international climate change regime. Further, African country NDCs have included elements that link climate action to development such as poverty reduction, adaptation among others, mirroring the age-old divergence in the framing of the climate issue.

But perhaps a more compelling example was the recent collapse of negotiations towards a Global Compact for the Environment. One of the main reasons for the collapse was the fallout between industrialised and developing countries, whereby the latter demanded support for implementation, while the former rejected the obligation to provide the support.[103] In addition, the proponents of the Global Compact for the Environment sought to open principles such as CBDR to renegotiation, an objective that was rejected outright by developing countries. Finally, the Compact sought to make environmental litigation easier, while developing countries wanted to limit its scope to identifying gaps in international law. Except for a few states, these proposals did not enjoy widespread support from African states.[104]

A further dilution of the CBDR principle could be in the form of long-term climate neutrality targets. As almost all African countries have adopted a long-term emissions reduction target, mostly in the form of net zero by the year 2050, the effects of the Great Climate Transformation have been locked in.[105] For African countries, realising the net zero targets is a firm policy commitment, thus bringing into sharp focus the prospects of realising a just transition. Key possible questions for African policy makers would include, for instance, how their respective countries can realise their net zero targets while also exploiting their increasingly large fossil fuel reserves, or even power carbon-intensive industrialisation. Significant trade-offs would need to be made, but the key point here is the dilemma posed by the Great Climate Transformation and the growing momentum for continental economic transformation.

3.6   CONCLUSION

This chapter has articulated a conceptual framework for understanding how Africa as a continent is operating in conditions that are far from equilibrium in so far as pursuit its developmental goals in the context of evolving climate governance is concerned. African contemporary history, punctuated by colonisation and the struggle for independence, left Africa in a situation akin to chaos and uncertainty. Ironically it was during this time that equilibrium models of global economic and institutional design were embedded into the emerging international order, including multilateral environmental governance. These dynamics created conditions to approach multilateral climate cooperation with much reluctance and contestation. It is out of this contestation that a compromise that exchanged participation and legitimacy for meaningful mainstreaming of developmental concerns within the global environmental agenda was forged, creating conditions for Africa's engagement in the climate discourse. However, events following this framing of global environmental problems including climate change have shown that Africa's balancing act is situated in irreversible conditions that are far from the status quo. Changes in the global climate discourse coupled with internal geo-economic dynamics have not only produced high levels of uncertainty but also novelty as reflected through internal institutions and responses to changes in the global climate regime. These internal processes especially in the economic space were not designed along a predetermined path. Instead, they have been a consequence of policy experimentation in a search for solutions to Africa's unique socio-economic issues.

To better manage what appears to be increasingly existential concerns, African states must thus adjust their diplomatic approach accordingly and harness this growing wedge to create even more policy innovations. This will require a systems approach that emphasises developing greater internal interactions while harnessing the diversity that comes with the continent's national identities. Balancing between the global climate mitigation goal and its own socio-economic development will also require the continent to redefine its position in the new era of climate and developmental governance. These are unpredictable processes that will likely involve incremental experimentation over time. Current regional integration efforts are representative of the scale of policy innovation that will be required to usher Africa into prosperity in a twenty-first century that will be characterised by a drive towards net zero emissions and a complete restructuring of the global economic system.

NOTES

1. Dumisani Chirambo, 'Towards the Achievement of SDG 7 in Sub-Saharan Africa: Creating Synergies Between Power Africa, Sustainable Energy for All and Climate Finance In-Order to Achieve Universal Energy Access Before 2030', *Renewable and Sustainable Energy Reviews* 94 (1 October 2018): 600–608, https://doi.org/10.1016/j.rser.2018.06.025; David Ciplet and J. Timmons Roberts, 'Splintering South: Ecologically Unequal Exchange Theory in a Fragmented Global Climate', *Journal of World-Systems Research* 23, no. 2 (11 August 2017): 372–98, https://doi.org/10.5195/jwsr.2017.669; David Ciplet, J. Timmons Roberts, and Mizan Khan, 'The Politics of International Climate Adaptation Funding: Justice and Divisions in the Greenhouse', *Global Environmental Politics* 13, no. 1 (18 December 2012): 49–68, https://doi.org/10.1162/GLEP_a_00153.

2. Peter Newell and Harriet Bulkeley, 'Landscape for Change? International Climate Policy and Energy Transitions: Evidence from Sub-Saharan Africa', *Climate Policy* 17, no. 5 (2017): 650–63, https://doi.org/10.1080/14693062.2016.1173003; Ana Pueyo and Pedro Linares, 'Renewable Technology Transfer to Developing Countries: One Size Does Not Fit All', *IDS Working Papers* 2012, no. 412 (2012): 1–39, https://doi.org/10.1111/j.2040-0209.2012.00412.x.

3. Adil Najam, 'Developing Countries and Global Environmental Governance: From Contestation to Participation to Engagement', *International Environmental Agreements: Politics, Law and Economics* 5, no. 3 (1 September 2005): 303–21, https://doi.org/10.1007/s10784-005-3807-6.

4. Reuben Makomere and Kennedy Liti Mbeva, 'Squaring the Circle: Development Prospects Within the Paris Agreement', *Carbon & Climate Law Review* 12, no. 1 (2018): 31–40, https://doi.org/10.21552/cclr/2018/1/7.

5. Ciplet, Roberts, and Khan, 'The Politics of International Climate Adaptation Funding'; Chukwumerije Okereke, 'Climate Justice and the International Regime', *WIREs Climate Change* 1, no. 3 (2010): 462–74, https://doi.org/10.1002/wcc.52; J. Timmons Roberts, Martin Stadelmann, and Saleemul Huq, 'Copenhagen's Climate Finance Promise: Six Key Questions', Briefing (London, UK: International Institute for Environment and Development (IIED), 2010), https://www.osti.gov/etdeweb/servlets/purl/22041098; Martin Stadelmann, J. Timmons Roberts, and Axel Michaelowa, 'New and Additional to What? Assessing

Options for Baselines to Assess Climate Finance Pledges', *Climate and Development* 3, no. 3 (2011): 175–92, https://doi.org/10.1080/175 65529.2011.599550.

6. Joseph L. Love, 'Raul Prebisch and the Origins of the Doctrine of Unequal Exchange', *Latin American Research Review* 15, no. 3 (1980): 45–72; Raúl Prebisch, 'The Economic Development of Latin America and Its Principal Problems', 27 April 1950, https://repositorio.cepal.org/handle/11362/29973.

7. Andrea Maneschi, *Comparative Advantage in International Trade: A Historical Perspective* (Edward Elgar Publishing, 1998).

8. Joseph L. Love, 'Raul Prebisch and the Origins of the Doctrine of Unequal Exchange', 14.

9. Francis Mangeni and Calestous Juma, *Emergent Africa. Evolution of Regional Economic Integration* (Terra Alta, WV: Headline Books, 2019), 29.

10. Tom Burgis, *The Looting Machine: Warlords, Tycoons, Smugglers, and the Systematic Theft of Africa's Wealth* (UK: William Collins, 2015).

11. 'Africa's Population Will Double by 2050', *The Economist*, March 2020, https://www.economist.com/special-report/2020/03/26/africas-pop ulation-will-double-by-2050.

12. Mangeni and Juma, *Emergent Africa. Evolution of Regional Economic Integration*, 32.

13. Mangeni and Juma, 20.

14. Mahmood Mamdani, 'Historicizing Power and Responses to Power: Indirect Rule and Its Reform', *Social Research*, 1999, 859–86.

15. Mangeni and Juma, *Emergent Africa. Evolution of Regional Economic Integration*, 30–35.

16. John Mukum Mbaku, 'Constitutional Coups as a Threat to Democratic Governance in Africa', *International Comparative, Policy & Ethics Law Review* 2 (2019 2018): 77; Claude E. Welch, 'Emerging Patterns of Civil-Military Relations in Africa: Radical Coups d'Etat and Political Stability', in *African Security Issues: Sovereignty, Stability, and Solidarity* (Routledge, 1984).

17. Najam, 'Developing Countries and Global Environmental Governance', 303.

18. Sharachchandra M. Lélé, 'Sustainable Development: A Critical Review', *World Development* 19, no. 6 (1991): 607–21, https://doi.org/10.1016/0305-750X(91)90197-P; Marian A. Miller, *The Third World in Global Environmental Politics* (Boulder, Colorado: Lynne Rienner Publishers, 1995); Adil Najam, Saleemul Huq, and Youba Sokona, 'Climate Negotiations beyond Kyoto: Developing Countries Concerns and Interests', *Climate Policy* 3, no. 3 (1 January 2003): 221–31, https://doi.org/10.3763/cpol.2003.0329.

19. Ronald Hope Kempe, 'Climate Change and Poverty in Africa', *International Journal of Sustainable Development & World Ecology* 16, no. 6 (2009): 451–61, https://doi.org/10.1080/13504500903354424; Sheona E. Shackleton and Charlie M. Shackleton, 'Linking Poverty, HIV/AIDS and Climate Change to Human and Ecosystem Vulnerability in Southern Africa: Consequences for Livelihoods and Sustainable Ecosystem Management', *International Journal of Sustainable Development & World Ecology* 19, no. 3 (2012): 275–86, https://doi.org/10.1080/13504509.2011.641039; Youba Sokona and Fatma Denton, 'Climate Change Impacts: Can Africa Cope with the Challenges?', *Climate Policy* 1, no. 1 (1 January 2001): 117–23, https://doi.org/10.3763/cpol.2001.0110.

20. Robert W. Cox, 'Social Forces, States and World Orders: Beyond International Relations Theory', *Millennium* 10, no. 2 (1 June 1981): 126–55, https://doi.org/10.1177/03058298810100020501; Karl P. Sauvant and Hajo Hasenpflug, *The New International Economic Order: Confrontation or Cooperation Between North and South?* (Routledge, 2019); Robin C. A. White, 'A New International Economic Order', *International & Comparative Law Quarterly* 24, no. 3 (1975): 542–52, https://doi.org/10.1093/iclqaj/24.3.542.

21. Report of Experts Convened by the Secretary General of the United Nations Conference on the Human Environment, 'Environment and Development: The Founex Report on Development and Environment' (Founex: Carnegie Endowment for International Peace, 1972), 1.

22. Report of Experts Convened by the Secretary General of the United Nations Conference on the Human Environment, 1–2.

23. Najam, 'Developing Countries and Global Environmental Governance', 308.

24. David A. Kay and Eugene B. Skolnikoff, 'World Eco-Crisis', 1972.

25. Susanna Hecht and Alexander Cockburn, 'Rhetoric and Reality in Rio', *Nation* 254, no. 24 (1992): 848–53.

26. Najam, 'Developing Countries and Global Environmental Governance', 308.

27. Najam, 308.

28. Report of Experts Convened by the Secretary General of the United Nations Conference on the Human Environment, 'Environment and Development'.

29. Report of Experts Convened by the Secretary General of the United Nations Conference on the Human Environment, 5–6.

30. Report of Experts Convened by the Secretary General of the United Nations Conference on the Human Environment, 'Environment and Development'.

31. UN, 'Declaration of the United Nations Conference on the Human Environment' (United Nations, 1972), https://legal.un.org/avl/ha/dunche/dunche.html.
32. UNEP, 'In Defence of the Earth. The Basic Texts on Environment: Founex. Stockholm. Cocoyoc', Executive Series (Nairobi, Kenya: United Nations Environment Programme, 1981), viii.
33. Mahbub ul Haq, *The Poverty Curtain: Choices for the Third World* (New York: Columbia University Press, 1976).
34. Andronico O. Adede, 'International Environmental Law from Stockholm to Rio: An Overview of Past Lessons and Future Challenges', *Journal of Environmental Law and Policy* 22 (1992): 88.
35. UN, 'United Nations Conference on Environment and Development (UNCED), Earth Summit' (Rio de Janeiro, 1992), https://sustainabledevelopment.un.org/milestones/unced.
36. Najam, 'Developing Countries and Global Environmental Governance', 311.
37. UN, 'United Nations Conference on Environment and Development (UNCED), Earth Summit'.
38. Andronico O. Adede, 'International Environmental Law from Stockholm to Rio'.
39. Daniel Bodansky, 'The History of the Global Climate Change Regime', *International Relations and Global Climate Change* 23, no. 23 (2001): 23–40.
40. Bodansky, 24.
41. Bodansky, 31.
42. Bodansky, 23–24.
43. Simon Chin-Yee, Tobias Dan Nielsen, and Lau Øfjord Blaxekjær, 'One Voice, One Africa: The African Group of Negotiators', in *Coalitions in the Climate Change Negotiations* (Routledge, 2020).
44. David Held and Charles Roger, 'Three Models of Global Climate Governance: From Kyoto to Paris and Beyond', *Global Policy* 9, no. 4 (2018): 527–37, https://doi.org/10.1111/1758-5899.12617; UN, 'Protection of Global Climate for Present and Future Generations of Mankind' (UN, 17 January 1991), http://digitallibrary.un.org/record/196769.
45. Bodansky, 'The History of the Global Climate Change Regime', 32; Held and Roger, 'Three Models of Global Climate Governance', 528.
46. UN, 'United Nations Conference on Environment and Development (UNCED), Earth Summit', Art 1(3).
47. UN, Art 4.
48. COP-1 met in Berlin. Among its significant outcomes, the Berlin meeting decided to inter alia establish an ad hoc committee to negotiate a protocol or other legal instrument by 1997 containing additional commitments for industrialised countries for the post-2000 period. This

was known as the Berlin Mandate and the new negotiating committee became known as the Ad Hoc Group on the Berlin Mandate (AGBM). See https://unfccc.int/cop3/fccc/info/backgrod.htm#:~:text=The%20Berlin%20Mandate%20calls%20on,new%20commitments%20for%20developing%20countries. Accessed on the 25 December 2020.

49. Christopher Napoli, 'Understanding Kyoto's Failure', *SAIS Review of International Affairs* 32, no. 2 (2012): 183–96; Amanda M. Rosen, 'The Wrong Solution at the Right Time: The Failure of the Kyoto Protocol on Climate Change', *Politics & Policy* 43, no. 1 (2015): 30–58, https://doi.org/10.1111/polp.12105; Jeffrey McGee and Jens Steffek, 'The Copenhagen Turn in Global Climate Governance and the Contentious History of Differentiation in International Law', *Journal of Environmental Law* 28, no. 1 (1 March 2016): 37–63, https://doi.org/10.1093/jel/eqw003.

50. Pieter Pauw, Kennedy Mbeva, and Harro van Asselt, 'Subtle Differentiation of Countries' Responsibilities Under the Paris Agreement', *Palgrave Communications* 5, no. 1 (30 July 2019): 1–7, https://doi.org/10.1057/s41599-019-0298-6; Thomas Deleuil, 'The Common but Differentiated Responsibilities Principle: Changes in Continuity After the Durban Conference of the Parties', *Review of European Community & International Environmental Law* 21, no. 3 (2012): 271–81, https://doi.org/10.1111/j.1467-9388.2012.00758.x.

51. Gwyn Prins and Steve Rayner, 'Time to Ditch Kyoto', *Nature* 449, no. 7165 (25 October 2007): 973–75, https://doi.org/10.1038/449973a; Robyn Eckersley, 'Ambushed: The Kyoto Protocol, the Bush Administration's Climate Policy and the Erosion of Legitimacy', *International Politics* 44, no. 2 (1 March 2007): 306–24, https://doi.org/10.1057/palgrave.ip.8800190; Peter Christoff, 'Post-Kyoto? Post-Bush? Towards an Effective "Climate Coalition of the Willing"', *International Affairs* 82, no. 5 (1 September 2006): 831–60, https://doi.org/10.1111/j.1468-2346.2006.00574.x; John Hovi and Tora Skodvin, eds., 'Climate Governance and the Paris Agreement', *Politics and Governance* 4, no. 3 (2016).

52. Prins and Rayner, 'Time to Ditch Kyoto'; Christoph Böhringer and Carsten Vogt, 'The Dismantling of a Breakthrough: The Kyoto Protocol as Symbolic Policy', *European Journal of Political Economy* 20, no. 3 (1 September 2004): 597–617, https://doi.org/10.1016/j.ejpoleco.2004.02.004; William Nordhaus and Joseph Boyer, 'Requiem for Kyoto: An Economic Analysis of the Kyoto Protocol', *The Energy Journal* 20 (1999): 93–130.

53. Ngwadla Xolisa, 'Equitable Access to Sustainable Development: Relevance to Negotiations and Actions on Climate Change' (Cape Town, South Africa: Mitigation Action Plan & Scenarios (MAPS),

2013), http://www.mapsprogramme.org/wp-content/uploads/EASD-Relevance-to-negotiations_Paper.pdf.

54. Climate finance, as used here, is in the form of grants, and not commercial lending packages.

55. David Ockwell and Rob Byrne, 'Improving Technology Transfer Through National Systems of Innovation: Climate Relevant Innovation-System Builders (CRIBs)', *Climate Policy* 16, no. 7 (2 October 2016): 836–54, https://doi.org/10.1080/14693062.2015.1052958.

56. Natalie Sauer, 'Mozambique "Faces Climate Debt Trap" as Cyclone Kenneth Follows Idai', *Climate Home News*, 26 April 2019, https://www.climatechangenews.com/2019/04/26/mozambique-faces-cli mate-debt-trap-cyclone-kenneth-follows-idai/.

57. Prins and Rayner, 'Time to Ditch Kyoto'; McGee and Steffek, 'The Copenhagen Turn in Global Climate Governance and the Contentious History of Differentiation in International Law'.

58. McGee and Steffek, 'The Copenhagen Turn in Global Climate Governance and the Contentious History of Differentiation in International Law', 55.

59. McGee and Steffek, 'The Copenhagen Turn in Global Climate Governance and the Contentious History of Differentiation in International Law'.

60. McGee and Steffek, 55.

61. McGee and Steffek, 'The Copenhagen Turn in Global Climate Governance and the Contentious History of Differentiation in International Law'.

62. Robert Falkner, 'The Paris Agreement and the New Logic of International Climate Politics', *International Affairs* 92, no. 5 (1 September 2016): 1107–25, https://doi.org/10.1111/1468-2346.12708.

63. McGee and Steffek, 'The Copenhagen Turn in Global Climate Governance and the Contentious History of Differentiation in International Law', 60.

64. Daniel Bodansky, 'The Legal Character of the Paris Agreement', *Review of European, Comparative & International Environmental Law* 25, no. 2 (2016): 142–50, https://doi.org/10.1111/reel.12154; Falkner, 'The Paris Agreement and the New Logic of International Climate Politics'.

65. Thomas Hale, 'Catalytic Cooperation', *Global Environmental Politics* 20, no. 4 (1 November 2020): 73–98, https://doi.org/10.1162/glep_a_00561; Falkner, 'The Paris Agreement and the New Logic of International Climate Politics'; Robert O. Keohane and Michael Oppenheimer, 'Paris: Beyond the Climate Dead End Through Pledge and Review?', *Politics and Governance* 4, no. 3 (8 September 2016): 142–51, https://doi.org/10.17645/pag.v4i3.634.

66. McGee and Steffek, 'The Copenhagen Turn in Global Climate Governance and the Contentious History of Differentiation in International Law'.
67. Falkner, 'The Paris Agreement and the New Logic of International Climate Politics'.
68. McGee and Steffek, 'The Copenhagen Turn in Global Climate Governance and the Contentious History of Differentiation in International Law', 60.
69. McGee and Steffek, 61.
70. UNFCCC, 'Decision -/CP.20. Lima Call for Climate Action' (United Nations Framework Convention on Climate Change [UNFCCC], 2014), https://unfccc.int/files/meetings/lima_dec_2014/application/pdf/auv_cop20_lima_call_for_climate_action.pdf.
71. Joeri Rogelj et al., 'Paris Agreement Climate Proposals Need a Boost to Keep Warming Well Below 2 °C', *Nature* 534, no. 7609 (30 June 2016): 631–39, https://doi.org/10.1038/nature18307; Sander Chan, Paula Ellinger, and Oscar Widerberg, 'Exploring National and Regional Orchestration of Non-State Action for a <1.5 °C World', *International Environmental Agreements: Politics, Law and Economics* 18, no. 1 (1 February 2018): 135–52, https://doi.org/10.1007/s10784-018-9384-2; P. Pauw et al., 'Beyond Headline Mitigation Numbers: We Need More Transparent and Comparable NDCs to Achieve the Paris Agreement on Climate Change', *Climatic Change* 147, no. 1 (1 March 2018): 23–29, https://doi.org/10.1007/s10584-017-2122-x.
72. Piero Morseletto, Frank Biermann, and Philipp Pattberg, 'Governing by Targets: Reductio Ad Unum and Evolution of the Two-Degree Climate Target', *International Environmental Agreements: Politics, Law and Economics* 17, no. 5 (1 October 2017): 655–76, https://doi.org/10.1007/s10784-016-9336-7.
73. Piero Morseletto, Frank Biermann, and Philipp Pattberg.
74. Pier Vellinga and Robert Swart, 'The Greenhouse Marathon: A Proposal for Global Strategy', *Climatic Change; (Netherlands)* 18, no. 1 (1 January 1991), https://doi.org/10.1007/BF00142501.
75. J. Edmonds and S. Smith, 'The Technology of Two Degrees, "Avoiding Dangerous Climate Change". HJ Schellenhuber, W. Cramer, N. Nakicenovic, T. Wrigley, and G. Yohe' (Cambridge University Press, 2006).
76. Council of the European Union, 'Presidency Conclusions—Brussels, 22 and 23 March 2005—IV. Climate Change, 7619/1/05 REV 1 CONCL 1' (Brussels: European Council, 2005), http://www.consilium.europa.eu/uedocs/cms_data/docs/pressdata/en/ec/84335.pdf.
77. UNFCCC, *Paris Agreement on Climate Change* (New York: United Nations, 2015), https://unfccc.int/sites/default/files/english_paris_agreement.pdf.

78. Mangeni and Juma, *Emergent Africa. Evolution of Regional Economic Integration*, 9.
79. Mangeni and Juma, 10.
80. Mangeni and Juma, 4–12.
81. Mangeni and Juma, *Emergent Africa. Evolution of Regional Economic Integration*.
82. Mangeni and Juma.
83. Mangeni and Juma, 11.
84. Mangeni and Juma, 11.
85. Mangeni and Juma, 11.
86. Vahit Güntay, '(Is) African Spring in Chinese Foreign Policy (?)', *Asia Europe Journal* 19, no. 3 (1 September 2021): 275–90, https://doi.org/10.1007/s10308-021-00602-w.
87. 2022 CARI, 'Data: Chinese Investment in Africa', China Africa Research Initiative, 2022, http://www.sais-cari.org/chinese-investment-in-africa.
88. CARI.
89. Mangeni and Juma, *Emergent Africa. Evolution of Regional Economic Integration*, 12.
90. Mangeni and Juma, *Emergent Africa. Evolution of Regional Economic Integration*.
91. Mangeni and Juma.
92. John Mearsheimer, 'The Inevitable Rivalry: America, China, and the Tragedy of Great-Power Politics', *Foreign Affairs* 100, no. 48 (2021).
93. CARI, 'Data'.
94. Masuma Farooki and Raphael Kaplinsky, *The Impact of China on Global Commodity Prices: The Global Reshaping of the Resource Sector* (Routledge, 2013).
95. Deborah Brautigam, 'A Critical Look at Chinese "Debt-Trap Diplomacy": The Rise of a Meme', *Area Development and Policy* 5, no. 1 (2020): 1–14; Masuma Farooki and Raphael Kaplinsky, *The Impact of China on Global Commodity Prices*.
96. Mangeni and Juma, *Emergent Africa. Evolution of Regional Economic Integration*, 16.
97. Mangeni and Juma, 16.
98. Makomere and Mbeva, 'Squaring the Circle'.
99. Karen O'Brien et al., 'Why Different Interpretations of Vulnerability Matter in Climate Change Discourses', *Climate Policy* 7, no. 1 (1 January 2007): 73–88, https://doi.org/10.1080/14693062.2007.9685639; Mary E. Pettenger, *The Social Construction of Climate Change: Power, Knowledge, Norms, Discourses* (Ashgate Publishing, Ltd., 2013); René Audet, 'Climate Justice and Bargaining Coalitions: A Discourse Analysis', *International Environmental Agreements: Politics, Law and Economics* 13, no. 3 (1 September 2013): 369–86, https://doi.org/10.1007/s10784-012-9195-9.

100. Thomas Hale, '"All Hands on Deck": The Paris Agreement and Nonstate Climate Action', *Global Environmental Politics* 16, no. 3 (15 July 2016): 12–22, https://doi.org/10.1162/GLEP_a_00362.
101. Makomere and Mbeva, 'Squaring the Circle'.
102. Makomere and Mbeva.
103. IISD, 'ENB Report | Global Pact for the Environment OEWG-3 | 20–22 May 2019 | Nairobi, Kenya | IISD Reporting Services', *Earth Negotiations Bulletin (ENB)*, 22 May 2019, http://enb.iisd.org/vol35/enb 3503e.html.
104. IISD.
105. Thomas Hale et al., *Net Zero Tracker* (Oxford, UK: Energy and Climate Intelligence Unit, Data-Driven EnviroLab, NewClimate Institute, Oxford Net Zero, 2021), https://zerotracker.net/.

References

Adede, Andronico O. 'International Environmental Law from Stockholm to Rio: An Overview of Past Lessons and Future Challenges'. *Journal of Environmental Law and Policy* 22 (1992): 88.

Audet, René. 'Climate Justice and Bargaining Coalitions: A Discourse Analysis'. *International Environmental Agreements: Politics, Law and Economics* 13, no. 3 (1 September 2013): 369–86. https://doi.org/10.1007/s10784-012-9195-9.

Bodansky, Daniel. 'The History of the Global Climate Change Regime'. *International Relations and Global Climate Change* 23, no. 23 (2001): 23–40.

———. 'The Legal Character of the Paris Agreement'. *Review of European, Comparative & International Environmental Law* 25, no. 2 (2016): 142–50. https://doi.org/10.1111/reel.12154.

Böhringer, Christoph, and Carsten Vogt. 'The Dismantling of a Breakthrough: The Kyoto Protocol as Symbolic Policy'. *European Journal of Political Economy* 20, no. 3 (1 September 2004): 597–617. https://doi.org/10.1016/j.ejpoleco.2004.02.004.

Brautigam, Deborah. 'A Critical Look at Chinese "Debt-Trap Diplomacy": The Rise of a Meme'. *Area Development and Policy* 5, no. 1 (2020): 1–14.

Burgis, Tom. *The Looting Machine: Warlords, Tycoons, Smugglers, and the Systematic Theft of Africa's Wealth.* UK: William Collins, 2015.

CARI, 2022. 'Data: Chinese Investment in Africa'. China Africa Research Initiative, 2022. http://www.sais-cari.org/chinese-investment-in-africa.

Chan, Sander, Paula Ellinger, and Oscar Widerberg. 'Exploring National and Regional Orchestration of Non-State Action for a <1.5 °C World'. *International Environmental Agreements: Politics, Law and Economics* 18, no. 1 (1 February 2018): 135–52. https://doi.org/10.1007/s10784-018-9384-2.

Chin-Yee, Simon, Tobias Dan Nielsen, and Lau Øfjord Blaxekjær. 'One Voice, One Africa: The African Group of Negotiators'. In *Coalitions in the Climate Change Negotiations*. Routledge, 2020.

Chirambo, Dumisani. 'Towards the Achievement of SDG 7 in Sub-Saharan Africa: Creating Synergies Between Power Africa, Sustainable Energy for All and Climate Finance In-Order to Achieve Universal Energy Access Before 2030'. *Renewable and Sustainable Energy Reviews* 94 (1 October 2018): 600–608. https://doi.org/10.1016/j.rser.2018.06.025.

Christoff, Peter. 'Post-Kyoto? Post-Bush? Towards an Effective "Climate Coalition of the Willing"'. *International Affairs* 82, no. 5 (1 September 2006): 831–60. https://doi.org/10.1111/j.1468-2346.2006.00574.x.

Ciplet, David, and J. Timmons Roberts. 'Splintering South: Ecologically Unequal Exchange Theory in a Fragmented Global Climate'. *Journal of World-Systems Research* 23, no. 2 (11 August 2017): 372–98. https://doi.org/10.5195/jwsr.2017.669.

Ciplet, David, J. Timmons Roberts, and Mizan Khan. 'The Politics of International Climate Adaptation Funding: Justice and Divisions in the Greenhouse'. *Global Environmental Politics* 13, no. 1 (18 December 2012): 49–68. https://doi.org/10.1162/GLEP_a_00153.

Council of the European Union. 'Presidency Conclusions—Brussels, 22 and 23 March 2005—IV. Climate Change, 7619/1/05 REV 1 CONCL 1'. Brussels: European Council, 2005. http://www.consilium.europa.eu/uedocs/cms_data/docs/pressdata/en/ec/84335.pdf.

Cox, Robert W. 'Social Forces, States and World Orders: Beyond International Relations Theory'. *Millennium* 10, no. 2 (1 June 1981): 126–55. https://doi.org/10.1177/03058298810100020501.

Deleuil, Thomas. 'The Common but Differentiated Responsibilities Principle: Changes in Continuity After the Durban Conference of the Parties'. *Review of European Community & International Environmental Law* 21, no. 3 (2012): 271–81. https://doi.org/10.1111/j.1467-9388.2012.00758.x.

Eckersley, Robyn. 'Ambushed: The Kyoto Protocol, the Bush Administration's Climate Policy and the Erosion of Legitimacy'. *International Politics* 44, no. 2 (1 March 2007): 306–24. https://doi.org/10.1057/palgrave.ip.8800190.

Edmonds, J., and S. Smith. 'The Technology of Two Degrees, "Avoiding Dangerous Climate Change". HJ Schellenhuber, W. Cramer, N. Nakicenovic, T. Wrigley, and G. Yohe'. Cambridge University Press, 2006.

Falkner, Robert. 'The Paris Agreement and the New Logic of International Climate Politics'. *International Affairs* 92, no. 5 (1 September 2016): 1107–25. https://doi.org/10.1111/1468-2346.12708.

Farooki, Masuma, and Raphael Kaplinsky. *The Impact of China on Global Commodity Prices: The Global Reshaping of the Resource Sector*. Routledge, 2013.

Güntay, Vahit. '(Is) African Spring in Chinese Foreign Policy (?)'. *Asia Europe Journal* 19, no. 3 (1 September 2021): 275–90. https://doi.org/10.1007/s10308-021-00602-w.

Hale, Thomas. '"All Hands on Deck": The Paris Agreement and Nonstate Climate Action'. *Global Environmental Politics* 16, no. 3 (15 July 2016): 12–22. https://doi.org/10.1162/GLEP_a_00362.

———. 'Catalytic Cooperation'. *Global Environmental Politics* 20, no. 4 (1 November 2020): 73–98. https://doi.org/10.1162/glep_a_00561.

Hale, Thomas, Takeshi Kuramochi, John Lang, Brendan Mapes, Steve Smith, Ria Aiyer, Richard Black, et al. *Net Zero Tracker*. Oxford, UK: Energy and Climate Intelligence Unit, Data-Driven EnviroLab, NewClimate Institute, Oxford Net Zero, 2021. https://zerotracker.net/.

Haq, Mahbub ul. *The Poverty Curtain: Choices for the Third World*. New York: Columbia University Press, 1976.

Held, David, and Charles Roger. 'Three Models of Global Climate Governance: From Kyoto to Paris and Beyond'. *Global Policy* 9, no. 4 (2018): 527–37. https://doi.org/10.1111/1758-5899.12617.

Hecht, Susanna, and Alexander Cockburn. 'Rhetoric and Reality in Rio.' *Nation* 254, no. 24 (1992): 848–53.

Hovi, John, and Tora Skodvin, eds. 'Climate Governance and the Paris Agreement'. *Politics and Governance* 4, no. 3 (2016).

IISD. 'ENB Report | Global Pact for the Environment OEWG-3 | 20–22 May 2019 | Nairobi, Kenya | IISD Reporting Services'. *Earth Negotiations Bulletin (ENB)*, 22 May 2019. http://enb.iisd.org/vol35/enb3503e.html.

Kay, David A., and Eugene B. Skolnikoff. 'World Eco-Crisis.' 1972.

Kempe, Ronald Hope. 'Climate Change and Poverty in Africa'. *International Journal of Sustainable Development & World Ecology* 16, no. 6 (2009): 451–61. https://doi.org/10.1080/13504500903354424.

Keohane, Robert O., and Michael Oppenheimer. 'Paris: Beyond the Climate Dead End Through Pledge and Review?' *Politics and Governance* 4, no. 3 (8 September 2016): 142–51. https://doi.org/10.17645/pag.v4i3.634.

Lélé, Sharachchandra M. 'Sustainable Development: A Critical Review'. *World Development* 19, no. 6 (1991): 607–21. https://doi.org/10.1016/0305-750 X(91)90197-P.

Love, Joseph L. 'Raul Prebisch and the Origins of the Doctrine of Unequal Exchange'. *Latin American Research Review* 15, no. 3 (1980): 45–72.

Makomere, Reuben, and Kennedy Liti Mbeva. 'Squaring the Circle: Development Prospects Within the Paris Agreement'. *Carbon & Climate Law Review* 12, no. 1 (2018): 31–40. https://doi.org/10.21552/cclr/2018/1/7.

Mamdani, M. 'Historicizing Power and Responses to Power: Indirect Rule and Its Reform'. *Social Research*, 1999, 859–86.

Maneschi, Andrea. *Comparative Advantage in International Trade: A Historical Perspective*. Edward Elgar Publishing, 1998.

Mangeni, Francis, and Calestous Juma. *Emergent Africa. Evolution of Regional Economic Integration*. Terra Alta, WV: Headline Books, 2019.

Mbaku, John Mukum. 'Constitutional Coups as a Threat to Democratic Governance in Africa'. *International Comparative, Policy & Ethics Law Review* 2 (2018/2019): 77.

McGee, Jeffrey, and Jens Steffek. 'The Copenhagen Turn in Global Climate Governance and the Contentious History of Differentiation in International Law'. *Journal of Environmental Law* 28, no. 1 (1 March 2016): 37–63. https://doi.org/10.1093/jel/eqw003.

Mearsheimer, John. 'The Inevitable Rivalry: America, China, and the Tragedy of Great-Power Politics'. *Foreign Affairs* 100, no. 48 (2021).

Miller, Marian A. *The Third World in Global Environmental Politics*. Boulder, Colorado: Lynne Rienner Publishers, 1995.

Morseletto, Piero, Frank Biermann, and Philipp Pattberg. 'Governing by Targets: Reductio Ad Unum and Evolution of the Two-Degree Climate Target'. *International Environmental Agreements: Politics, Law and Economics* 17, no. 5 (1 October 2017): 655–76. https://doi.org/10.1007/s10784-016-9336-7.

Najam, Adil. 'Developing Countries and Global Environmental Governance: From Contestation to Participation to Engagement'. *International Environmental Agreements: Politics, Law and Economics* 5, no. 3 (1 September 2005): 303–21. https://doi.org/10.1007/s10784-005-3807-6.

Najam, Adil, Saleemul Huq, and Youba Sokona. 'Climate Negotiations Beyond Kyoto: Developing Countries Concerns and Interests'. *Climate Policy* 3, no. 3 (1 January 2003): 221–31. https://doi.org/10.3763/cpol.2003.0329.

Napoli, Christopher. 'Understanding Kyoto's Failure'. *SAIS Review of International Affairs* 32, no. 2 (2012): 183–96.

Newell, Peter, and Harriet Bulkeley. 'Landscape for Change? International Climate Policy and Energy Transitions: Evidence from Sub-Saharan Africa'. *Climate Policy* 17, no. 5 (2017): 650–63. https://doi.org/10.1080/14693062.2016.1173003.

Nordhaus, William, and Joseph Boyer. 'Requiem for Kyoto: An Economic Analysis of the Kyoto Protocol'. *The Energy Journal* 20 (1999): 93–130.

O'Brien, Karen, Siri Eriksen, Lynn Nygaard, and Ane Schjolden. 'Why Different Interpretations of Vulnerability Matter in Climate Change Discourses'. *Climate Policy* 7, no. 1 (1 January 2007): 73–88. https://doi.org/10.1080/14693062.2007.9685639.

Ockwell, David, and Rob Byrne. 'Improving Technology Transfer Through National Systems of Innovation: Climate Relevant Innovation-System Builders (CRIBs)'. *Climate Policy* 16, no. 7 (2 October 2016): 836–54. https://doi.org/10.1080/14693062.2015.1052958.

Okereke, Chukwumerije. 'Climate Justice and the International Regime'. *WIREs Climate Change* 1, no. 3 (2010): 462–74. https://doi.org/10.1002/wcc.52.

Pauw, P., Richard J. T. Klein, Kennedy Mbeva, Adis Dzebo, Davide Cassanmagnago, and Anna Rudloff. 'Beyond Headline Mitigation Numbers: We Need More Transparent and Comparable NDCs to Achieve the Paris Agreement on Climate Change'. *Climatic Change* 147, no. 1 (1 March 2018): 23–29. https://doi.org/10.1007/s10584-017-2122-x.

Pauw, Pieter, Kennedy Mbeva, and Harro van Asselt. 'Subtle Differentiation of Countries' Responsibilities Under the Paris Agreement'. *Palgrave Communications* 5, no. 1 (30 July 2019): 1–7. https://doi.org/10.1057/s41599-019-0298-6.

Pettenger, Mary E. *The Social Construction of Climate Change: Power, Knowledge, Norms, Discourses.* Ashgate Publishing, Ltd., 2013.

Prebisch, R. 'The Economic Development of Latin America and Its Principal Problems', 27 April 1950. https://repositorio.cepal.org/handle/11362/29973.

Prins, Gwyn, and Steve Rayner. 'Time to Ditch Kyoto'. *Nature* 449, no. 7165 (25 October 2007): 973–75. https://doi.org/10.1038/449973a.

Pueyo, Ana, and Pedro Linares. 'Renewable Technology Transfer to Developing Countries: One Size Does Not Fit All'. *IDS Working Papers* 2012, no. 412 (2012): 1–39. https://doi.org/10.1111/j.2040-0209.2012.00412.x.

Report of Experts Convened by the Secretary General of the United Nations Conference on the Human Environment. In *Environment and Development: The Founex Report on Development and Environment.* Founex: Carnegie Endowment for International Peace, 1972.

Roberts, J. Timmons, Martin Stadelmann, and Saleemul Huq. *Copenhagen's Climate Finance Promise: Six Key Questions.* Briefing. London, UK: International Institute for Environment and Development (IIED), 2010. https://www.osti.gov/etdeweb/servlets/purl/22041098.

Rogelj, Joeri, Michel den Elzen, Niklas Höhne, Taryn Fransen, Hanna Fekete, Harald Winkler, Roberto Schaeffer, Fu Sha, Keywan Riahi, and Malte Meinshausen. 'Paris Agreement Climate Proposals Need a Boost to Keep Warming Well Below 2 °C'. *Nature* 534, no. 7609 (30 June 2016): 631–39. https://doi.org/10.1038/nature18307.

Rosen, Amanda M. 'The Wrong Solution at the Right Time: The Failure of the Kyoto Protocol on Climate Change'. *Politics & Policy* 43, no. 1 (2015): 30–58. https://doi.org/10.1111/polp.12105.

Sauer, Natalie. 'Mozambique "Faces Climate Debt Trap" as Cyclone Kenneth Follows Idai'. *Climate Home News*, 26 April 2019. https://www.climatechangenews.com/2019/04/26/mozambique-faces-climate-debt-trap-cyclone-kenneth-follows-idai/.

Sauvant, Karl P., and Hajo Hasenpflug. *The New International Economic Order: Confrontation or Cooperation between North and South?* Routledge, 2019.

Shackleton, Sheona E., and Charlie M. Shackleton. 'Linking Poverty, HIV/AIDS and Climate Change to Human and Ecosystem Vulnerability in Southern Africa: Consequences for Livelihoods and Sustainable Ecosystem Management'. *International Journal of Sustainable Development & World Ecology* 19, no. 3 (2012): 275–86. https://doi.org/10.1080/13504509.2011.641039.

Sokona, Youba, and Fatma Denton. 'Climate Change Impacts: Can Africa Cope with the Challenges?' *Climate Policy* 1, no. 1 (1 January 2001): 117–23. https://doi.org/10.3763/cpol.2001.0110.

Stadelmann, Martin, J. Timmons Roberts, and Axel Michaelowa. 'New and Additional to What? Assessing Options for Baselines to Assess Climate Finance Pledges'. *Climate and Development* 3, no. 3 (2011): 175–92. https://doi.org/10.1080/17565529.2011.599550.

The Economist. 'Africa's Population Will Double by 2050', March 2020. https://www.economist.com/special-report/2020/03/26/africas-population-will-double-by-2050.

UN. 'Declaration of the United Nations Conference on the Human Environment'. United Nations, 1972. https://legal.un.org/avl/ha/dunche/dunche.html.

———. 'Protection of Global Climate for Present and Future Generations of Mankind'. UN, 17 January 1991. http://digitallibrary.un.org/record/196769.

———. 'United Nations Conference on Environment and Development (UNCED), Earth Summit'. Rio de Janeiro, 1992. https://sustainabledevelopment.un.org/milestones/unced.

UNEP. 'In Defence of the Earth. The Basic Texts on Environment: Founex. Stockholm. Cocoyoc'. Executive Series. Nairobi, Kenya: United Nations Environment Programme, 1981.

UNFCCC. 'Decision -/CP.20. Lima Call for Climate Action'. United Nations Framework Convention on Climate Change (UNFCCC), 2014. https://unfccc.int/files/meetings/lima_dec_2014/application/pdf/auv_cop20_lima_call_for_climate_action.pdf.

———. *Paris Agreement on Climate Change*. New York: United Nations, 2015. https://unfccc.int/sites/default/files/english_paris_agreement.pdf.

Vellinga, Pier, and Robert Swart. 'The Greenhouse Marathon: A Proposal for Global Strategy'. *Climatic Change; (Netherlands)* 18, no. 1 (1 January 1991). https://doi.org/10.1007/BF00142501.

Welch, Claude E. 'Emerging Patterns of Civil-Military Relations in Africa: Radical Coups d'Etat and Political Stability'. In *African Security Issues: Sovereignty, Stability, and Solidarity*. Routledge, 1984.

White, Robin C. A. 'A New International Economic Order'. *International & Comparative Law Quarterly* 24, no. 3 (1975): 542–52. https://doi.org/10.1093/iclqaj/24.3.542.

Xolisa, Ngwadla. *Equitable Access to Sustainable Development: Relevance to Negotiations and Actions on Climate Change*. Cape Town, South Africa: Mitigation Action Plan & Scenarios (MAPS), 2013. http://www.mapsprogramme.org/wp-content/uploads/EASD-Relevance-to-negotiations_Paper.pdf.

CHAPTER 4

The Evolving Geopolitics of Climate Change

In his critically acclaimed book *Born in Blackness: Africa, Africans, and the Making of the Modern World*, Howard French has persuasively sought to reclaim Africa's central position in the history of the making of the modern world.[1] But in the post Second World War order, Africa has striven to pursue its continental policy objectives especially in the shadow of great power politics in engaging in international regimes. Like many other areas of international cooperation, hegemonic leadership has been central to the creation, operation, and reform of the multilateral climate change regime. The United States was instrumental in establishing several international environmental regimes, including the landmark and highly successful multilateral treaties to address ozone depletion.[2] Thus, great powers have exercised their unrivalled capability to significantly shape and reshape multilateral climate cooperation.[3] After all, great powers shape the geopolitical environment within which all other actors operate.[4]

This chapter examines how the shifting geopolitics over the last three decades have influenced Africa's engagement the international climate regime. The chapter argues that the establishment of the multilateral climate regime at the onset of the unipolar moment in international politics shaped the design of the regime. But the emergence of China as a great power, the rise of other major emerging economies, as well

© The Author(s), under exclusive license to Springer Nature Switzerland AG 2023
K. Mbeva et al., *Africa's Right to Development in a Climate-Constrained World*, Contemporary African Political Economy,
https://doi.org/10.1007/978-3-031-22887-2_4

85

as the emergence of the attendant spheres of influence, have significantly led to the contestation of the core assumptions that underpinned the initial design of the multilateral climate change regime. At the centre of this contestation is the differentiation of country groups and their concomitant obligations including the provisions of support to developing countries to implement their climate commitments. China's classification as a developing country has been one of the salient issues in the controversy.

The chapter first sketches the broader contours of the geopolitics of climate change, before proceeding to provide a historical backdrop against which the multilateral climate change regime was established. Subsequent sections of the chapter examine the establishment of the multilateral climate change regime, focusing on the UNFCCC. Failure of the Kyoto Protocol is then examined, especially its design that excluded the major emerging economies in particular China. As countries sought a new agreement, they had to abandon some of the foundational notions of the regime, especially on differentiation and support for implementation. The penultimate section of the chapter examines the growing importance of spheres of geopolitical influence as an emerging locus of international climate cooperation, and draws out the implications for Africa.

4.1 Africa in Multilateral Climate Cooperation

For African countries, the initial design of the multilateral climate change regime, through the UNFCCC, was favourable, as they were not expected to commit to climate action. But the shift towards a more dynamic regime based on universal participation of countries and the strengthening of climate pledges over time has meant that African countries, alongside other countries, would be expected to undertake increasingly ambitious climate obligations over time. Moreover, the geopolitics of climate change are shifting the focus of cooperation outside of the multilateral forum, and into spheres of influence managed by the great and major powers.

At the multilateral level, the bifurcated approach to differentiated responsibilities, where the US and to some extent the EU undertook a disproportionate burden of addressing global climate change has eventually been watered down in favour of a more universal approach where all countries make contributions. Consequently, developing countries, including those in Africa, are under pressure to undertake significantly greater responsibilities to address global climate change.[5] Africa's case is especially concerning given that the continent has contributed a very small fraction—about four per cent—of greenhouse gas emissions while suffering disproportionately from the impacts of climate change.[6] Moreover, great powers, especially the US, EU and China, have are also increasingly focusing on maintaining, and enhancing their economic and political spheres of influence in Africa. These shifts in effect call for a reconsideration of Africa's approach to engagement in global climate change. Instead, we argue that African countries should pro-actively rethink its engagement with the great powers and focus on aligning strategic issues such as infrastructure development with climate policy goals. Doing so would necessitate reframing the climate question as pertains to the continent and the quest for achieving just transition from a normative to strategic one.

To preview this argument, and to show the limits of Africa's agency in the multilateral climate change regime, consider a salient episode in UN climate negotiations whereby Africa countries, under the aegis of the African Group of Negotiators (AGN), did not secure the crucial policy objective identifying Africa as a unique formal category based on "special needs and circumstances", despite intense lobbying. Instead, the Alliance of Small Island States (AOSIS) secured the vulnerability designation, as it managed to garner consensus on the issue.[7] This episode underscored the incredible challenge of African countries securing key policy objectives through the UNFCCC.

To be clear, Africa has made significant contributions to international climate cooperation.[8] This include the design of the multilateral climate change regime, especially on adaptation and international support through climate finance, technology and capacity building.[9] But Africa has not been as successful in restructuring official country categories to be recognised as a unique category at the UNFCCC. In effect, not securing such categorical recognition has limited efforts to secure policy priorities targeted and tailor-made for the continent, with significant geopolitical implications.

This evolving politics, combined with the relatively limitations of Africa's engagement has necessitated the need to re-explore engagement in the global climate regime from the vantage point of evolution and novelty.[10] That is, the multilateral climate regime has shifted from a logic of cooperation that allowed greater flexibility and voluntary engagement for developing countries, including those in Africa, to one where each country is expected to engage and strengthen their contribution over time. Moreover, the reliance on industrialised countries to provide material support to developing countries has also shifted such that African states are now increasingly required to drawing on available and acquired resources to implement their climate policy commitments. Within this new dissipative state, they are thus required to take up greater responsibility in addressing global climate change, while also competing with the rest of the developing world to access international support in the form of climate finance, technology transfer and capacity building. The shift in China's role from the leader of developing countries to great power status, co-equal with the US, has had significant influence on the bargaining strategies of developing countries.[11] This rise has not only affected the existing spheres of influence but is also reflected in the dynamics of international climate cooperation.

Subsequent sections in the chapter demonstrate how Africa's prospects have changed in tandem with the geopolitical landscape, and the need for exploring and strengthening engagement in alternative forums. An important caveat, however, is that the chapter's scope is limited to the implications of the change from unipolarity to multipolarity for Africa's diplomatic strategy in international climate policy. Hence, the chapter does not delve into a detailed analysis of Africa's significant contribution to the multilateral climate change regime, which has been covered in detail elsewhere.[12] Instead, it focuses on the transformation of the geopolitical landscape and the subsequent implications on Africa's climate change policy and diplomatic strategy.

4.2   THE POST-WORLD WAR CONSENSUS

It is important to first examine the geopolitical environment and developments that emerged after the Second World War, before turning to the establishment of the multilateral climate change regime. Just before the Second World War, the geopolitical environment was characterised by multipolarity; that is, there were several great powers. But by the end of the war, only two great powers emerged—the US and the Union of Soviet Socialist Republics (USSR).[13] Immediately after the end of the world war, the US enjoyed preeminence due to its unilateral possession of nuclear weapons, but the USSR joined shortly afterwards. Both great powers then engaged in intense security competition, leading to the Cold War.[14]

4.2.1 In the Shadow of the Cold War

While the US and the USSR were allies during the Second World War, they soon set off an intense geopolitical rivalry. Each of the great powers tried to establish its sphere of influence, thus leading to the Cold War pitting the U.S led capitalist and the communist USSR. The rivalries ushered in a bipolar international order, as both powers sought to gain advantage and influence across the world.

However, competition between the US and the USSR was not the only key development in the aftermath of the Second World War. Decolonisation was emerging as a powerful force of change in international politics, whereby colonised countries sought to become sovereign states.[15] Great power competition and decolonisation thus intersected in a manner that would shape future political engagement in global climate governance. The US and the USSR each sought to influence the newly independent states to take their ideological side.[16] But many of the newly independent states rejected such overtures, leading to the non-aligned movement (NAM) led by India.

Consequently, international cooperation was marked by clamours for ideological dominance as well as a normative critique of empire as embodied by decolonisation. Adom Getachew aptly captured this zeitgeist as 'world making after empire'.[17] Getachew's main argument was that some of the innovative ideas on international cooperation, centred on decolonisation, were advanced by the newly independent states, However, ideas that were predicated on reorganizing the international political order along the line of decolonization failed to take root and were consequently well reflected in the key Cold War international institutions. Self-determination was central to the efforts by newly independent states to decolonise and create a fairer international political system.

These dynamics played out in multilateral cooperation especially under the auspices of United Nations. African countries, were instrumental in the decolonisation movement and the push for a reorganized international order. The critique of the empire thus not only included the quest for independence, but also redress for the harms caused by colonisation.[18]

Two key features marked post-war multilateral cooperation. One key feature was that the US, with the support of other Western liberal states, took the lead in developing multilateral institutions. Indeed, the UN charter, which established the United Nations, has at its core liberal norms,[19] including inalienable individual rights; open markets for the movement of goods, and institutionalised cooperation based on sovereignty.[20] A second key feature, largely driven by newly independent states, was the need for support and redress by industrialised countries and former imperial powers to enable the newly independent states meet their development objectives.

4.2.2 Advent of Derived Development

Multilateral cooperation was shaped by the dynamic forces of creating a liberal international order (LIO), and a reparative force under the banner of a New International Economic Order (NIEO). To bridge these two phenomena, the field of international development emerged under the UN. Specialised UN agencies were created to promote international development, based on the concept of 'derived development'. Derived development sought to promote the transfer of resources from industrialised to newly independent states. Several UN institutions were created to fulfil this mandate, and they included institutions such as the United Nations Development Program (UNDP), UN Centre for Science and Technology for Development, the UN Fund on Science and Technology for Development, and the UN Commission for Science and Technology for Development, among others.[21]

A key pillar of the US-led LIO included a global financial architecture that was based on a system that entrenched the dominance of donor countries.[22] Dubbed the Bretton Woods system, the global financial architecture would be dominated by the ideas of the major Western powers including on development policy. Given the significant role for government involvement in the economy envisioned by the Bretton Woods system, thanks to its Keynesian underpinnings, the notion of derived development was a natural fit for the major powers that controlled the system.[23] As aptly captured by the American Central Banker Henry Wallich in the debate on fostering development especially in the global South, resource transfers from the global North to the South would be a central mechanism of cooperation. Crucially, these technologies would not be cutting edge, arguing that developing countries were yet to acquire the capacity to absorb novel technologies.[24] Western dominance of the Bretton Woods system, with the push by developing countries for resource transfers under the NIEO, the transfer of technologies, capacity and finance, derived development took a stronghold in development initiatives especially at the UN. This can be distinguished from other aid models such as the Marshall Plan for Europe that incorporated assumptions of limited capacity.[25] Indeed, the Washington Consensus and its Structural Adjustment Programs (SAPs) manifested the power imbalances and the outsize influence the donor countries had on developing countries, especially in Africa.[26]

It is therefore no accident that the design of multilateral environmental agreements included resource transfers, in the form of means of implementation, as a key pillar for securing international cooperation. In theoretical terms, multilateral cooperation after the Second World War had taken an Olsonian logic.[27] That is, a small group of countries (the k-group) had taken up relatively greater responsibilities in providing global public goods, while also facilitating side-payments (selective incentives) through the transfer of resources especially to newly independent states. It would also create conditions for hegemonic leadership.[28] The Olsonian model based on leadership by industrialised countries would underpin much of multilateral (climate) cooperation for several decades.

4.2.3 *The Emergence of Multilateral Environmental Governance*

Multilateral environmental cooperation came into prominence from the 1970s. Cognisant of the growing challenges of environmental cooperation, countries under the banner of the UN organised the first multilateral summit on the environment in 1972 in Stockholm, Sweden.[29] While the initiative for such a summit sought a global remit, only a few Western industrialised countries were enthusiastic in convening such a summit. Part of the reason is that many of the transboundary environmental problems were acute in industrialised countries, as a consequence of industrialisation.[30]

In contrast, developing countries, many of which were newly independent, were more interested in addressing developmental issues, especially the eradication of poverty. Decades, if not centuries, of underdevelopment had led to a significant divergence between developing and industrialised states.[31] It was therefore evident that there were divergent conceptions of environmental problems. For industrialised countries, environmental problems were a result of polluting industrial activities. But for developing countries, environmental problems were a result of poverty and underdevelopment.[32]

To bridge these divergent views on environmental problems and their subsequent resolution, the organisers of what became the Stockholm Conference of 1972 articulated an agenda that sought to be inclusive. The eventual title of the conference, 'United Nations Conference on the Human Environment', highlighted the connection between the environmental and human dimension. The final resolution of the conference outlined an Olsonian template where industrialised countries would take the lead by committing to relatively greater commitments while also providing support through transfer of resources to developing countries.[33]

4.3 Establishment of the Multilateral Climate Regime

Two decades after the Stockholm Conference of 1972, countries met once again in Rio in 1992. They adopted multilateral environmental agreements on three issue areas: climate change; biodiversity; and desertification.[34] While there were many similarities between the 1972 Stockholm Conference and the 1992 Rio Conference, the political environments were quite different. The Stockholm Conference was convened at the height of the Cold War which was bipolar, while the Rio Conference was convened at the Unipolar moment following the collapse of the Soviet Union and the emergence of the US as the sole superpower.[35]

4.3.1 Hegemonic Leadership and Differentiation

The unipolar geopolitical environment ensured that there was much momentum in cooperation, as the US clearly took the helm of global leadership. Momentum for the Olsonian logic of cooperation increased, as the US sought to establish a liberal international order. Differentiation in the rights and obligations of the k-group that led the cooperation, and the other countries, was apparent. The Rio Conference marked a watershed moment in international environmental law by codifying the differentiation, through the principle of Common But Differentiated Responsibility (CBDR) and its derivations. Related concepts such as equity and fairness were also included in the multilateral treaties that were adopted following the Rio Conference.[36] Even though CBDR was formally articulated in Rio, in substance it has a long history across the 1972 Stockholm Declaration and the General Agreement on Tariffs and Trade (GATT).[37]

As one of the three treaties adopted at the Rio Conference, the United Nations Framework Convention on Climate Change (UNFCCC) was the first multilateral regime to address climate change. The UNFCCC was designed as a framework convention; that is, it would provide the general framework within which subsequent treaties, which would be more precise, would be developed. This 'bifurcated' approach, based on differentiation via obligation and annexes, laid the foundation for multilateral cooperation on climate change. A list of countries, known as 'Annex I', would take the lead in drastically reducing their greenhouse gas emissions, while the other (developing) countries would only make voluntary commitments. Moreover, the Annex I countries, which were industrialised economies, would transfer resources in the form of finance, technology and capacity to developing countries.[38] So deep was the divide between the two groups of countries that some scholars referred to it as the 'bifurcated firewall' that is 'dysfunctional'.[39] Initially, dysfunction in this case had less to do with the extent of the divide, but more to do with assessing the outcomes of the divide. But over time, as the emissions profiles of countries changed, the extent of the divide gained more traction especially at the turn of the millennium and henceforth.[40]

For African countries, the bifurcated approach to international cooperation was ideal, and one that they also advocated for, since they were not obligated to undertake any commitments, and they were entitled to receiving resources from industrialised countries. Thus, it was arguably in the best interest of African countries to advocate and ensure the persistence of this model of multilateral climate cooperation for two primary reasons. First, African countries would not be under any pressure to commit to reducing emissions. And second, they would receive much external support and not have to allocate scarce domestic resources to implement increasingly ambitious climate commitments. Crucially, African countries would also have to contend with opportunity costs, such as the prospects of foregoing the exploitation of abundant fossil fuel resources to support and promote industrialisation across the continent. After all, Affirmative Multilateralism, as some scholars termed this model of cooperation, resonated with the postcolonial critique and the attendant derived development model, which were supported by African countries.[41] To be sure, climate mitigation is not a burden per se, but it takes unique salience in the African context especially when viewed vis-à-vis opportunity costs, which might overshadow the co-benefits of ambitious climate mitigation.[42]

4.4 Kyoto and the 'China' Question

In a unipolar world, the Olsonian logic of cooperation, which was underpinned by hegemonic global leadership, made sense. But as the geopolitical environment changed, so did the prospects for such a model of cooperation. The shift from unipolarity to the onset of multipolarity had a significant effect on multilateral cooperation in general, and multilateral climate cooperation in particular.[43]

To operationalise the UNFCCC, countries embarked on the development of a new protocol. There was much momentum in the development of the treaty, which culminated in the adoption of the Kyoto Protocol in 1997. In many ways, the Kyoto Protocol was a mirror of the UNFCCC, albeit with finer details. The Protocol adopted a regulatory approach to cooperation, as it laid out a timetable of emissions reductions to be undertaken by the Annex I countries. In addition, these countries would also provide support to developing countries through resource transfers.[44]

4.4.1 An Unsustainable Model

Even though the Kyoto Protocol was adopted, its ratification proved problematic. The US, which had led the multilateral climate change negotiations, could not get the Kyoto Protocol ratified by the US Senate.[45] Canada ratified the Protocol but eventually withdrew from it in 2011.[46] Australia initially refused to ratify the treaty, but eventually did so only after the Protocol had entered into force.[47] A common thread across the three countries was that the Protocol did not include mandatory emissions reductions especially for emerging economies, showing changing ideas from the previous consensus in UNFCCC itself.[48] Moreover, the stringent targets for the Annex I countries were deemed to be too onerous and lacking sufficient flexibility. Major emitters such as Russia experienced a lengthy ratification process, due to the contestation of the various domestic political interests including on fossil fuels.[49] A letter by then US President George Bush in response to a letter by some US Senators clearly articulated the issue, noting,

> As you know, I oppose the Kyoto Protocol because it exempts 80 percent of the world, including major population centers such as China and India, from compliance, and would cause serious harm to the U.S. economy. The Senate's vote, 95-0, shows that there is a clear consensus that the Kyoto

Protocol is an unfair and ineffective means of addressing global climate change concerns.[50]

4.4.1.1 The 'China' Question

President Bush's sentiments were echoed by the rationales articulated by Canada and Australia in rejecting the Kyoto Protocol. That the Protocol did not include commitments by major emerging economies, especially China, made it untenable for some Annex I countries. It was thus evidently becoming clear that the Kyoto Protocol model could not be sustained.[51]

It has been shown that fossil fuel special interests have been lobbying the US federal government in particular, and other governments in general.[52] Hence, the key point is here was the geopolitical perception occasioned by such an omission, exacerbated by the problem of relative gains.[53] Indeed, subsequent US presidents after Bush emphasised the need to cooperate closely with China, with Donald Trump withdrawing from the Paris Agreement based on the argument that the agreement favoured China.[54]

Theoretically, the shape of multilateral climate cooperation was increasingly responding to the sensitivities associated with the shift from absolute to relative gains. Absolute gains make international cooperation easier as countries only worry about their domestic gains without much regard to other countries. But in the context of relative gains, countries are concerned with their gains vis-à-vis other countries.[55] Importantly, the underlying model that had underpinned multilateral climate cooperation was brought into question. The k-group of countries that had provided hegemonic leadership, through the Annex I categorisation, were no longer willing to do so. Other countries would have to undertake a more significant share of the burden in providing the public good of a safe global climate.[56] A key argument advanced by the k-group of countries was that the shifting pattern of annual global emissions (i.e. by 2006/7 China would become the net largest emitter) changed the baseline against which burden-sharing is perceived.

In the face of the failure of the Kyoto Protocol, a new approach and treaty were needed; one that could deal with the issues raised by the onset of multipolarity. It could thus be concluded that the multilateral climate regime was at the threshold of shifting from one dissipate structure (a bifurcated approach) to a more universal approach.[57] And this shift would continue to evolve, as the geopolitical environment was also transforming from unipolarity to multipolarity.

4.5 A UNIVERSAL APPROACH

Given the limits of the Kyoto Protocol's top-down regulatory approach, and the changing geopolitical environment, it was imperative that new legal instruments be developed under the UNFCCC. Two key features would be necessary in the design of the new instrument. One would be universal participation, where all countries would take up climate commitments. The other would be softening of a bifurcated approach to a more dynamic approach of differentiation.[58]

4.5.1 In Search of a Universal Approach

Securing universal participation in the new multilateral climate change instrument would nevertheless be a challenging task. After the election of President George Bush in the new millennium, the US lost momentum in leading multilateral climate change negotiations. Security issues, especially the infamous War on Terror, would be the central focus of the new US administration. Thus, in the absence of US leadership, there were no major developments in the design of the new legal instrument that would replace the Kyoto Protocol.[59] It was not until after Copenhagen was there a recognition that Kyoto would be 'replaced' post-2020 rather than co-exist. Universal mitigation commitments was a longstanding US goal even at Kyoto, but European countries came to this conclusion only much later on.[60]

Prospects, however, changed with the election of President Barack Obama as the US President. While there had been developments at the UNFCCC towards a new legal instrument, there wasn't much leadership from the US. But as President Obama identified multilateral climate cooperation as one of his key foreign policy objectives, the US engagement renewed impetus in negotiations.[61]

4.5.2 The Copenhagen Climate Talks

US re-engagement in leadership in multilateral climate change cooperation however began with a hitch. Expectations were high in the year 2009 that a treaty successor to the Kyoto Protocol would be adopted. Instead, the climate change negotiations, which were held in Copenhagen that year, ended in acrimony. The acrimony culminated from lack of agreement between the US and China, as well as other major emerging economies, on a universal approach to mandating emissions reduction.[62]

But from the failure of the Copenhagen conference emerged a kernel that salvaged hopes for a universally applicable legal instrument to succeed the Kyoto Protocol. The Copenhagen Accord, the main outcome of the conference, included a commitment to adopt a universally applicable legal instrument.[63] This was a major shift in multilateral climate cooperation, since the initial approach was the application of legally binding commitments only to Annex I countries. By implication, another change was the commitment to abandon the bifurcated approach of differentiation of commitments.[64] Taken together, the universal applicability of the new legal instrument and the adoption of a more dynamic approach to differentiation marked a critical juncture in the transformation of multilateral climate change cooperation.[65]

4.5.3 *The Paris Agreement and Catalytic Cooperation*

Abandoning the Kyoto Protocol approach, as well as the bifurcated approach to differentiation, meant that a new model had to be adopted. In other words, the logic of multilateral climate cooperation had to change. As earlier noted, the new instrument would include universal participation of countries and dynamic differentiation. The issue of dynamic differentiation arose from the concern that over time, emerging countries would be the main emitters of greenhouse gases. Hence, it was important to create a legal instrument that would account for this dynamic element.

An additional component was also incorporated into the consideration of the design for the new legal instrument. The Copenhagen Accord included a global temperature goal of two degrees Celsius. Such a global target would provide a convergence point for a country's commitments.[66] But meeting the global target would necessitate iterative commitments from countries, which would be strengthened over time. However, it is important to note that the reason for iterative commitments is not so much the temperature goal itself, but the inadequacy of current commitments—so to meet the temperature goal, the commitments would have to be iterated (i.e. if current commitments were on a 2-degree pathway, there would be no need for iteration and the periodic raising of ambition).

A pledge-review-ratchet model thus emerged as the most suitable for the new legal instrument. The pledges would be submitted by each party, there would be a review process to assess the adequacy of the commitments, and the commitments would be strengthened over time.[67] The Paris Agreement on Climate Change, which embodies this logic, was adopted in 2015. It was a landmark agreement in its design, given its dynamic approach. Additionally, the Paris Agreement was more politically feasible, and its rapid ratification underscored this fact.[68]

It is important to note that the Paris Agreement was a culmination of prior iterations of pledge and review approaches and mechanisms. Countries have been practising a pledge and review system for climate cooperation for decades. Many countries have pledges dating back to the 1980s (Toronto targets), followed by Kyoto (legally binding for developed countries, Nationally Appropriate Mitigation Actions [NAMA] for developing countries), pre-Copenhagen pledges, post-Copenhagen pledges, etc. During this time, there had been informal reviews (both by initiatives such as the Climate Action Tracker and others, as well as at COP), and a review every five years as part of the IPCC Assessment Reports.[69] The Paris Agreement can thus be viewed more as the most politically feasible model that could garner and foster universal political support.

4.5.4   Elusive Solidarity: Paris and Beyond

Even though the Paris Agreement was widely deemed a great political success, it also posed significant challenges, some of which are directly applicable to African countries. Most importantly, African countries did not secure special recognition as a distinct category, with greater flexibility of commitments and enhanced access to resources. Not receiving the special recognition meant that African countries would be viewed within the broader context of other developing countries.[70]

Moreover, China's emergence as a great power changed the dynamics of bargaining coalitions in multilateral climate change negotiations. Initially, the leader of the G77 group and de facto representative of developing countries, China's role as one of the key influences in the successful adoption of the Paris Agreement meant that developing countries had less leverage to promote the continuation of the bifurcated differentiation of commitments.[71] The US and China concluded a significant bilateral agreement on climate change which served as the precursor to the Paris

Agreement. But even so, US leadership has waned and waxed between leading and undermining the multilateral climate regime.[72]

For developing countries in general, and African countries in particular, the onset of multipolarity has fundamentally transformed the basis of multilateral cooperation from a normative to a strategic one. As their share of global emissions rise, and their national economic circumstances improve, they would be expected to strengthen their contribution to the global climate cooperation effort.[73]

4.5.5 Continental Climate Coordination in Africa

Due to their significant numbers, African countries established the Africa Group of Negotiators (AGN) to coordinate their efforts in multilateral climate change negotiations. The AGN has been effective in providing a unified voice. But its effectiveness in achieving continental climate policy objectives remains unclear. AGN's effectiveness as a coordinating platform has also not been consistent.[74] As Fig. 4.1 shows, the number of submissions by the AGN, as part of the negotiations, has been sporadic.

In the lead up to adoption of the Paris Agreement in 2015, African countries used the AGN to coordinate their positions and submissions.

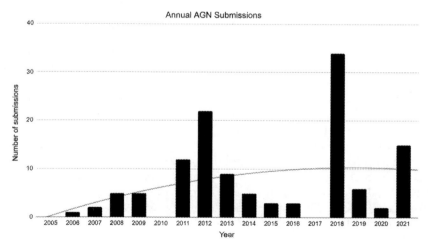

Fig. 4.1 Annual number of AGN submissions in climate change negotiations under the UNFCCC (*Source* Authors, with data from the UNFCCC website)

But the number of submissions, vis-à-vis those of individual countries or other negotiation groups that African countries are part of, is very low, as illustrated in Fig. 4.1. What can therefore be inferred is that solidarity and effectiveness in using the AGN as a strategic coordinating platform by African countries has been limited, if not elusive.

4.6 Emerging Spheres of Climate Influence

Outside of the multilateral cooperation forums in particular the UNFCCC, the geopolitical transformations also had significant implications for climate cooperation. Great powers (the US and China), major powers (the EU) and emerging powers (such as BRICS) have sought to establish spheres of influence to promote their geopolitical objectives.[75] While diverse in many ways, these forums share an underlying logic, whereby the dominant power has hegemonic influence over others in their region. Such spheres of climate influence are organised in tandem with the logic of orders. It is not unexpected that great powers will likely seek to create spheres of influence on aspects of multilateral cooperation including climate governance to promote their norms and strategic interests.[76]

The impacts of such dynamics on climate governance can be reflected in several ways including the already intensifying race for critical materials needed for the transition to low-carbon economies.[77] Major powers, in a bid to decarbonise their economies and expand their renewable energy infrastructure, have sought to secure the requisite natural resources and supply lines that will be used to facilitate the transition to a low-carbon economy. As such, African countries, some of which host many of these minerals such as cobalt in the Democratic Republic of Congo, have been caught in the competition for such resources.[78]

Africa is also emerging as a strategic sphere of influence including on international climate cooperation.[79] However, the increasingly intense dynamics of contemporary geopolitical competition poses a significant strategic challenge. While the multilateral climate forum has offered a viable platform for articulating and coordinating a normative approach to climate cooperation, geopolitical competition is driven by *realpolitik* such that strategic considerations trump normative ones.

Nonetheless, the emergence of climate spheres of influence has also presented opportunities for African countries to pursue policy objectives that had been unviable in the multilateral forum. There are opportunities for more meaningful engagement with Africa including on climate cooperation. What is also important to note is that the emerging spheres of climate influence are also creating opportunities for more strategic engagement on the issue of African development as opposed to primary reliance on the derived development approach of transferring resources.

4.6.1 South-South Cooperation

Premised on solidarity, South-South Cooperation (SSC) arose to create a shared platform for global South countries to cooperate on issues of mutual interest.[80] SSC differs from North-South cooperation given that the former has less emphasis on normative aspects such as preparation, but embraces solidarity. Moreover, cooperation within the South-South context is relatively less contested in terms of power imbalances and coercion, which have their roots primarily in the (post)colonial relations between the North and the South. In tandem with its ascendance as a great power, China has increasingly taken up leadership in developing and promoting the SSC model and its attendant institutions.[81] Focus has been on technical and scientific cooperation, including provision of aid. Several of these initiatives are of immediate and direct relevance to African countries.[82]

China's establishment of a climate change fund to support SSC is perhaps the clearest indication of the country's role in promoting climate cooperation in the global South. In 2015, China established the China South-South Climate Cooperation Fund, and initially capitalised it with US$3.1 billion 'to help developing countries tackle climate change'.[83] In doing so, China was strengthening not only its engagement, but also leadership in South-South cooperation. Numerous other initiatives have also sought to advance South-South cooperation including on climate change, as outlined below.

Forum for China-Africa Cooperation (FOCAC): For the past two decades or so, Sino-African relations have brought in significant transformations. Under the auspices of FOCAC, China and African countries have engaged in high-level cooperation on development. A major success of FOCAC has been in coordinating trade and development, especially in infrastructure development, between African countries and China. Moreover, FOCAC has provided a political framework for the engagement of African countries as a bloc, thus providing greater coordination with China.[84]

While initial efforts under FOCAC focused on developmental issues, broadly understood, recent initiatives have brought in a focus on climate change. For the first time, the FOCAC summit in 2021, held in Senegal, included a stand-alone commitment on climate change.[85] In the meeting's joint communiqué, the commitment on climate cooperation, and its underpinning logic, was clear, emphasising mutually shared commitments such as upholding the principle of common but differentiated responsibilities; taking into account the challenging issues faced by developing countries; and strengthening the transfer of technology and the capacity of African countries to respond to climate change.[86]

What is interesting about the FOCAC declaration on climate change is the logic of cooperation: even though China is now a great power, it did not leverage its huge market power to coerce African countries to enhance climate ambition through sanctions. Trade sanctions, or the threat of their use are absent from the cooperation. Instead, the logic is one of solidarity at the multilateral level, and support at the bilateral level, based on mutual trust and understanding. This approach reflects the broader strategy of Sino-African relations, where diplomacy and mutual understanding play a key role in cooperation.

Belt and Road Initiative (BRI): In tandem, the BRI has been instrumental in bilateral cooperation between China and Africa.[87] Designed as China's main geopolitical instrument, the BRI has mainly focused on infrastructure projects. For African countries, the BRI presented an important opportunity to close the significant infrastructure gap in the continent. Part of the infrastructure investment has included fossil fuels and renewable energy. But China has indicated that it will no longer fund the construction of coal power plants overseas.[88] Already, coal power plants had been controversial in Africa, and faced local opposition, a prime example being the successful opposition to the construction of a China-financed coal power plant in the pristine Lamu marine park in Kenya.[89] China's pledge not to fund new overseas coal plants might be understood to be in line with global efforts to phase out the use of coal, and less to do with local opposition to such investments overseas.[90]

Coupled with major investments in solar and wind power plants in several parts of Africa, China's shift in focus to climate-compatible infrastructure investment in Africa will have a major impact on Africa's climate policy. Furthermore, since the BRI has been a major source of technology and support, it has in many ways diminished the significance of means of implementation mechanisms developed at the multilateral level. African countries have always found accessing resources through the multilateral mechanisms to be quite challenging; consider that African countries only managed to access less than three per cent of Clean Development Mechanisms (CDM) under the Kyoto Protocol, of which a disproportionate share of the resources were accrued by South Africa.[91] In the long run, the increased importance of BRI will entrench the multipolar dimension of climate cooperation.[92]

International Solar Alliance (ISA): As an emerging power, India has also sought to foster international climate cooperation.[93] India's establishment of the International Solar Alliance (ISA) is perhaps the most salient signal of leveraging its power to promote international climate cooperation. Through the ISA, India has tried to leverage its status as a major power by establishing and maintaining the institution. Moreover, the ISA reflects India's focus on the role of solar energy especially in the context of developing countries.[94] Established in 2015, in partnership with France, the stated objective of the ISA is to

> develop and deploy cost-effective and transformational energy solutions powered by the sun to help member countries develop low-carbon growth trajectories, with particular focus on delivering impact in countries categorized as Least Developed Countries (LDCs) and the Small Island Developing States (SIDS). Being a global platform, ISA's partnerships with multilateral development banks (MDBs), development financial institutions (DFIs), private and public sector organisations, civil society and other international institutions is key to delivering the change it seeks to see in the world going ahead.[95]

EU-Africa Green New Deal: Not surprisingly, Europe has also sought to strategically engage with African countries including on climate cooperation. Historical relations between Europe and Africa go back many centuries, many of them characterised by the scourge of colonialism and later on neocolonialism and postcolonial continuity.[96] Thus, Africa-Europe relations have been tenuous. Being a major power and instrumental in multilateral climate change cooperation, the EU has been keen to leverage its bilateral relations to promote climate change cooperation.

In response to China's growing geopolitical influence in Africa, Europe especially through the European Union (EU) has revamped its approach to the African continent. The initial approach by Europe was premised on delivering support for means of implementation as part of their commitments and obligations through the multilateral system. Yet, recent bilateral initiatives have been more tightly coupled with strategic geopolitical considerations. In 2021, the EU proposed the establishment of a Green Deal with Africa as a bilateral forum for cooperation on climate change.[97] The Green Deal would be part of a broader strategic initiative of the EU termed 'Towards a Comprehensive Strategy with Africa'. More recently, the EU has also announced the EU Global Gateway initiative as an alternative to the BRI, with the claimed differentiating factor being that the former will explicitly promote climate cooperation.[98]

Also, the EU's introduction of trade sanctions to promote climate action has added a strategic dimension to international cooperation. Called the Carbon Border Adjustment Mechanism (CBAM), the policy instrument will impose taxes on exports to the EU deemed to be carbon intensive.[99] The objective of the CBAM is to induce countries to increase their climate ambition especially through cleaner production processes, and to stem carbon leakage and ensure a fair playing field for EU domestic producers. African countries and other developing countries have decried the CBAM as undercutting equity.[100] That the CBAM does not explicitly exclude Least Developed Countries (LDCs), majority of which are in Africa, has been a cause for concern. Also, since the EU is a major export market for African countries, and African countries have embraced industrialisation as the main development policy, the CBAM poses major challenges.[101] The sanctioned-based approach of the EU could transform the international climate cooperation, with significant implications for African countries.

US B3W: The United States (US) has also been active in establishing its own spheres of influence, including on climate cooperation in Africa. An initial approach focused on closing the energy infrastructure gap in Africa. Through the Power Africa Initiative, the US promoted private sector investment in clean energy in Africa.[102] Later on, the US established the Build Back Better World (B3W) initiative as 'a values-driven, high-standard, and transparent infrastructure partnership led by major democracies to help narrow the $40+ trillion infrastructure need in the developing world...Through B3W, the G7 and other like-minded partners will coordinate in mobilizing private-sector capital in four areas of focus—climate, health and health security, digital technology, and gender equity and equality'.[103]

Other Africa+1 Initiatives: Beyond the great and major powers, some emerging powers are also establishing strategic bilateral relationships with Africa. Turkey, for instance, has established high-level bilateral cooperation with African countries as a bloc. The Turkey-Africa partnership was formalised in 2018, under the Africa-Turkey Joint Implementation Plan.[104] It includes cooperation in trade and investment including on energy. Other 'Africa+1' initiatives are more likely to proliferate.[105] Whether the Africa+1 summits will foster climate cooperation, and the logic of cooperation they will adopt, remains to be seen. What is apparent though is that such initiatives will continue reshaping the geopolitical environment.

Strategic Partnerships: Apart from the continental engagement with great and middle powers, African countries are also seeking strategic partnerships to foster international climate cooperation. In partnership with France, Germany, the United Kingdom and the US , South Africa has launched a long-term Just Energy Transition Partnership to support the country's decarbonisation efforts. The partnership has mobilised an initial investment of US$8.5 billion.[106] It is important, however, to note that South Africa is an outlier in Africa, given its disproportionate capacity to attract significant investments especially when compared with most African countries that have limited capacity, as well as its relatively high emissions profile.[107] The EU-Africa partnership on climate change and COVID pandemic recovery, which is based on efforts to renew and strengthen EU-Africa strategic relations, is another example of the evolving geopolitics and their implications on climate cooperation.[108]

4.7 Conclusion

Geopolitical dynamics have been instrumental in shaping international climate cooperation. In the last three decades, the international system has transformed from a bipolar to unipolar and eventually a multipolar system. As this chapter has argued, the changes in the geopolitical environment continue to shape international climate change cooperation. The most significant change has been the shift in emphasis from normative to strategic considerations in international climate cooperation.

For African countries, which had long advocated for a more equitable approach to international climate cooperation, the increasingly competitive geopolitical environment has meant that these countries have had to take up a significant portion of responsibility in providing a safe climate as a public good, while the multilateral sources of support have been largely constrained. Moreover, the changing emissions profile whereby emerging and developing countries' emissions are bound to rise in the future, will exacerbate the geopolitical dimension of climate cooperation, as these countries would be expected to significantly enhance their contributions to global climate cooperation. As has been demonstrated in the chapter, Africa's climate policy and diplomacy would need to be fit for purpose to effectively engage in the evolving geopolitical environment. Specifically, such an approach would have to adapt to the dynamic notions of international equity, an issue elaborated in the next chapter.

NOTES

1. Howard W. French, *Born in Blackness: Africa, Africans, and the Making of the Modern World, 1471 to the Second World War* (New York: Liveright Publishing Corporation, 2021).
2. Robert Falkner, 'American Hegemony and the Global Environment', *International Studies Review* 7, no. 4 (1 December 2005): 585–99, https://doi.org/10.1111/j.1468-2486.2005.00534.x.
3. Robert Falkner and Barry Buzan, eds., *Great Powers, Climate Change, and Global Environmental Responsibilities* (Oxford, New York: Oxford University Press, 2022).
4. John J. Mearsheimer, *The Tragedy of Great Power Politics* (New York: W. W. Norton & Company, 2001).
5. Pieter Pauw, Kennedy Mbeva, and Harro van Asselt, 'Subtle Differentiation of Countries' Responsibilities Under the Paris Agreement', *Palgrave Communications* 5, no. 1 (30 July 2019): 1–7, https://doi.org/10.1057/s41599-019-0298-6; Reuben Makomere and Kennedy Liti Mbeva, 'Squaring the Circle: Development Prospects Within the Paris Agreement', *Carbon & Climate Law Review* 12, no. 1 (2018): 31–40, https://doi.org/10.21552/cclr/2018/1/7.
6. Lacour M. Ayompe, Steven J. Davis, and Benis N. Egoh, 'Trends and Drivers of African Fossil Fuel CO_2 Emissions 1990–2017', *Environmental Research Letters* 15, no. 12 (December 2020): 124039, https://doi.org/10.1088/1748-9326/abc64f.

7. Nicholas Chan, '"Special Circumstances" and the Politics of Climate Vulnerability: African Agency in the UN Climate Change Negotiations', *Africa Spectrum*, 24 June 2021, 2, https://doi.org/10.1177/000203 9721991151.

8. e.g. see Adom Getachew, *Worldmaking After Empire: The Rise and Fall of Self-Determination* (New Jersey: Princeton University Press, 2020); Sabelo J. Ndlovu-Gatsheni, 'Decoloniality in Africa: A Continuing Search for a New World Order', *The Australasian Review of African Studies* 36, no. 2 (2015): 22–50, https://doi.org/10.3316/informit.640531 150387614.

9. Charles Roger and Satishkumar Belliethathan, 'Africa in the Global Climate Change Negotiations', *International Environmental Agreements: Politics, Law and Economics* 16, no. 1 (1 February 2016): 91–108, https://doi.org/10.1007/s10784-014-9244-7.

10. Ilya Prigogine, 'Time, Structure, and Fluctuations', *Science*, 1 September 1978, https://doi.org/10.1126/science.201.4358.777.

11. Chan, '"Special Circumstances" and the Politics of Climate Vulnerability', 316.

12. E.g. see Roger and Belliethathan, 'Africa in the Global Climate Change Negotiations'; Simon Chin-Yee, 'Briefing: Africa and the Paris Climate Change Agreement', *African Affairs* 115, no. 459 (1 April 2016): 359–68, https://doi.org/10.1093/afraf/adw005; Joanes Odiwuor Atela et al., 'Exploring the Agency of Africa in Climate Change Negotiations: The Case of REDD+', *International Environmental Agreements: Politics, Law and Economics* 17, no. 4 (1 August 2017): 463–82, https://doi.org/10.1007/s10784-016-9329-6.

13. Kenneth N. Waltz, 'The Stability of a Bipolar World', *Daedalus* 93, no. 3 (1964): 881–909.

14. Waltz; Henry A. Kissinger, *Nuclear Weapons and Foreign Policy* (Boulder, Colorado: Westview Press, 1957).

15. Miles Larmer, 'Leslie James, George Padmore and Decolonisation from Below: Pan-Africanism, the Cold War and the End of Empire', *Journal of Contemporary History* 53, no. 2 (1 April 2018): 462–64, https://doi.org/10.1177/0022009417749502m; John Darwin, *Britain and Decolonisation: The Retreat from Empire in the Post-War World* (Macmillan International Higher Education, 1988); Christopher J. Lee, 'At the Rendezvous of Decolonization', *Interventions* 11, no. 1 (1 March 2009): 81–93, https://doi.org/10.1080/136980109027 52806.

16. Wai-Li Chu, 'Cold War and Decolonisation', in *Hong Kong History: Themes in Global Perspective*, ed. Man-Kong Wong and Chi-Man Kwong, Hong Kong Studies Reader Series (Singapore: Springer, 2022), 83–113, https://doi.org/10.1007/978-981-16-2806-1_4.

17. Getachew, *Worldmaking After Empire*.
18. Biko Agozino, 'Reparative Justice: The Final Stage of Decolonization', *Punishment & Society* 23, no. 5 (1 December 2021): 613–30, https://doi.org/10.1177/14624745211024342.
19. G. John Ikenberry, 'America's Liberal Hegemony', *Current History; Philadelphia*, January 1999.
20. Michael N. Barnett, 'Bringing in the New World Order: Liberalism, Legitimacy, and the United Nations', ed. Boutros Boutros-Ghali et al., *World Politics* 49, no. 4 (1997): 526–51.
21. Calestous Juma, 'Complexity, Innovation, and Development: Schumpeter Revisited', *Policy and Complex Systems* 1, no. 1 (2014): 15, https://doi.org/10.18278/jpcs.1.1.1.
22. Matías Vernengo, 'The Consolidation of Dollar Hegemony After the Collapse of Bretton Woods: Bringing Power Back In', *Review of Political Economy* 33, no. 4 (2 October 2021): 529–51, https://doi.org/10.1080/09538259.2021.1950966.
23. Adrien Faudot, 'The Keynes Plan and Bretton Woods Debates: The Early Radical Criticisms by Balogh, Schumacher and Kalecki', *Cambridge Journal of Economics* 45, no. 4 (1 July 2021): 751–70, https://doi.org/10.1093/cje/beab018; Robert Skidelsky, 'Keynes, Globalisation and the Bretton Woods Institutions in the Light of Changing Ideas About Markets', *World Economics* 6, no. 1 (2005): 15–30.
24. Juma, 'Complexity, Innovation, and Development: Schumpeter Revisited', 9–10.
25. Dambisa Moyo, *Dead Aid: Why Aid Is Not Working and How There Is a Better Way for Africa*, Reprint edition (Farrar, Straus and Giroux, 2010); Dambisa Moyo, 'Why Foreign Aid Is Hurting Africa', *Wall Street Journal*, 22 March 2009, sec. World News, https://www.wsj.com/articles/SB123758895999200083.
26. J. Barry Riddell, 'Things Fall Apart Again: Structural Adjustment Programmes in Sub-Saharan Africa', *The Journal of Modern African Studies* 30, no. 1 (1992): 53–68; Joseph Stiglitz, *Globalization and Its Discontents* (W. W. Norton & Company, 2002).
27. Mancur Olson, *The Logic of Collective Action. Public Goods and the Theory of Groups* (Cambridge, MA: Harvard University Press, 1965).
28. Duncan Snidal, 'The Limits of Hegemonic Stability Theory', *International Organization* 39, no. 4 (ed 1985): 579–614, https://doi.org/10.1017/S002081830002703X.
29. Eric Paglia, 'The Swedish Initiative and the 1972 Stockholm Conference: The Decisive Role of Science Diplomacy in the Emergence of Global

Environmental Governance', *Humanities and Social Sciences Communications* 8, no. 1 (5 January 2021): 1–10, https://doi.org/10.1057/s41 599-020-00681-x; Lars Emmelin, 'The Stockholm Conferences', *Ambio* 1, no. 4 (1972): 135–40.

30. Adil Najam, 'Developing Countries and Global Environmental Governance: From Contestation to Participation to Engagement', *International Environmental Agreements: Politics, Law and Economics* 5, no. 3 (1 September 2005): 307, https://doi.org/10.1007/s10784-005-3807-6.

31. Agarwala A.N., *The Economics of Underdevelopment* (Oxford University Press, 1961); Walter Rodney, *How Europe Underdeveloped Africa*, Revised edition (Washington, DC: Howard Univ Pr, 1981).

32. Najam, 'Developing Countries and Global Environmental Governance', 308–9.

33. UN, *Declaration of the United Nations Conference on the Human Environment* (United Nations, 1972), https://legal.un.org/avl/ha/dun che/dunche.html.

34. UN, *Rio Declaration on Environment and Development* (Rio de Janeiro: United Nations General Assembly, 1992), https://www.un.org/en/development/desa/population/migration/generalassembly/docs/glo balcompact/A_CONF.151_26_Vol.I_Declaration.pdf; UN, *Agenda 21* (Rio de Janeiro: United Nations, 1992), https://sustainabledevelop ment.un.org/content/documents/Agenda21.pdf.

35. Charles Krauthammer, 'The Unipolar Moment', *Foreign Affairs* 70, no. 1 (1990): 23–33, https://doi.org/10.2307/20044692.

36. Phillip Stalley, 'Norms from the Periphery: Tracing the Rise of the Common but Differentiated Principle in International Environmental Politics', *Cambridge Review of International Affairs* 31, no. 2 (4 March 2018): 144, https://doi.org/10.1080/09557571.2018.1481824.

37. Christopher D. Stone, 'Common But Differentiated Responsibilities in International Law', *American Journal of International Law* 98, no. 2 (April 2004): 276–301, https://doi.org/10.2307/3176729.

38. Jutta Brunnée and Charlotte Streck, 'The UNFCCC as a Negotiation Forum: Towards Common but More Differentiated Responsibilities', *Climate Policy* 13, no. 5 (1 September 2013): 589–607, https://doi.org/10.1080/14693062.2013.822661; Jeffrey McGee and Jens Steffek, 'The Copenhagen Turn in Global Climate Governance and the Contentious History of Differentiation in International Law', *Journal of Environmental Law* 28, no. 1 (1 March 2016): 37–63, https://doi.org/10.1093/jel/eqw003; Lavanya Rajamani, 'The Principle of Common but Differentiated Responsibilities and Respective Capabilities in the International Climate Change Regime', in *Research Handbook on Climate Disaster Law*, ed. Rosemary Lyster and Robert

Verchick (Cheltenham, UK and Northampton, MA: Edward Elgar, 2018), 46–60, https://www.elgaronline.com/view/edcoll/978178643 0021/9781786430021.00009.xml.

39. Joanna Depledge and Farhana Yamin, 'The Global Climate-Change Regime: A Defence', in *The Economics and Politics of Climate Change*, ed. Dieter Helm and Cameron Hepburn (Oxford: Oxford University Press, 2009), 443, https://doi.org/10.1093/acprof:osobl/978019957 3288.003.0021.

40. Falkner and Buzan, *Great Powers, Climate Change, and Global Environmental Responsibilities*, 284.

41. Robyn Eckersley, 'Moving Forward in the Climate Negotiations: Multilateralism or Minilateralism?', *Global Environmental Politics* 12, no. 2 (20 March 2012): 31, https://doi.org/10.1162/GLEP_a_00107; Kennedy Mbeva and Reuben Makomere, 'The End of Affirmative Multilateralism?', SSRN Scholarly Paper (Rochester, NY: Social Science Research Network, 7 May 2021), https://doi.org/10.2139/ssrn.384 1282.

42. Edward King, 'Africa's "Buyer's Remorse" over Paris Climate Deal', Climate Home, 3 November 2016, http://www.climatechangenews. com/2016/11/03/africas-buyers-remorse-over-paris-climate-deal/; Victoria R. Nalule, 'Transitioning to a Low Carbon Economy: Is Africa Ready to Bid Farewell to Fossil Fuels?', in *The Palgrave Handbook of Managing Fossil Fuels and Energy Transitions*, ed. Geoffrey Wood and Keith Baker (Cham: Springer International Publishing, 2020), 261–86, https://doi.org/10.1007/978-3-030-28076-5_10.

43. J. Timmons Roberts, 'Multipolarity and the New World (Dis)order: US Hegemonic Decline and the Fragmentation of the Global Climate Regime', *Global Environmental Change, Symposium on Social Theory and the Environment in the New World (Dis)order*, 21, no. 3 (1 August 2011): 776–84, https://doi.org/10.1016/j.gloenvcha.2011. 03.017; Hari M. Osofsky, 'The Complexities of Multipolar Approaches to Climate Change: Lessons from Litigation and Local Action', *Proceedings of the ASIL Annual Meeting* 107 (ed 2013): 73–75, https://doi. org/10.5305/procannmeetasil.107.0073.

44. Christoph Böhringer, 'The Kyoto Protocol: A Review and Perspectives', *Oxford Review of Economic Policy* 19, no. 3 (1 September 2003): 451– 66, https://doi.org/10.1093/oxrep/19.3.451.

45. Robyn Eckersley, 'Ambushed: The Kyoto Protocol, the Bush Administration's Climate Policy and the Erosion of Legitimacy', *International Politics* 44, no. 2 (1 March 2007): 306–24, https://doi.org/10.1057/ palgrave.ip.8800190.

46. Staff, 'Canada Pulls Out of Kyoto Protocol', *The Guardian*, 13 December 2011, sec. Environment, https://www.theguardian.com/env ironment/2011/dec/13/canada-pulls-out-kyoto-protocol.
47. Kate Crowley, 'Is Australia Faking It? The Kyoto Protocol and the Greenhouse Policy Challenge', *Global Environmental Politics* 7, no. 4 (1 November 2007): 118–39, https://doi.org/10.1162/glep.2007.7.4.118.
48. Ingrid Barnsley, 'Dealing with Change: Australia, Canada and the Kyoto Protocol to the Framework Convention on Climate Change', *The Round Table* 95, no. 385 (1 July 2006): 399–410, https://doi.org/10.1080/00358530600748358.
49. Alexander Gusev, 'Evolution of Russian Climate Policy: From the Kyoto Protocol to the Paris Agreement', *L'Europe En Formation* 380, no. 2 (2016): 39–52; Igor Makarov, 'Climate Change Policies and Resource Abundance: The Case of Russia', *Handbook of Sustainable Politics and Economics of Natural Resources*, 10 December 2021, https://www.elgaronline.com/view/edcoll/978 1789908763/9781789908763.00017.xml.
50. President George W. Bush, 'Text of a Letter from the President to Senators Hagel, Helms, Craig, and Roberts', 13 March 2001, https://georgewbush-whitehouse.archives.gov/news/releases/2001/03/200 10314.html.
51. Steve Rayner and Gwyn Prins, 'The Wrong Trousers: Radically Rethinking Climate Policy', Other Working Paper (Oxford, UK: James Martin Institute for Science and Civilization, University of Oxford and the MacKinder Centre for the Study of Long-Wave Events, London School of Economics, 2007), http://www.sbs.ox.ac.uk/centres/insis/Documents/TheWrongTrousers.pdf; Dieter Helm, 'The Kyoto Approach Has Failed', *Nature* 491, no. 7426 (November 2012): 663–65, https://doi.org/10.1038/491663a; Gwyn Prins and Steve Rayner, 'Time to Ditch Kyoto', *Nature* 449, no. 7165 (25 October 2007): 973–75, https://doi.org/10.1038/449973a.
52. Leah Cardamore Stokes, *Short Circuiting Policy: Interest Groups and the Battle Over Clean Energy and Climate Policy in the American States* (Oxford University Press, 2020); Michaël Aklin and Matto Mildenberger, 'Prisoners of the Wrong Dilemma: Why Distributive Conflict, Not Collective Action, Characterizes the Politics of Climate Change', *Global Environmental Politics* 20, no. 4 (1 November 2020): 4–27, https://doi.org/10.1162/glep_a_00578.
53. Joseph Grieco, Robert Powell, and Duncan Snidal, 'The Relative-Gains Problem for International Cooperation', *The American Political Science Review* 87, no. 3 (1993): 727–43, https://doi.org/10.2307/2938747.
r

54. Luke Kemp, 'Better Out Than In', *Nature Climate Change* 7 (22 May 2017): 458; Luke Kemp, 'US-Proofing the Paris Climate Agreement', *Climate Policy* 17, no. 1 (2 January 2017): 86–101, https://doi.org/10.1080/14693062.2016.1176007.
55. Grieco, Powell, and Snidal, 'The Relative-Gains Problem for International Cooperation'; Frank Grundig, 'Patterns of International Cooperation and the Explanatory Power of Relative Gains: An Analysis of Cooperation on Global Climate Change, Ozone Depletion, and International Trade', *International Studies Quarterly* 50, no. 4 (1 December 2006): 781–801, https://doi.org/10.1111/j.1468-2478.2006.00425.x.
56. Roberts, 'Multipolarity and the New World (Dis)order'.
57. Daniel Bodansky, 'A Tale of Two Architectures: The Once and Future U.N. Climate Change Regime', *Climate Change and Environmental Hazards Related to Shipping: An International Legal Framework*, 1 January 2013, 35–51, https://doi.org/10.1163/9789004244955_005.
58. Daniel Bodansky, 'Legal Form of a New Climate Agreement: Avenues and Options', *Center for Climate and Energy Solutions* (blog), 15 April 2009, https://www.c2es.org/document/legal-form-of-a-new-climate-agreement-avenues-and-options/.
59. Luke Kemp, 'Bypassing the "Ratification Straitjacket": Reviewing US Legal Participation in a Climate Agreement', *Climate Policy* 16, no. 8 (16 November 2016): 1011–28, https://doi.org/10.1080/14693062.2015.1061472.
60. Bodansky, 'A Tale of Two Architectures'.
61. Barack Obama, 'The Irreversible Momentum of Clean Energy', *Science* 355, no. 6321 (13 January 2017), https://doi.org/10.1126/science.aam6284.
62. Navroz K. Dubash, 'Copenhagen: Climate of Mistrust', *Economic and Political Weekly* 44, no. 52 (2009): 8–11.
63. McGee and Steffek, 'The Copenhagen Turn in Global Climate Governance and the Contentious History of Differentiation in International Law'.
64. Christina Voigt and Felipe Ferreira, '"Dynamic Differentiation": The Principles of CBDR-RC, Progression and Highest Possible Ambition in the Paris Agreement', *Transnational Environmental Law* 5, no. 2 (October 2016): 285–303, https://doi.org/10.1017/S20471025160 00212; Pauw, Mbeva, and van Asselt, 'Subtle Differentiation of Countries' Responsibilities under the Paris Agreement'.
65. Daniel Bodansky, 'The Paris Climate Change Agreement: A New Hope?', *American Journal of International Law* 110, no. 2 (April 2016): 288–319, https://doi.org/10.5305/amerjintelaw.110.2.0288.
66. Piero Morseletto, Frank Biermann, and Philipp Pattberg, 'Governing by Targets: Reductio Ad Unum and Evolution of the Two-Degree

Climate Target', *International Environmental Agreements: Politics, Law and Economics* 17, no. 5 (1 October 2017): 655–76, https://doi.org/10.1007/s10784-016-9336-7.

67. Robert O. Keohane and Michael Oppenheimer, 'Paris: Beyond the Climate Dead End Through Pledge and Review?', *Politics and Governance* 4, no. 3 (8 September 2016): 142–51, https://doi.org/10.17645/pag.v4i3.634; Bård Harstad, 'Pledge-and-Review Bargaining', SSRN Scholarly Paper (Rochester, NY: Social Science Research Network, 2018), https://doi.org/10.2139/ssrn.3338622.

68. Jen Iris Allan et al., 'Making the Paris Agreement: Historical Processes and the Drivers of Institutional Design', *Political Studies*, 6 October 2021, 00323217211049294, https://doi.org/10.1177/00323217211049294; Thomas Hale, 'Catalytic Cooperation', *Global Environmental Politics* 20, no. 4 (1 November 2020): 73–98, https://doi.org/10.1162/glep_a_00561.

69. Daniel Bodansky, 'The Copenhagen Climate Change Conference: A Postmortem', *American Journal of International Law* 104, no. 2 (April 2010): 230–40, https://doi.org/10.5305/amerjintelaw.104.2.0230; Keohane and Oppenheimer, 'Paris'.

70. Chan, '"Special Circumstances" and the Politics of Climate Vulnerability', 314.

71. Chan, 327.

72. Kemp, 'Better Out than In'; Kemp, 'US-Proofing the Paris Climate Agreement'; Jonathan Pickering et al., 'The Impact of the US Retreat from the Paris Agreement: Kyoto Revisited?', *Climate Policy* 0, no. 0 (18 December 2017): 1–10, https://doi.org/10.1080/14693062.2017.1412934; Johannes Urpelainen and Thijs Van de Graaf, 'United States Non-Cooperation and the Paris Agreement', *Climate Policy* 18, no. 7 (9 August 2018): 839–51, https://doi.org/10.1080/14693062.2017.1406843.

73. Falkner and Buzan, *Great Powers, Climate Change, and Global Environmental Responsibilities*, 284.

74. Chan, '"Special Circumstances" and the Politics of Climate Vulnerability', 315.

75. Graham Allison, 'The New Spheres of Influence: Sharing the Globe with Other Great Powers', *Foreign Affairs*, 19 October 2021, https://www.foreignaffairs.com/articles/united-states/2020-02-10/new-spheres-influence.

76. John J. Mearsheimer, 'Bound to Fail: The Rise and Fall of the Liberal International Order', *International Security* 43, no. 4 (1 April 2019): 11–12, https://doi.org/10.1162/isec_a_00342.

77. Meghan O'Sullivan, Indra Overland, and David Sandalow, 'The Geopolitics of Renewable Energy', Working Paper (New York, NY; and

Cambridge, MA: Center on Global Energy Policy, Columbia University|SIPA; and The Geopolitics of Energy Project, Belfer Center for Science and International Affairs, Harvard Kennedy School, 2017), https://www.belfercenter.org/sites/default/files/files/publication/Geopolitics%20Renewables%20-%20final%20report%206.26.17.pdf; Marjolein de Ridder, *The Geopolitics of Mineral Resources for Renewable Energy Technologies* (The Hague Centre for Strategic Studies, 2013); Roman Vakulchuk, Indra Overland, and Daniel Scholten, 'Renewable Energy and Geopolitics: A Review', *Renewable and Sustainable Energy Reviews* 122 (1 April 2020): 109547, https://doi.org/10.1016/j.rser.2019.109547.

78. Sophia Kalantzakos, 'The Race for Critical Minerals in an Era of Geopolitical Realignments', *The International Spectator* 55, no. 3 (2 July 2020): 9, https://doi.org/10.1080/03932729.2020.1786926.

79. Horace Campbell, 'China in Africa: Challenging US Global Hegemony', *Third World Quarterly* 29, no. 1 (1 February 2008): 89–105, https://doi.org/10.1080/01436590701726517.

80. Kevin Gray and Barry K. Gills, 'South–South Cooperation and the Rise of the Global South', *Third World Quarterly* 37, no. 4 (2 April 2016): 557–74, https://doi.org/10.1080/01436597.2015.1128817.

81. Li Sheng and Dmitri Felix do Nascimento, *The Belt and Road Initiative in South–South Cooperation: The Impact on World Trade and Geopolitics* (Springer Nature, 2021).

82. Doctor Padraig Carmody, *The Rise of the BRICS in Africa: The Geopolitics of South-South Relations* (Zed Books Ltd., 2013).

83. Martin Khor, 'China's Boost to South-South Cooperation', *South Bulletin* 90 (16 May 2016), https://www.southcentre.int/question/chinas-boost-to-south-south-cooperation/.

84. Ian Taylor, *The Forum on China-Africa Cooperation (FOCAC)* (London: Routledge, 2010), https://doi.org/10.4324/9780203835005.

85. MFA, 'Declaration on China-Africa Cooperation on Combating Climate Change', 2 December 2021, https://www.fmprc.gov.cn/mfa_eng/wjdt_665385/2649_665393/202112/t20211203_10461772.html.

86. MFA, 'Dakar Declaration of the Eighth Ministerial Conference of the Forum on China-Africa Cooperation', 3 December 2021, para. 24, https://www.fmprc.gov.cn/mfa_eng/wjdt_665385/2649_665393/202112/t20211203_10461779.html.

87. Xiao Han and Michael Webber, 'From Chinese Dam Building in Africa to the Belt and Road Initiative: Assembling Infrastructure Projects and Their Linkages', *Political Geography* 77 (1 March 2020): 102102, https://doi.org/10.1016/j.polgeo.2019.102102.

88. Yixian Sun, 'China Will No Longer Build Overseas Coal Power Plants—What Energy Projects Will It Invest in Instead?', *The Conversation*,

28 September 2021, http://theconversation.com/china-will-no-lon ger-build-overseas-coal-power-plants-what-energy-projects-will-it-invest-in-instead-168614; Jonathan Watts, 'China Pledge to Stop Funding Coal Projects "Buys Time for Emissions Target"', *The Guardian*, 22 September 2021, sec. World news, https://www.theguardian.com/world/2021/sep/22/china-pledge-to-stop-funding-coal-projects-buys-time-for-emissions-target.

89. Michael Boulle, 'The Hazy Rise of Coal in Kenya: The Actors, Interests, and Discursive Contradictions Shaping Kenya's Electricity Future', *Energy Research & Social Science* 56 (1 October 2019): 101205, https://doi.org/10.1016/j.erss.2019.05.015; Nanjala Nyabola, 'Cashing in on Coal: Kenya's Unnecessary Power Plant', *World Policy Journal* 34, no. 3 (2017): 69–75.

90. Cecilia Han Springer, 'China's Withdrawal from Overseas Coal in Context', *World Development Perspectives* 25 (1 March 2022): 100397, https://doi.org/10.1016/j.wdp.2022.100397.

91. David Ockwell and Rob Byrne, 'Improving Technology Transfer Through National Systems of Innovation: Climate Relevant Innovation-System Builders (CRIBs)', *Climate Policy* 16, no. 7 (2 October 2016): 844, https://doi.org/10.1080/14693062.2015.1052958.

92. Thomas Hale, Chuyu Liu, and Johannes Urpelainen, *Belt and Road Decision-Making in China and Recipient Countries: How and to What Extent Does Sustainability Matter?* (Oxford, UK: Blavatnik School of Government, Initiative for Sustainable Energy Policy (ISEP), and ClimateWorks Foundation, 24 April 2020).

93. Alyssa Ayres, *Our Time Has Come: How India Is Making Its Place in the World* (Oxford, New York: Oxford University Press, 2018); Navroz K. Dubash, ed., *India in a Warming World: Integrating Climate Change and Development* (Oxford, New York: Oxford University Press, 2019).

94. Arunabha Ghosh and Kanika Chawla, 'The Role of International Solar Alliance in Advancing the Energy Transition in Asia', in *Renewable Energy Transition in Asia: Policies, Markets and Emerging Issues*, ed. Nandakumar Janardhanan and Vaibhav Chaturvedi (Singapore: Springer, 2021), 63–87, https://doi.org/10.1007/978-981-15-8905-8_4.

95. ISA, 'International Solar Alliance', n.d., https://isolaralliance.org/about/background.

96. Kwame Nkrumah, *Neo-Colonialism: The Last Stage of Imperialism* (Panaf, 1974).

97. Joana Gomes, 'Von Der Leyen Calls for African Green Deal', EURACTIV, 23 April 2021, https://www.euractiv.com/section/energy-environment/news/von-der-leyen-calls-for-african-green-deal/.

98. E3G, '"Global Gateway": The EU Green Deal Goes Global', E3G, 1 December 2021, https://www.e3g.org/news/global-gateway-eu-green-deal-goes-global/.

99. Michael A. Mehling et al., 'Designing Border Carbon Adjustments for Enhanced Climate Action', *American Journal of International Law* 113, no. 3 (July 2019): 433–81, https://doi.org/10.1017/ajil.2019.22.

100. Catherine Early, 'The EU Can Expect Heavy Pushback on Its Carbon Border Tax', *China Dialogue* (blog), 1 September 2020, https://chinadialogue.net/en/business/eu-can-expect-heavy-pushback-carbon-border-tax/.

101. EurActiv, 'African Countries Deem EU Carbon Border Levy "Protectionist"', ECEEE, 25 March 2021, https://www.eceee.org/all-news/news/african-countries-deem-eu-carbon-border-levy-protectionist/.

102. Todd Moss and Morgan Bazilian, 'Signalling, Governance, and Goals: Reorienting the United States Power Africa Initiative', *Energy Research & Social Science* 39 (1 May 2018): 74–77, https://doi.org/10.1016/j.erss.2017.11.001.

103. USGOV, 'FACT SHEET: President Biden and G7 Leaders Launch Build Back Better World (B3W) Partnership', The White House, 12 June 2021, https://www.whitehouse.gov/briefing-room/statements-releases/2021/06/12/fact-sheet-president-biden-and-g7-leaders-launch-build-back-better-world-b3w-partnership/.

104. Federico Donelli, 'The Ankara Consensus: The Significance of Turkey's Engagement in Sub-Saharan Africa', *Global Change, Peace & Security* 30, no. 1 (2 January 2018): 57–76, https://doi.org/10.1080/14781158.2018.1438384.

105. Folashadé Soulé, '"Africa+1" Summit Diplomacy and the "New Scramble" Narrative: Recentering African Agency', *African Affairs* 119, no. 477 (1 October 2020): 1, https://doi.org/10.1093/afraf/adaa015.

106. EC, 'Just Energy Transition Partnership with South Africa', Press Release, European Commission—European Commission, 2 November 2021, https://ec.europa.eu/commission/presscorner/detail/en/IP_21_5768.

107. Harald Winkler et al., 'Just Transition Transaction in South Africa: An Innovative Way to Finance Accelerated Phase Out of Coal and Fund Social Justice', *Journal of Sustainable Finance & Investment* 0, no. 0 (3 September 2021): 1–24, https://doi.org/10.1080/20430795.2021.1972678.

108. Chloe Teevan et al., *A New Multilateralism for the Post-COVID World: What Role for the EU-Africa Partnership?* (Bonn: European think Tanks Group, 2021), https://ettg.eu/wp-content/uploads/2021/04/ETTG_new_multilateralism_post-Covid-April_2021_final.pdf.

4 THE EVOLVING GEOPOLITICS OF CLIMATE CHANGE 117

REFERENCES

Agozino, Biko. 'Reparative Justice: The Final Stage of Decolonization'. *Punishment & Society* 23, no. 5 (1 December 2021): 613–30. https://doi.org/10.1177/14624745211024342.

Aklin, Michaël, and Matto Mildenberger. 'Prisoners of the Wrong Dilemma: Why Distributive Conflict, Not Collective Action, Characterizes the Politics of Climate Change'. *Global Environmental Politics* 20, no. 4 (1 November 2020): 4–27. https://doi.org/10.1162/glep_a_00578.

Allan, Jen Iris, Charles B. Roger, Thomas N. Hale, Steven Bernstein, Yves Tiberghien, and Richard Balme. 'Making the Paris Agreement: Historical Processes and the Drivers of Institutional Design'. *Political Studies*, 6 October 2021, 00323217211049294. https://doi.org/10.1177/003232 17211049294.

Allison, Graham. 'The New Spheres of Influence: Sharing the Globe with Other Great Powers'. *Foreign Affairs*, 19 October 2021. https://www.foreignaffairs.com/articles/united-states/2020-02-10/new-spheres-influence.

Agarwala, A.N. *The Economics of Underdevelopment*. Oxford University Press, 1961.

Atela, Joanes Odiwuor, Claire Hellen Quinn, Albert A. Arhin, Lalisa Duguma, and Kennedy Liti Mbeva. 'Exploring the Agency of Africa in Climate Change Negotiations: The Case of REDD+'. *International Environmental Agreements: Politics, Law and Economics* 17, no. 4 (1 August 2017): 463–82. https://doi.org/10.1007/s10784-016-9329-6.

Ayompe, Lacour M., Steven J. Davis, and Benis N. Egoh. 'Trends and Drivers of African Fossil Fuel CO2 Emissions 1990–2017'. *Environmental Research Letters* 15, no. 12 (December 2020): 124039. https://doi.org/10.1088/1748-9326/abc64f.

Ayres, Alyssa. *Our Time Has Come: How India Is Making Its Place in the World*. Oxford, New York: Oxford University Press, 2018.

Barnett, Michael N. 'Bringing in the New World Order: Liberalism, Legitimacy, and the United Nations'. Edited by Boutros Boutros-Ghali, Commission on Global Governance, Gareth Evans, and Report of the Independent Working Group on the Future of the United Nations. *World Politics* 49, no. 4 (1997): 526–51.

Barnsley, Ingrid. 'Dealing with Change: Australia, Canada and the Kyoto Protocol to the Framework Convention on Climate Change'. *The Round Table* 95, no. 385 (1 July 2006): 399–410. https://doi.org/10.1080/003 58530600748358.

Bodansky, Daniel. 'A Tale of Two Architectures: The Once and Future U.N. Climate Change Regime'. *Climate Change and Environmental Hazards Related to Shipping: An International Legal Framework*, 1 January 2013, 35–51. https://doi.org/10.1163/9789004244955_005.

————. 'Legal Form of a New Climate Agreement: Avenues and Options'. *Center for Climate and Energy Solutions* (blog), 15 April 2009. https://www.c2es.org/document/legal-form-of-a-new-climate-agreement-avenues-and-options/.

————. 'The Copenhagen Climate Change Conference: A Postmortem'. *American Journal of International Law* 104, no. 2 (April 2010): 230–40. https://doi.org/10.5305/amerjintelaw.104.2.0230.

————. 'The Paris Climate Change Agreement: A New Hope?' *American Journal of International Law* 110, no. 2 (April 2016): 288–319. https://doi.org/10.5305/amerjintelaw.110.2.0288.

Böhringer, Christoph. 'The Kyoto Protocol: A Review and Perspectives'. *Oxford Review of Economic Policy* 19, no. 3 (1 September 2003): 451–66. https://doi.org/10.1093/oxrep/19.3.451.

Boulle, Michael. 'The Hazy Rise of Coal in Kenya: The Actors, Interests, and Discursive Contradictions Shaping Kenya's Electricity Future'. *Energy Research & Social Science* 56 (1 October 2019): 101205. https://doi.org/10.1016/j.erss.2019.05.015.

Brunnée, Jutta, and Charlotte Streck. 'The UNFCCC as a Negotiation Forum: Towards Common but More Differentiated Responsibilities'. *Climate Policy* 13, no. 5 (1 September 2013): 589–607. https://doi.org/10.1080/14693062.2013.822661.

Campbell, Horace. 'China in Africa: Challenging US Global Hegemony'. *Third World Quarterly* 29, no. 1 (1 February 2008): 89–105. https://doi.org/10.1080/01436590701726517.

Carmody, Doctor Padraig. *The Rise of the BRICS in Africa: The Geopolitics of South-South Relations.* Zed Books Ltd., 2013.

Chan, Nicholas. '"Special Circumstances" and the Politics of Climate Vulnerability: African Agency in the UN Climate Change Negotiations'. *Africa Spectrum*, 24 June 2021, 0002039721991151. https://doi.org/10.1177/0002039721991151.

Chin-Yee, Simon. 'Briefing: Africa and the Paris Climate Change Agreement'. *African Affairs* 115, no. 459 (1 April 2016): 359–68. https://doi.org/10.1093/afraf/adw005.

Chu, Wai-Li. 'Cold War and Decolonisation'. In *Hong Kong History: Themes in Global Perspective*, edited by Man-Kong Wong and Chi-Man Kwong, 83–113. Hong Kong Studies Reader Series. Singapore: Springer, 2022. https://doi.org/10.1007/978-981-16-2806-1_4.

Crowley, Kate. 'Is Australia Faking It? The Kyoto Protocol and the Greenhouse Policy Challenge'. *Global Environmental Politics* 7, no. 4 (1 November 2007): 118–39. https://doi.org/10.1162/glep.2007.7.4.118.

Darwin, John. *Britain and Decolonisation: The Retreat from Empire in the Post-War World.* Macmillan International Higher Education, 1988.

Depledge, Joanna, and Farhana Yamin. 'The Global Climate-Change Regime: A Defence'. In *The Economics and Politics of Climate Change*, edited by Dieter Helm and Cameron Hepburn. Oxford: Oxford University Press, 2009. https://doi.org/10.1093/acprof:osobl/9780199573288.003.0021.

Donelli, Federico. 'The Ankara Consensus: The Significance of Turkey's Engagement in Sub-Saharan Africa'. *Global Change, Peace & Security* 30, no. 1 (2 January 2018): 57–76. https://doi.org/10.1080/14781158.2018.1438384.

Dubash, Navroz K. 'Copenhagen: Climate of Mistrust'. *Economic and Political Weekly* 44, no. 52 (2009): 8–11.

———, ed. *India in a Warming World: Integrating Climate Change and Development*. Oxford, New York: Oxford University Press, 2019.

E3G. '"Global Gateway": The EU Green Deal Goes Global'. E3G, 1 December 2021. https://www.e3g.org/news/global-gateway-eu-green-deal-goes-global/.

Early, Catherine. 'The EU Can Expect Heavy Pushback on Its Carbon Border Tax'. *China Dialogue* (blog), 1 September 2020. https://chinadialogue.net/en/business/eu-can-expect-heavy-pushback-carbon-border-tax/.

EC. 'Just Energy Transition Partnership with South Africa'. Press Release. European Commission—European Commission, 2 November 2021. https://ec.europa.eu/commission/presscorner/detail/en/IP_21_5768.

Eckersley, Robyn. 'Ambushed: The Kyoto Protocol, the Bush Administration's Climate Policy and the Erosion of Legitimacy'. *International Politics* 44, no. 2 (1 March 2007): 306–24. https://doi.org/10.1057/palgrave.ip.8800190.

———. 'Moving Forward in the Climate Negotiations: Multilateralism or Minilateralism?' *Global Environmental Politics* 12, no. 2 (20 March 2012): 24–42. https://doi.org/10.1162/GLEP_a_00107.

Emmelin, Lars. 'The Stockholm Conferences'. *Ambio* 1, no. 4 (1972): 135–40.

EurActiv. 'African Countries Deem EU Carbon Border Levy "Protectionist"'. ECEEE, 25 March 2021. https://www.eceee.org/all-news/news/african-countries-deem-eu-carbon-border-levy-protectionist/.

Falkner, Robert. 'American Hegemony and the Global Environment'. *International Studies Review* 7, no. 4 (1 December 2005): 585–99. https://doi.org/10.1111/j.1468-2486.2005.00534.x.

Falkner, Robert, and Barry Buzan, eds. *Great Powers, Climate Change, and Global Environmental Responsibilities*. Oxford, New York: Oxford University Press, 2022.

Faudot, Adrien. 'The Keynes Plan and Bretton Woods Debates: The Early Radical Criticisms by Balogh, Schumacher and Kalecki'. *Cambridge Journal of Economics* 45, no. 4 (1 July 2021): 751–70. https://doi.org/10.1093/cje/beab018.

French, Howard W. *Born in Blackness: Africa, Africans, and the Making of the Modern World, 1471 to the Second World War*. New York: Liveright Publishing Corporation, 2021.

Getachew, Adom. *Worldmaking After Empire: The Rise and Fall of Self-Determination*. New Jersey: Princeton University Press, 2020.

Ghosh, Arunabha, and Kanika Chawla. 'The Role of International Solar Alliance in Advancing the Energy Transition in Asia'. In *Renewable Energy Transition in Asia: Policies, Markets and Emerging Issues*, edited by Nandakumar Janardhanan and Vaibhav Chaturvedi, 63–87. Singapore: Springer, 2021. https://doi.org/10.1007/978-981-15-8905-8_4.

Gomes, Joana. 'Von Der Leyen Calls for African Green Deal'. EURACTIV, 23 April 2021. https://www.euractiv.com/section/energy-environment/news/von-der-leyen-calls-for-african-green-deal/.

Gray, Kevin, and Barry K. Gills. 'South–South Cooperation and the Rise of the Global South'. *Third World Quarterly* 37, no. 4 (2 April 2016): 557–74. https://doi.org/10.1080/01436597.2015.1128817.

Grieco, Joseph, Robert Powell, and Duncan Snidal. 'The Relative-Gains Problem for International Cooperation'. *The American Political Science Review* 87, no. 3 (1993): 727–43. https://doi.org/10.2307/2938747.

Grundig, Frank. 'Patterns of International Cooperation and the Explanatory Power of Relative Gains: An Analysis of Cooperation on Global Climate Change, Ozone Depletion, and International Trade'. *International Studies Quarterly* 50, no. 4 (1 December 2006): 781–801. https://doi.org/10.1111/j.1468-2478.2006.00425.x.

Gusev, Alexander. 'Evolution of Russian Climate Policy: From the Kyoto Protocol to the Paris Agreement'. *L'Europe En Formation* 380, no. 2 (2016): 39–52.

Hale, Thomas. 'Catalytic Cooperation'. *Global Environmental Politics* 20, no. 4 (1 November 2020): 73–98. https://doi.org/10.1162/glep_a_00561.

Hale, Thomas, Chuyu Liu, and Johannes Urpelainen. *Belt and Road Decision-Making in China and Recipient Countries: How and to What Extent Does Sustainability Matter?* Oxford, UK: Blavatnik School of Government, Initiative for Sustainable Energy Policy (ISEP), and ClimateWorks Foundation, 24 April 2020.

Han, Xiao, and Michael Webber. 'From Chinese Dam Building in Africa to the Belt and Road Initiative: Assembling Infrastructure Projects and Their Linkages'. *Political Geography* 77 (1 March 2020): 102102. https://doi.org/10.1016/j.polgeo.2019.102102.

Harstad, Bård. 'Pledge-and-Review Bargaining'. SSRN Scholarly Paper. Rochester, NY: Social Science Research Network, 2018. https://doi.org/10.2139/ssrn.3338622.

Helm, Dieter. 'The Kyoto Approach Has Failed'. *Nature* 491, no. 7426 (November 2012): 663–65. https://doi.org/10.1038/491663a.

Ikenberry, G. John. 'America's Liberal Hegemony'. *Current History; Philadelphia*, January 1999.

ISA. 'International Solar Alliance', n.d. https://isolaralliance.org/about/background.

Juma, Calestous. 'Complexity, Innovation, and Development: Schumpeter Revisited'. *Policy and Complex Systems* 1, no. 1 (2014): 4–21. https://doi.org/10.18278/jpcs.1.1.1.

Kalantzakos, Sophia. 'The Race for Critical Minerals in an Era of Geopolitical Realignments'. *The International Spectator* 55, no. 3 (2 July 2020): 1–16. https://doi.org/10.1080/03932729.2020.1786926.

Kemp, Luke. 'Better Out Than In'. *Nature Climate Change* 7 (22 May 2017): 458.

———. 'Bypassing the "Ratification Straitjacket": Reviewing US Legal Participation in a Climate Agreement'. *Climate Policy* 16, no. 8 (16 November 2016): 1011–28. https://doi.org/10.1080/14693062.2015.1061472.

———. 'US-Proofing the Paris Climate Agreement'. *Climate Policy* 17, no. 1 (2 January 2017): 86–101. https://doi.org/10.1080/14693062.2016.1176007.

Keohane, Robert O., and Michael Oppenheimer. 'Paris: Beyond the Climate Dead End Through Pledge and Review?' *Politics and Governance* 4, no. 3 (8 September 2016): 142–51. https://doi.org/10.17645/pag.v4i3.634.

Khor, Martin. 'China's Boost to South-South Cooperation'. *South Bulletin* 90 (16 May 2016). https://www.southcentre.int/question/chinas-boost-to-south-south-cooperation/.

King, Edward. 'Africa's "Buyer's Remorse" over Paris Climate Deal'. Climate Home, 3 November 2016. http://www.climatechangenews.com/2016/11/03/africas-buyers-remorse-over-paris-climate-deal/.

Kissinger, Henry A. *Nuclear Weapons and Foreign Policy*. Boulder, Colorado: Westview Press, 1957.

Krauthammer, Charles. 'The Unipolar Moment'. *Foreign Affairs* 70, no. 1 (1990): 23–33. https://doi.org/10.2307/20044692.

Larmer, Miles. 'Leslie James, George Padmore and Decolonisation from Below: Pan-Africanism, the Cold War and the End of Empire'. *Journal of Contemporary History* 53, no. 2 (1 April 2018): 462–64. https://doi.org/10.1177/0022009417749502m.

Lee, Christopher J. 'At the Rendezvous of Decolonization'. *Interventions* 11, no. 1 (1 March 2009): 81–93. https://doi.org/10.1080/13698010902752806.

Makarov, Igor. 'Climate Change Policies and Resource Abundance: The Case of Russia'. *Handbook of Sustainable Politics and Economics of Natural Resources,*

10 December 2021. https://www.elgaronline.com/view/edcoll/978178990 8763/9781789908763.00017.xml.

Makomere, Reuben, and Kennedy Liti Mbeva. 'Squaring the Circle: Development Prospects Within the Paris Agreement'. *Carbon & Climate Law Review* 12, no. 1 (2018): 31–40. https://doi.org/10.21552/cclr/2018/1/7.

Mbeva, Kennedy, and Reuben Makomere. 'The End of Affirmative Multilateralism?' SSRN Scholarly Paper. Rochester, NY: Social Science Research Network, 7 May 2021. https://doi.org/10.2139/ssrn.3841282.

McGee, Jeffrey, and Jens Steffek. 'The Copenhagen Turn in Global Climate Governance and the Contentious History of Differentiation in International Law'. *Journal of Environmental Law* 28, no. 1 (1 March 2016): 37–63. https://doi.org/10.1093/jel/eqw003.

Mearsheimer, John J. 'Bound to Fail: The Rise and Fall of the Liberal International Order'. *International Security* 43, no. 4 (1 April 2019): 7–50. https://doi.org/10.1162/isec_a_00342.

———. *The Tragedy of Great Power Politics*. New York: W. W. Norton & Company, 2001.

Mehling, Michael A., Harro van Asselt, Kasturi Das, Susanne Droege, and Cleo Verkuijl. 'Designing Border Carbon Adjustments for Enhanced Climate Action'. *American Journal of International Law* 113, no. 3 (July 2019): 433–81. https://doi.org/10.1017/ajil.2019.22.

MFA. 'Dakar Declaration of the Eighth Ministerial Conference of the Forum on China-Africa Cooperation', 3 December 2021. https://www.fmprc.gov.cn/mfa_eng/wjdt_665385/2649_665393/202112/t20211203_10461779.html.

———. 'Declaration on China-Africa Cooperation on Combating Climate Change', 2 December 2021. https://www.fmprc.gov.cn/mfa_eng/wjdt_665385/2649_665393/202112/t20211203_10461772.html.

Morseletto, Piero, Frank Biermann, and Philipp Pattberg. 'Governing by Targets: Reductio Ad Unum and Evolution of the Two-Degree Climate Target'. *International Environmental Agreements: Politics, Law and Economics* 17, no. 5 (1 October 2017): 655–76. https://doi.org/10.1007/s10784-016-9336-7.

Moss, Todd, and Morgan Bazilian. 'Signalling, Governance, and Goals: Reorienting the United States Power Africa Initiative'. *Energy Research & Social Science* 39 (1 May 2018): 74–77. https://doi.org/10.1016/j.erss.2017.11.001.

Moyo, Dambisa. *Dead Aid: Why Aid Is Not Working and How There Is a Better Way for Africa*. Reprint edition. Farrar, Straus and Giroux, 2010.

———. 'Why Foreign Aid Is Hurting Africa'. *Wall Street Journal*, 22 March 2009, sec. World News. https://www.wsj.com/articles/SB123758895999200083.

Najam, Adil. 'Developing Countries and Global Environmental Governance: From Contestation to Participation to Engagement'. *International Environmental Agreements: Politics, Law and Economics* 5, no. 3 (1 September 2005): 303–21. https://doi.org/10.1007/s10784-005-3807-6.

Nalule, Victoria R. 'Transitioning to a Low Carbon Economy: Is Africa Ready to Bid Farewell to Fossil Fuels?' In *The Palgrave Handbook of Managing Fossil Fuels and Energy Transitions*, edited by Geoffrey Wood and Keith Baker, 261–86. Cham: Springer International Publishing, 2020. https://doi.org/10.1007/978-3-030-28076-5_10.

Ndlovu-Gatsheni, Sabelo J. 'Decoloniality in Africa: A Continuing Search for a New World Order'. *The Australasian Review of African Studies* 36, no. 2 (2015): 22–50. https://doi.org/10.3316/informit.640531150387614.

Nkrumah, Kwame. *Neo-Colonialism: The Last Stage of Imperialism*. Panaf, 1974.

Nyabola, Nanjala. 'Cashing in on Coal: Kenya's Unnecessary Power Plant'. *World Policy Journal* 34, no. 3 (2017): 69–75.

Obama, Barack. 'The Irreversible Momentum of Clean Energy'. *Science* 355, no. 6321 (13 January 2017). https://doi.org/10.1126/science.aam6284.

Ockwell, David, and Rob Byrne. 'Improving Technology Transfer Through National Systems of Innovation: Climate Relevant Innovation-System Builders (CRIBs)'. *Climate Policy* 16, no. 7 (2 October 2016): 836–54. https://doi.org/10.1080/14693062.2015.1052958.

Olson, Mancur. *The Logic of Collective Action. Public Goods and the Theory of Groups*. Cambridge, MA: Harvard University Press, 1965.

Osofsky, Hari M. 'The Complexities of Multipolar Approaches to Climate Change: Lessons from Litigation and Local Action'. *Proceedings of the ASIL Annual Meeting* 107 (ed 2013): 73–75. https://doi.org/10.5305/procannmeetasil.107.0073.

O'Sullivan, Meghan, Indra Overland, and David Sandalow. 'The Geopolitics of Renewable Energy'. Working Paper. New York, NY; and Cambridge, MA: Center on Global Energy Policy, Columbia University|SIPA; and The Geopolitics of Energy Project, Belfer Center for Science and International Affairs, Harvard Kennedy School, 2017. https://www.belfercenter.org/sites/default/files/files/publication/Geopolitics%20Renewables%20-%20final%20report%206.26.17.pdf.

Paglia, Eric. 'The Swedish Initiative and the 1972 Stockholm Conference: The Decisive Role of Science Diplomacy in the Emergence of Global Environmental Governance'. *Humanities and Social Sciences Communications* 8, no. 1 (5 January 2021): 1–10. https://doi.org/10.1057/s41599-020-00681-x.

Pauw, Pieter, Kennedy Mbeva, and Harro van Asselt. 'Subtle Differentiation of Countries' Responsibilities Under the Paris Agreement'. *Palgrave Communications* 5, no. 1 (30 July 2019): 1–7. https://doi.org/10.1057/s41599-019-0298-6.

Pickering, Jonathan, Jeffrey S. McGee, Tim Stephens, and Sylvia I. Karlsson-Vinkhuyzen. 'The Impact of the US Retreat from the Paris Agreement: Kyoto Revisited?' *Climate Policy* 0, no. 0 (18 December 2017): 1–10. https://doi.org/10.1080/14693062.2017.1412934.

President George W. Bush. 'Text of a Letter from the President to Senators Hagel, Helms, Craig, and Roberts', 13 March 2001. https://georgewbush-whitehouse.archives.gov/news/releases/2001/03/20010314.html.

Prigogine, Ilya. 'Time, Structure, and Fluctuations'. *Science*, 1 September 1978. https://doi.org/10.1126/science.201.4358.777.

Prins, Gwyn, and Steve Rayner. 'Time to Ditch Kyoto'. *Nature* 449, no. 7165 (25 October 2007): 973–75. https://doi.org/10.1038/449973a.

Rajamani, Lavanya. 'The Principle of Common but Differentiated Responsibilities and Respective Capabilities in the International Climate Change Regime'. In *Research Handbook on Climate Disaster Law*, edited by Rosemary Lyster and Robert Verchick, 46–60. Cheltenham, UK and Northampton, MA: Edward Elgar, 2018. https://www.elgaronline.com/view/edcoll/978178643 0021/9781786430021.00009.xml.

Rayner, Steve, and Gwyn Prins. 'The Wrong Trousers: Radically Rethinking Climate Policy'. Other Working Paper. Oxford, UK: James Martin Institute for Science and Civilization, University of Oxford and the MacKinder Centre for the Study of Long-Wave Events, London School of Economics, 2007. http://www.sbs.ox.ac.uk/centres/insis/Documents/TheWrongTrousers.pdf.

Riddell, J. Barry. 'Things Fall Apart Again: Structural Adjustment Programmes in Sub-Saharan Africa'. *The Journal of Modern African Studies* 30, no. 1 (1992): 53–68.

Ridder, Marjolein de. *The Geopolitics of Mineral Resources for Renewable Energy Technologies*. The Hague Centre for Strategic Studies, 2013.

Roberts, J. Timmons. 'Multipolarity and the New World (Dis)order: US Hegemonic Decline and the Fragmentation of the Global Climate Regime'. *Global Environmental Change*, Symposium on Social Theory and the Environment in the New World (Dis)order, 21, no. 3 (1 August 2011): 776–84. https://doi.org/10.1016/j.gloenvcha.2011.03.017.

Rodney, Walter. *How Europe Underdeveloped Africa*. Revised edition. Washington, DC: Howard Univ Pr, 1981.

Roger, Charles, and Satishkumar Belliethathan. 'Africa in the Global Climate Change Negotiations'. *International Environmental Agreements: Politics, Law and Economics* 16, no. 1 (1 February 2016): 91–108. https://doi.org/10.1007/s10784-014-9244-7.

Sheng, Li, and Dmitri Felix do Nascimento. *The Belt and Road Initiative in South–South Cooperation: The Impact on World Trade and Geopolitics*. Springer Nature, 2021.

Skidelsky, Robert. 'Keynes, Globalisation and the Bretton Woods Institutions in the Light of Changing Ideas About Markets'. *World Economics* 6, no. 1 (2005): 15–30.

Snidal, Duncan. 'The Limits of Hegemonic Stability Theory'. *International Organization* 39, no. 4 (ed 1985): 579–614. https://doi.org/10.1017/S00 2081830002703X.

Soulé, Folashadé. '"Africa+1" Summit Diplomacy and the "New Scramble" Narrative: Recentering African Agency'. *African Affairs* 119, no. 477 (1 October 2020): 633–46. https://doi.org/10.1093/afraf/adaa015.

Springer, Cecilia Han. 'China's Withdrawal from Overseas Coal in Context'. *World Development Perspectives* 25 (1 March 2022): 100397. https://doi.org/10.1016/j.wdp.2022.100397.

Staff. 'Canada Pulls Out of Kyoto Protocol'. *The Guardian*, 13 December 2011, sec. Environment. https://www.theguardian.com/environment/2011/dec/13/canada-pulls-out-kyoto-protocol.

Stalley, Phillip. 'Norms from the Periphery: Tracing the Rise of the Common but Differentiated Principle in International Environmental Politics'. *Cambridge Review of International Affairs* 31, no. 2 (4 March 2018): 141–61. https://doi.org/10.1080/09557571.2018.1481824.

Stiglitz, Joseph. *Globalization and Its Discontents*. W. W. Norton & Company, 2002.

Stokes, Leah Cardamore. *Short Circuiting Policy: Interest Groups and the Battle over Clean Energy and Climate Policy in the American States*. Oxford University Press, 2020.

Stone, Christopher D. 'Common but Differentiated Responsibilities in International Law'. *American Journal of International Law* 98, no. 2 (April 2004): 276–301. https://doi.org/10.2307/3176729.

Sun, Yixian. 'China Will No Longer Build Overseas Coal Power Plants—What Energy Projects Will It Invest in Instead?' *The Conversation*, 28 September 2021. http://theconversation.com/china-will-no-longer-build-overseas-coal-power-plants-what-energy-projects-will-it-invest-in-instead-168614.

Taylor, Ian. *The Forum on China- Africa Cooperation (FOCAC)*. London: Routledge, 2010. https://doi.org/10.4324/9780203835005.

Teevan, Chloe, Luca Barana, Daniele Fattibene, Daniela Iacobuta, Silke Weinlich, and Steffen Bauer. 'A New Multilateralism for the Post-COVID World: What Role for the EU-Africa Partnership?' N. Bonn: European think Tanks Group, 2021. https://ettg.eu/wp-content/uploads/2021/04/ETTG_new_multilateralism_post-Covid-April_2021_final.pdf.

UN. *Agenda 21*. Rio de Janeiro: United Nations, 1992. https://sustainabledevelopment.un.org/content/documents/Agenda21.pdf.

———. 'Declaration of the United Nations Conference on the Human Environment'. United Nations, 1972. https://legal.un.org/avl/ha/dunche/dunche.html.

———. *Rio Declaration on Environment and Development.* Rio de Janeiro: United Nations General Assembly, 1992. https://www.un.org/en/development/desa/population/migration/generalassembly/docs/globalcompact/A_CONF.151_26_Vol.I_Declaration.pdf.

Urpelainen, Johannes, and Thijs Van de Graaf. 'United States Non-Cooperation and the Paris Agreement'. *Climate Policy* 18, no. 7 (9 August 2018): 839–51. https://doi.org/10.1080/14693062.2017.1406843.

USGOV. 'FACT SHEET: President Biden and G7 Leaders Launch Build Back Better World (B3W) Partnership'. The White House, 12 June 2021. https://www.whitehouse.gov/briefing-room/statements-releases/2021/06/12/fact-sheet-president-biden-and-g7-leaders-launch-build-back-better-world-b3w-partnership/.

Vakulchuk, Roman, Indra Overland, and Daniel Scholten. 'Renewable Energy and Geopolitics: A Review'. *Renewable and Sustainable Energy Reviews* 122 (1 April 2020): 109547. https://doi.org/10.1016/j.rser.2019.109547.

Vernengo, Matías. 'The Consolidation of Dollar Hegemony After the Collapse of Bretton Woods: Bringing Power Back In'. *Review of Political Economy* 33, no. 4 (2 October 2021): 529–51. https://doi.org/10.1080/09538259.2021.1950966.

Voigt, Christina, and Felipe Ferreira. '"Dynamic Differentiation": The Principles of CBDR-RC, Progression and Highest Possible Ambition in the Paris Agreement'. *Transnational Environmental Law* 5, no. 2 (October 2016): 285–303. https://doi.org/10.1017/S2047102516000212.

Waltz, Kenneth N. 'The Stability of a Bipolar World'. *Daedalus* 93, no. 3 (1964): 881–909.

Watts, Jonathan. 'China Pledge to Stop Funding Coal Projects "Buys Time for Emissions Target"'. *The Guardian*, 22 September 2021, sec. World news. https://www.theguardian.com/world/2021/sep/22/china-pledge-to-stop-funding-coal-projects-buys-time-for-emissions-target.

Winkler, Harald, Emily Tyler, Samantha Keen, and Andrew Marquard. 'Just Transition Transaction in South Africa: An Innovative Way to Finance Accelerated Phase out of Coal and Fund Social Justice'. *Journal of Sustainable Finance & Investment* 0, no. 0 (3 September 2021): 1–24. https://doi.org/10.1080/20430795.2021.1972678.

CHAPTER 5

Dynamic Differentiation

Issues of equity and fairness have been central to international cooperation. Differentiation of rights and obligations is a common feature of international regimes. Depending on the nature of the transboundary problem being addressed, various countries or groups of countries usually have varying responsibilities. In international climate cooperation, differentiation has been an important notion, hence its centrality in the regime. Viewed within the context of the Great Climate Transformation, differentiation has significantly evolved. A crucial development has been the shift away from a bifurcated differentiation system whereby industrialised countries would take disproportionate climate commitments while also providing support for means of implementation to developing countries. Instead, dynamic differentiation based on prevailing national circumstances has been adopted as the main form of differentiation. In other words, there has been a shift from "bifurcated" to dynamic differentiation.

This chapter argues that while the shift towards dynamic differentiation in the international climate regime has facilitated cooperation, it has also set in motion a dynamic that may diminish the salience of differentiation, with significant implications for African countries. As countries undertake increasingly ambitious commitments under the Paris Agreement,

---

© The Author(s), under exclusive license to Springer Nature Switzerland AG 2023
K. Mbeva et al., *Africa's Right to Development in a Climate-Constrained World*, Contemporary African Political Economy,
https://doi.org/10.1007/978-3-031-22887-2_5

and their emission profiles change over time—a decline in the emissions of industrialised countries and the concomitant rise of the emissions of developing countries—differentiation will become a less important factor. Prevailing national circumstances, instead, will be the main locus of differentiation. Perhaps in response to the uncertainties and inadequacies of international support for means of implementation, almost all African countries have made their NDCs conditional on international support. That African countries would make their NDCs conditional on international support for means of implementation, in spite of the Paris Agreement including provisions for such support, underscores the limits of differentiation as conventionally understood.

The shift towards dynamic differentiation implies that as African countries' socio-economic conditions improve, their case for support for means of implementation will diminish in significance. Thus, African countries will have to increasingly draw on their domestic resources to meet their climate commitments. Moreover, almost all African countries have expressed an interest in or adopted long-term climate targets, especially on achieving carbon neutrality by mid-century—the so-called net zero targets. Following the logic of the net zero target to its logical conclusion, it is apparent that African countries would have to harmonise their climate standards with the rest of the world within a few decades. In the long run, differentiation will diminish in significance as national climate targets converge to net zero, across the world.

To elaborate this argument, the chapter first lays out the theoretical underpinnings on differentiation and incentives in international cooperation, elaborating on the theoretical argument presented in Chapter one. The section shows the limits of the differentiation between industrialised and developing countries, as well as the role of incentives through the multilateral climate regime. The chapter then sketches a historical backdrop of differentiation in international environmental and climate change negotiations, focusing on the principle of Common but Differentiated Responsibilities (CBDR). To illustrate the limits of the CBDR and the shift towards dynamic differentiation, the chapter then critically examines how and why African countries have made their climate pledges (NDCs) conditional on international support for means of implementation. In the penultimate section, the chapter shows the structural transformation set in motion by the adoption of climate neutrality targets by African countries, which would lead to the global harmonisation of global standards. The chapter then considers the long-run policy implications of the argument presented herein, before concluding.

5.1 Hegemonic Leadership and Selective Incentives

Before proceeding with examining the shifting notion of differentiation in international climate cooperation, it is important to recap and elaborate the theoretical underpinnings of the argument we advance in the chapter. As discussed in preceding chapters, the multilateral climate regime was established at the end of the Cold War and the onset of Unipolarity. Since the end of the Second World War, the US-led Liberal International Order (LIO) has dominated international cooperation.[1] The US and its Western allies led the development of many of the Multilateral Environmental Agreements (MEAs), while developing countries—many of which were newly independent states—reluctantly engaged.[2] It is important to keep this point in mind, as the notion of hegemonic leadership would be instrumental in the establishment of the multilateral climate regime.

In addition to being the demandeur of global environmental cooperation, the global North also took up the obligation of providing assistance to developing countries to implement their environmental commitments.[3] The support was underpinned by the twin impetus of providing incentives to spur collective action, as well as the demands for reparative justice from developing countries who argued that they had contributed the least to global environmental problems.[4] Moreover, the reparative dimension was linked to the broader efforts by developing countries to secure a fairer international order, especially through the New International Economic Order (NIEO).[5]

It is within this context that differentiation of rights and responsibilities has been undertaken in international environmental cooperation. In theoretical terms, the Olsonian logic of cooperation that marked the initial phase of multilateral climate cooperation included two key elements: a privileged group; and the use of selective incentives.[6] Industrialised countries were the privileged group (or k-group), as they accounted for the bulk of greenhouse gas emissions, and they were the demandeurs of the regime. Industrialised countries were also obligated to provide support for means of implementation to developing countries. The principle of CBDR, which was central to the multilateral climate change regime, embodied the two dimensions of the Olsonian logic of cooperation.[7] But as the Great Climate Transformation has shown, the Olsonian logic of cooperation proved untenable, as indicated by the failure of the Kyoto Protocol which was designed using this logic. A catalytic logic of cooperation was instead adopted, as reflected in the Paris Agreement, whereby universal participation, dynamic differentiation in the light of national circumstances and ratcheting up NDCs would be central to the implementation of the Agreement.[8]

It can be argued, therefore, that the Great Climate Transformation revealed the limits of the hegemonic leadership upon which the multilateral climate regime and its notion of differentiation were predicated. As Duncan Snidal convincingly showed, the Olsonian logic of cooperation could only be sustained so long as the differences between the k-group (Hegemonic leaders) and the rest of the group remained significant. Should there be convergence between the two groups, the Olsonian logic of cooperation would break down.[9] In the multilateral climate change realm, the rise of emerging countries and their corresponding rising emissions, in particular China, made the global North reluctant to undertake any significant emission reductions without the emerging countries on board. Instead of a binary industrialised/developing countries differentiation which was the hallmark of the Kyoto Protocol, a dynamic approach that was premised on prevailing national circumstances was adopted.[10] A core assumption of the dynamic approach to differentiation was that as countries improved their socio-economic conditions, they would undertake more significant responsibilities in international climate cooperation. This dynamic and progressive approach ensured that the binary distinction between industrialised and developing countries that has persisted in multilateral negotiations and rhetoric would diminish, if not disappear, over time.

Related, and turning to "selective incentives"—which is the second element of the Olsonian logic of cooperation—it follows that as differentiation diminishes, the role of such incentives correspondingly diminishes. After all, the notion of changing national circumstances, as articulated in the Paris Agreement, assumes that as countries become more capable, their need for international support would reduce.[11] Capability, and not incentives, thus becomes the central mechanism for generating more ambitious climate commitments and action. Despite the provision of means of implementation (finance, technology transfer and capacity) being central to the multilateral climate regime, the provision of the support has been a very contested issue. Debates have persisted on whether adequate support has been provided, as well as the nature of the support—in particular the prevalence of loans over grants in climate financing. Moreover, many developing countries have made their NDCs conditional on international support for means of implementation, despite the Paris Agreement including such provisions. By contrast, industrialised countries have been reluctant to include commitments for support for means of implementation in their NDCs. In the long run, therefore, "selective incentives" will diminish in importance in the international climate change regime.

Based on the foregoing, our main argument in this chapter is that the conditions that would support an Olsonian logic of cooperation are being replaced by those that make dynamic differentiation more tenable in international climate politics. An implication of this development is that African countries will have to reduce overreliance on multilateral support for means of implementation, and instead draw more from a diversity of resources in implementing their NDCs. While this development departs from cherished and justifiable notions that have underpinned bifurcated differentiation, the embrace of a dynamic approach opens up opportunities for novel policymaking in Africa that would strengthen the alignment between development and climate policy, through a strategic notion of the just transition. The rest of the chapter empirically elaborates this argument.

5.2 The Origins of Differentiation in Multilateral Environmental Governance

The year 1992 was undoubtedly the annus mirabilis for global environmental cooperation. Efforts to address global climate change gained international prominence and support when states convened the landmark UN Conference on Environment and Development (UNCED), popularly known as the Rio Conference, in 1992.[12] The conference saw the consolidation of key multilateral achievements including mainstreaming of the concept of sustainable development and the birth of three landmark international environmental agreements covering climate change, biodiversity and desertification.[13] Importantly, while the three conventions differed in their subject matter, governance arrangements and the political dynamics therein, they all incorporated and operationalised differentiation through the principle of common but differentiated responsibilities and respective capacities (principle 7 CBDR & RC).

The CBDR and RC principle was based on the notion that even though all countries were responsible for addressing global environmental degradation, their individual share of responsibility was not equal (some were more responsible than others).[14] In this sense, addressing global environmental challenges was to be done against the backdrop of the significant differences in socio-economic and even political development between different states. These differences were linked to the level of responsibility, their abilities to address the problems and the subsequent contributions made to solve these challenges.[15] It provided a basis through which rights and obligations could be allocated to states based on their differentiated contribution to the challenges and capabilities to their capacity to address the problems.

The organising debates around differentiation through the CBDR principle did not however begin in 1992. The debates can be tracked to the early days of global environmental governance, flowing along historical, political and economic fault lines.[16] Twenty years earlier, the flagship 1972 United Nations Conference on the Human Environment (UNCHE) immediately saw this divergence materialise as developing countries emphasised the need to focus on socio-economic development, while the more industrialised countries seemed to lean more towards enhancing environmental integrity through the development of norms and standards of global environmental governance.[17]

This impasse subsequently created a scenario where developing countries assumed the role of contesting entities and not *demandeurs* in global environmental governance, a status quo that would result in a delicate compromise known as the Stockholm Declaration of 1972.[18] Even so, these ideological differences continued to persist as developing nations continued to contest how global environmental governance was being conceived and designed.[19]

Key in the thinking behind developing countries' approach to international environmental governance was that the notion of pollution could be classified into two key groups. (1) Pollution arising from poverty and the lack of development and (2) pollution arising from rapid industrialisation and associated wealth and development.[20] The preamble of the Stockholm Declaration reflected this fundamental difference in reading in part, and worth quoting at length:

In the developing countries most of the environmental problems are caused by under-development. Millions continue to live far below the minimum levels required for a decent human existence, deprived of adequate food and clothing, shelter and education, health, and sanitation. Therefore, the developing countries must direct their efforts to development, bearing in mind their priorities and the need to safeguard and improve the environment. For the same purpose, the industrialized countries should make efforts to reduce the gap themselves and the developing countries. In the industrialized countries, environmental problems are generally related to industrialization and technological development....[21]

This provision captured important aspects of global environmental and later climate change multilateralism: a) that environment and development were inextricably linked; b) the primary focus of developing countries was socio-economic development; c) and that developed countries should assist their developing countries in reducing the socio-economic gap between them. This early understanding set the stage for the onset of an affirmative form of environmental multilateralism, the tone and context for future contestation around environmental governance. Affirmative multilateralism 'provides a form of reverse discrimination in favor of developing countries in order to reduce asymmetries in power, wealth, income, risk and opportunity between the developed and developing world'.[22] This was especially the case such that by the time the World Commission on Environment and Development (WCED) was releasing its famous Brundtland Report in 1987, the environment-development link coupled with the idea of differentiation in favour of developing countries had been firmly established as a core piece of the environmental governance discourse.[23]

The preeminent place of affirmative multilateralism in international politics was further affirmed by the subsequent 1989 Hague Declaration on the Environment and UN Resolution 44/228.[24] For instance, UN Resolution 44/228 explicitly articulated the responsibility of developed states in limiting environmental damage and providing support to developing states by primarily attributing global environmental degradation to poverty and unsustainable patterns of production and consumption in particularly industrialised countries.[25] It was therefore no accident that affirmative multilateral cooperation had by this time become important to securing the participation of developing states in multilateral environmental governance.

Similarly, it was also not by chance that the 1992 Rio conference convened by Resolution 44/228 was formally referred to as the United Nations Conference on Environment and Development (UNCED) instead of the 2nd United Nations Conference on the Human Environment (UNCHE) as first proposed by developed states.[26] In essence, the two decades since the 1972 UNCHE had seen the dawn and entrenchment of affirmative multilateralism as a principle organising logic of global environmental governance, with far reaching imprints in subsequent climate change governance.

5.3 Common but Differentiated Responsibilities in the Multilateral Climate Change Regime

The global climate change regime's development set off in full earnest in the late 1980s, right around the time discussions on the environmental-development nexus were at their apex (see also discussion above).[27] The World Climate Conference was convened as far back as 1979 to draw both scientific and possibly political attention to the issue.[28] However, these early efforts had limited participation from states and governments, let alone developing countries.

Furthermore, international law had thus far provided exiguous (small in amount), if any, guidance on addressing climate change.[29] It was not until about 1988 when it finally became a global environmental policy issue for discussion in major intergovernmental forums including the UN General Assembly and the Toronto Conference on Changing the Atmosphere.[30] Crucially, it was during this late 1980s period that Resolution 45/212 was passed, triggering negotiations for developing a new multilateral agreement on climate change at the end of 1990 and the Intergovernmental Panel on Climate Change (IPCC) was established.[31]

This is a crucial detail since this developmental stage also overlapped with the period when debates on pursuing an affirmative approach to environmental governance were at their peak. The chasms between developing and developed states were therefore transferred to climate change governance in these early years. Coming soon after the developing countries achieved success in negotiating a special fund to help implement the Montreal Protocol on Substances that Deplete the Ozone Layer, they sought to transpose this affirmative multilateralism approach into the climate governance architecture.[32] This enabled developing states to successfully argue for subsequent negotiations to be hosted at the UN

General Assembly instead of the more technical IPCC, UNEP or the WMO as preferred by more developed states.[33] In this regard, an affirmative approach to climate change governance was now firmly entrenched in the negotiations for the design of the then new multilateral climate regime.

5.3.1 A Bifurcated Approach

States eventually adopted the United Nations Framework Convention on Climate Change (UNFCCC) at the 1992 UNCED conference after about 3 years of negotiations through the Intergovernmental Negotiating Committee for a Framework Convention on Climate Change (INC/FCCC).[34] Less than 2 years later, the UNFCCC entered into force on the 21st of March 1994.[35] Contained in the UNFCCC were key provisions that institutionalised an affirmative approach to multilateral climate governance including inter alia the provision and/or transfer of support from industrialised to developing countries for implementation of the Convention's objectives and Common but Differentiated Responsibilities that primarily favoured developing countries.[36] The preamble and Article 3 of the UNFCCC outline these obligations.[37]

As soon as the UNFCCC was established, new negotiations for an agreement that would operationalise the Convention kicked off at Berlin in 1995. Under the Berlin Mandate, states discussed the contours of the then new agreement and consequently, a new global legally binding agreement (Kyoto Protocol) was adopted in 1997 in what proved to be a comparatively quick turnaround for multilateral environmental governance.[38]

Importantly, the Kyoto Protocol set an overall greenhouse gas emission reduction target (5% below 1990 levels for developed countries during its first commitment period of 2008–2012) and once individual targets were set, they would be legally binding on states. In essence, industrialised countries were obligated to take on binding emission reduction and/or limitation targets along strict timelines (regulated binding targets and timetables approach) for its commitment period.[39] It did also exempt developing countries from new obligations, only allowing them to engage voluntarily. This bifurcation would later be christened as 'the firewall'.[40] Through a dichotomous system, industrialised countries the were listed as Annex I, and afterwards 'Annex I' became a way to point at categorisation, while developing countries were listed as non-Annex I. This design was premised on the strict application of the CBDR and RC principle that had already been enshrined in the UNFCCC Convention.[41] A key argument underpinning this approach was that of historical responsibility for the climate problem and the large inequalities between both developing and developing countries. In this sense, the Protocol not only represented a perpetuation of the 1987 Montreal Protocol model, but crucially crystallised an affirmative approach to multilateral cooperation in international environmental governance institutions.

5.3.2 From Limited to Universal Participation

At this juncture, it is crucial to emphasise that the relatively quick entrenchment of affirmative multilateralism in global climate governance was not without serious challenge from the developed states.[42] Indeed, this contestation had and continues to exert constant pressure on the climate regime. However, as seen above, creating the space for affirmative multilateralism in climate change governance was necessary to, inter alia, bring already reluctant developing countries to the table and have a chance at solving the climate crisis. Consequently, the intensity of distributeonal conflicts at the time, while relatively high, still enabled the entrenchment of this form of multilateral cooperation in global climate governance architecture.

Nonetheless, this intensity of distributional conflicts continued to increase as especially the large industrialised countries continued to experience rapid economic growth and the problem structure of multilateral cooperation changed accordingly. The conflicts carried over from pre-Kyoto Protocol days, coupled with the rapid changes in particularly the large developing economies meant that the affirmative multilateralism in climate governance was bound to face intense challenges from the start. The Kyoto Protocol had already received a lukewarm reception following its adoption in 1997, despite some arguing that the Protocol represented a first step towards global multilateral climate governance cooperation.[43] Several reasons have been cited for this reception ranging from design shortcomings to its differentiated approach to states' obligations which excluded particularly large developing nations and the inadequacy of its scope.[44] Consequently, some scholars christened the Protocol as a "wrong solution at the right time".[45]

However, it is perhaps the unwillingness of the US to participate in the Kyoto Protocol that best captures the significance of increased problem structure intensity in so far as affirmative multilateralism in climate governance is concerned.[46] One of the primary drivers for the US' recalcitrance in the aftermath of the Kyoto Protocol was the design of the affirmative approach to climate change multilateral cooperation alluded to above. Consequently, developing countries, including large developing economies, were effectively excluded from taking on new obligations under the Kyoto Protocol's bifurcated design. This would ultimately lead to the Bush administration's withdrawal in March 2001 as it felt that the distributional costs would hurt its economy.[47] This withdrawal had the immediate effect of not only undermining the effectiveness of the Protocol but also the appeal and efficacy of affirmative multilateralism as one of the key logics underpinning international climate cooperation. It brought into sharp focus the question of whether future global cooperation on climate change was tenable unless there were significant changes to the configuration of this affirmative differentiated approach to climate governance.

Contestations around the affirmative approach to climate governance and the design of differentiation continued at several instances well after the withdrawal of the US. For instance, the European Union highlighted the issue of future developing country emissions at the 2002 8th Conference of Parties to the UNFCCC in New Delhi, India. In response, developing countries sharply contested the European Union's attempts to focus on that topic, emphasising once again the primacy of socio-economic development and retaining the status quo.[48] The Bush administration also sponsored several bilateral and mini-lateral arrangements around themes like enhanced research, mitigation, technology development, among others.

Importantly, these arrangements eschewed the key distributional concerns that fuelled the dominant affirmative multilateral approach to climate governance.[49] The 2005 Asia Pacific Partnership on Clean Development and Climate brought together seven countries, most importantly India and China to design a mini-lateral arrangement that was aimed at enhancing cooperation around areas such as economic and technological development, climate change and pollution.[50] Crucially, while it set no joint goals, targets and/or objectives, it encouraged each participating state to set its own domestic targets for mitigating greenhouse gas emissions.[51] This represented one of the first explicit attempts to design an international climate governance arrangement that expressly took up a voluntary pledge-based framework and focused on self-differentiation and national climate pledges as opposed to the top-down approach to target-setting in the Kyoto Protocol.

It is these efforts that eventually culminated in the first major shift from the affirmative approach through the Copenhagen Accord following the 15th session of the Conference of Parties (COP) to the UNFCCC.[52] The Accord contained a few crucial provisions that would later become critical to the eventual design of a post-Kyoto climate regime. Importantly, it abandoned the bifurcated binding targets approach in the Kyoto Protocol with 1990 as the baseline year, in favour of more universal nationally determined voluntary non-binding pledges, echoing the initiatives sponsored by the US before the talks.[53] This approach was confirmed in the subsequent decision of the 16th session of the UNFCCC's COP in Cancun after failure of the Copenhagen talks to reach a formal COP decision.[54] Even though the differentiation between countries remained a key feature of the accords, the structure of global cooperation had changed such that the status quo that had previously allowed it to underpin an affirmative multilateral model of climate change cooperation was no longer tenable. Importantly, the second commitment period of the Kyoto Protocol was a failure in the sense that even fewer countries committed to new targets for the period 2012–2020.[55]

While this does not mean that this shift from an affirmative approach happened overnight, it was reflected in subsequent climate change negotiations that followed COPs 15 and 16. For instance, states decided that they would design their own intended nationally determined contributions (INDCs) on key climate change related issues including emission targets at the 19th COP in Warsaw, departing from the bifurcated differentiated approach that had been a core pillar of the Kyoto led regime.[56] Similarly, the 20th COP in Lima culminated in inter alia the tempering of the CBDR principle through a rider that it be considered 'in light of different national circumstances'.[57] This less forceful version of the CBDR principle was once again a reiteration of the push to get rid of the bifurcated differentiation seen in the Kyoto climate regime and perhaps importantly came just one year before the landmark Paris Climate Agreement was adopted in 2015.

5.4 Towards Dynamic Differentiation: The Paris Agreement and Beyond

The landmark 2015 Paris Climate Agreement was arguably the culmination of efforts to shift the affirmative approach of global climate cooperation from its original design under the Kyoto Protocol-led regime. The Agreement ushered in a more hybrid (bottom-up and top-down features), pledge and review approach to multilateral climate cooperation as opposed to the regulated, top-down, targets and timetables approach of the Kyoto Protocol.[58,59] Importantly, it did away with the strict, bifurcated categorisation of countries along differentiation lines and applied to all countries. Even though CBDR & RC was to continue to be a key feature of global climate governance, its application had fundamentally changed such that universal self-differentiation would prevail over the Annex I/Non-Annex model. The universality of NDCs was coupled with self-determined ambitions and priorities and thereby still allows for differentiation.[60] Crucially, it also enshrined the non-binding nationally determined contributions mechanisms as a medium through which universal action and self-differentiation could be enhanced as opposed to the previous model where developing countries large and small were excluded from mandatory mitigation obligations. It is important to note that while the NDCs themselves are binding, their targets per so are not.[61]

5.4.1 Subtle and Dynamic Differentiation

In departing from the bifurcated approach to differentiation, the Paris Agreement ushered in a dynamic and subtle form of differentiation of rights and responsibilities.[62] Subtle and dynamic differentiation differed from the bifurcated approach in several significant ways. Fundamentally, the Paris Agreement regime embraced dynamic differentiation. The 'subtle differentiation' goes beyond the developed-developing countries bifurcation and concerns the extensive inclusion of Least Developed Countries (LDCs) and Small Island Developing States (SIDS) in the Paris Agreement, and tests whether this 'subtle differentiation' is also reflected in NDCs.[63]

First, the Paris Agreement outlined collective climate goals. For mitigation, two targets were adopted. One was the commitment to 'holding the increase in the global average temperature to well below 2 °C above pre-industrial levels and pursuing efforts to limit the temperature increase to 1.5 °C above pre-industrial levels, recognizing that this would significantly reduce the risks and impacts of climate change'.[64] Another mitigation target was to ensure a balance between GHG emissions and absorption; in other words a global net zero target. These two mitigation targets would provide a convergence point for all parties to the UNFCCC.

The second difference was the abandonment, in principle, of the bifurcated classification of countries outlined in the UNFCCC. While the Paris Agreement still includes references to the different rights and obligations of industrialised and developing countries, its inclusion of the dynamic element of 'in light of different national circumstances' is of greater interest for our argument.[65] Bearing in mind that the global GHG emissions profile would change over time, especially developing countries overtaking the industrialised ones as the main GHG emitters, differentiation under the Paris Agreement would be based on changing national circumstances. The phrase 'in light of different national circumstances' would therefore ensure that the analysis of countries' commitments would be dynamic.

Third, the Paris Agreement adopted a logic of progressive commitments. Parties to the UNFCCC would be expected to strengthen their NDCs every five years. Over time, this ratchet mechanism would significantly raise the ambition of the NDCs in line with the global goals of the Paris Agreement. Clearly a stark departure from the static equilibrium approach of the UNFCCC and the Kyoto Protocol, the Paris Agreement has embraced a logic of catalytic cooperation.[66]

5.4.2 *Conditionality as an Insurance Policy*

Many NDCs, especially from developing countries, are conditional on international support for means of implementation from industrialised countries.[67] This has perhaps been best demonstrated through the studies that have illustrated a significant gap in meeting the 2-degree temperature increase target if these conditions are not met.[68] Importantly, the controversies around affirmative multilateral cooperation have also manifested in subsequent climate talks following the adoption of the Paris Agreement. For instance, operationalising the CBDR & RC under the Agreement remained one of the more difficult issues at the negotiations for developing the Paris Agreement Rule Book.[69] Some groups of developing countries even called for a return to the bifurcated and more assertive differentiated separation of developed and developing countries in some areas during the negotiations.[70]

5.4.2.1 Conditionality in African NDCs

For African countries, the commitments on support for means of implementation (MoI) in the Paris Agreement could have been deemed insufficient.[71] Making their NDC conditional on support was therefore the most pragmatic approach for African countries. The adoption of the conditionality approach enabled African countries to commit to submit their national contributions but also maintain the role of external support for MoI as part of the climate change regime.

Conditionality in African countries' NDCs includes several elements. Broadly, conditionality takes the form of three themes: climate finance; technology development and finance; and capacity building. Figure 5.1 below presents a detailed overview of the various elements of conditionality in the NDCs of African countries, with data from the NDC Explorer.[72]

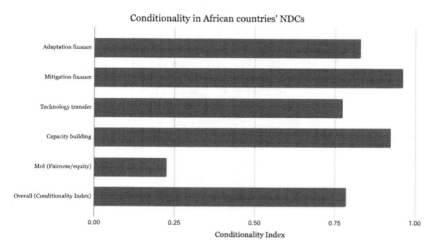

Fig. 5.1 Overview of the variation in the degree of conditionality of African NDCs (*Data source* NDC Explorer. Please note that there are countries who make their NDC fully conditional, and those who only make it partially conditional, but we don't distinguish between the two types)

Of the conditionality categories analysed, technology needs was the most prevalent category. All the African country NDCs included the transfer of technology as a condition to committing to greater climate ambition. That this category is the most prevalent underscores the importance of climate technologies in the realisation of climate policy goals. Mitigation finance was the second most prevalent conditionality category. Mitigation incurs abatement costs and has been the most prominent aspect of global climate policy. Hence, many African countries included two mitigation commitments: one based on their domestic resources; and additional mitigation action based on external support especially from industrialised countries. Adaptation finance and capacity building were also included in many African countries' NDCs, indicating their continued importance for African countries.

Surprisingly, the link between conditionality and fairness and equity was only made by a few African NDCs. Since the inception of the multilateral climate regime, African countries have always emphasised the role of historical emissions in apportioning rights and responsibilities for climate action. Industrialised countries, which account for the bulk of historical emissions, have been allocated greater mitigation responsibility relative to developing countries. It is important, however, to note that there are many countries who make their NDCs conditional upon support, but who do not mention this support in their fairness section. One could argue that the option to put an ambitious NDC forward but to make implementation conditional upon support increases the relevance and importance of this support.[73] But there is no guarantee that the support would be fully provided.

But the weak link between conditionality and fairness and equity is surprising because it implies that African countries have accepted that the climate change regime has moved into a new dispensation where historical responsibility has become passé. In theoretical terms, it might be inferred that African countries are coming to terms with the transition of the climate regime into a new dissipative structure which has been concretised by the Paris Agreement. In this new dispensation, universal application of the regime and its hybrid architecture which is anchored on the bottom-up NDCs means that African countries are not exempt from committing to climate action. These findings are consistent with broader, global analysis of conditionality in NDCs.[74]

Overall, about three quarters of African countries' NDCs include a conditional element. This means that for these countries, there is need

5 DYNAMIC DIFFERENTIATION   143

to include conditionality of commitments to external MoI support as insurance policy, even though the Paris Agreement includes provisions for MoI. Perhaps the continued poor record of the transfer of MoI has necessitated the design and adoption of conditionality as an insurance policy.

Viewed in a geographical context, it is apparent that the adoption of conditionality varies across countries, as illustrated in Fig. 5.2.

Even though African countries often present a common position in the UN climate change negotiations, it is apparent that there are significant variations in the design of climate policy at the national level. As can be discerned from Fig. 5.2, conditionality is most prevalent in a few African countries, especially on the eastern side of the continent. NDCs of North and West African countries include relatively fewer elements of conditionality as compared to those on the north-east, east and southern Africa.

Of course, African countries vary in many ways. But that most of the countries have a relatively limited notion of conditionality suggests that the differences deserve greater scrutiny. It is beyond the scope of the present chapter to probe the causes of the differences in the adoption of

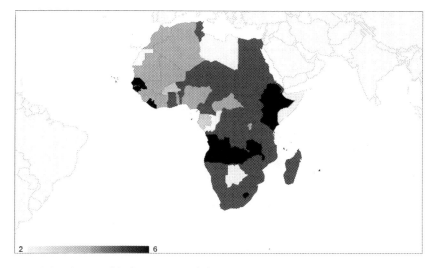

Fig. 5.2 Geographical overview of the variation in the degree of conditionality of African NDCs (*Data source* NDC Explorer)

conditionality in African NDCs. But it does suffice to note the importance of the geographical variation in the analysis of climate policy in Africa.

What can be generally inferred from the foregoing discussion on conditionality is that African countries still consider the notion of CBDR as being important in multilateral climate cooperation. Uncertainty over the ability of the multilateral mechanisms of MoI to deliver is also clearly apparent. If such uncertainty was not an issue, then conditionality would not be included in the NDCs.

At a more fundamental level, conditionality can be understood as an attempt to maintain the differentiation regime of the multilateral climate change regime. The shift from bifurcation to subtle and dynamic differentiation in the regime meant that African countries could no longer be excluded from making significant contributions. The shift also shows the limitations of the bifurcated approach of the earlier MoI regime premised on bifurcation. In tandem with Prigogine's theoretical articulation of systems in disequilibrium, the subtle and dynamic approach to differentiation has meant that African countries must adopt a different tact to ensure that they still have flexibility in implementing their NDCs. Adoption of conditionality also indicates the attempts by African countries to maintain the necessity of MoI as a crucial component of climate action.

In a broader context, the emergence and prevalence of conditionality also suggests attempts to maintain the connection between climate change and sustainable development, given the centrality of MoI in both international development and climate cooperation. Indeed, many African NDCs have been framed within the context of sustainable development. Conditionality, therefore, presents a policy option to preserve the flexibilities necessary to realise sustainable development in African countries.[75] Kenya's NDC, for instance, emissions from fossil fuel extraction are excluded from the mitigation commitments. Instead, the NDC has focused on the need for greater external support in the access and deployment of renewable energy technologies and the capacity to reduce emissions from the extraction of the recently discovered fossil fuels in the country.

5.5   Net Zero and Structural Transformation

While the argument that conditionality in NDCs is an insurance policy for African countries may not be entirely convincing for some, the additional consideration of the long-term climate targets that African countries have undertaken would perhaps alleviate such scepticism. Consider that almost all African countries have expressed interest in or adopted long-term climate neutrality goals—net zero targets. While the Paris Agreement included a commitment to achieving negative emissions reductions in the second half of the twenty-first century, only a few countries had initially adopted net zero targets. Table 5.1 shows the types of climate neutrality targets that African countries are considering or have adopted.

To fully appreciate the structural transformations that could be induced by the net zero, it is important to consider their logical implications. That net zero targets cover 88% of the global emissions, 90% of GDP and 85% of the global population indicates the scale of transformation that the net zero targets would generate should they be fully implemented.[77] For African countries that have or will commit to net zero targets, they would need to eventually implement them, thus aligning their climate standards with the rest of the net zero countries. Whether adequate international support for means would be provided remains an open question, but what

Table 5.1 Long-term climate neutrality targets indicated by African countries[76]

	Percentage of African countries (%)
End-target	
Net zero target	58
1.5 degrees	2
Absolute emissions target	2
Emissions intensity target	2
Emissions reduction target	4
Reduction vs BAU	13
Other target	13
End-target	
2000	6
2030	34
2050	51
2060	2
Open	2
End-target status	
Achieved/self-declared	8
Declaration/pledge	17
In law	2
In policy document	21
Proposed/in discussion	47

Data source Net Zero Tracker

is instructive is that net zero will eventually phase out differentiation, at least to a significant degree.

5.6 Implications of Dynamic Differentiation for African Countries

Several implications for Africa's climate policy follow from the foregoing discussion. First, it is clear that the differentiation mechanism has moved from the bifurcation characterised by the Olsonian logic, to a more dynamic catalytic approach that acknowledges the expected changes in national contexts. By adopting such a dynamic approach, the multilateral climate change regime has ushered in the possibility that as their economies and capabilities grow, African countries would be expected to increase their contribution to the global climate change effort. It is important to note that the Paris Agreement expects all countries to move towards economy wide reduction targets over time.[78]

Second, the catalytic approach of the Paris Agreement, which is premised on disequilibrium, means that as African countries strengthen their NDCs over time by increasing the ambition of commitments and targets, and as the role of MoI diminishes, these countries will have to utilise more of their domestic resources to meet their climate targets. For African countries, the chasm between normative multilateral appeals for MoI and greater flexibility will be negated—if not overturned—by the tightening vice of the ambition mechanism of the Paris Agreement. Moreover, the net zero targets that are or will be widely adopted by African countries will lock in structural transformation towards the global net zero goal, thus reinforcing the ratchet mechanism of the NDCs.

Third, the relationship between sustainable development and climate action might increasingly be tenuous for African countries. As they would be expected to strengthen their NDCs every five years, African countries would have to reconcile the need to allocate more resources required for the implementation of the NDCs, with the pressure to address other pressing development issues. While the debates on the climate action and sustainable development nexus have been ongoing for decades, the Paris Agreement regime has shifted focus to implementation. Squaring this circle of climate and development policy will definitely pose a significant challenge for African countries. Of critical importance is how African countries will reconcile rapid industrialisation, which may lead to an overall rise in emissions, with deep emissions reductions in line with the climate commitments adopted by these countries.

Finally, the shift from bifurcation to dynamic differentiation will necessitate the re-examination of long-run climate policy for African countries. While differentiation has been a core pillar of the multilateral climate regime, the recent adoption of common targets, especially net zero, points towards a harmonisation of domestic climate standards. While it is true that net zero targets can be differentiated, especially as regards the end-year of the target, the main point of emphasis herein is the structural transformation effects of the targets. Viewed in this long-term perspective, differentiation might end up giving way to harmonisation. The costs of this transition will be significant for African countries. Already, many African countries have pledged net zero target, with some of them adopting the target, thus indicating that this prognosis is not far-fetched; in fact, it is imminent.

5.7 CONCLUSION

This chapter has argued that the shift from bifurcated to dynamic and subtle differentiation poses significant challenges to African countries. Differentiation of rights and responsibilities has been central to the pursuit of equity and fairness in the multilateral climate change regime. But as this chapter has demonstrated, differentiation in the climate change regime has evolved from bifurcation to dynamic and subtle differentiation. Bifurcated differentiation, which was premised on a worldview of static equilibrium, articulated differentiation between industrialised and developing countries. As the regime evolved and grew in complexity, and tended towards disequilibrium, the notion of differentiation changed from a normative to strategic consideration.

For African countries, bifurcated differentiation enabled them to agree to addressing climate change in the UNFCCC and the Kyoto Protocol— but they did not set commitments on targets as they were not among the Annex I countries. But the shift to subtle and dynamic differentiation, which underpins the catalytic Paris Agreement regime, will in the long-run diminish the salience of the role of MoI in international climate cooperation. To be clear, the persistence of the importance of MoI does not necessarily mean that this will correspond to the persistence of the mechanism in practice for reasons articulated earlier in the chapter; but we present this as a conjecture. As African countries submit enhanced

NDCs over time, they would have to incur greater costs to do so. Moreover, the interest in and the adoption of long-term climate neutrality/net zero targets has set in motion a structural transformation towards the global harmonisation of climate standards, with significant implications for African countries. The next chapter examines how non-state actors, who are less encumbered with the politics of differentiation, can reinforce state-led climate action.

NOTES

1. Charles P. Kindleberger, *The World in Depression, 1929–1939: Revised and Enlarged Edition* (University of California Press, 1973), 305; Michael C. Webb and Stephen D. Krasner, 'Hegemonic Stability Theory: An Empirical Assessment', *Review of International Studies* 15, no. 2 (1989): 183–98; Robert O. Keohane, 'The Theory of Hegemonic Stability and Changes in International Economic Regimes, 1967–1977', in *Change in the International System* (Routledge, 1980).
2. Adil Najam, 'Developing Countries and Global Environmental Governance: From Contestation to Participation to Engagement', *International Environmental Agreements: Politics, Law and Economics* 5, no. 3 (1 September 2005): 303–21, https://doi.org/10.1007/s10784-005-3807-6.
3. Lavanya Rajamani, *Differential Treatment in International Environmental Law*, Oxford Monographs in International Law (Oxford, New York: Oxford University Press, 2006).
4. Chukwumerije Okereke, 'North–South Inequity and Global Environmental Governance', in *Routledge Handbook of Global Sustainability Governance* (Routledge, 2019).
5. Jagdish N. (ed) Bhagwati, 'The New International Economic Order: The North–South Debate', *MIT Bicentennial Studies (USA)*, 1977, https://agris.fao.org/agris-search/search.do?recordID=US8003918; Jeffrey A. Hart, *The New International Economic Order: Conflict and Cooperation in North–South Economic Relations, 1974–77* (Springer, 1983).
6. Mancur Olson, *The Logic of Collective Action. Public Goods and the Theory of Groups* (Cambridge, MA: Harvard University Press, 1965).
7. Lavanya Rajamani, 'The Principle of Common but Differentiated Responsibilities and Respective Capabilities in the International Climate Change Regime', in *Research Handbook on Climate Disaster Law*, ed. Rosemary Lyster and Robert Verchick (Cheltenham, UK and Northampton, MA: Edward Elgar, 2018), 46–60, https://www.elgaronline.com/view/edcoll/9781786430021/9781786430021.00009.xml.

8. Thomas Hale, 'Catalytic Cooperation', *Global Environmental Politics* 20, no. 4 (1 November 2020): 73–98, https://doi.org/10.1162/glep_a_00561.
9. Duncan Snidal, 'The Limits of Hegemonic Stability Theory', *International Organization* 39, no. 4 (ed 1985): 598–603, https://doi.org/10.1017/S002081830002703X.
10. Robert Falkner, 'The Paris Agreement and the New Logic of International Climate Politics', *International Affairs* 92, no. 5 (1 September 2016): 1107–25, https://doi.org/10.1111/1468-2346.12708.
11. Pieter Pauw, Kennedy Mbeva, and Harro van Asselt, 'Subtle Differentiation of Countries' Responsibilities under the Paris Agreement', *Palgrave Communications* 5, no. 1 (30 July 2019): 1–7, https://doi.org/10.1057/s41599-019-0298-6.
12. UN, 'United Nations Conference on Environment and Development (UNCED), Earth Summit' (Rio de Janeiro, 1992), https://sustainabledevelopment.un.org/milestones/unced.
13. UNCED, 'Agenda 21' (Rio de Janeiro: United Nations, 1992), https://sustainabledevelopment.un.org/outcomedocuments/agenda21.
14. Rajamani, *Differential Treatment in International Environmental Law*, 56; see also Rio Principles, Principle 7 https://www.cbd.int/doc/ref/rio-declaration.shtml.
15. Najam, 'Developing Countries and Global Environmental Governance'; Rajamani, *Differential Treatment in International Environmental Law*, 3.
16. Najam, 'Developing Countries and Global Environmental Governance', 307–10; Rajamani, *Differential Treatment in International Environmental Law*, 35–38.
17. Najam, 'Developing Countries and Global Environmental Governance'; Rajamani, *Differential Treatment in International Environmental Law*.
18. Günther Handl, 'Declaration of the United Nations Conference on the Human Environment - Main Page' (United Nations, 1972), https://legal.un.org/avl/ha/dunche/dunche.html.
19. Rajamani, *Differential Treatment in International Environmental Law*, 56; Najam, 'Developing Countries and Global Environmental Governance', 308.
20. Rajamani, *Differential Treatment in International Environmental Law*, 56.
21. Preamble to Stockholm Declaration, also known as the United Nations Conference on the Human Environment 1972.
22. Robyn Eckersley, 'Moving Forward in the Climate Negotiations: Multilateralism or Minilateralism?', *Global Environmental Politics* 12, no. 2 (20 March 2012): 31, https://doi.org/10.1162/GLEP_a_00107.
23. Gru Brundtland et al., 'Our Common Future ('Brundtland Report')', 1987.

24. UNGA, 'UN Conference on Environment and Development': (New York: United Nations, 22 March 1990), http://digitallibrary.un.org/record/82555; UN, 'Hague Declaration on the Environment *', *International Legal Materials* 28, no. 5 (September 1989): 1308–10, https://doi.org/10.1017/S0020782900022750.
25. UNGA, 'UN Conference on Environment and Development', para 9.
26. Najam, 'Developing Countries and Global Environmental Governance', 311; Rajamani, *Differential Treatment in International Environmental Law*, 57.
27. Daniel Bodansky, 'The History of the Global Climate Change Regime', *International Relations and Global Climate Change* 23, no. 23 (2001): 23–40.
28. Brundtland et al., 'Our Common Future ('Brundtland Report')'.
29. Bodansky, 'The History of the Global Climate Change Regime'.
30. UN, 'Hague Declaration on the Environment *'; Brundtland et al., 'Our Common Future ('Brundtland Report')'.
31. UN, 'Protection of Global Climate for Present and Future Generations of Mankind': (UN, 17 January 1991), http://digitallibrary.un.org/record/196769; Bodansky, 'The History of the Global Climate Change Regime', 30; David Held and Charles Roger, 'Three Models of Global Climate Governance: From Kyoto to Paris and Beyond', *Global Policy* 9, no. 4 (2018): 527–37, https://doi.org/10.1111/1758-5899.12617.
32. Bodansky, 'The History of the Global Climate Change Regime', 30.
33. UN, 'Protection of Global Climate for Present and Future Generations of Mankind'; Bodansky, 'The History of the Global Climate Change Regime', 30; Pieter Pauw et al., 'Different Perspectives on Differentiated Responsibilities. A State-of-the-Art Review of the Notion of Common but Differentiated Responsibilities in International Negotiations', Discussion Paper (Bonn, Germany: German Development Institute/Deutsches Institut für Entwicklungspolitik (DIE), 2014), https://www.die-gdi.de/uploads/media/DP_6.2014..pdf.
34. Bodansky, 'The History of the Global Climate Change Regime'.
35. United Nations Framework Convention on Climate Change, art. 1(3), Mar. 21, 1994, 1771 U.N.T.S. 107.
36. United Nations Framework Convention on Climate Change, art. 1(3), Mar. 21, 1994, 1771 U.N.T.S. 107 Article 4.
37. *Preamble: Noting that the largest share of historical and current global emissions of greenhouse gases has originated in developed countries, that per capita emissions in developing countries are still relatively low and that the share of global emissions originating in developing countries will grow to meet their social and development needs. Article 3 (Principles): (i) The Parties should protect the climate system for the benefit of present and future generations of humankind, on the basis of equity and in accordance with*

their common but differentiated responsibilities and respective capabilities. Accordingly, the developed country Parties should take the lead in combating climate change and the adverse effects thereof.

38. COP-1 met in Berlin. Among its significant outcomes, the Berlin meeting decided to inter alia establish an ad hoc committee to negotiate a protocol or other legal instrument by 1997 containing additional commitments for industrialized countries for the post-2000 period. This was known as the Berlin Mandate and the new negotiating committee became known as the Ad Hoc Group on the Berlin Mandate (AGBM). See UNEP, 'Press Backgrounder: A Brief History of the Climate Change Convention' (Bonn, Germany: Information Unit for Conventions, United Nations Environment Programme, 1997), https://unfccc.int/cop3/fccc/info/backgrod.htm#:~:text=The%20Berlin%20Mandate%20calls%20on,new%20commitments%20for%20developing%20countries.

39. Christopher Napoli, 'Understanding Kyoto's Failure', *SAIS Review of International Affairs* 32, no. 2 (2012): 183–96; Amanda M. Rosen, 'The Wrong Solution at the Right Time: The Failure of the Kyoto Protocol on Climate Change', *Politics & Policy* 43, no. 1 (2015): 30–58, https://doi.org/10.1111/polp.12105; Jeffrey McGee and Jens Steffek, 'The Copenhagen Turn in Global Climate Governance and the Contentious History of Differentiation in International Law', *Journal of Environmental Law* 28, no. 1 (1 March 2016): 38, https://doi.org/10.1093/jel/eqw003.

40. Falkner, 'The Paris Agreement and the New Logic of International Climate Politics'.

41. Rajamani, *Differential Treatment in International Environmental Law*, 182.

42. McGee and Steffek, 'The Copenhagen Turn in Global Climate Governance and the Contentious History of Differentiation in International Law', 51–55.

43. Rosen, 'The Wrong Solution at the Right Time'.

44. Napoli, 'Understanding Kyoto's Failure', 183; Rosen, 'The Wrong Solution at the Right Time', 31; McGee and Steffek, 'The Copenhagen Turn in Global Climate Governance and the Contentious History of Differentiation in International Law', 38.

45. Rosen, 'The Wrong Solution at the Right Time'.

46. David E. Sanger, 'Bush Will Continue to Oppose Kyoto Pact on Global Warming', *The New York Times*, 12 June 2001, sec. World, https://www.nytimes.com/2001/06/12/world/bush-will-continue-to-oppose-kyoto-pact-on-global-warming.html.

47. USGOV, 'Text of a Letter From The President' (Washington DC: The White House, 13 March 2001), https://georgewbush-whitehouse.archives.gov/news/releases/2001/03/20010314.html.

48. Napoli, 'Understanding Kyoto's Failure', 194.

49. McGee and Steffek, 'The Copenhagen Turn in Global Climate Governance and the Contentious History of Differentiation in International Law', 55.
50. McGee and Steffek, 'The Copenhagen Turn in Global Climate Governance and the Contentious History of Differentiation in International Law'.
51. Falkner, 'The Paris Agreement and the New Logic of International Climate Politics'.
52. McGee and Steffek, 'The Copenhagen Turn in Global Climate Governance and the Contentious History of Differentiation in International Law'.
53. Falkner, 'The Paris Agreement and the New Logic of International Climate Politics'.
54. McGee and Steffek, 'The Copenhagen Turn in Global Climate Governance and the Contentious History of Differentiation in International Law', 60.
55. Rosen, 'The Wrong Solution at the Right Time'.
56. Joeri Rogelj et al., 'Paris Agreement Climate Proposals Need a Boost to Keep Warming Well below 2 °C', *Nature* 534, no. 7609 (30 June 2016): 631, https://doi.org/10.1038/nature18307; Yann Robiou du Pont et al., 'Equitable Mitigation to Achieve the Paris Agreement Goals', *Nature Climate Change* 7, no. 1 (January 2017): 38, https://doi.org/10.1038/nclimate3186; Reuben Makomere and Kennedy Liti Mbeva, 'Squaring the Circle: Development Prospects Within the Paris Agreement', *Carbon & Climate Law Review* 12, no. 1 (2018): 35, https://doi.org/10.21552/cclr/2018/1/7.
57. UNFCCC, 'Decision 1/CP.20, Lima Call for Climate Action' (2 February 2015) FCCC/CP/2014/10/Add.1.
58. Daniel Bodansky, 'The Legal Character of the Paris Agreement', *Review of European, Comparative & International Environmental Law* 25, no. 2 (2016): 142–50, https://doi.org/10.1111/reel.12154; Falkner, 'The Paris Agreement and the New Logic of International Climate Politics'.
59. Bodansky, 'The Legal Character of the Paris Agreement'; Falkner, 'The Paris Agreement and the New Logic of International Climate Politics'.
60. Caroline Zimm and Nebojsa Nakicenovic, 'What Are the Implications of the Paris Agreement for Inequality?', *Climate Policy* 20, no. 4 (20 April 2020): 458–67, https://doi.org/10.1080/14693062.2019.1581048; Pauw, Mbeva, and van Asselt, 'Subtle Differentiation of Countries' Responsibilities under the Paris Agreement'; Lavanya Rajamani, 'The Principle of Common but Differentiated Responsibilities and Respective Capabilities in the International Climate Change Regime', in *Research Handbook on Climate Disaster Law*, ed. Rosemary Lyster and Robert Verchick (Cheltenham, UK and Northampton, MA: Edward Elgar,

2018), 46–60, https://www.elgaronline.com/view/edcoll/978178643 0021/9781786430021.00009.xml.

61. Daniel Bodansky and Lavanya Rajamani, 'The Evolution and Governance Architecture of the United Nations Climate Change Regime', in *Global Climate Policy: Actors, Concepts, and Enduring Challenges*, ed. Urs Luterbacher and Detlef F. Sprinz (MIT Press, 2018); Daniel Bodansky and Lavanya Rajamani, 'The Issues That Never Die', *Carbon & Climate Law Review* 12, no. 3 (2018): 184–90, https://doi.org/10.21552/cclr/201 8/3/4.

62. Pauw, Mbeva, and van Asselt, 'Subtle Differentiation of Countries' Responsibilities under the Paris Agreement'.

63. Pauw, Mbeva, and van Asselt.

64. Art 2(a).

65. Bodansky and Rajamani, 'The Evolution and Governance Architecture of the United Nations Climate Change Regime'; Pauw, Mbeva, and van Asselt, 'Subtle Differentiation of Countries' Responsibilities under the Paris Agreement'; Christina Voigt and Felipe Ferreira, '"Dynamic Differentiation": The Principles of CBDR-RC, Progression and Highest Possible Ambition in the Paris Agreement', *Transnational Environmental Law* 5, no. 2 (October 2016): 285–303, https://doi.org/10.1017/S20471025 16000212.

66. Hale, 'Catalytic Cooperation'.

67. Makomere and Mbeva, 'Squaring the Circle'.

68. Rogelj et al., 'Paris Agreement Climate Proposals Need a Boost to Keep Warming Well below 2 °C', 631; Pont et al., 'Equitable Mitigation to Achieve the Paris Agreement Goals', 35.

69. Bodansky and Rajamani, 'The Evolution and Governance Architecture of the United Nations Climate Change Regime'.

70. Bodansky and Rajamani, 189.

71. Georgia Savvidou et al., 'Quantifying International Public Finance for Climate Change Adaptation in Africa', *Climate Policy* 21, no. 8 (14 September 2021): 1020–36, https://doi.org/10.1080/14693062.2021. 1978053.

72. Pieter Pauw et al., *NDC Explorer* (Bonn, Germany and Nairobi, Kenya: German Development Institute/Deutsches Institut für Entwicklungspolitik (DIE), and African Centre for Technology Studies (ACTS), 2016), http://klimalog.die-gdi.de/ndc/.

73. W. Pauw et al., 'Conditional Nationally Determined Contributions in the Paris Agreement: Foothold for Equity or Achilles Heel?', *Climate Policy* 20, no. 4 (20 April 2020): 468–84, https://doi.org/10.1080/ 14693062.2019.1635874.

74. Pauw et al.

75. Makomere and Mbeva, 'Squaring the Circle'.

76. Thomas Hale et al., 'Net Zero Tracker' (Oxford, UK: Energy and Climate Intelligence Unit, Data-Driven EnviroLab, NewClimate Institute, Oxford Net Zero, 2021), https://zerotracker.net/.
77. Hale et al.
78. Anders Bjørn, Shannon Lloyd, and Damon Matthews, 'From the Paris Agreement to Corporate Climate Commitments: Evaluation of Seven Methods for Setting "Science-Based" Emission Targets', *Environmental Research Letters*, 2021, https://doi.org/10.1088/1748-9326/abe57b; Christina Hood and Carly Soo, 'Accounting for Mitigation Targets in Nationally Determined Contributions under the Paris Agreement', 2017, https://www.oecd-ilibrary.org/content/paper/63937a2b-en.

References

Bhagwati, Jagdish N. (ed). 'The New International Economic Order: The North-South Debate'. *MIT Bicentennial Studies (USA)*, 1977. https://agris.fao.org/agris-search/search.do?recordID=US8003918.

Bjørn, Anders, Shannon Lloyd, and Damon Matthews. 2021. From the Paris Agreement to Corporate Climate Commitments: Evaluation of Seven Methods for Setting "Science-Based" Emission Targets. *Environmental Research Letters*. https://doi.org/10.1088/1748-9326/abe57b.

Bodansky, Daniel. 2001. The History of the Global Climate Change Regime. *International Relations and Global Climate Change* 23 (23): 23–40.

Bodansky, Daniel. 2016. The Legal Character of the Paris Agreement. *Review of European, Comparative & International Environmental Law* 25 (2): 142–150. https://doi.org/10.1111/reel.12154.

Bodansky, Daniel, and Lavanya Rajamani. 'The Evolution and Governance Architecture of the United Nations Climate Change Regime'. In *Global Climate Policy: Actors, Concepts, and Enduring Challenges*, edited by Urs Luterbacher and Detlef F. Sprinz. MIT Press, 2018.

———. 'The Issues That Never Die'. *Carbon & Climate Law Review* 12, no. 3 (2018): 184–90. https://doi.org/10.21552/cclr/2018/3/4.

Brundtland, Gru, Mansour Khalid, Susanna Agnelli, Sali Al-Athel, Bernard Chidzero, Lamina Fadika, Volker Hauff, Istvan Lang, Ma Shijun, and Margarita Morino de Botero. 'Our Common Future ('Brundtland Report')', 1987.

Eckersley, Robyn. 'Moving Forward in the Climate Negotiations: Multilateralism or Minilateralism?' *Global Environmental Politics* 12, no. 2 (20 March 2012): 24–42. https://doi.org/10.1162/GLEP_a_00107.

Falkner, Robert. 'The Paris Agreement and the New Logic of International Climate Politics'. *International Affairs* 92, no. 5 (1 September 2016): 1107–25. https://doi.org/10.1111/1468-2346.12708.

Hale, Thomas. 'Catalytic Cooperation'. *Global Environmental Politics* 20, no. 4 (1 November 2020): 73–98. https://doi.org/10.1162/glep_a_00561.

Hale, Thomas, Takeshi Kuramochi, John Lang, Brendan Mapes, Steve Smith, Ria Aiyer, Richard Black, et al. 'Net Zero Tracker'. Oxford, UK: Energy and Climate Intelligence Unit, Data-Driven EnviroLab, NewClimate Institute, Oxford Net Zero, 2021. https://zerotracker.net/.

Handl, Günther. 'Declaration of the United Nations Conference on the Human Environment—Main Page'. United Nations, 1972. https://legal.un.org/avl/ha/dunche/dunche.html.

Hart, Jeffrey A. *The New International Economic Order: Conflict and Cooperation in North-South Economic Relations, 1974–77*. Springer, 1983.

Held, David, and Charles Roger. 2018. Three Models of Global Climate Governance: From Kyoto to Paris and Beyond. *Global Policy* 9 (4): 527–537. https://doi.org/10.1111/1758-5899.12617.

Hood, Christina, and Carly Soo. 'Accounting for Mitigation Targets in Nationally Determined Contributions under the Paris Agreement', 2017. https://www.oecd-ilibrary.org/content/paper/63937a2b-en.

Keohane, Robert O. 'The Theory of Hegemonic Stability and Changes in International Economic Regimes, 1967–1977'. In *Change in the International System*. Routledge, 1980.

Kindleberger, Charles P., and Ford International Professor of Economics Charles P. Kindleberger. *The World in Depression, 1929–1939: Revised and Enlarged Edition*. University of California Press, 1973.

Makomere, Reuben, and Kennedy Liti Mbeva. 'Squaring the Circle: Development Prospects Within the Paris Agreement'. *Carbon & Climate Law Review* 12, no. 1 (2018): 31–40. https://doi.org/10.21552/cclr/2018/1/7.

McGee, Jeffrey, and Jens Steffek. 'The Copenhagen Turn in Global Climate Governance and the Contentious History of Differentiation in International Law'. *Journal of Environmental Law* 28, no. 1 (1 March 2016): 37–63. https://doi.org/10.1093/jel/eqw003.

Najam, Adil. 'Developing Countries and Global Environmental Governance: From Contestation to Participation to Engagement'. *International Environmental Agreements: Politics, Law and Economics* 5, no. 3 (1 September 2005): 303–21. https://doi.org/10.1007/s10784-005-3807-6.

Napoli, Christopher. 2012. Understanding Kyoto's Failure. *SAIS Review of International Affairs* 32 (2): 183–196.

Okereke, Chukwumerije. 2019. *North-South Inequity and Global Environmental Governance*. In Routledge Handbook of Global Sustainability Governance: Routledge.

Olson, Mancur. *The Logic of Collective Action. Public Goods and the Theory of Groups*. Cambridge, MA: Harvard University Press, 1965.

Pauw, Pieter, Steffen Bauer, Carmen Richerzhagen, Clara Brandi, and Hannah Schmole. 'Different Perspectives on Differentiated Responsibilities. A State-of-the-Art Review of the Notion of Common but Differentiated Responsibilities in International Negotiations'. Discussion Paper. Bonn, Germany: German Development Institute / Deutsches Institut für Entwicklungspolitik (DIE), 2014. https://www.die-gdi.de/uploads/media/DP_6.2014..pdf.

Pauw, Pieter, Davide Cassanmagnano, Kennedy Mbeva, Jonas Hein, Alejandro Guarin, Clara Brandi, Thomas Bock, et al. *NDC Explorer*. Bonn, Germany and Nairobi, Kenya: German Development Institute/Deutsches Institut für Entwicklungspolitik (DIE), and African Centre for Technology Studies (ACTS), 2016. http://klimalog.die-gdi.de/ndc/.

Pauw, Pieter, Kennedy Mbeva, and Harro van Asselt. 'Subtle Differentiation of Countries' Responsibilities under the Paris Agreement'. *Palgrave Communications* 5, no. 1 (30 July 2019): 1–7. https://doi.org/10.1057/s41599-019-0298-6.

Pauw, W., P. Castro, J. Pickering, and S. Bhasin. 'Conditional Nationally Determined Contributions in the Paris Agreement: Foothold for Equity or Achilles Heel?' *Climate Policy* 20, no. 4 (20 April 2020): 468–84. https://doi.org/10.1080/14693062.2019.1635874.

Pont, Yann Robiou du, M. Louise Jeffery, Johannes Gütschow, Joeri Rogelj, Peter Christoff, and Malte Meinshausen. 'Equitable Mitigation to Achieve the Paris Agreement Goals'. *Nature Climate Change* 7, no. 1 (January 2017): 38–43. https://doi.org/10.1038/nclimate3186.

Rajamani, Lavanya. *Differential Treatment in International Environmental Law.* Oxford Monographs in International Law. Oxford, New York: Oxford University Press, 2006.

———. 'The Principle of Common but Differentiated Responsibilities and Respective Capabilities in the International Climate Change Regime'. In *Research Handbook on Climate Disaster Law*, edited by Rosemary Lyster and Robert Verchick, 46–60. Cheltenham, UK and Northampton, MA: Edward Elgar, 2018. https://www.elgaronline.com/view/edcoll/9781786430021/9781786430021.00009.xml.

Rogelj, Joeri, Michel den Elzen, Niklas Höhne, Taryn Fransen, Hanna Fekete, Harald Winkler, Roberto Schaeffer, Fu Sha, Keywan Riahi, and Malte Meinshausen. 'Paris Agreement Climate Proposals Need a Boost to Keep Warming Well below 2 °C'. *Nature* 534, no. 7609 (30 June 2016): 631–39. https://doi.org/10.1038/nature18307.

Rosen, Amanda M. 2015. The Wrong Solution at the Right Time: The Failure of the Kyoto Protocol on Climate Change. *Politics & Policy* 43 (1): 30–58. https://doi.org/10.1111/polp.12105.

Sanger, David E. 'Bush Will Continue to Oppose Kyoto Pact on Global Warming'. *The New York Times*, 12 June 2001, sec. World. https://www.nyt imes.com/2001/06/12/world/bush-will-continue-to-oppose-kyoto-pact-on-global-warming.html.

Savvidou, Georgia, Aaron Atteridge, Kulthoum Omari-Motsumi, and Christopher H. Trisos. 'Quantifying International Public Finance for Climate Change Adaptation in Africa'. *Climate Policy* 21, no. 8 (14 September 2021): 1020–36. https://doi.org/10.1080/14693062.2021.1978053.

Snidal, Duncan. 'The Limits of Hegemonic Stability Theory'. *International Organization* 39, no. 4 (ed 1985): 579–614. https://doi.org/10.1017/S00 2081830002703X.

UN. 'Hague Declaration on the Environment *'. *International Legal Materials* 28, no. 5 (September 1989): 1308–10. https://doi.org/10.1017/S00207 82900022750.

———. 'Protection of Global Climate for Present and Future Generations of Mankind ': UN, 17 January 1991. http://digitallibrary.un.org/record/ 196769.

———. 'United Nations Conference on Environment and Development (UNCED), Earth Summit'. Rio de Janeiro, 1992. https://sustainabledeve lopment.un.org/milestones/unced.

UNCED. 'Agenda 21'. Rio de Janeiro: United Nations, 1992. https://sustainab ledevelopment.un.org/outcomedocuments/agenda21.

UNEP. 'Press Backgrounder: A Brief History of the Climate Change Convention'. Bonn, Germany: Information Unit for Conventions, United Nations Environment Programme, 1997. https://unfccc.int/cop3/fccc/info/bac kgrod.htm#:~:text=The%20Berlin%20Mandate%20calls%20on,new%20comm itments%20for%20developing%20countries.

UNGA. 'UN Conference on Environment and Development ': New York: United Nations, 22 March 1990. http://digitallibrary.un.org/record/82555.

USGOV. 'Text of a Letter From The President'. Washington DC: The White House, 13 March 2001. https://georgewbush-whitehouse.archives. gov/news/releases/2001/03/20010314.html.

Voigt, Christina, and Felipe Ferreira. October 2016. "Dynamic Differentiation": The Principles of CBDR-RC, Progression and Highest Possible Ambition in the Paris Agreement. *Transnational Environmental Law* 5 (2): 285–303. https://doi.org/10.1017/S2047102516000212.

Webb, Michael C., and Stephen D. Krasner. 1989. Hegemonic Stability Theory: An Empirical Assessment. *Review of International Studies* 15 (2): 183–98.

Zimm, Caroline, and Nebojsa Nakicenovic. 'What Are the Implications of the Paris Agreement for Inequality?' *Climate Policy* 20, no. 4 (20 April 2020): 458–67. https://doi.org/10.1080/14693062.2019.1581048.

CHAPTER 6

The Rise of Non-state Actors

In many ways, the rise of non- and sub-state actors (hereafter non-state actors, NSAs) has transformed the international climate policy landscape. Alongside national governments, many actors such as businesses, civil societies and sub-national governments have engaged in climate policy. Moreover, such actors often collaborate across state borders. Scholars have long identified this phenomenon, and termed it as transnational governance. Applied to climate change, the phenomenon has been called transnational climate governance (TCG).[1]

Scholars have sought to determine the nature and extent of TCG.[2] While there is much literature on the extent and dynamics of TCG in the global North, there is limited scholarship on the global South. Moreover, most of the studies on TCG in the global South are limited to national case studies.[3] This chapter contributes to addressing this gap by undertaking a detailed analysis of TCG in an African context. Focusing on an empirical case study of TCG in Kenya, the chapter argues that like in other parts of the world, TCG is a growing phenomenon in Africa. A crucial assumption of the case study, though, is that it is illustrative, but not necessarily representative, of other African countries, especially given that Kenya has been a pioneer on climate policy in Africa by among others being the first country in Africa to enact a climate change law.[4] As a consequence, international climate policy in the region is becoming more

© The Author(s), under exclusive license to Springer Nature Switzerland AG 2023
K. Mbeva et al., *Africa's Right to Development in a Climate-Constrained World*, Contemporary African Political Economy,
https://doi.org/10.1007/978-3-031-22887-2_6

159

complex, evolving to include more actors and climate-related issues. TCG will therefore be an integral component of international climate policy in Africa, hence the need to better understand its dynamics.

From a conceptual point, understanding the rise of NSAs and TCG points to the growing complexity of the climate governance landscape at global and continental level. While such an observation is interesting, it is only a starting point for more detailed investigations into the phenomenon. Moreover, if TCG and non- and sub-state action generate additional complexity, is this a positive development, or does it pose an additional challenge especially to African governments that have always struggled with limited capacity? As demonstrated in the chapter, NSA climate action and TCG present an important dimension to augment national climate policy in African countries. But it also faces constraints which, when overcome, can unlock greater potential for more ambitious climate action in Africa.

6.1   Non-state and Transnational Climate Governance

Transnational climate governance has emerged as an important pillar of the international climate policy landscape. In addition to the nation-state, other actors contribute to addressing climate change in various ways. Viewed through a functionalist lens, TCG largely arose to fill the gap and inadequacies arising from inadequate multilateral responses to global climate change.[5] But other sources of the phenomenon, and its diffusion, can also be connected to socialisation of actors to engage with the initiative, as well as through donors and other actors especially from the global North.[6]

On sustainability issues, NSAs have been active in developing and participating in various governance regimes. Private actors such as companies and the civil society have developed governance arrangements that have sought to complement the policies of national governments.[7] In many cases, such initiatives have included the establishment of novel institutions to govern sustainability challenges. A salient example is the Forest Stewardship Council (FSC) which has been influential in forest governance.[8]Non-state actors have therefore become agents and entrepreneurs in global environmental governance.[9]

The role of NSAs in transnational relations and governance is not new. In the 1970s, scholars theorised the rise of such transnational actors, and hypothesised how the NSAs were affecting global governance. The initial strand of scholarship focused on multinational cooperation, examining whether they were replacing the nation-state as the primary actors in international politics.[10] Over the years, the literature on transnational environmental and climate governance has proliferated.[11] The growth of this literature can be linked to the growing role of non-state actors in climate change policy, especially at the multilateral level. As countries negotiated a climate change treaty to replace the Kyoto Protocol, private sector actors, civil society and other actors became increasingly engaged in the process.[12]

Initially, the main international response to climate change involved multilateral cooperation through the establishment of the UNFCCC. Over time, national governments tried to develop international legal instruments to implement the multilateral commitments outlined in the UNFCCC. But the design and adoption of a universally accepted instrument, one that was also politically elusive, proved challenging.[13] Only after about three decades did the adoption of the Paris Agreed break the gridlock in multilateral climate cooperation.[14] Moreover, the Paris Agreement and its attendant process acknowledged the role of NSAs in addressing climate change. The launch of the Non-state Zone for Climate Action (NAZCA) in 2014 to track NSAs' contributions under the UNFCCC, which was also referred to in the Conference of Parties (COP) decision during the adoption of the Paris Agreement, marked a major milestone.[15]

But while there has been growth in the recorded climate actions of NSAs, there is an apparent geographical imbalance. Much of the recorded action is in the global North, thus raising the question as to whether TCG is indeed present and prevalent in the global South. Table 6.1 clearly illustrates the proliferation but geographically imbalance phenomenon of non-state climate action.

As Table 6.1 shows, the imbalance is especially acute in Africa, as only 3% of the actors are from Africa, including at the national level.

To probe this pattern of geographical imbalance, the following sections examine in detail a case study of transnational and non-state climate action in Kenya. Understanding such climate action within the context of an African country is critical, as it would allow the examination of whether there are unique factors that shape the climate action. Moreover, an in-depth analysis would provide a useful heuristic for similar analysis in other African countries.

Table 6.1 Non- and sub-state climate action in Africa vis-à-vis the global perspective

	Number of climate actions	
Actors	*Africa*	*Global*
Companies	234	9979
Investors	40	1441
Organisations	277	3219
Regions	18	283
Cities	233	11,191
Countries	54	196
Total	856	26,309
Percentage (%)	3	100

Data source NAZCA[16]

If indeed transnational, non- and sub-state climate action is a significant dimension of climate governance in Africa, then the scholarly and policy discourses need to evolve and incorporate it. In doing so, a clearer picture would also emerge on whether the phenomenon is particular to certain countries in Africa, or whether it is much more prevalent and effective in fostering climate action across the continent.

6.2 Non-state Climate Action in Kenya

Transnational and non-state climate action in Kenya operates within a broader national context of climate policy. Kenya has developed a suite of national policies and laws to address climate change. These regulatory instruments have been either pursuant to the implementation of international climate change commitments, or a direct response to national climate and climate-related challenges.

6.2.1 National Climate Landscape in Kenya

Overall, Kenya has numerous regulatory instruments to address climate change. According to the Climate Laws database, these regulatory instruments include five laws, fourteen policies and seven climate targets. In addition, climate-related jurisprudence in Kenya is emerging.[17]

The main national regulatory instrument in Kenya is the Climate Change Law of 2017. As the first to be adopted in Africa, Kenya's Climate Change Law provides the legal basis for climate action in the country.[18] At the multilateral level, Kenya has submitted a nationally determined contribution (NDCs) outlining the country's commitment to the Paris Agreement. While the NDC is the central instrument connecting national and international dimensions of climate action in Kenya, there are other important policy instruments. The National Climate Change Action Plan 2018–2022, for instance, elaborates on a programme for climate change implementation over five year periods.[19]

Given the growing number of climate and climate-related regulatory instruments, the national climate policy landscape in Kenya is characterised by increasing complexity. And since many of the regulatory instruments include provisions on the importance of non-state climate action, it can be concluded that NSAs are an important set of actors in addressing climate change in Kenya. During the development of its NDC, for instance, the Kenya government involved sub-national governments, civil society, academia and the private sector. These actors also have been identified in the NDCs as playing an important role in its implementation.[20]

6.2.2 Mapping Non-state Climate Action in Kenya

To probe the extent and nature of non-state and transnational climate action in the global South, the ClimateSouth project was developed by leading scholars. It includes the global and national comparative analysis of Kenya and India. In this chapter, only the Kenya case study is analysed, and data is drawn from the project.

A mixed-methods approach was used to collect data on non-state and transnational climate action in Kenya. Combining desk research, surveys and focused group discussions, data on climate action by companies and County (sub-national governments) was collected. In total, sixty four (64) stock-listed companies, eighty two (82) small and medium enterprises (SMEs) and 47 County governments were analysed. Data was collected between the years 2017–2020. In addition, two workshops with key stakeholders, designed as focused group discussions, were convened to probe the data and findings from the surveys.[21] Analysis was conducted along the themes of institutional design, exposure to climate risks, target-setting and engagement in domestic and transnational climate initiatives.

Taken together, the data (both qualitative and quantitative) presents a novel database of non- sub-state and transnational climate governance in Kenya. The main finding from the analysis is that although non-state and sub-national climate action is prevalent in Kenya, it is largely under-reported in global datasets. There is, thus, a "visibility gap".[22] Also, while many of the actors surveyed had adopted various climate targets and plans, there is a challenge in terms of implementation. Another key finding is that much of the climate action is framed within the broader context of sustainable development, in line with the long-running argument especially by developing countries that stresses the developmental dimension of climate action.[23]

6.2.2.1 Non-State (Companies) Climate Action

Climate action by companies was examined across the themes of perceptions of climate risks, institutional arrangements, target-setting, reporting and participation in domestic and transnational climate initiatives. Overall, many companies in Kenya have taken up some form of climate action. Stock-listed companies, however, have more institutionalised arrangement to support climate compared to SMEs, as the Nairobi Securities Exchange has clear sustainability reporting guidelines.[24] A cross-cutting theme across the two categories of companies is the prevalence of informal climate targets.

Perception of climate risks

Turning first to the companies, we find that the main climate risks facing these actors are those of energy security (reliability of supply) and climate drought. Energy supply is a major issue in Kenya, hence power outages are sometimes a common occurrence. Part of the reason is that a significant proportion of Kenya's energy supply is from hydropower. Since droughts have been prevalent in the country, water levels in dams have often dropped to unsustainable levels.[25] Energy supply, however, was perceived as a relatively major challenge for stock-listed companies compared to SMEs.

A related climate risk, as identified from the surveys, was the increase in the frequency and intensity of droughts. Relatively speaking, this challenge was more acute for SMEs than for stock-listed companies. Kenya's economy is primarily based on agriculture, and many of the SMEs are in the agricultural sector. Frequent and more intense droughts therefore lead to increased food insecurity, thus affecting crop yields and agricultural and related supply chains.[26]

Institutional arrangements

To address climate change, a significant number of the companies have established governance institutions. Sustainability and corporate social responsibility (CSR) offices are the most common institutional feature of climate policy, as identified by the surveyed companies. Only less than one-third of the companies have established a climate office. In this sense, private sector companies in Kenya predominantly viewed climate change issues within the broader context of business and economic sustainability.

Target-setting

Targets setting has been a crucial feature of transnational and non-state climate action.[27] Just like governments, NSAs and sub-national governments have set various kinds of climate targets. These range from broad to narrow or sectoral sustainability targets. The most widely adopted target in Kenya is on Sustainability, whereby ninety-two per cent (92%) of all companies surveyed include some form of sustainability target.

As regards climate-specific targets, the three most prevalent are energy efficiency targets (71%), greenhouse targets (64%) and resilience targets (53%). That energy efficiency targets are the most common indicates that issues of reliability of energy supply, as identified above, are a motivation for switching to renewable energy sources such as solar. The resilience target also shows that companies, especially those in the agricultural sector are keen to make their operations more resilient to the impacts of climate change.

An important feature of the climate targets set by the companies is that most of them are voluntary. Only a small fraction of the targets are legally mandated by the government. This implies that most of the companies have taken voluntary initiatives to introduce the climate targets. It is important, however, to note that the Nairobi Securities Exchange (NSE), the sole bourse in the country, requires sustainability reporting by all listed companies.[28] The NSE is also a member of the United Nations Sustainable Stock Exchanges Initiative, thus illustrating a socialisation element.[29] The reporting mandate does not include climate commitments in particular. For the SMEs, there is no similar institutional requirement. Still, it can be concluded that both types of companies have voluntarily adopted climate targets.

Also, and in particular for the SMEs, most of the targets outlined are informal in nature. This is in contrast to the conventional approach, whereby companies usually set quantitative targets that are easily measurable. For most companies in Kenya, the targets are largely framed in qualitative ways that are difficult to quantify. A typical response to sustainability targets would, for instance, entail engagement in corporate social responsibility. Moreover, most of the targets were aspirational, and not clearly defined with measuring, verification, and reporting frameworks. A reason for the use of informal targets might be the limited capacity in adopting and implementing standardised targets.

Reporting

Reporting of performance on meeting targets is crucial. For many Kenyan companies, reporting of climate commitments is mainly undertaken within the context of annual organizational reports. That is, there are no stand-alone reports on climate action. Moreover, climate actions are also reported within the context of CSR. Such a reporting approach is different from more established ones, whereby there is a rigorous reporting and assessment of climate action. Some of the non-state actors based in Kenya report their initiatives to global data aggregation portals. NAZSCA, for example, includes 41 companies, 2 investor firms, 24 organisations and 1 subregion.[30]

Participation in domestic and transnational initiatives

Regarding engagement in domestic and/or transnational initiatives, findings show that domestic associations are the most common way of engaging on climate change issues. This is not a surprising finding, given that most Kenyan companies belong to two main domestic business associations: the Kenya Association of Manufacturing (KAM) and the Kenya Private Sector Alliance (KEPSA). These two associations present a platform for companies to lobby and engage in climate policy.[31]

Indeed, such associations are powerful and highly effective in shaping climate policy in Kenya. When the first version of the Climate Change Bill was passed in parliament without inputs from the business community, the then president vetoed it. Only after the Bill was returned to parliament, and the business sector had been substantively engaged, did the Bill get assented to by the president to become law.[32] In the revised version, the Bill included a more comprehensive participatory process in both the design and implementation phases. The private sector has also played a substantive role in the development of the various climate regulations, often through KAM and KEPSA.[33]

Companies in Kenya have also been engaging in domestic climate initiatives. Such initiatives include policy roundtables, as well as other multi-stakeholder meetings. Moreover, companies have used their business associations to convene climate initiatives, as well as coordinating their attendance and participation in domestic climate initiatives through the associations.[34]

Transnational initiatives have also been an important locus for companies in Kenya to engage with climate change issues.[35] Participation in transnational business, sustainability and climate networks is often undertaken by about one-third of the initiatives. Only a small fraction of the companies, however, have taken up leadership roles in the initiatives. Not surprising, most of the initiatives are led by better resourced companies, mainly from the global North. Figure 6.1 presents an illustration of the main findings on how companies engage in climate action in Kenya.

6.2.2.2 Sub-national Climate Action

Despite being a novel feature in Kenya's governance landscape, County governments have become an integral actor in facilitating sub-national climate action. There are currently forty-seven (47) County governments in Kenya, and they perform a devolved policy function.[37] It is within this context that County governments have been playing an increasingly important role in promoting climate action in Kenya.[38]

It is important to note the socio-economic context within which the County governments operate. On average, half the population in Kenyan Counties lives below the poverty line—under US$1.5 a day. In addition, only 20% of the population has access to reliable energy. Viewed in this context, the developmental dimension of climate action is quite clear.

Perceived climate risks

Drought is the most significant climate risk identified by County governments. Almost all County governments identified drought as a major risk. That Kenya's economy relies on agriculture might explain the disproportionate importance attached to drought as a climate risk.[39] Extreme temperatures, which often occur concurrently with droughts, were also identified as an important climate risk.

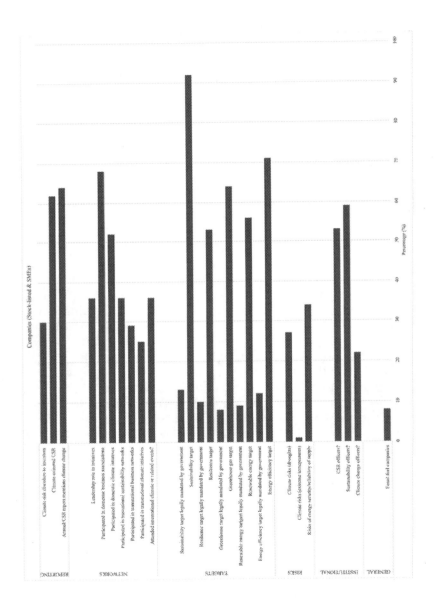

Fig. 6.1 Non-state (companies) climate action in Kenya (*Data source* ClimateSouth project)[36]

Kenya has developed several climate change regulatory instruments, as earlier noted. Climate change adaptation has been identified as the overriding policy priority in many of these regulatory instruments. In Kenya's NDC, for instance, climate change adaptation is prioritised over adaptation.[40] Also, the national government has developed a stand-alone climate change adaptation plan to tackle climate impacts. It might be therefore understood that the Counties are following national climate change policies and their attendant priorities. But it can also be argued that by focusing on climate risks that have a disproportionate impact on the economy and livelihoods, County governments are responding to their socio-economic contexts. Whatever the reason, the prevalence of drought and extreme temperatures as the main climate risks underscores the link between climate action and the socio-economic impacts within which they are implemented.

Institutional arrangements

County governments have developed various institutional arrangements related to climate governance. The most common institution established by County governance is on energy governance. Renewable energy is critical to the realisation of climate policy objectives. In Kenya, access to electricity and energy has been a key policy priority, mainly in poverty eradication. Significant efforts and resources have therefore been allocated to realise universal energy access, especially renewable energy.

More than 80% of the County governments have established energy offices. Related, more than two thirds of the Counties have empowered the energy agencies with funding and regulatory powers. In effect, this means that the energy agencies would not only be able to promote renewable energy, but also have the necessary resources to implement the programmes.

To a relatively lesser extent, County governments have also established climate change agencies/offices with funding and regulatory powers. That almost half of the County governments have a climate office/agency indicates the intent to mainstream climate change in sub-national governance. It could be argued that the County governments have established the climate agencies in response to the policy focus brought by the enactment of the national climate law and policy. But the fact that some County governments have established such an office, while others have not done so, suggests a variation in the importance of institutionalising climate governance. What is important, though, is that almost half of the County governments have such an office, even though the sub-national government has been in existence for less than a decade.

Target-setting

Targets are also an important feature of climate governance arrangements at the County level. County governments have adopted a wide array of targets and attendant policies to address climate change. Most of the local targets are mitigation focused, whereby almost all (96%) County governments have adopted the target. In a general sense, the broad adoption of the mitigation target can be understood to imply that reducing greenhouse gas emissions is an integral issue for the County governments. While the national government has often prioritised adaptation over mitigation, it may be that mitigation targets are easier to formulate than adaptation targets, especially in a quantitative manner.

Energy mitigation and land-use targets are the next most common targets adopted by County governments. As earlier noted, renewable energy is an important part of the energy mix and also climate policy, in Kenya.[41] Thus, the pursuit of universal access to energy, coupled with the promotion of renewable energy, has presented an important emissions abatement option. Also, the wide adoption of the land-use mitigation targets is in line with efforts to reduce deforestation. In technical analyses of how Kenya can meet its NDC mitigation targets, land-use planning has been identified as one of the sectors with the highest abatement potential.[42] Land-use management is also closely tied to agriculture, the mainstay of Kenya's economy.[43]

An interesting finding on the design of climate targets by the County governments is that very few of them are mandated by the national government. While there exist national climate change policies that serve as overarching legal frameworks, there are roles apportioned for the national and County governments. Most of the policies identified in the survey were voluntary, meaning that the County governments took the initiative to design, adopt and implement the policies.

Participation in domestic and transnational initiatives

County governments have participated in various domestic and transnational climate initiatives. Like the companies, County governments have been the most active in domestic associations and climate initiatives.

Indeed, Counties coordinate their policies and activities through the Council of Governance (CoG). The CoG brings together County Governors, who are the chief executives of the sub-national government. To illustrate the salience of climate policy at County government-level, the CoG organised the 2021 annual devolution conference around the theme '*Multilevel governance for climate action: Sub-National mobilisation in unlocking the full potential of climate action during and after pandemics*'.[44]

Even though the devolution conference was convened at the height of the COVID-19 pandemic, that the CoG brought together the themes of climate change and pandemic response indicates a growing importance of the former. Convening of the conference also indicates the political importance accorded to climate policy by the County governments, and the relation to other levels of government.[45]

Engagement of County governments in domestic climate initiatives has taken several forms. At the policy level, County governments have contributed to the development of national climate change policies and other regulatory instruments. In doing so, the County governments not only bring their perspectives and interests to bear, but they also take up the responsibility of implementing climate policy. Such engagement is often undertaken through the Council of Governors.

About two thirds of the County governments have engaged in transnational climate initiatives. Transnational actors such as international NGOs, international donors and think tanks, among others, have been active in the climate policy space in Kenya. After all, Kenya hosts the United Nations Environment Programme (UNEP), as well many other international organisations working on climate change and sustainability. Kenya is also a popular destination for international environmental and climate change conferences and other events. County governments thus have access to such transnational actors and initiatives, engaging on various climate policy issues.

As an example of a successful transnational partnership, consider the case of County governments working with transnational partners to establish climate change institutions. Makueni County, for instance, established a County Climate Change Fund, with support from the UK's Department for International Development (DFID) through the Adaptation Consortium—a transnational climate initiative. Moreover, in the regulation establishing the Climate Change Fund, the Steering Committee includes 'Two Representatives of Participating Development Partners; and Two Representatives of non-state financial supporters'.[46]

A few County governments, though, have also participated in international climate change governance negotiations. Some of the reasons identified for the low participation include limited financial and technical resources. Coordination of participation in international climate meetings through the Council of Governors has also meant that only a few select County government officials could attend the meetings. But the engagement of County governments in both national and international climate policy is instructive. But to be clear, participation of sub-national government officials in international climate conferences and other forums does not necessarily indicate substantive sub-national governance. Instead, the Council of Governors could be seen as an important conduit that links global and domestic climate governance.

In contrast, most of the County governments have engaged in transnational sustainability networks, thus indicating that climate policy might be perceived by these governments as a derivation of sustainable development. In many ways, this approach of placing climate action within the broader context of sustainability is consistent with the approach undertaken by the national government and the companies.

Figure 6.2 presents an overview of how County governments engage in climate policy in Kenya.

Table 6.2 presents a summary of the key findings from the analysis of non-, sub-state and transnational climate action in Kenya.

6.3   RECONCEPTUALISING NON-STATE AND TRANSNATIONAL CLIMATE GOVERNANCE

Based on the foregoing results, it is necessary to reconceptualise non-state and transnational climate action. First, it is important to close the "visibility gap".[49] As has been demonstrated in the chapter and elsewhere, there is much value in broadening the empirical base of non-state and transnational climate action. Only by having an empirical base that is truly global can we have a fuller picture of the phenomenon.

Other important issues also arise, with important implications for Africa. That many developing countries in general, and African countries in particular, submitted NDCs that explicitly frame climate action within the broader context of sustainable development brings into focus the need to examine how non-state and transnational climate actions are framed.[50]

6 THE RISE OF NON-STATE ACTORS 173

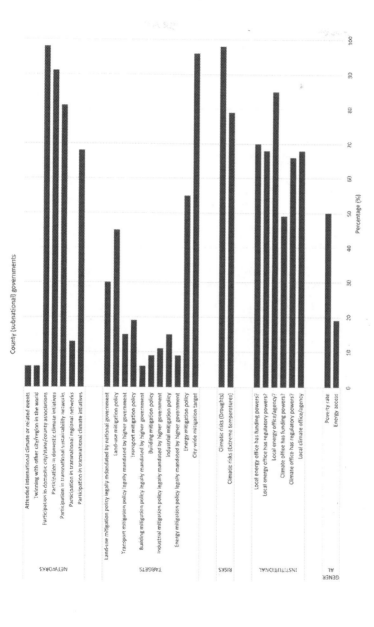

Fig. 6.2 Sub-national (County government) climate action in Kenya (*Data source* ClimateSouth project)[47]

Table 6.2 Summary of non- and sub-state climate action in Kenya

Category	Companies	County governments
Institutional	Limited institutionalisation of climate issues, but significant institutionalisation of sustainability Stock-listed companies have greater institutionalisation of their initiatives than SMEs	High institutionalisation of climate change and energy, with agencies having regulatory and funding powers
Risks	Energy security (reliability of supply) and droughts main risk identified by both stock-listed companies and SMEs	Droughts most prevalent risks, followed by extreme temperatures
Targets	Energy efficiency target, GHG target, sustainability target, and resilience targets most prevalent	County-wide mitigation targets, energy mitigation targets, and land-use mitigation targets most prevalent. Most targets not mandated by national government, showing County leadership
Networks	Participation in domestic climate activities and business associations most common; limited leadership roles in initiatives, as well as limited attendance of international climate events; participation in transnational sustainability initiatives more than climate ones Stock-listed companies engage in domestic and transnational networks more than SMEs	High participation in domestic county associations, domestic climate initiatives, transnational sustainability networks, and transnational climate initiatives

Data source ClimateSouth project[48]

In Kenya, the national government has framed its NDC within the sustainable development context. Companies and County governments in Kenya have followed the conceptual approach. It can therefore be postulated that a narrow conception of TCG is ill-suited for the global South context where development challenges persist. Framing TCG and non-state climate action within the broader sustainable development context, such as through linking Sustainable Development Goals (SDGs), is an important step forward.[51]

The prevalence of non-state and transnational climate action is a welcome development especially in light of strengthening and scaling ambitious climate action. But this very aspect also adds a layer of complexity to climate governance, raising concerns as to whether such action undermines or complements national climate action. Some cross-national studies have found that TCG initiatives are complements and not substitutes to national climate policy. Moreover, national policy contexts significantly shape TCG action.[52] Kenya's and many African countries' NDCs, for instance, include roles for NSAs in their implementation.[53] TCG, thus, adds an important dimension to the climate policy landscape, making it more complex.

Capacity is another critical issue that would determine the significance of TCG in Africa. Capacity is an important issue for non- and sub-state actors for actors in the global South to effectively participate in TCG.[54] Perhaps limited capacity could account for the limited leadership role these actors from the global South play in transnational initiatives, despite engaging in them. Combined with the "visibility gap", capacity can enhance the participation and leadership of global South actors in transnational climate initiatives.

In other African countries with a relatively less vibrant climate policy landscape, TCG could be assumed to have a less significant effect. Studies have shown that only a handful of countries in Africa have attracted a disproportionate amount of aid.[55] But this could only be one of several factors that account for the diffusion of TCGs initiatives, since networks and other actors can also contribute to the diffusion. Related, it might be that only a few African countries that have certain characteristics have vibrant TCG, non- and sub-state climate action. At a broader level, the levels of capacity might determine the extent to which transnational, non- and sub-state climate actors engage, especially in sharing information captured in aggregated portals such as NAZCA.

Alignment of transnational, non- and sub-state climate action with national climate policy is also important. Many countries have noted the importance of such actors and actions in their NDCs. A study examining how NDCs link with transnational, non- and sub-state actors showed that there was strong linkage, and developing countries were more likely to reference such actors in their NDCs. A key limitation identified by the authors, however, was that many NDCs identified the role of NSAs within and not across sectors.[56] This is an interesting finding that raises the spectre of such actors making a significant contribution to the implementation of national climate policy, pursuant to multilateral commitments especially under the Paris Agreement.[57] How such potential can be realised is an important element in understanding how such actors can enhance national, transnational and sub-national climate governance.

Whether transnational, non- and sub-state actions are effective remains an open question. That such action exists is important. But more important is whether such action is actually contributing to the broader climate policy objectives including of African countries.[58] To be sure, TCG and non- and sub-state climate action holds much promise when it is effective. But there remain challenges which undermine the full realisation of such climate action. Identifying the degree of effectiveness, as well as the gaps and opportunities for scaling such action, will be critical going forward.[59]

6.4   Conclusion

Transnational, non- and sub-state climate action is becoming an important component of international climate policy. In many ways, this novel type of climate action has transformed international climate policy. But there is much significant geographical imbalance, whereby datasets that aggregate such action mostly capture initiatives from the global North. It could be that there is much more action in the global North compared to the South. But the gap poses an important question on the extent of transnational, non- and sub-state climate action in the global South. As has been shown, just a small number of NSAs have been captured by global aggregation datasets such as NAZCA, yet the chapter has shown that there is extensive climate action being undertaken by these actors.

This chapter has examined the proliferation of transnational, non- and sub-state climate action in the global South. Focusing on companies and county (sub-national) governments in Kenya, the chapter has shown that indeed non-state climate action is prevalent especially at local level. It is however markedly different from the patterns identified especially in similar actions from the global North. In a broad sense, transnational, non- and sub-state climate action has emerged as an important dimension of climate policy. But while it holds much promise, several challenges remain that inhibit the full potential of the initiatives. Prospectively, TCG will be a critical component of climate policy in Africa, but much more research is needed to understand its extent and effectiveness. In addition, support for transnational linkages between the UNFCCC and the national and sub-national levels in Africa will be important. That notwithstanding, the rise of transnational, non- and sub-state actors has significantly transformed climate policy, and will continue doing so in the medium and long-term. Whether this transformation manifests across Africa remains an open question.

Notes

1. Liliana B. Andonova, Michele M. Betsill, and Harriet Bulkeley, 'Transnational Climate Governance', *Global Environmental Politics* 9, no. 2 (May 2009): 52–73; Harriet Bulkeley et al., *Transnational Climate Change Governance* (Cambridge: Cambridge University Press, 2014), https://doi.org/10.1017/CBO9781107706033; Thomas Hale, 'Transnational Actors and Transnational Governance in Global Environmental Politics', *Annual Review of Political Science* 23, no. 1 (2020): null, https://doi.org/10.1146/annurev-polisci-050718-032644.
2. Sander Chan, Clara Brandi, and Steffen Bauer, 'Aligning Transnational Climate Action with International Climate Governance: The Road from Paris', *Review of European, Comparative & International Environmental Law* 25, no. 2 (2016): 238–47, https://doi.org/10.1111/reel.12168; Andonova, Betsill, and Bulkeley, 'Transnational Climate Governance'; Bulkeley et al., *Transnational Climate Change Governance*; Thomas Hale and Charles Roger, 'Orchestration and Transnational Climate Governance', *The Review of International Organizations* 9, no. 1 (2014): 59–82.
3. Sander Chan et al., 'Effective and Geographically Balanced? An Output-Based Assessment of Non-state Climate Actions', *Climate Policy* 18, no. 1 (2 January 2018): 24–35, https://doi.org/10.1080/14693062.2016.1248343.
4. Clarice Wambua, 'The Kenya Climate Change Act 2016: Emerging Lessons From a Pioneer Law', *Carbon & Climate Law Review* 13, no. 4 (2019): 257–69, https://doi.org/10.21552/cclr/2019/4/6.
5. Bulkeley et al., *Transnational Climate Change Governance*.
6. Sander Chan et al., 'A Momentum for Change? Systemic Effects and Catalytic Impacts of Transnational Climate Action', *Earth System Governance* 9 (1 September 2021): 100119, https://doi.org/10.1016/j.esg.2021.100119.
7. Hale, 'Transnational Actors and Transnational Governance in Global Environmental Politics'.
8. Stephen Bell and Andrew Hindmoor, 'Governance Without Government? The Case of the Forest Stewardship Council', *Public Administration* 90, no. 1 (2012): 144–59, https://doi.org/10.1111/j.1467-9299.2011.01954.x; Axel Marx and Dieter Cuypers, 'Forest Certification as a Global Environmental Governance Tool: What Is the Macro-Effectiveness of the Forest Stewardship Council?', *Regulation & Governance* 4, no. 4

(2010): 408–34, https://doi.org/10.1111/j.1748-5991.2010.01088.x; Philipp Pattberg, 'What Role for Private Rule-Making in Global Environmental Governance? Analysing the Forest Stewardship Council (FSC)', *International Environmental Agreements: Politics, Law and Economics* 5, no. 2 (1 June 2005): 175–89, https://doi.org/10.1007/s10784-005-0951-y.

9. Jessica F. Green, *Rethinking Private Authority: Agents and Entrepreneurs in Global Environmental Governance*, Illustrated edition (Princeton: Princeton University Press, 2013).

10. Joseph S. Nye and Robert O. Keohane, 'Transnational Relations and World Politics: An Introduction', *International Organization* 25, no. 3 (1971): 329–49.

11. Bulkeley et al., *Transnational Climate Change Governance*.

12. Chan, Brandi, and Bauer, 'Aligning Transnational Climate Action with International Climate Governance'.

13. Robert Falkner, 'The Paris Agreement and the New Logic of International Climate Politics', *International Affairs* 92, no. 5 (1 September 2016): 1107–25, https://doi.org/10.1111/1468-2346.12708.

14. Thomas Hale, 'Catalytic Cooperation', *Global Environmental Politics* 20, no. 4 (1 November 2020): 73–98, https://doi.org/10.1162/glep_a_00561.

15. Thomas Hale, '"All Hands on Deck": The Paris Agreement and Nonstate Climate Action', *Global Environmental Politics* 16, no. 3 (15 July 2016): 12–22, https://doi.org/10.1162/GLEP_a_00362.

16. https://climateaction.unfccc.int/.

17. https://climate-laws.org/geographies/kenya.

18. Wambua, 'The Kenya Climate Change Act 2016'.

19. Meissy Janet Naeku, 'Climate Change Governance: An Analysis of the Climate Change Legal Regime in Kenya', *Environmental Law Review* 22, no. 3 (1 September 2020): 170–83, https://doi.org/10.1177/146145 2920958398.

20. GoK, 'Kenya's Updated Nationally Determined Contribution (NDC)' (Government of Kenya, 2020), https://www4.unfccc.int/sites/ndcsta ging/PublishedDocuments/Kenya%20First/Kenya%27s%20First%20 20NDC%20(updated%20version).pdf.

21. For a detailed overview of the ClimateSouth project through which data was collected, see Thomas Hale et al., 'Global Performance & Delivery in the Global South. Preliminary Findings of the ClimateSouth Project for the Global Climate Action Summit', GCAS Brief, Cooperative Climate Action (Oxford, UK: Global Economic Governance Programme, 10 September 2018), https://www.geg.ox.ac.uk/publication/cooperative-cli mate-action-global-performance-delivery-global-south.

22. Hale et al.

6 THE RISE OF NON-STATE ACTORS   179

23. Reuben Makomere and Kennedy Liti Mbeva, 'Squaring the Circle: Development Prospects Within the Paris Agreement', *Carbon & Climate Law Review* 12, no. 1 (2018): 31–40, https://doi.org/10.21552/cclr/2018/1/7.

24. NSE, 'Nairobi Securities Exchange ESG Disclosure Guidance Manual' (Nairobi Securities Exchange, 30 July 2021), https://sseinitiative.org/wp-content/uploads/2021/12/NSE-ESG-Disclosures-Guidance.pdf.

25. Ochieng Willis Owino et al., 'An Analytical Assessment of Climate Change Trends and Their Impacts on Hydropower in Sondu Miriu River Basin, Kenya', *African Journal of Environmental Science and Technology* 15, no. 12 (31 December 2021): 519–28, https://doi.org/10.5897/AJEST2021.3064; Feyera A. Hirpa et al., 'Finding Sustainable Water Futures in Data-Sparse Regions under Climate Change: Insights from the Turkwel River Basin, Kenya', *Journal of Hydrology: Regional Studies* 19 (1 October 2018): 124–35, https://doi.org/10.1016/j.ejrh.2018.08.005.

26. Kate Elizabeth Gannon et al., 'What Role for Multi-Stakeholder Partnerships in Adaptation to Climate Change? Experiences from Private Sector Adaptation in Kenya', *Climate Risk Management* 32 (1 January 2021): 100319, https://doi.org/10.1016/j.crm.2021.100319.

27. Monica Di Gregorio et al., 'Building Authority and Legitimacy in Transnational Climate Change Governance: Evidence from the Governors' Climate and Forests Task Force', *Global Environmental Change* 64 (1 September 2020): 102126, https://doi.org/10.1016/j.gloenvcha.2020.102126; Piero Morseletto, Frank Biermann, and Philipp Pattberg, 'Governing by Targets: Reductio Ad Unum and Evolution of the Two-Degree Climate Target', *International Environmental Agreements: Politics, Law and Economics* 17, no. 5 (1 October 2017): 655–76, https://doi.org/10.1007/s10784-016-9336-7.

28. NSE, 'Nairobi Securities Exchange ESG Disclosure Guidance Manual'.

29. UNCTAD, 'Nairobi Securities Exchange Joins United Nations Sustainable Stock Exchanges Initiative | UNCTAD', UNCTAD | Prosperity for All, 10 March 2015, https://unctad.org/news/nairobi-securities-exchange-joins-united-nations-sustainable-stock-exchanges-initiative.

30. UNFCCC, 'GCAP UNFCCC—Home Page', Global Climate Action—NAZCA, 2022, https://climateaction.unfccc.int/.

31. Lars Otto Naess et al., 'Climate Policy Meets National Development Contexts: Insights from Kenya and Mozambique', *Global Environmental Change* 35 (1 November 2015): 534–44, https://doi.org/10.1016/j.gloenvcha.2015.08.015.

32. Joseph M. Njoroge, Beate M.W. Ratter, and Lucy Atieno, 'Climate Change Policy-Making Process in Kenya: Deliberative Inclusionary Processes in Play', *International Journal of Climate Change Strategies and*

Management 9, no. 4 (1 January 2017): 535–54, https://doi.org/10.1108/IJCCSM-10-2016-0154.

33. UNDP and GoK, 'Private Sector Engagement and Coordination Framework for the Implementation of the National Climate Change Action Plan in Kenya' (New York; Nairobi: United Nations Development Program (UNDP); Government of Kenya, April 2019), https://www1.undp.org/content/dam/LECB/docs/pubs-reports/undp-ndcsp-kenya-private-sector-framework-final.pdf.

34. UNDP and GoK; Gannon et al., 'What Role for Multi-Stakeholder Partnerships in Adaptation to Climate Change?'; Lauren M. MacLean and Jennifer N. Brass, 'Foreign Aid, NGOs and the Private Sector: New Forms of Hybridity in Renewable Energy Provision in Kenya and Uganda', *Africa Today* 62, no. 1 (2015): 57–82, https://doi.org/10.2979/africatoday.62.1.57.

35. Hale et al., 'Global Performance & Delivery in the Global South. Preliminary Findings of the ClimateSouth Project for the Global Climate Action Summit'; Gannon et al., 'What Role for Multi-Stakeholder Partnerships in Adaptation to Climate Change?'.

36. Hale et al., 'Global Performance & Delivery in the Global South. Preliminary Findings of the ClimateSouth Project for the Global Climate Action Summit'.

37. Samuel Ngigi and Doreen Busolo, 'Devolution in Kenya: The Good, the Bad and the Ugly', *Public Policy and Administration Research* 9, no. 6 (2019).

38. Naeku, 'Climate Change Governance'.

39. Benjamin Kipkemboi Kogo, Lalit Kumar, and Richard Koech, 'Climate Change and Variability in Kenya: A Review of Impacts on Agriculture and Food Security', *Environment, Development and Sustainability* 23, no. 1 (1 January 2021): 23–43, https://doi.org/10.1007/s10668-020-00589-1; Jane Kabubo-Mariara and Fredrick K. Karanja, 'The Economic Impact of Climate Change on Kenyan Crop Agriculture: A Ricardian Approach', *Global and Planetary Change* 57, no. 3 (1 June 2007): 319–30, https://doi.org/10.1016/j.gloplacha.2007.01.002.

40. GoK, 'Kenya's Updated Nationally Determined Contribution (NDC)'.

41. Peter Newell et al., 'The Political Economy of Low Carbon Energy in Kenya', *IDS Working Papers* 2014, no. 445 (2014): 1–38, https://doi.org/10.1111/j.2040-0209.2014.00445.x; Mirko Dal Maso et al., 'Sustainable Development Impacts of Nationally Determined Contributions: Assessing the Case of Mini-Grids in Kenya', *Climate Policy* 20, no. 7 (8 August 2020): 815–31, https://doi.org/10.1080/14693062.2019.1644987.

42. GoK, 'Kenya: Second National Communication to the United Nations Framework Convention on Climate Change' (Government of Kenya, 2015), https://unfccc.int/sites/default/files/resource/Kennc2.pdf.

43. Aggrey Ochieng Adimo et al., 'Land Use and Climate Change Adaptation Strategies in Kenya', *Mitigation and Adaptation Strategies for Global Change* 17, no. 2 (1 February 2012): 153–71, https://doi.org/10.1007/s11027-011-9318-6; Florence Bernard et al., 'REDD + Projects and National-Level Readiness Processes: A Case Study from Kenya', *Climate Policy* 14, no. 6 (2 November 2014): 788–800, https://doi.org/10.1080/14693062.2014.905440.

44. CoG, '7th Annual Devolution Conference 2021', Maarifa Centre | Council of Governors, 23 November 2021, https://maarifa.cog.go.ke/221/7th-annual-devolution-conference-2021/.

45. Presidency, 'Speech by H.E. President Uhuru Kenyatta C.G.H. During the Official Opening of the 7TH Annual Devolution Conference in Makueni County on 24th November, 2021 | The Presidency' (Office of the President of Kenya, 24 November 2021), https://www.president.go.ke/2021/11/24/speech-by-h-e-president-uhuru-kenyatta-c-g-h-during-the-official-opening-of-the-7th-annual-devolution-conference-in-makueni-county-on-24th-november-2021/.

46. GoM, 'The Public Finance Management Act Regulations, 2015 Arrangement of Regulations | Climate Change' (Government of Makueni County, 2015), https://www.makueni.go.ke/site/files/2018/11/Makueni-County-Climate-Change-Fund-Regulations-2015.pdf.

47. Hale et al., 'Global Performance & Delivery in the Global South. Preliminary Findings of the ClimateSouth Project for the Global Climate Action Summit'.

48. Hale et al.

49. Hale et al.

50. Makomere and Mbeva, 'Squaring the Circle'.

51. Sander Chan et al., 'Climate Ambition and Sustainable Development for a New Decade: A Catalytic Framework', *Global Policy* 12, no. 3 (2021): 245–59, https://doi.org/10.1111/1758-5899.12932.

52. Liliana B. Andonova, Thomas Hale, and Charles B. Roger, 'National Policy and Transnational Governance of Climate Change: Substitutes or Complements?', *International Studies Quarterly* 61, no. 2 (1 June 2017): 253–68, https://doi.org/10.1093/isq/sqx014.

53. Angel Hsu et al., 'Exploring Links between National Climate Strategies and Non-State and Subnational Climate Action in Nationally Determined Contributions (NDCs)', *Climate Policy* 20, no. 4 (20 April 2020): 443–57, https://doi.org/10.1080/14693062.2019.1624252.

54. Sander Chan et al., 'Promises and Risks of Nonstate Action in Climate and Sustainability Governance', *Wiley Interdisciplinary Reviews: Climate Change* 10, no. 3 (2019): e572, https://doi.org/10.1002/wcc.572.
55. David Landry, 'Under a Money Tree? Comparing the Determinants of Western and Chinese Development Finance Flows to Africa', *Oxford Development Studies* 49, no. 2 (3 April 2021): 149–68, https://doi.org/10.1080/13600818.2020.1865901; Jeffery I. Round and Matthew Odedokun, 'Aid Effort and Its Determinants', *International Review of Economics & Finance*, Aid Allocations and Development Financing, 13, no. 3 (1 January 2004): 293–309, https://doi.org/10.1016/j.iref.2003.11.006.
56. Hsu et al., 'Exploring Links between National Climate Strategies and Non-State and Subnational Climate Action in Nationally Determined Contributions (NDCs)'.
57. Chan et al., 'A Momentum for Change?'.
58. Sander Chan et al., 'Reinvigorating International Climate Policy: A Comprehensive Framework for Effective Nonstate Action', *Global Policy* 6, no. 4 (2015): 466–73, https://doi.org/10.1111/1758-5899.12294.
59. Chan, Brandi, and Bauer, 'Aligning Transnational Climate Action with International Climate Governance'.

References

Adimo, Aggrey Ochieng, John Bosco Njoroge, Leaven Claessens, and Leonard S. Wamocho. 'Land Use and Climate Change Adaptation Strategies in Kenya'. *Mitigation and Adaptation Strategies for Global Change* 17, no. 2 (1 February 2012): 153–71. https://doi.org/10.1007/s11027-011-9318-6.

Andonova, Liliana B., Michele M. Betsill, and Harriet Bulkeley. May2009. Transnational Climate Governance. *Global Environmental Politics* 9 (2): 52–73.

Andonova, Liliana B., Thomas Hale, and Charles B. Roger. 'National Policy and Transnational Governance of Climate Change: Substitutes or Complements?' *International Studies Quarterly* 61, no. 2 (1 June 2017): 253–68. https://doi.org/10.1093/isq/sqx014.

Bell, Stephen, and Andrew Hindmoor. 2012. Governance Without Government? The Case of the Forest Stewardship Council. *Public Administration* 90 (1): 144–159. https://doi.org/10.1111/j.1467-9299.2011.01954.x.

Bernard, Florence, Peter A. Minang, Bryan Adkins, and Jeremy T. Freund. 'REDD+Projects and National-Level Readiness Processes: A Case Study from Kenya'. *Climate Policy* 14, no. 6 (2 November 2014): 788–800. https://doi.org/10.1080/14693062.2014.905440.

Bulkeley, Harriet, Liliana B. Andonova, Michele M. Betsill, Daniel Compagnon, Thomas Hale, Matthew J. Hoffmann, Peter Newell, Matthew Paterson, Charles Roger, and Stacy D. VanDeveer. *Transnational Climate Change Governance*. Cambridge: Cambridge University Press, 2014. https://doi.org/10.1017/CBO9781107706033.

Chan, Sander, Harro van Asselt, Thomas Hale, Kenneth W. Abbott, Marianne Beisheim, Matthew Hoffmann, Brendan Guy, et al. 'Reinvigorating International Climate Policy: A Comprehensive Framework for Effective Nonstate Action'. *Global Policy* 6, no. 4 (2015): 466–73. https://doi.org/10.1111/1758-5899.12294.

Chan, Sander, Idil Boran, Harro van Asselt, Paula Ellinger, Miriam Garcia, Thomas Hale, Lukas Hermwille, et al. 'Climate Ambition and Sustainable Development for a New Decade: A Catalytic Framework'. *Global Policy* 12, no. 3 (2021): 245–59. https://doi.org/10.1111/1758-5899.12932.

Chan, Sander, Idil Boran, Harro van Asselt, Gabriela Iacobuta, Navam Niles, Katharine Rietig, Michelle Scobie, et al. 'Promises and Risks of Nonstate Action in Climate and Sustainability Governance'. *Wiley Interdisciplinary Reviews: Climate Change* 10, no. 3 (2019): e572. https://doi.org/10.1002/wcc.572.

Chan, Sander, Clara Brandi, and Steffen Bauer. 2016. Aligning Transnational Climate Action with International Climate Governance: The Road from Paris. *Review of European, Comparative & International Environmental Law* 25 (2): 238–247. https://doi.org/10.1111/reel.12168.

Chan, Sander, Friederike Eichhorn, Frank Biermann, and Aron Teunissen. 'A Momentum for Change? Systemic Effects and Catalytic Impacts of Transnational Climate Action'. *Earth System Governance* 9 (1 September 2021): 100119. https://doi.org/10.1016/j.esg.2021.100119.

Chan, Sander, Robert Falkner, Matthew Goldberg, and Harro van Asselt. 'Effective and Geographically Balanced? An Output-Based Assessment of Non-State Climate Actions'. *Climate Policy* 18, no. 1 (2 January 2018): 24–35. https://doi.org/10.1080/14693062.2016.1248343.

CoG. '7th Annual Devolution Conference 2021'. Maarifa Centre | Council of Governors, 23 November 2021. https://maarifa.cog.go.ke/221/7th-annual-devolution-conference-2021/.

Dal Maso, Mirko, Karen Holm Olsen, Yan Dong, Mathilde Brix Pedersen, and Michael Zwicky Hauschild. 'Sustainable Development Impacts of Nationally Determined Contributions: Assessing the Case of Mini-Grids in Kenya'. *Climate Policy* 20, no. 7 (8 August 2020): 815–31. https://doi.org/10.1080/14693062.2019.1644987.

Di Gregorio, Monica, Kate Massarella, Heike Schroeder, Maria Brockhaus, and Thuy Thu Pham. 'Building Authority and Legitimacy in Transnational Climate Change Governance: Evidence from the Governors' Climate and

Forests Task Force'. *Global Environmental Change* 64 (1 September 2020): 102126. https://doi.org/10.1016/j.gloenvcha.2020.102126.

Falkner, Robert. 'The Paris Agreement and the New Logic of International Climate Politics'. *International Affairs* 92, no. 5 (1 September 2016): 1107–25. https://doi.org/10.1111/1468-2346.12708.

Gannon, Kate Elizabeth, Florence Crick, Joanes Atela, and Declan Conway. 'What Role for Multi-Stakeholder Partnerships in Adaptation to Climate Change? Experiences from Private Sector Adaptation in Kenya'. *Climate Risk Management* 32 (1 January 2021): 100319. https://doi.org/10.1016/j.crm.2021.100319.

GoK. 'Kenya: Second National Communication to the United Nations Framework Convention on Climate Change'. Government of Kenya, 2015. https://unfccc.int/sites/default/files/resource/Kennc2.pdf.

———. 'Kenya's Updated Nationally Determined Contribution (NDC)'. Government of Kenya, 2020. https://www4.unfccc.int/sites/ndcstaging/PublishedDocuments/Kenya%20First/Kenya%27s%20First%20%20NDC%20(updated%20version).pdf.

GoM. 'The Public Finance Management Act Regulations, 2015 Arrangement of Regulations | Climate Change'. Government of Makueni County, 2015. https://www.makueni.go.ke/site/files/2018/11/Makueni-County-Climate-Change-Fund-Regulations-2015.pdf.

Green, Jessica F. 2013. *Rethinking Private Authority: Agents and Entrepreneurs in Global Environmental Governance*. Illustrated. Princeton: Princeton University Press.

Hale, Thomas. '"All Hands on Deck": The Paris Agreement and Nonstate Climate Action'. *Global Environmental Politics* 16, no. 3 (15 July 2016): 12–22. https://doi.org/10.1162/GLEP_a_00362.

———. 'Catalytic Cooperation'. *Global Environmental Politics* 20, no. 4 (1 November 2020): 73–98. https://doi.org/10.1162/glep_a_00561.

———. 'Transnational Actors and Transnational Governance in Global Environmental Politics'. *Annual Review of Political Science* 23, no. 1 (2020): null. https://doi.org/10.1146/annurev-polisci-050718-032644.

Hale, Thomas, Sander Chan, Kennedy Mbeva, Manish Shrivastava, Jacopo Bencini, Victoria Chengo, Ganesh Gorti, et al. 'Global Performance & Delivery in the Global South. Preliminary Findings of the ClimateSouth Project for the Global Climate Action Summit'. GCAS Brief. Cooperative Climate Action. Oxford, UK: Global Economic Governance Programme, 10 September 2018. https://www.geg.ox.ac.uk/publication/cooperative-climate-action-global-performance-delivery-global-south.

Hale, Thomas, and Charles Roger. 2014. Orchestration and Transnational Climate Governance. *The Review of International Organizations* 9 (1): 59–82.

Hirpa, Feyera A., Ellen Dyer, Rob Hope, Daniel O. Olago, and Simon J. Dadson. 'Finding Sustainable Water Futures in Data-Sparse Regions under Climate Change: Insights from the Turkwel River Basin, Kenya'. *Journal of Hydrology: Regional Studies* 19 (1 October 2018): 124–35. https://doi.org/10.1016/j.ejrh.2018.08.005.

Hsu, Angel, John Brandt, Oscar Widerberg, Sander Chan, and Amy Weinfurter. 'Exploring Links between National Climate Strategies and Non-State and Subnational Climate Action in Nationally Determined Contributions (NDCs)'. *Climate Policy* 20, no. 4 (20 April 2020): 443–57. https://doi.org/10.1080/14693062.2019.1624252.

Kabubo-Mariara, Jane, and Fredrick K. Karanja. 'The Economic Impact of Climate Change on Kenyan Crop Agriculture: A Ricardian Approach'. *Global and Planetary Change* 57, no. 3 (1 June 2007): 319–30. https://doi.org/10.1016/j.gloplacha.2007.01.002.

Kogo, Benjamin Kipkemboi, Lalit Kumar, and Richard Koech. 'Climate Change and Variability in Kenya: A Review of Impacts on Agriculture and Food Security'. *Environment, Development and Sustainability* 23, no. 1 (1 January 2021): 23–43. https://doi.org/10.1007/s10668-020-00589-1.

Landry, David. 'Under a Money Tree? Comparing the Determinants of Western and Chinese Development Finance Flows to Africa'. *Oxford Development Studies* 49, no. 2 (3 April 2021): 149–68. https://doi.org/10.1080/13600818.2020.1865901.

MacLean, Lauren M., and Jennifer N. Brass. 2015. Foreign Aid, NGOs and the Private Sector: New Forms of Hybridity in Renewable Energy Provision in Kenya and Uganda. *Africa Today* 62 (1): 57–82. https://doi.org/10.2979/africatoday.62.1.57.

Makomere, Reuben, and Kennedy Liti Mbeva. 'Squaring the Circle: Development Prospects Within the Paris Agreement'. *Carbon & Climate Law Review* 12, no. 1 (2018): 31–40. https://doi.org/10.21552/cclr/2018/1/7.

Marx, Axel, and Dieter Cuypers. 2010. Forest Certification as a Global Environmental Governance Tool: What Is the Macro-Effectiveness of the Forest Stewardship Council? *Regulation & Governance* 4 (4): 408–434. https://doi.org/10.1111/j.1748-5991.2010.01088.x.

Naeku, Meissy Janet. 'Climate Change Governance: An Analysis of the Climate Change Legal Regime in Kenya'. *Environmental Law Review* 22, no. 3 (1 September 2020): 170–83. https://doi.org/10.1177/1461452920958398.

Naess, Lars Otto, Peter Newell, Andrew Newsham, Jon Phillips, Julian Quan, and Thomas Tanner. 'Climate Policy Meets National Development Contexts: Insights from Kenya and Mozambique'. *Global Environmental Change* 35 (1 November 2015): 534–44. https://doi.org/10.1016/j.gloenvcha.2015.08.015.

Newell, Peter, Jon Phillips, Ana Pueyo, Edith Kirumba, Nicolas Ozor, and Kevin Urama. 'The Political Economy of Low Carbon Energy in Kenya'. *IDS Working Papers* 2014, no. 445 (2014): 1–38. https://doi.org/10.1111/j.2040-0209.2014.00445.x.

Ngigi, Samuel, and Doreen Busolo. 'Devolution in Kenya: The Good, the Bad and the Ugly'. *Public Policy and Administration Research* 9, no. 6 (2019).

Njoroge, Joseph M., Beate M.W. Ratter, and Lucy Atieno. 'Climate Change Policy-Making Process in Kenya: Deliberative Inclusionary Processes in Play'. *International Journal of Climate Change Strategies and Management* 9, no. 4 (1 January 2017): 535–54. https://doi.org/10.1108/IJCCSM-10-2016-0154.

NSE. 'Nairobi Securities Exchange ESG Disclosure Guidance Manual'. Nairobi Securities Exchange, 30 July 2021. https://sseinitiative.org/wp-content/upl oads/2021/12/NSE-ESG-Disclosures-Guidance.pdf.

Nye, Joseph S., and Robert O. Keohane. 1971. Transnational Relations and World Politics: An Introduction. *International Organization* 25 (3): 329–349.

Owino, Ochieng Willis, Oludhe Christopher, Dulo Simeon, and Olaka Lydia. 'An Analytical Assessment of Climate Change Trends and Their Impacts on Hydropower in Sondu Miriu River Basin, Kenya'. *African Journal of Environmental Science and Technology* 15, no. 12 (31 December 2021): 519–28. https://doi.org/10.5897/AJEST2021.3064.

Pattberg, Philipp. 'What Role for Private Rule-Making in Global Environmental Governance? Analysing the Forest Stewardship Council (FSC)'. *International Environmental Agreements: Politics, Law and Economics* 5, no. 2 (1 June 2005): 175–89. https://doi.org/10.1007/s10784-005-0951-y.

Piero Morseletto, Frank Biermann, and Philipp Pattberg. 'Governing by Targets: Reductio Ad Unum and Evolution of the Two-Degree Climate Target'. *International Environmental Agreements: Politics, Law and Economics* 17, no. 5 (1 October 2017): 655–76. https://doi.org/10.1007/s10784-016-9336-7.

Presidency. 'Speech by H.E. President Uhuru Kenyatta C.G.H. During the Official Opening of the 7TH Annual Devolution Conference in Makueni County on 24th November, 2021 | The Presidency'. Office of the President of Kenya, 24 November 2021. https://www.president.go.ke/2021/11/24/speech-by-h-e-president-uhuru-kenyatta-c-g-h-during-the-official-opening-of-the-7th-annual-devolution-conference-in-makueni-county-on-24th-nov ember-2021/.

Round, Jeffery I., and Matthew Odedokun. 'Aid Effort and Its Determinants'. *International Review of Economics & Finance, Aid Allocations and Development Financing* 13, no. 3 (1 January 2004): 293–309. https://doi.org/10.1016/j.iref.2003.11.006.

UNCTAD. 'Nairobi Securities Exchange Joins United Nations Sustainable Stock Exchanges Initiative | UNCTAD'. UNCTAD | Prosperity for All, 10 March 2015. https://unctad.org/news/nairobi-securities-exchange-joins-united-nations-sustainable-stock-exchanges-initiative.

UNDP, and GoK. 'Private Sector Engagement and Coordination Framework for the Implementation of the National Climate Change Action Plan in Kenya'. New York; Nairobi: United Nations Development Program (UNDP); Government of Kenya, April 2019. https://www1.undp.org/content/dam/LECB/docs/pubs-reports/undp-ndcsp-kenya-private-sector-framework-final.pdf.

UNFCCC. 'GCAP UNFCCC—Home Page'. Global Climate Action—NAZCA, 2022. https://climateaction.unfccc.int/.

Wambua, Clarice. 'The Kenya Climate Change Act 2016: Emerging Lessons From a Pioneer Law'. *Carbon & Climate Law Review* 13, no. 4 (2019): 257–69. https://doi.org/10.21552/cclr/2019/4/6.

CHAPTER 7

Emergent Climate-Related Policy Issues

As the preceding chapters have demonstrated, the international climate regime has rapidly evolved and is increasingly characterised by complexity. In addition to the main drivers of the complexity identified in the chapters, there are recent and emergent policy developments that will continue to increase the complexity of the regime. Moreover, these policy developments are irreversible, thus leading to continued evolution of the regime. While some of the policy developments might pose strategic challenges, others would open up novel opportunities for realising both development and climate goals in Africa.

This chapter examines these recent and emergent policy developments, and how they will make the international climate change regime more complex and drive it further away from equilibrium. It shall be argued that these policy developments need to be included in the long-run analysis of international climate cooperation by African countries. While it is difficult, and almost impossible, to accurately predict the future, it would be prudent for policy makers and scholars alike to acknowledge and embrace the growing complexity of the international climate regime, albeit from a different conceptual vantage point. Doing so would open possibilities for creating policy choices that would otherwise pose major challenges if not anticipated and dealt with in advance. In other words, scholars and policy

© The Author(s), under exclusive license to Springer Nature   189
Switzerland AG 2023
K. Mbeva et al., *Africa's Right to Development in a Climate-Constrained World*, Contemporary African Political Economy,
https://doi.org/10.1007/978-3-031-22887-2_7

makers have to perceive international climate policy as one characterised by dynamism, complexity and disequilibrium.

7.1 Long-Run Policy Developments

While the catalytic climate regime ushered in by the Paris Agreement has been celebrated as a major global policy win, its inception marked a significant change for Africa's engagement with the regime.[1] By adopting a catalytic logic, where actors' preferences are shifted towards a desired common outcome over time, the Paris Agreement embraced a dynamic and evolutionary approach.[2] But its catalytic effect also means that it is meant to stimulate similar developments in climate-related policies.

As a consequence, the international climate change regime will only become more complex. In principle, such a consequence is good, as climate change is a 'super wicked' problem. Hence, all relevant policies can contribute to addressing the problem. But complexity also brings to the fore challenges of harnessing and navigating it. For African countries of which many still struggle with numerous other policy challenges, increasing policy complexity can pose an additional challenge.

In the analysis of long-run international climate cooperation, anticipating and dealing with emerging and frontier policy issues is critical. What is important in such a situation is not necessarily finding a solution to all the policy challenges, but the shifting the conceptual approach to the challenge. In this context, the following sections will outline some of the emerging climate-related policy issues, as well as the challenges and opportunities they present. To be clear, African countries have already begun taking steps to address some of these policy developments, for example by developing initiatives such as the AU Climate Change and Resilient Development Strategy and Action Plan to guide, coordinate and support the Continent's response to Climate Change for the period 2022–2032.[3] To address the more recent challenge of the COVID-19 pandemic, African countries have adopted the African Union Green Recovery Action Plan 2021–2027.[4] What this chapter seeks to do is to identify these policy challenges, and not to necessarily assess the adequacy of African countries' responses to them.

7.2 Strategic Challenges

7.2.1 The Tightening Vice of Climate Ambition

A key innovation of the Paris Agreement on Climate Change was the inclusion of a ratchet mechanism.[5] The ratchet mechanism ensures that countries submit more ambitious successive NDCs every five years, with the aim of reaching global targets. That is, the Paris Agreement is based on a pledge-review-ratchet mechanism. Conceptually, this approach means that countries would also have to submit more ambitious NDCs over time, especially to meet the global temperate goal of keeping global warming below two degrees Celsius, with an aspirational target of 1.5 degrees Celsius. A convergence of NDCs towards a common global target sets in motion, for the first time, a harmonisation of domestic climate mitigation targets. This is clearly a stark departure from the bifurcated approach, whereby industrialised countries would undertake the significant bulk of the mitigation effort, as well as provide resources to developing countries. Put differently, the Paris Agreement abandoned the static equilibrium approach of bifurcation, in favour of a catalytic logic that is characterised by disequilibrium given its evolutionary dynamic. The ratchet mechanism, therefore, presents what can be termed as *a tightening vice of ambition*. For African countries, whose total emissions are about four per cent of the global emissions, the tightening vice of ambition would significantly reduce the scope for future emissions.[6]

Raising ambition through rapid and deeper emission reduction cuts poses a major challenge for African countries. If African countries are to rapidly reduce their emissions, they would also need to commit more material resources. That is why most African countries' NDCs have a conditionality component.[7] Conditionality means that African countries would only commit to more ambitious climate action only if they receive the requisite eternal support for means of implementation (MoI) such as through transfers of climate finance, technology and capacity building. But the past decades of MoI support under the UNFCCC and its various legal instruments have shown that African countries have received a miniscule amount of the support.[8] Thus, the requirement of raising climate ambition and the inadequate MoI support are conceptually incongruent.

That African countries have made their NDCs conditional on external MoI support, even though the Paris Agreement includes provisions for support, indicates their reluctance and the effect of the tightening vice of ambition. In Eastern Africa, for instance, of the eleven updated NDCs, only Tanzania has a fully conditional NDC; the rest of the NDCs include more significant aspects of self-financing. By extrapolation, African countries would have to commit more of their resources in their contribution to global climate action as they strengthen their NDCs. Already, some of the African countries are struggling with implementing their first NDC. Consider the case of Chad, whose challenge to implement their overly ambitious NDC was articulated by one of their key climate policy makers who expressed buyer's remorse, and noted that their country had committed to significant emissions reductions while not addressing broader sustainable development challenges.[9] In its updated NDC, Chad only included a more modest target of 19.3% emissions reduction against the Business as Usual (BAU) trend.[10]

7.2.2 Divestment and Fossil Fuel Extraction

African countries find themselves in a dilemma where, on the one hand, the emissions reduction targets they have adopted would drastically reduce the scope of future emissions. But, on the other hand, the present and future energy mix of many African countries includes the extraction of fossil fuels, given that investments are a critical element of the energy infrastructure and industrialisation. In recent years, however, there has been a big push to shift investments away from fossil fuels.[11] Given impetus by students in their universities, divestment from fossil fuels has grown to a powerful transnational movement.[12] The idea behind divestment is a simple one. Its ethical foundation is that investing in climate-damaging fuels is untenable, hence the need to move investments from fossil fuels to renewable and clean energy.[13]

Divestment movements initially focused on universities, where students sought to pressure leadership to divest the significant investments of endowment funds from fossil fuels.[14] Over time, the divestment movement has grown to include other civil society and religious groups. The Vatican, which is a major religious institution, has deemed divestment from fossil fuels as a moral imperative.[15] Other major entities such as national sovereign wealth funds, including the Norwegian fund which is the largest in the world, have also pledged to divest from fossil fuels.[16] Major financial markets have also joined the efforts to divest from fossil fuels. Activist shareholders, who are concerned about climate change, are also pressuring their respective companies to divest from fossil fuels.[17]

7 EMERGENT CLIMATE-RELATED POLICY ISSUES   193

At the international policy level, divestment has also gained much traction.[18] Earlier this year, the International Energy Agency (IEA), which is an intergovernmental institution, released a roadmap that detailed the need for the countries to rapidly divest from fossil fuels.[19] The IEA's authoritative analysis added much impetus to the divestment movement especially in the energy sector.[20]

Divestment presents a significant challenge to African countries in various ways. In a bid to power its industrialisation, African countries have been prospecting fossil fuel reserves, with great success.[21] Many of the countries have engaged foreign multinational companies to prospect and develop the fossil fuel reserves. But divestment poses a major challenge, as the divestment movement seeks to starve these companies of the necessary capital to carry out the exploitation of fossil fuels. It is, therefore, questionable whether African countries can fully exploit their fossil fuel reserves given the structural pressures from divestment.[22]

Moreover, as more African countries are discovering huge fossil fuel reserves, especially oil and gas, the push for divestment from fossil fuels poses other a major challenges. Should African countries forego the new found resources, or should they use them to improve human development? For these countries, many of which have limited resources, exploiting the fossil fuels would provide additional revenues which can be used to fund development projects. But since a bulk of the technical knowledge and funding for fossil fuel exploitation comes from overseas, especially from countries where the domestic push for divestment is significant, it is not guaranteed that African countries will have the necessary capacity to fully exploit the fossil fuel resources. Also, China, which is Africa's development partner and main financier of infrastructure projects, has committed to stop funding overseas coal projects. It is, therefore, clear that the push for divestment from fossil fuels will impact Africa's ability to exploit its fossil fuel resources.

7.2.3   Climate-Related Trade Measures

Much of multilateral climate cooperation has been based on consensus building and voluntary, non-punitive compliance.[23] The non-punitive compliance mechanism of the Paris Agreement is testament to this approach, especially when contrasted with the more punitive third-party dispute settlement mechanism of the World Trade Organization

(WTO).[24] A long-standing norm of compliance in international environmental cooperation has been the avoidance of sanctions and other punitive tools. Trade restrictions have been the focus of such debates, given their potency. Only in addressing exceptional transboundary environmental problems such as ozone depletion and illegal trafficking of wildlife have trade restrictions been embraced as a viable and preferred compliance and enforcement policy tool.

Coercive policy instruments have thus been largely avoided in international climate cooperation.[25] But this is now changing. Trade-restrictive measures have been one such controversial climate policy measure in debates on how to enhance climate action.[26] The logic behind trade-restrictive measures is that they make access to export markets conditional on meeting certain environmental and climate change standards. The European Union (EU), a major economic power and export market, recently announced a Carbon Border Adjustment Mechanism (CBAM).[27] Imports into the EU from countries deemed to have lower climate change standards would be taxed at the European Borders. The US is also considering a CBAM akin to that of the EU.[28]

As one could predict, the EU CBAM generated much controversy and was rejected by many developing countries.[29] CBAMs are controversial in that they seek to level national climate change standards; contrast this with the international climate change regime which is premised on the heterogeneity of national climate change standards.[30] Such trade-restrictive policy tools are also controversial in the sense that they can undermine equity, especially for least developed and other vulnerable countries. Furthermore, if the sanctions are levied by major polluters against vulnerable countries, the equity and justice concerns are more acute.

CBAM poses a major challenge for African countries. Given that the EU is a major export market for African countries, exports from the continent would be subject to the CBAM once it comes into effect.[31] This would be akin to equalising EU and African countries' climate standards, a proposition that would be outrightly rejected were it proposed under the auspices of multilateral climate change negotiations. Moreover, for African countries that do not yet have adequate technology that would meet the EU requirements, the CBAM presents a major challenge to industrialisation in the continent. Exporters to the EU would thus have to incur increased compliance costs.[32] Moreover, continental industrialisation powered by fossil fuels would be heavily penalised under CBAMs and other carbon border measures.

Developments in continental trade policy would also have significant impacts on climate policy in Africa. The adoption of AfCFTA marked a major milestone in continental economic integration in Africa. But that AfCFTA does not include provisions on climate change commitments is of major interest. Given the rising salience of linking free trade agreements with climate policy goals, AfCFTA's 'silence' on climate policy is striking.[33] Even considering the broader environmental policy issue, AfCFTA only includes provisions in its preamble that acknowledge the right of signatories to regulate environmental issues at the domestic level.[34]

7.2.4 *Transformative Structural Climate Targets*

A related economic development is the rise in the importance of transformative climate targets based on market forces. Consumers in major economies are exercising their market power to foster greater sustainability.[35] By demanding imported products that adhere to high climate standards, these consumers are shaping markets and forcing exporters to integrate climate change considerations into their exports.[36]

Another major development that has significantly shaped markets, but also national climate change policy, is the adoption of net zero targets.[37] The global net zero target, as enshrined in the Paris Agreement, requires countries to absorb more greenhouse gases than they emit.[38] A wave of adoption of net zero national targets has unfolded over the past few years.[39] As at the time of writing, 131 countries representing 88% of global emissions and 90% of the GDP, and 85% of the global population have adopted or are considering adopting a net zero target.[40] Net zero flips the logic of differentiated multilateral climate change cooperation on its head by ensuring that countries are converging towards a common climate standard. Many countries are also not on target to meet their NDC commitments, thus suggesting that greater climate ambition would be needed to meet these targets.[41]

Sub-state and non-state actors have also taken up net zero targets, especially the private sector.[42] Adoption of the net zero targets especially by the private sector will unleash a significant transformation of the global market, including critical supply chains. It may also catalyse the push towards enshrining voluntary net zero targets in policy and law in the form of regulatory standards.[43] Intergovernmental organisations such as the IEA, as earlier mentioned, have developed detailed global net zero roadmaps. By developing a global energy roadmap for net zero, the IEA has set an important international climate policy benchmark, as this will significantly shape energy policies across the globe. It is also a clear policy signal that the continued exploitation of fossil fuels is untenable.

African countries are currently grappling with how to handle the sustainability standards and net zero challenge. Almost all African countries (50) have adopted a long-term emissions reduction target, thus setting in motion the structural transformation towards the global net zero goal.[44] An emerging theme is the need to ensure Africa's divergent globalisation, especially through regional economic integration, is compatible with global climate goals. Net zero is, therefore, not a preserve of industrialised countries, but a major climate policy tool whose transnational consequences will be significant, especially for African countries. The implications of the long-term climate targets on the development prospects of the continent also remain an open question.

7.2.5 Proliferation of Anti-Fossil Fuel Norms

Another strategic challenge for African countries is the proliferation of anti-fossil fuel norms. Initially confined to industrialised countries with the intention of turning the public opinion against fossil fuels, anti-fossil fuel norms have now proliferated.[45] As a consequence, exploitation of fossil fuels in African countries would face significant opposition should the anti-fossil fuel norms take hold in the continent.

Consider the example of the highly controversial proposed coal power plant in Kenya. Backed by the national government and other actors, the coal plant was set to be built in Lamu, which hosts a pristine marine ecosystem. Much of the opposition came from Lamu citizens, and their national counterparts and other transnational actors lobbied for the project to be abandoned. Public pressure and opinion, opposition from Kenya's Ministry of Environment prevailed, backed by a court ruling stopping the project on environmental grounds, converged, and the coal power plant project was abandoned.[46]

A youth-led climate movement has also grown across the African continent.[47] Led by youth, these movements are promoting anti-fossil fuel norms, targeting in particular initiatives that aim to exploit significant fossil fuel reserves. Should public opinion drawing on anti-fossil fuel norms prevail, further exploitation of fossil fuel reserves in the continent will prove challenging.

7.2.6 Nexus Policy Issues

Other emergent global challenges have also had a significant impact on climate policy. Most recently, the COVID-19 pandemic, which shut down the entire world, is the most salient example. Only a century ago was there a pandemic that affected a significant proportion of the global population—the Spanish flu. In a globalised and highly interconnected world, pandemics can spread very rapidly, as the COVID-19 pandemic did.

In contrast to slow onset events like global climate change, pandemics unravel rapidly, requiring urgent political attention. Moreover, the impacts of pandemics are immediate, thus necessitating urgent policy responses. In many ways, the world over has struggled to contain the pandemic. But as the pandemic unfolds, it is becoming apparent that its impacts will not only be on public health. Spillover effects of the pandemic are already manifesting, including on climate change. For Africa, the impacts of the pandemic, coupled with the impacts of vaccine inequity, are disproportionate.

In the medium and long run, COVID-19 will have a significant impact on climate policy in Africa in several ways. For many African countries, resource constraints have been a persistent challenge. When the pandemic struck, many African countries had to quickly re-allocate public funds to support the attendant policy response measures. Given the scarcity of resources, the funds had to be diverted from other policy issues. Public health policy measures such as securing vaccines, purchasing personal protective equipment (PPE) and also securing vaccines have drained the public coffers of African governments. In the medium and longer term, African countries will find it challenging to allocate sufficient resources to implement their increasingly ambitious NDCs. But the "all of society" approach adopted by African countries, especially on implementation, would broaden the scope of climate action.

An immediate impact of the pandemic has been the shutting down of economies to contain the spread of the virus. Governments injected billions and even trillions of dollars to their economies to stimulate them as they began emerging out of the lockdown. Attempts have been made to tie the economic recovery packages with other policy objectives, including on climate change.[48] While some governments have managed to do so, many others haven't made the connection. The expected synergy of addressing other policy challenges while responding to the pandemic has not been fully realised.[49] African countries have already made the policy connection, as outlined in the African Union Green Recovery Action Plan (2021–2027).[50]

Data collected through various initiatives tracking COVID-19 recovery spending have highlighted the disconnect between pandemic response and other policy issues, especially climate change. As one prominent estimate has shown, only about thirty per cent (30%) of recovery spending has been earmarked for 'green policies' in general, equating to 0.97 trillion dollars of the 3.11 Trillion dollars spent on pandemic recovery. In Africa, the disconnect is acute.

In addition to leading to reallocation of precious public resources, the COVID-19 pandemic has also exacerbated debt distress, especially in Africa. Prior to the pandemic, debt distress had been a major challenge, as many African countries borrowed significant amounts of funds to finance infrastructure and support domestic public expenditure.[51] But as these countries were finding it increasingly difficult to service the debt, they also allocated scarce resources that could have been used to address other development challenges.[52] Thus when the pandemic hit, many of these countries were faced with a double dilemma—should they continue paying the debts or should they re-allocate domestic resources to addressing the pandemic? Zambia's debt default in 2020 raised concerns that other African countries would also default on their loans, especially given the adverse impacts of the pandemic on the economies of African countries.[53]

To address this dilemma, some multilateral initiatives have been suggested. The most prominent initiative has been to link debt relief with climate policy, in particular through the International Monetary Fund, which is the lender of last resort.[54] In restructuring the debt repayment, the IMF would be implementing its infamous structural adjustment programme, albeit this time with a climate policy dimension. Climate-debt swaps, which have long been suggested, have also been revisited as a way of simultaneously dealing with the pandemic-induced debt distress and climate action.[55]

African countries will, therefore, continue to face the long-term impacts of alleviating debt distress while also strengthening their climate commitments especially through their NDCs. While it is not clear whether this will be accomplished, it is evident that the debt distress, which has been exacerbated by the COVID-19 pandemic, has added another layer of complexity to climate policy in Africa. If the synergy is harnessed, it can simultaneously lead to enhanced climate action and reduced debt distress. But if left unaddressed, a prolonged debt distress could end up undermining the case realisation of more ambitious climate policy in Africa. The adoption of the African Union Green Recovery Action Plan (2021–2027) lays a policy foundation in addressing this issue.[56]

7.3 Strategic Opportunities

The aforementioned challenges notwithstanding, there are significant opportunities that Africa can harness. This section explores some of these opportunities, which would in principle entail leveraging the emerging policy developments to also enhance climate action in Africa. What is apparent, though, is that while the emerging strategic opportunities are adding to the complexity of climate policy, they also provide important new policy avenues to enhance climate action. As Prigogine aptly noted on the opportunities for novelty that are opened up by the transition from one phase to another,

> If we turn now to discuss large, nonlinearly interacting systems that are maintained far from...equilibrium, then we find that the bifurcating solutions...can lead to the appearance of a wealth of possible new structures and organizations. When bifurcation occurs, then the stability of the existing state of the system breaks down, allowing the amplification of some small, random fluctuation to occur and to carry the system off to one of the possible, new branches of solution.[57]

7.3.1 Renewable and Clean Energy Supply Chains

There is also a rapid global shift towards renewable energy. A critical component of decarbonisation and the transition to a low-carbon economy will depend on the deployment of large-scale renewable energy. As the cost of technologies such as wind and solar keep falling, the technologies are becoming more ubiquitous and accessible, the transition to a climate-compatible society has been gaining momentum. Or as has been well noted, we are now in the age of exponential innovation.[58]

Africa is well positioned to take advantage of the accessible clean technologies especially in its large energy infrastructure projects. Several clean energy mega projects have been implemented in the continent, including geothermal, solar and wind power plants.[59] Countries such as Kenya, which are endowed with significant geothermal energy, have managed to develop a clean energy grid. Moreover, Kenya has been able to export geothermal power. Inefficient cooking systems, which primarily rely on biomass, are also a major challenge.[60] As such, the significant energy infrastructure gap indeed offers an important opportunity to build a clean energy infrastructure in Africa.[61]

Another important strategic opportunity for Africa is to contribute to the global decarbonisation and renewable energy efforts through the provision of the necessary critical materials. Endowed with significant amounts of critical minerals necessary for clean and renewable energy, African countries stand to benefit from this transformation.[62] Already, there is a geopolitical race to secure the critical minerals, with Africa being the centre stage given its significant share of minerals.[63]

Harnessing the global value chains for renewable energy would be a critical opportunity for African countries. Many industrialised and emerging countries are transforming their grids to generate energy from renewable energy. In addition, the rapid adoption of electric cars has generated significant demand for the critical minerals necessary to produce the batteries and other components.[64] Cobalt, for instance, is one of the central critical minerals in the development of batteries that power electric cars and other appliances. Congo accounts for about seventy per cent (70%) of cobalt reserves, thus illustrating the geopolitical importance of how the country engages with the supply chain.[65]

Tapping into the supply chains will be necessary but insufficient. African countries would also need to move up the global value chains, especially by linking industrialisation with the emerging clean and renewable energy markets and trends.[66] Some African countries are already positioning themselves to be suppliers of materials necessary for decarbonisation. Heavy industry, especially the production of steel and aluminium, has been a major source of greenhouse gas emissions, as they have relied on coal to run their furnaces and kilns. Since abatement costs for the heavy industries have been very high, transitioning to cleaner energy for such sectors has been challenging. But the emergence of hydrogen has raised interest since it is a cheaper and reliable substitute to coal. Also, the promise of hydrogen has generated much geopolitical interest.[67]

South Africa and Namibia have emerged as potential early adopters of using hydrogen fuel to produce steel and aluminium. Namibia is positioning itself as one of the ideal locations for the production of hydrogen fuel.[68] South Africa is also exploring using hydrogen to ensure its position as a manufacturing powerhouse in Africa and beyond. South Africa's consideration of hydrogen fuelled steel and aluminium production has also been clearly linked with the strategic opportunity of decarbonisation.[69] Given that many African countries are keen on scaling industrialisation in anticipation of accessing the continental and global markets, adopting clean energy would be important. Also, options such as hydrogen energy would be useful in developing an industrial base built on clean energy. An added benefit of such heavy industry clean energy would be the exclusion of industries in Africa using such energy from trade measures such as CBAM.[70] Regional linkage of energy infrastructure across the African continent could also power the growing industrial base in Africa.[71]

7.3.2   Continental Just Transition

African countries have traditionally sought equity, justice and fairness at the multilateral level, including on climate change.[72] Through lesser obligations and pledges for support through means of implementation, African countries have been successful in securing the inclusion of these normative concerns into multilateral agreements.[73] But the realisation of these commitments has not been forthcoming. That African countries only accounted for less than three per cent of the allocations of the Clean Development Mechanism of the Kyoto Protocol is illustrative of this challenge.[74]

In light of the aforementioned challenges, it would be prudent for African countries to consider a continental strategy for a just transition. Such a plan would include mitigating the effects of stranded fossil fuel assets and securing resources for the transition to a climate friendly future. Countries such as Norway and some of the Gulf States have demonstrated the importance of investing the proceeds from fossil fossils into sovereign wealth funds (SWFs) that are a social safety net and insurance policy.[75] African countries such as Ghana have also adopted a similar approach.[76] Reducing reliance on multilateral appeals and developing endogenous institutional arrangements to shield African countries would be a viable solution.

Some African countries have already started securing their just transition. In a clear departure from multilateral appeals for support, South Africa engaged some of the major industrialised countries to access finance, technology and capacity to transform the country's electricity grid. Termed as the 'Just Energy Transition Partnership', the initiative 'aims to accelerate the decarbonisation of South Africa's economy, with a focus on the electricity system, to help it achieve the ambitious goals set out in its updated Nationally Determined Contribution emissions goals'.[77] Based on seed funding of US$ 8.5 billion dollars, the partnership will support South Africa's decarbonisation efforts while, crucially, also ensuring a just transition. The justice dimension is important, as it brings into focus the concerns of marginalised and vulnerable groups in a practical manner. South Africa is indeed an outlier in Africa, given its disproportionate economic power, reliance of its energy grid on coal and incessant power cuts, but its approach to just transition offers an important heuristic for other African countries.[78]

7.3.3   Aligning Regional Integration with Climate Policy

At a time when economic globalisation has slowed and is even being reversed, African countries have taken a divergent approach. The recent adoption of the landmark Africa continental free trade agreement (AfCFTA) is indicative of this shift. It is also a bold indication of Africa's shift towards self-reliance and industrialisation.[79] Africa is thus charting its divergent globalisation in a world that is rapidly deglobalising.[80] At the broader policy level, the adoption of the landmark African Union Agenda 2063 marked a major milestone in orienting Africa's development trajectory.

But in a world where economic policy is being increasingly constrained by climate change considerations, African countries would have to seriously consider the implications of ambitious climate policy. While climate and development policy can go hand in hand, the rapid transformation of the international climate policy regime poses significant challenges, such as those dealing with stranded fossil fuel assets. But a closer and pragmatic alignment between climate and development policy could alleviate some of those challenges, and even open up important strategic opportunities. Coordination at the continental and sub-regional levels is especially important.

Some of the regional bodies in Africa have already taken up this challenge, especially at the continental level, the African Union.[81] To ensure political momentum at the highest levels, the Meeting of the Committee of African Heads of State and Government on Climate Change (CAHOSCC) coordinates climate cooperation among African countries.[82] At the sub-regional level, the East African Community (EAC), for instance, has adopted a suite of regional climate policy tools and developed the attendant institutions. These regional arrangements include a draft climate change law, a climate change policy, master plan, climate change fund and a climate change department at the EAC Secretariat.[83] By including climate policy and cooperation into regional cooperation, the EAC and its partner countries have opened up strategic opportunities, such as establishing a regional climate change fund.[84]

Other regional institutions such as the African Development Bank (AfDB) have been active in promoting climate action in the continent.[85] As a pan-African bank, the AfDB is instrumental in funding continental projects, especially on infrastructure. The AfDB bank has established an Africa Climate Change Fund, and it also engages in multilateral climate change negotiations.[86] Given its importance, the AfDB presents an important coordinating platform for the continent. A key challenge for the bank, however, will be to reconcile the funding of fossil fuel projects as it invests in renewable energy projects in the continent. Other regional platforms such as the New Partnership for African Development (NEPAD)—which has since been upgraded to the AUDA-NEPAD—have primarily focused on climate change adaptation, and can provide an important coordination platform to reconcile climate and development policy, as it is also a crucial institution in supporting regional integration. In particular, the AUDA-NEPAD can leverage its formidable peer review mechanism to promote coordination.[87]

In the long run, the political momentum towards continental economic integration can be harnessed to promote climate policy. While such linkage is rhetorically simple, its implementation will be challenging. Viewing the alignment of the two policies in a longer time horizon, especially within the context of a rapidly changing international climate change regime, will be important.

7.3.4 Reconsidering Multilateral Cooperation

Due to the impacts of the Paris Agreement, multilateral cooperation now primarily plays a coordination more than a regulatory role. Moreover, the proliferation of other policy levers and developments means that climate policy is not solely developed under the auspices of the UNFCCC.[88] It is true that the Paris Agreement has a compliance mechanism, but it has been designed to be non-punitive and facilitative.[89] For African countries, the Paris Agreement should be viewed as a focal point for coordinating their climate policies. Much more diplomatic attention and resources should be directed to continental, sub-regional and national efforts to reconcile climate and development policy. In doing so, African countries would have adopted a much more pragmatic approach while also engaging in multilateral climate diplomacy.

Africa's diplomatic attention and resources should also be devoted to addressing the emerging climate policy issues in other policy domains. Already, at the World Trade Organization (WTO), for instance, governments are developing initiatives to align trade policy with climate goals.[90] African countries are conspicuously missing in these initiatives, an oversight that may prove to be costly should the measures undermine some of Africa's development policy objectives.[91] By contributing to agenda-setting, African countries can ensure that their concerns and views are captured from the onset.

Another emerging strategic opportunity is in addressing the international investment and climate policy nexus. Scholarly and policy efforts are currently underway to address the climate policy dimensions of international investment treaties. A crucial element is the susceptibility of climate policy to the Investor-State Dispute Settlement System (ISDS), where international investors can use the mechanism to sue governments for introducing domestic climate policies that may be perceived to negatively affect investments.[92] Since international investment agreements are central to Africa's renewed push for infrastructure investment, including in fossil fuel infrastructure, African governments can carve out policy space for climate regulations. Doing so would shield the African governments from the potent ISDS mechanism and create greater regulatory certainty. Developments in the reform of the Energy Charter Treaty can serve as an important heuristic.[93]

7.3.5 South-South Cooperation

Emerging economies especially China and India are significant actors in international climate change policy, and their profile keeps rising. China's rise as a great power poses an important opportunity for African countries. In tandem with the shifts in the global distribution of power, the geography and availability of clean and climate technology have also changed.[94]

While the initial phases of the multilateral climate regime were marked by costly climate technology mostly from industrialised countries, China's rise as a clean and climate technology giant calls for a consideration of technology transfer.[95] Unlike industrialised countries, China is not obligated to support African countries through finance and technology transfers and capacity building. Also, climate technologies are now cheaper than before, strengthening the case for their adoption and diffusion.[96]

African countries can harness South-South cooperation as an important platform to strengthen development cooperation.[97] Already, African countries and China are cooperating under the Forum for China-Africa Cooperation (FOCAC) forum including on climate change.[98] China's recent commitment of about three billion dollars in support to developing countries' climate action also presents a welcome opportunity for African countries.[99]

Continental-level cooperation especially on climate-compatible infrastructure is important. For example, Kenya's Geothermal Development Cooperation and the Kenya Electricity Generating Company (KenGen) are working with their Ethiopia and Tanzania counterparts on regional geothermal development.[100] Other countries in Africa are also engaging in the sale of electricity to neighbouring countries in Southern Africa.[101]

7.4 Conclusion

Already, the international climate change regime has evolved to a 'regime complex'. Recent and emergent climate and climate-related policy developments will only increase the complexity of the regime. Moreover, these developments are evolutionary and irreversible, leading to constant change in the international climate regime. In other policy domains such as international trade, investment, finance and even global public health, climate policy issues have been emerging.

As this chapter has shown, a long-run analysis of international climate cooperation shows that climate policy designers will have to take into account the dynamic nature of the regime. In addition, they would also have to anticipate and manage the emerging policy dimensions that touch on climate change. That climate change is a cross-cutting super wicked problem, hence the need to leverage other policy domains to address it means that policy makers will have to navigate the increasingly complex policy landscape. Such developments present both strategic challenges and opportunities. At the very least, African policy makers should anticipate and prepare to effectively engage in such a policy environment.

NOTES

1. Simon Chin-Yee, 'Briefing: Africa and the Paris Climate Change Agreement', *African Affairs* 115, no. 459 (1 April 2016): 367–68, https://doi.org/10.1093/afraf/adw005.
2. Thomas Hale, 'Catalytic Cooperation', *Global Environmental Politics* 20, no. 4 (1 November 2020): 73–98, https://doi.org/10.1162/glep_a_00561.
3. AU, 'African Leaders Push for Adequate Financial and Technical Support to Address Climate Change Challenges in the Lead up to COP27. | African Union', *African Union*, 6 February 2022, https://au.int/es/node/41467.
4. AU, 'African Union Green Recovery Action Plan 2021–2027' (Addis Ababa, Ethiopia: African Union, 2021), https://au.int/sites/default/files/newsevents/workingdocuments/40567-wd-AU_Green_Recovery_Action_Plan_ENGLISH.pdf.
5. Frauke Röser et al., 'Ambition in the Making: Analysing the Preparation and Implementation Process of the Nationally Determined Contributions under the Paris Agreement', *Climate Policy* 20, no. 4 (20 April 2020): 415–29, https://doi.org/10.1080/14693062.2019.1708697; Michael Pahle et al., 'Sequencing to Ratchet up Climate Policy Stringency', *Nature Climate Change* 8, no. 10 (October 2018): 861–67, https://doi.org/10.1038/s41558-018-0287-6.
6. Lacour M. Ayompe, Steven J. Davis, and Benis N. Egoh, 'Trends and Drivers of African Fossil Fuel CO2 Emissions 1990–2017', *Environmental Research Letters* 15, no. 12 (December 2020): 124039, https://doi.org/10.1088/1748-9326/abc64f.
7. Reuben Makomere and Kennedy Liti Mbeva, 'Squaring the Circle: Development Prospects Within the Paris Agreement', *Carbon & Climate Law Review* 12, no. 1 (2018): 31, https://doi.org/10.21552/cclr/2018/1/7.

8. David Ockwell and Rob Byrne, 'Improving Technology Transfer through National Systems of Innovation: Climate Relevant Innovation-System Builders (CRIBs)', *Climate Policy* 16, no. 7 (2 October 2016): 844, https://doi.org/10.1080/14693062.2015.1052958.

9. Edward King, 'Africa's "Buyer's Remorse" over Paris Climate Deal', Climate Home, 3 November 2016, http://www.climatechangenews.com/2016/11/03/africas-buyers-remorse-over-paris-climate-deal/.

10. Pieter Pauw et al., *NDC Explorer* (Bonn, Germany and Nairobi, Kenya: German Development Institute / Deutsches Institut für Entwicklungspolitik (DIE), and African Centre for Technology Studies (ACTS), 2016), http://klimalog.die-gdi.de/ndc/.

11. Chelsie Hunt and Olaf Weber, 'Fossil Fuel Divestment Strategies: Financial and Carbon-Related Consequences', *Organization & Environment* 32, no. 1 (1 March 2019): 41–61, https://doi.org/10.1177/1086026618773985.

12. Jessica Grady-Benson and Brinda Sarathy, 'Fossil Fuel Divestment in US Higher Education: Student-Led Organising for Climate Justice', *Local Environment* 21, no. 6 (2 June 2016): 661–81, https://doi.org/10.1080/13549839.2015.1009825.

13. Yiping Zhang and Olaf Weber, 'Investors' Moral and Financial Concerns—Ethical and Financial Divestment in the Fossil Fuel Industry', *Sustainability* 14, no. 4 (January 2022): 1952, https://doi.org/10.3390/su14041952.

14. Grady-Benson and Sarathy, 'Fossil Fuel Divestment in US Higher Education'.

15. Arthur Neslen, 'Catholic Church to Make Record Divestment from Fossil Fuels', *The Guardian*, 3 October 2017, sec. Environment, https://www.theguardian.com/environment/2017/oct/03/catholic-church-to-make-record-divestment-from-fossil-fuels.

16. Matthew Rimmer, 'Investing in the Future: Norway, Climate Change, and Fossil Fuel Divestment', SSRN Scholarly Paper (Rochester, NY: Social Science Research Network, 2016), https://papers.ssrn.com/abstract=2770844.

17. Caroline Flammer, Michael W. Toffel, and Kala Viswanathan, 'Shareholder Activism and Firms' Voluntary Disclosure of Climate Change Risks', *Strategic Management Journal* 42, no. 10 (2021): 1850–79, https://doi.org/10.1002/smj.3313.

18. Neil Gunningham, 'Review Essay: Divestment, Nonstate Governance, and Climate Change', *Law & Policy* 39, no. 4 (2017): 309–24, https://doi.org/10.1111/lapo.12085.

19. Margaret Gleeson, 'International Energy Agency Calls Time on New Fossil Fuels', *Green Left Weekly*, no. 1311 (n.d.): 10, https://doi.org/10.3316/informit.849458544850871.

20. 'The Path to Net Zero by 2050 Is Narrow and Challenging', *Emerald Expert Briefings* oxan-db, no. oxan-db (1 January 2021), https://doi.org/10.1108/OXAN-DB263035.

21. Noreen Kidunduhu, 'Energy Transition in Africa: Context, Barriers and Strategies', in *Energy Transitions and the Future of the African Energy Sector: Law, Policy and Governance*, ed. Victoria R. Nalule (Cham: Springer International Publishing, 2021), 73–111, https://doi.org/10.1007/978-3-030-56849-8_3; Damian Carrington, '"Hypocrisy": 90% of UK-Africa Summit's Energy Deals Were in Fossil Fuels', *The Guardian*, 24 January 2020, sec. Environment, https://www.theguardian.com/environment/2020/jan/24/90-pe-cent-uk-africa-energy-deals-fossil-fuels.

22. Carrington, '"Hypocrisy"'.

23. Christina Voigt, 'The Compliance and Implementation Mechanism of the Paris Agreement', *Review of European, Comparative & International Environmental Law* 25, no. 2 (2016): 161–73, https://doi.org/10.1111/reel.12155.

24. Peter Lawrence and Daryl Wong, 'Soft Law in the Paris Climate Agreement: Strength or Weakness?', *Review of European, Comparative & International Environmental Law* 26, no. 3 (2017): 277, https://doi.org/10.1111/reel.12210.

25. Daniel Bodansky, 'The Legal Character of the Paris Agreement', *Review of European, Comparative & International Environmental Law* 25, no. 2 (2016): 142–50, https://doi.org/10.1111/reel.12154.

26. Jacob Werksman, 'Compliance and the Use of Trade Measures', in *Promoting Compliance in an Evolving Climate Regime*, ed. Jutta Brunnée, Lavanya Rajamani, and Meinhard Doelle (Cambridge: Cambridge University Press, 2011), 262–85, https://doi.org/10.1017/CBO9780511979286.017.

27. Stuart Evans et al., 'Border Carbon Adjustments and Industrial Competitiveness in a European Green Deal', *Climate Policy* 21, no. 3 (16 March 2021): 307–17, https://doi.org/10.1080/14693062.2020.1856637.

28. Lisa Friedman, 'Democrats Propose a Border Tax Based on Countries' Greenhouse Gas Emissions', *The New York Times*, 19 July 2021, sec. Climate, https://www.nytimes.com/2021/07/19/climate/democrats-border-carbon-tax.html.

29. Catherine Early, 'The EU Can Expect Heavy Pushback on Its Carbon Border Tax', *China Dialogue* (blog), 1 September 2020, https://chinadialogue.net/en/business/eu-can-expect-heavy-pushback-carbon-border-tax/.

30. Robyn Eckersley, 'The Politics of Carbon Leakage and the Fairness of Border Measures', *Ethics & International Affairs* 24, no. 4 (ed 2010): 367–93, https://doi.org/10.1111/j.1747-7093.2010.00277.x.

31. EurActiv, 'African Countries Deem EU Carbon Border Levy "Protectionist"', ECEEE, 25 March 2021, https://www.eceee.org/all-news/news/african-countries-deem-eu-carbon-border-levy-protectionist/.
32. EurActiv.
33. Christopher Frey, 'Mega-Regional Trade Agreements and Post-2015 Climate Protection: Bridging the Gap', *Journal for European Environmental & Planning Law* 12, no. 3–4 (8 December 2015): 264–85, https://doi.org/10.1163/18760104-01204003.
34. AU, 'Agreement Establishing the African Continental Free Trade Area', 2018, https://au.int/sites/default/files/treaties/36437-treaty-consolidated_text_on_cfta_-_en.pdf.
35. Maria L. Loureiro and Justus Lotade, 'Do Fair Trade and Eco-Labels in Coffee Wake up the Consumer Conscience?', *Ecological Economics* 53, no. 1 (1 April 2005): 129–38, https://doi.org/10.1016/j.ecolecon.2004.11.002; Jung-Ah Hwang, Youkyoung Park, and Yeonbae Kim, 'Why Do Consumers Respond to Eco-Labels? The Case of Korea', *SpringerPlus* 5, no. 1 (4 November 2016): 1915, https://doi.org/10.1186/s40064-016-3550-1.
36. e.g. see Linda Lisa Maria Turunen and Minna Halme, 'Communicating Actionable Sustainability Information to Consumers: The Shades of Green Instrument for Fashion', *Journal of Cleaner Production* 297 (15 May 2021): 126605, https://doi.org/10.1016/j.jclepro.2021.126605.
37. Helen Mountford and Mauricio Cárdenas, 'How to Reach Net Zero', Project Syndicate, 20 July 2021, https://www.project-syndicate.org/commentary/five-ways-to-reach-net-zero-emissions-by-mid-century-by-helen-mountford-and-mauricio-cardenas-2021-07.
38. Niklas Höhne et al., 'Wave of Net Zero Emission Targets Opens Window to Meeting the Paris Agreement', *Nature Climate Change*, 16 September 2021, 1–3, https://doi.org/10.1038/s41558-021-01142-2.
39. Höhne et al.
40. Heleen L. van Soest, Michel G. J. den Elzen, and Detlef P. van Vuuren, 'Net-Zero Emission Targets for Major Emitting Countries Consistent with the Paris Agreement', *Nature Communications* 12, no. 1 (9 April 2021): 2140, https://doi.org/10.1038/s41467-021-22294-x.
41. CA, '1.5 °C National Pathway Explorer' (Climate Analytics, 2022), https://1p5ndc-pathways.climateanalytics.org/.
42. Joeri Rogelj et al., 'Net-Zero Emissions Targets Are Vague: Three Ways to Fix', *Nature* 591, no. 7850 (March 2021): 365–68, https://doi.org/10.1038/d41586-021-00662-3.
43. Thomas Hale, 'Governing Net Zero: The Conveyor Belt', Policy Memo (Oxford, UK: Blavatnik School of Government, 2021), https://www.bsg.ox.ac.uk/sites/default/files/2021-11/2021-11%20Hale%20Net%20Zero%20Policy%20Memo.pdf.

44. Thomas Hale et al., 'Net Zero Tracker' (Oxford, UK: Energy and Climate Intelligence Unit, Data-Driven EnviroLab, NewClimate Institute, Oxford Net Zero, 2021), https://zerotracker.net/.
45. Fergus Green, 'Anti-Fossil Fuel Norms', *Climatic Change* 150, no. 1 (1 September 2018): 103–16, https://doi.org/10.1007/s10584-017-2134-6.
46. Kalume Kazungu, 'Kenya: Lamu County Puts Coal-Fired Power Plant On Hold', *Daily Nation*, 9 August 2016, http://allafrica.com/stories/201608100091.html; 'Kenya Halts Lamu Coal Power Project at World Heritage Site', *BBC News*, 26 June 2019, sec. Africa, https://www.bbc.com/news/world-africa-48771519.
47. 'African Youth Initiative on Climate Change (AYICC) | Devex', accessed 27 September 2021, https://www.devex.com/organizations/african-youth-initiative-on-climate-change-ayicc-101004.
48. Philippe Le Billon et al., 'Fossil Fuels, Climate Change, and the COVID-19 Crisis: Pathways for a Just and Green Post-Pandemic Recovery', *Climate Policy* 21, no. 10 (26 November 2021): 1347–56, https://doi.org/10.1080/14693062.2021.1965524; Johan A. Oldekop et al., 'COVID-19 and the Case for Global Development', *World Development* 134 (1 October 2020): 105044, https://doi.org/10.1016/j.worlddev.2020.105044; Cameron Hepburn et al., 'Will COVID-19 Fiscal Recovery Packages Accelerate or Retard Progress on Climate Change?', *Oxford Review of Economic Policy* 36, no. Supplement_1 (28 September 2020): S359–81, https://doi.org/10.1093/oxrep/graa015.
49. Erik Pihl et al., 'Ten New Insights in Climate Science 2020—A Horizon Scan', *Global Sustainability* 4 (ed 2021): 7, https://doi.org/10.1017/sus.2021.2.
50. AU, 'African Union Green Recovery Action Plan 2021–2027'.
51. Shantayanan Devarajan, Indermit S Gill, and Kenan Karakülah, 'Debt, Growth and Stability in Africa: Speculative Calculations and Policy Responses †', *Journal of African Economies* 30, no. Supplement_1 (8 November 2021): 174–102, https://doi.org/10.1093/jae/ejab022.
52. Arjuna Dibley, Thom Wetzer, and Cameron Hepburn, 'National COVID Debts: Climate Change Imperils Countries' Ability to Repay', *Nature* 592, no. 7853 (April 2021): 184–87, https://doi.org/10.1038/d41586-021-00871-w.
53. Ollie Williams, 'Zambia's Default Fuels Fears of African "debt Tsunami" as Covid Impact Bites', *The Guardian*, 25 November 2020, sec. Global development, https://www.theguardian.com/global-development/2020/nov/25/zambias-default-fuels-fears-of-african-debt-tsunami-as-covid-impact-bites.
54. Ulrich Volz et al., 'Debt Relief for a Green and Inclusive Recovery: Securing Private-Sector Participation and Creating Policy Space for

Sustainable Development' (Berlin, London, and Boston, MA: Heinrich Böll Stiftung; Boston University Global Development Policy Center; Centre for Sustainable Finance SOAS University of London, June 2021), https://eprints.soas.ac.uk/35254/1/DRGR%20Report%202021.pdf.

55. Dennis Essers, Danny Cassimon, and Martin Prowse, 'Debt-for-Climate Swaps: Killing Two Birds with One Stone?', *Global Environmental Change* 71 (1 November 2021): 102407, https://doi.org/10.1016/j.gloenvcha.2021.102407; Adelle Thomas and Emily Theokritoff, 'Debt-for-Climate Swaps for Small Islands', *Nature Climate Change* 11, no. 11 (November 2021): 889–91, https://doi.org/10.1038/s41558-021-01194-4.

56. AU, 'African Union Green Recovery Action Plan 2021–2027'.

57. Peter Allen and Ilya Prigogine, 'The Challenge of Complexity', in *Self-Organization and Dissipative Structures: Applications in the Physical and Social Sciences*, ed. William Schieve and Peter Allen (Austin: University of Texas Press, 2021), https://doi.org/10.7560/703544.

58. Calestous Juma, 'Exponential Innovation and Human Rights: Implications for Science and Technology Diplomacy', SSRN Scholarly Paper (Rochester, NY: Social Science Research Network, 27 February 2018), https://papers.ssrn.com/abstract=3131243.

59. Emmanuel Yeri Kombe and Joseph Muguthu, 'Geothermal Energy Development in East Africa: Barriers and Strategies', *Journal of Energy Research and Reviews*, 2019, 1–6, https://doi.org/10.9734/jenrr/2019/v2i129722; Ibrahim Kabiru Maji, 'Impact of Clean Energy and Inclusive Development on CO2 Emissions in Sub-Saharan Africa', *Journal of Cleaner Production* 240 (10 December 2019): 118186, https://doi.org/10.1016/j.jclepro.2019.118186; Nadia S. Ouedraogo, 'Opportunities, Barriers and Issues with Renewable Energy Development in Africa: A Comprehensible Review', *Current Sustainable/Renewable Energy Reports* 6, no. 2 (1 June 2019): 52–60, https://doi.org/10.1007/s40518-019-00130-7.

60. Yohannes Biru Aemro, Pedro Moura, and Aníbal T. de Almeida, 'Inefficient Cooking Systems a Challenge for Sustainable Development: A Case of Rural Areas of Sub-Saharan Africa', *Environment, Development and Sustainability* 23, no. 10 (1 October 2021): 14697–721, https://doi.org/10.1007/s10668-021-01266-7.

61. Nathalie Spittler et al., 'Implications of Renewable Resource Dynamics for Energy System Planning: The Case of Geothermal and Hydropower in Kenya', *Energy Policy* 150 (1 March 2021): 111,985, https://doi.org/10.1016/j.enpol.2020.111985; Kombe and Muguthu, 'Geothermal Energy Development in East Africa'.

62. Manfred Hafner, Simone Tagliapietra, and Lucia de Strasser, 'Prospects for Renewable Energy in Africa', in *Energy in Africa: Challenges and*

Opportunities, ed. Manfred Hafner, Simone Tagliapietra, and Lucia de Strasser, SpringerBriefs in Energy (Cham: Springer International Publishing, 2018), 47–75, https://doi.org/10.1007/978-3-319-922 19-5_3.

63. Lapo Pistelli, 'Addressing Africa's Energy Dilemma', in *The Geopolitics of the Global Energy Transition*, ed. Manfred Hafner and Simone Tagliapietra, Lecture Notes in Energy (Cham: Springer International Publishing, 2020), 151–74, https://doi.org/10.1007/978-3-030-390 66-2_7; Sophia Kalantzakos, 'The Race for Critical Minerals in an Era of Geopolitical Realignments', *The International Spectator* 55, no. 3 (2 July 2020): 1–16, https://doi.org/10.1080/03932729.2020.1786926; Gondia Sokhna Seck, Emmanuel Hache, and Charlène Barnet, 'Potential Bottleneck in the Energy Transition: The Case of Cobalt in an Accelerating Electro-Mobility World', *Resources Policy* 75 (1 March 2022): 102516, https://doi.org/10.1016/j.resourpol.2021.102516.

64. G. Mutezo and J. Mulopo, 'A Review of Africa's Transition from Fossil Fuels to Renewable Energy Using Circular Economy Principles', *Renewable and Sustainable Energy Reviews* 137 (1 March 2021): 110609, https://doi.org/10.1016/j.rser.2020.110609.

65. Seck, Hache, and Barnet, 'Potential Bottleneck in the Energy Transition'.

66. Ouedraogo, 'Opportunities, Barriers and Issues with Renewable Energy Development in Africa'.

67. Michel Noussan et al., 'The Role of Green and Blue Hydrogen in the Energy Transition—A Technological and Geopolitical Perspective', *Sustainability* 13, no. 1 (January 2021): 298, https://doi.org/10.3390/su13010298; Thijs Van de Graaf et al., 'The New Oil? The Geopolitics and International Governance of Hydrogen', *Energy Research & Social Science* 70 (1 December 2020): 101667, https://doi.org/10.1016/j.erss.2020.101667.

68. Detlof von Oertzen, 'Issues, Challenges and Opportunities to Develop Green Hydrogen in Namibia' (Windhoek, Namibia: Konrad Adenauer Stiftung, October 2021).

69. Hilton Trollip, Bryce McCall, and Chris Bataille, 'How Green Primary Iron Production in South Africa Could Help Global Decarbonization', *Climate Policy* 0, no. 0 (13 January 2022): 1–12, https://doi.org/10.1080/14693062.2021.2024123.

70. UNCTAD, 'A European Union Carbon Border Adjustment Mechanism: Implications for Developing Countries' (Geneva, Switzerland: United Nations Conference on Trade and Development., 2021), https://unctad.org/system/files/official-document/osginf2021d2_en.pdf.

71. Dumisani Chirambo, 'Towards the Achievement of SDG 7 in Sub-Saharan Africa: Creating Synergies between Power Africa, Sustainable Energy for All and Climate Finance in-Order to Achieve Universal

Energy Access before 2030', *Renewable and Sustainable Energy Reviews* 94 (1 October 2018): 600–608, https://doi.org/10.1016/j.rser.2018.06.025.

72. Joanes Odiwuor Atela et al., 'Exploring the Agency of Africa in Climate Change Negotiations: The Case of REDD + ', *International Environmental Agreements: Politics, Law and Economics* 17, no. 4 (1 August 2017): 463–82, https://doi.org/10.1007/s10784-016-9329-6; Nicholas Chan, '"Special Circumstances" and the Politics of Climate Vulnerability: African Agency in the UN Climate Change Negotiations', *Africa Spectrum*, 24 June 2021, 0002039721991151, https://doi.org/10.1177/0002039721991151.

73. Youba Sokona and Fatma Denton, 'Climate Change Impacts: Can Africa Cope with the Challenges?', *Climate Policy* 1, no. 1 (1 January 2001): 118, https://doi.org/10.3763/cpol.2001.0110.

74. Ockwell and Byrne, 'Improving Technology Transfer through National Systems of Innovation', 844.

75. Example see Sebastian Castelier, 'Gulf States' Quest to Find "New Oil" Turns to Hydrogen—Al-Monitor: The Pulse of the Middle East', *Al-Monitor*, 15 February 2021, https://www.al-monitor.com/originals/2021/02/gulf-states-quest-new-oil-hydrogen-green-energy-solar-wind.html; Rimmer, 'Investing in the Future'; Damian Carrington, 'World's Biggest Sovereign Wealth Fund Dumps Dozens of Coal Companies', *The Guardian*, 5 February 2015, sec. Environment, https://www.theguardian.com/environment/2015/feb/05/worlds-biggest-sovereign-wealth-fund-dumps-dozens-of-coal-companies.

76. Evaristus Oshionebo, 'Sovereign Wealth Funds in Developing Countries: A Case Study of the Ghana Petroleum Funds', *Journal of Energy & Natural Resources Law* 36, no. 1 (2 January 2018): 33–59, https://doi.org/10.1080/02646811.2017.1329120.

77. EC, 'Just Energy Transition Partnership with South Africa', Press Release, European Commission—European Commission, 2 November 2021, https://ec.europa.eu/commission/presscorner/detail/en/IP_21_5768.

78. Jacklyn Cock, 'Resistance to Coal Inequalities and the Possibilities of a Just Transition in South Africa', *Development Southern Africa* 36, no. 6 (2 November 2019): 860–73, https://doi.org/10.1080/0376835X.2019.1660859; Harald Winkler et al., 'Just Transition Transaction in South Africa: An Innovative Way to Finance Accelerated Phase out of Coal and Fund Social Justice', *Journal of Sustainable Finance & Investment* 0, no. 0 (3 September 2021): 1–24, https://doi.org/10.1080/20430795.2021.1972678.

79. Francis Mangeni and Calestous Juma, *Emergent Africa. Evolution of Regional Economic Integration* (Terra Alta, WV: Headline Books, 2019).

80. Markus Kornprobst and T V Paul, 'Globalization, Deglobalization and the Liberal International Order', *International Affairs* 97, no. 5 (1 September 2021): 1305–16, https://doi.org/10.1093/ia/iiab120; T V Paul, 'Globalization, Deglobalization and Reglobalization: Adapting Liberal International Order', *International Affairs* 97, no. 5 (1 September 2021): 1599–1620, https://doi.org/10.1093/ia/iiab072.
81. AU, 'Draft Africa Climate Change Strategy (2020–2030)' (Addis Ababa, Ethiopia: African Union, 2020), https://www.uneca.org/sites/default/files/ACPC/Africa-climate-change-strategy/AU%20CC%20Strategy%20REV-28-12-2020%20EN.pdf.
82. AU, 'Meeting of the Committee of African Heads of State and Government on Climate Change (CAHOSCC) | African Union' (African Union, 9 February 2019), https://au.int/en/newsevents/20190209/meeting-committee-african-heads-state-and-government-climate-change-cahoscc.
83. Example see James Farole Jarso, 'The East African Community and the Climate Change Agenda: An Inventory of the Progress, Hurdles, and Prospects', *Sustainable Development Law & Policy* 12 (2011): 19.
84. EAC, 'East African Climate Change Policy' (Arusha, Tanzania: East African Community Secretariat, 2011), http://repository.eac.int/bit stream/handle/11671/538/EAC%20Climate%20Change%20Policy_April%202011.pdf?sequence=1&isAllowed=y; EAC, 'East African Community Climate Change Master Plan 2011–2031' (Arusha, Tanzania: East African Community Secretariat, 2011), https://www.meteorwanda.gov.rw/fileadmin/Template/Policies/EAC_Climate_Change_Master_Plan.pdf.
85. Maarten Van Aalst, Molly Hellmuth, and Daniele Ponzi, 'Working Paper 89—Come Rain or Shine—Integrating Climate Risk Management into African Development Bank Operations', *Working Paper Series*, Working Paper Series (African Development Bank, 9 December 2007), https://ideas.repec.org/p/adb/adbwps/224.html.
86. African Development Bank, 'Africa Climate Change Fund', Text, African Development Bank—Building today, a better Africa tomorrow (African Development Bank Group, 16 April 2019), https://www.afdb.org/en/topics-and-sectors/initiatives-partnerships/africa-climate-change-fund.
87. Peace A. Jiboku and Kelly Omosat Osifo, 'Monitoring Democratic Governance: Modus Operandi of NEPAD's African Peer Review Mechanism', *Journal of African Union Studies* 10, no. 2 (August 2021): 27–50, https://doi.org/10.31920/2050-4306/2021/10n2a2.
88. Jonathan Kuyper, Heike Schroeder, and Björn-Ola Linnér, 'The Evolution of the UNFCCC', *Annual Review of Environment and Resources* 43, no. 1 (2018): 343–68, https://doi.org/10.1146/annurev-environ-102017-030119.

89. Voigt, 'The Compliance and Implementation Mechanism of the Paris Agreement'.
90. Harro van Asselt, 'The Prospects of Trade and Climate Disputes before the WTO', SSRN Scholarly Paper (Rochester, NY: Social Science Research Network, 2020), https://doi.org/10.2139/ssrn.365 8327; Carolyn Deere Birkbeck, 'How Can the WTO and Its Ministerial Conference in 2021 Be Used to Support Climate Action?', *One Earth* 4, no. 5 (21 May 2021): 595–98, https://doi.org/10.1016/j.oneear. 2021.05.001; Kasturi Das et al., 'Towards a Trade Regime That Works for the Paris Agreement', *Economic and Political Weekly* 54, no. 50 (5 June 2015): 7–8.
91. UNCTAD, 'A European Union Carbon Border Adjustment Mechanism: Implications for Developing Countries'.
92. Kyla Tienhaara, 'Regulatory Chill in a Warming World: The Threat to Climate Policy Posed by Investor-State Dispute Settlement', *Transnational Environmental Law* 7, no. 2 (July 2018): 229–50, https://doi. org/10.1017/S2047102517000309.
93. Kyla Tienhaara and Christian Downie, 'Risky Business? The Energy Charter Treaty, Renewable Energy, and Investor-State Disputes', *Global Governance: A Review of Multilateralism and International Organizations* 24, no. 3 (12 September 2018): 451–71, https://doi.org/10. 1163/19426720-02403009.
94. Juma, 'Exponential Innovation and Human Rights', 6.
95. Margret J. Kim and Robert E. Jones, 'China: Climate Change Superpower and the Clean Technology Revolution', *Natural Resources & Environment* 22, no. 3 (2008): 9–13.
96. Gregory F. Nemet, *How Solar Energy Became Cheap: A Model for Low-Carbon Innovation* (London: Routledge, 2019), https://doi.org/10. 4324/9780367136604.
97. Francesco Rampa, Sanoussi Bilal, and Elizabeth Sidiropoulos, 'Leveraging South–South Cooperation for Africa's Development', *South African Journal of International Affairs* 19, no. 2 (1 August 2012): 247–69, https://doi.org/10.1080/10220461.2012.709400.
98. Sven Grimm, 'Sustainability in China-Africa Relations—"Greening" FOCAC', *African East-Asian Affairs* 71 (18 June 2013), https://doi. org/10.7552/71-0-81.
99. Martin Khor, 'China's Boost to South-South Cooperation', *South Bulletin* 90 (16 May 2016), https://www.southcentre.int/question/chi nas-boost-to-south-south-cooperation/.
100. Kombe and Muguthu, 'Geothermal Energy Development in East Africa'.
101. R. Deshmukh, A. Mileva, and G. C. Wu, 'Renewable Energy Alternatives to Mega Hydropower: A Case Study of Inga 3 for Southern Africa', *Environmental Research Letters* 13, no. 6 (June 2018): 064020, https://doi.org/10.1088/1748-9326/aabf60.

REFERENCES

Aalst, Maarten Van, Molly Hellmuth, and Daniele Ponzi. 'Working Paper 89—Come Rain or Shine—Integrating Climate Risk Management into African Development Bank Operations'. *Working Paper Series*. Working Paper Series. African Development Bank, 9 December 2007. https://ideas.repec.org/p/adb/adbwps/224.html.

Aemro, Yohannes Biru, Pedro Moura, and Aníbal T. de Almeida. 'Inefficient Cooking Systems a Challenge for Sustainable Development: A Case of Rural Areas of Sub-Saharan Africa'. *Environment, Development and Sustainability* 23, no. 10 (1 October 2021): 14697–721. https://doi.org/10.1007/s10668-021-01266-7.

'African Youth Initiative on Climate Change (AYICC) | Devex'. Accessed 27 September 2021. https://www.devex.com/organizations/african-youth-initiative-on-climate-change-ayicc-101004.

Allen, Peter, and Ilya Prigogine. 'The Challenge of Complexity'. In *Self-Organization and Dissipative Structures: Applications in the Physical and Social Sciences*, edited by William Schieve and Peter Allen. Austin: University of Texas Press, 2021. https://doi.org/10.7560/703544.

Asselt, Harro van. 'The Prospects of Trade and Climate Disputes before the WTO'. SSRN Scholarly Paper. Rochester, NY: Social Science Research Network, 2020. https://doi.org/10.2139/ssrn.3658327.

Atela, Joanes Odiwuor, Claire Hellen Quinn, Albert A. Arhin, Lalisa Duguma, and Kennedy Liti Mbeva. 'Exploring the Agency of Africa in Climate Change Negotiations: The Case of REDD+'. *International Environmental Agreements: Politics, Law and Economics* 17, no. 4 (1 August 2017): 463–82. https://doi.org/10.1007/s10784-016-9329-6.

AU. 'African Leaders Push for Adequate Financial and Technical Support to Address Climate Change Challenges in the Lead up to COP27. | African Union'. *African Union*. 6 February 2022. https://au.int/es/node/41467.

———. 'African Union Green Recovery Action Plan 2021–2027'. Addis Ababa, Ethiopia: African Union, 2021. https://au.int/sites/default/files/newsevents/workingdocuments/40567-wd-AU_Green_Recovery_Action_Plan_ENGLISH.pdf.

———. 'Agreement Establishing the African Continental Free Trade Area', 2018. https://au.int/sites/default/files/treaties/36437-treaty-consolidated_text_on_cfta_-_en.pdf.

———. 'Draft Africa Climate Change Strategy (2020–2030)'. Addis Ababa, Ethiopia: African Union, 2020. https://www.uneca.org/sites/default/files/ACPC/Africa-climate-change-strategy/AU%20CC%20Strategy%20REV-28-12-2020%20EN.pdf.

———. 'Meeting of the Committee of African Heads of State and Government on Climate Change (CAHOSCC) | African Union'. African Union, 9

February 2019. https://au.int/en/newsevents/20190209/meeting-commit tee-african-heads-state-and-government-climate-change-cahoscc.

Ayompe, Lacour M., Steven J. Davis, and Benis N. Egoh. December 2020. Trends and Drivers of African Fossil Fuel CO2 Emissions 1990–2017. *Environmental Research Letters* 15 (12): 124039. https://doi.org/10.1088/1748-9326/abc64f.

Bank, African Development. 'Africa Climate Change Fund'. Text. African Development Bank—Building today, a better Africa tomorrow. African Development Bank Group, 16 April 2019. https://www.afdb.org/en/topics-and-sectors/initiatives-partnerships/africa-climate-change-fund.

Birkbeck, Carolyn Deere. 'How Can the WTO and Its Ministerial Conference in 2021 Be Used to Support Climate Action?' *One Earth* 4, no. 5 (21 May 2021): 595–98. https://doi.org/10.1016/j.oneear.2021.05.001.

Bodansky, Daniel. 2016. The Legal Character of the Paris Agreement. *Review of European, Comparative & International Environmental Law* 25 (2): 142–150. https://doi.org/10.1111/reel.12154.

CA. '1.5°C National Pathway Explorer'. Climate Analytics, 2022. https://1p5ndc-pathways.climateanalytics.org/.

Carrington, Damian. '"Hypocrisy": 90% of UK-Africa Summit's Energy Deals Were in Fossil Fuels'. *The Guardian*, 24 January 2020, sec. Environment. https://www.theguardian.com/environment/2020/jan/24/90-pe-cent-uk-africa-energy-deals-fossil-fuels.

———. 'World's Biggest Sovereign Wealth Fund Dumps Dozens of Coal Companies'. *The Guardian*, 5 February 2015, sec. Environment. https://www.theguardian.com/environment/2015/feb/05/worlds-biggest-sovereign-wealth-fund-dumps-dozens-of-coal-companies.

Castelier, Sebastian. 'Gulf States' Quest to Find "New Oil" Turns to Hydrogen—Al-Monitor: The Pulse of the Middle East'. *Al-Monitor*, 15 February 2021. https://www.al-monitor.com/originals/2021/02/gulf-states-quest-new-oil-hydrogen-green-energy-solar-wind.html.

Chan, Nicholas. June2021. "Special Circumstances" and the Politics of Climate Vulnerability: African Agency in the UN Climate Change Negotiations. *Africa Spectrum* 24: 0002039721991151. https://doi.org/10.1177/000203972 1991151.

Chin-Yee, Simon. 'Briefing: Africa and the Paris Climate Change Agreement'. *African Affairs* 115, no. 459 (1 April 2016): 359–68. https://doi.org/10. 1093/afraf/adw005.

Chirambo, Dumisani. 'Towards the Achievement of SDG 7 in Sub-Saharan Africa: Creating Synergies between Power Africa, Sustainable Energy for All and Climate Finance in-Order to Achieve Universal Energy Access before 2030'. *Renewable and Sustainable Energy Reviews* 94 (1 October 2018): 600–608. https://doi.org/10.1016/j.rser.2018.06.025.

Cock, Jacklyn. 'Resistance to Coal Inequalities and the Possibilities of a Just Transition in South Africa'. *Development Southern Africa* 36, no. 6 (2 November 2019): 860–73. https://doi.org/10.1080/0376835X.2019.1660859.

Das, Kasturi, Harro van Asselt, Susanne Droege, and Michael A. Mehling. 'Towards a Trade Regime That Works for the Paris Agreement'. *Economic and Political Weekly* 54, no. 50 (5 June 2015): 7–8.

Deshmukh, R., A. Mileva, and G.C. Wu. June2018. Renewable Energy Alternatives to Mega Hydropower: A Case Study of Inga 3 for Southern Africa. *Environmental Research Letters* 13 (6): 064020. https://doi.org/10.1088/1748-9326/aabf60.

Devarajan, Shantayanan, Indermit S Gill, and Kenan Karakülah. 'Debt, Growth and Stability in Africa: Speculative Calculations and Policy Responses†'. *Journal of African Economies* 30, no. Supplement_1 (8 November 2021): i74–102. https://doi.org/10.1093/jae/ejab022.

Dibley, Arjuna, Thom Wetzer, and Cameron Hepburn. April 2021. National COVID Debts: Climate Change Imperils Countries. *Ability to Repay'. Nature* 592 (7853): 184–187. https://doi.org/10.1038/d41586-021-00871-w.

EAC. 'East African Climate Change Policy'. Arusha, Tanzania: East African Community Secretariat, 2011. http://repository.eac.int/bitstream/handle/11671/538/EAC%20Climate%20Change%20Policy_April%202011.pdf?seq uence=1&isAllowed=y.

———. 'East African Community Climate Change Master Plan 2011–2031'. Arusha, Tanzania: East African Community Secretariat, 2011. https://www.meteorwanda.gov.rw/fileadmin/Template/Policies/EAC_Climate_Change_Master_Plan.pdf.

Early, Catherine. 'The EU Can Expect Heavy Pushback on Its Carbon Border Tax'. *China Dialogue* (blog), 1 September 2020. https://chinadialogue.net/en/business/eu-can-expect-heavy-pushback-carbon-border-tax/.

EC. 'Just Energy Transition Partnership with South Africa'. Press Release. European Commission—European Commission, 2 November 2021. https://ec.europa.eu/commission/presscorner/detail/en/IP_21_5768.

Eckersley, Robyn. 'The Politics of Carbon Leakage and the Fairness of Border Measures'. *Ethics & International Affairs* 24, no. 4 (ed 2010): 367–93. https://doi.org/10.1111/j.1747-7093.2010.00277.x.

Essers, Dennis, Danny Cassimon, and Martin Prowse. 'Debt-for-Climate Swaps: Killing Two Birds with One Stone?' *Global Environmental Change* 71 (1 November 2021): 102407. https://doi.org/10.1016/j.gloenvcha.2021.102407.

EurActiv. 'African Countries Deem EU Carbon Border Levy "Protectionist"'. ECEEE, 25 March 2021. https://www.eceee.org/all-news/news/african-cou ntries-deem-eu-carbon-border-levy-protectionist/.

Evans, Stuart, Michael A. Mehling, Robert A. Ritz, and Paul Sammon. 'Border Carbon Adjustments and Industrial Competitiveness in a European Green Deal'. *Climate Policy* 21, no. 3 (16 March 2021): 307–17. https://doi.org/10.1080/14693062.2020.1856637.

Flammer, Caroline, Michael W. Toffel, and Kala Viswanathan. 2021. Shareholder Activism and Firms' Voluntary Disclosure of Climate Change Risks. *Strategic Management Journal* 42 (10): 1850–1879. https://doi.org/10.1002/smj.3313.

Frey, Christopher. 'Mega-Regional Trade Agreements and Post-2015 Climate Protection: Bridging the Gap'. *Journal for European Environmental & Planning Law* 12, no. 3–4 (8 December 2015): 264–85. https://doi.org/10.1163/18760104-01204003.

Friedman, Lisa. 'Democrats Propose a Border Tax Based on Countries' Greenhouse Gas Emissions'. *The New York Times*, 19 July 2021, sec. Climate. https://www.nytimes.com/2021/07/19/climate/democrats-border-carbon-tax.html.

Gleeson, Margaret. 'International Energy Agency Calls Time on New Fossil Fuels'. *Green Left Weekly*, no. 1311 (n.d.): 10. https://doi.org/10.3316/informit.849458544850871.

Grady-Benson, Jessica, and Brinda Sarathy. 'Fossil Fuel Divestment in US Higher Education: Student-Led Organising for Climate Justice'. *Local Environment* 21, no. 6 (2 June 2016): 661–81. https://doi.org/10.1080/13549839.2015.1009825.

Green, Fergus. 'Anti-Fossil Fuel Norms'. *Climatic Change* 150, no. 1 (1 September 2018): 103–16. https://doi.org/10.1007/s10584-017-2134-6.

Grimm, Sven. 'Sustainability in China-Africa Relations—"Greening" FOCAC'. *African East-Asian Affairs* 71 (18 June 2013). https://doi.org/10.7552/71-0-81.

Gunningham, Neil. 2017. Review Essay: Divestment, Nonstate Governance, and Climate Change. *Law & Policy* 39 (4): 309–324. https://doi.org/10.1111/lapo.12085.

Hafner, Manfred, Simone Tagliapietra, and Lucia de Strasser. 'Prospects for Renewable Energy in Africa'. In *Energy in Africa: Challenges and Opportunities*, edited by Manfred Hafner, Simone Tagliapietra, and Lucia de Strasser, 47–75. SpringerBriefs in Energy. Cham: Springer International Publishing, 2018. https://doi.org/10.1007/978-3-319-92219-5_3.

Hale, Thomas. 'Catalytic Cooperation'. *Global Environmental Politics* 20, no. 4 (1 November 2020): 73–98. https://doi.org/10.1162/glep_a_00561.

———. 'Governing Net Zero: The Conveyor Belt'. Policy Memo. Oxford, UK: Blavatnik School of Government, 2021. https://www.bsg.ox.ac.uk/sites/default/files/2021-11/2021-11%20Hale%20Net%20Zero%20Policy%20Memo.pdf.

Hale, Thomas, Takeshi Kuramochi, John Lang, Brendan Mapes, Steve Smith, Ria Aiyer, Richard Black, et al. 'Net Zero Tracker'. Oxford, UK: Energy and Climate Intelligence Unit, Data-Driven EnviroLab, NewClimate Institute, Oxford Net Zero, 2021. https://zerotracker.net/.

Hepburn, Cameron, Brian O'Callaghan, Nicholas Stern, Joseph Stiglitz, and Dimitri Zenghelis. 'Will COVID-19 Fiscal Recovery Packages Accelerate or Retard Progress on Climate Change?' *Oxford Review of Economic Policy* 36, no. Supplement_1 (28 September 2020): S359–81. https://doi.org/10.1093/oxrep/graa015.

Höhne, Niklas, Matthew J. Gidden, Michel den Elzen, Frederic Hans, Claire Fyson, Andreas Geiges, M. Louise Jeffery, et al. 'Wave of Net Zero Emission Targets Opens Window to Meeting the Paris Agreement'. *Nature Climate Change*, 16 September 2021, 1–3. https://doi.org/10.1038/s41558-021-01142-2.

Hunt, Chelsie, and Olaf Weber. 'Fossil Fuel Divestment Strategies: Financial and Carbon-Related Consequences'. *Organization & Environment* 32, no. 1 (1 March 2019): 41–61. https://doi.org/10.1177/1086026618773985.

Hwang, Jung-Ah, Youkyoung Park, and Yeonbae Kim. 'Why Do Consumers Respond to Eco-Labels? The Case of Korea'. *SpringerPlus* 5, no. 1 (4 November 2016): 1915. https://doi.org/10.1186/s40064-016-3550-1.

Jarso, James Farole. 'The East African Community and the Climate Change Agenda: An Inventory of the Progress, Hurdles, and Prospects'. *Sustainable Development Law & Policy* 12 (2011): 19.

Jiboku, Peace A., and Kelly Omosat Osifo. 'Monitoring Democratic Governance: Modus Operandi of NEPAD's African Peer Review Mechanism'. *Journal of African Union Studies* 10, no. 2 (August 2021): 27–50. https://doi.org/10.31920/2050-4306/2021/10n2a2.

Juma, Calestous. 'Exponential Innovation and Human Rights: Implications for Science and Technology Diplomacy'. SSRN Scholarly Paper. Rochester, NY: Social Science Research Network, 27 February 2018. https://papers.ssrn.com/abstract=3131243.

Kalantzakos, Sophia. 'The Race for Critical Minerals in an Era of Geopolitical Realignments'. *The International Spectator* 55, no. 3 (2 July 2020): 1–16. https://doi.org/10.1080/03932729.2020.1786926.

Kazungu, Kalume. 'Kenya: Lamu County Puts Coal-Fired Power Plant On Hold'. *Daily Nation*. 9 August 2016. http://allafrica.com/stories/201608100091.html.

BBC News. 'Kenya Halts Lamu Coal Power Project at World Heritage Site', 26 June 2019, sec. Africa. https://www.bbc.com/news/world-africa-48771519.

Khor, Martin. 'China's Boost to South-South Cooperation'. *South Bulletin* 90 (16 May 2016). https://www.southcentre.int/question/chinas-boost-to-south-south-cooperation/.

Kidunduhu, Noreen. 'Energy Transition in Africa: Context, Barriers and Strategies'. In *Energy Transitions and the Future of the African Energy Sector: Law, Policy and Governance*, edited by Victoria R. Nalule, 73–111. Cham: Springer International Publishing, 2021. https://doi.org/10.1007/978-3-030-56849-8_3.

Kim, Margret J., and Robert E. Jones. 2008. China: Climate Change Superpower and the Clean Technology Revolution. *Natural Resources & Environment* 22 (3): 9–13.

King, Edward. 'Africa's "Buyer's Remorse" over Paris Climate Deal'. Climate Home, 3 November 2016. http://www.climatechangenews.com/2016/11/03/africas-buyers-remorse-over-paris-climate-deal/.

Kombe, Emmanuel Yeri, and Joseph Muguthu. 'Geothermal Energy Development in East Africa: Barriers and Strategies'. *Journal of Energy Research and Reviews*, 2019, 1–6. https://doi.org/10.9734/jenrr/2019/v2i129722.

Kornprobst, Markus, and T V Paul. 'Globalization, Deglobalization and the Liberal International Order'. *International Affairs* 97, no. 5 (1 September 2021): 1305–16. https://doi.org/10.1093/ia/iiab120.

Kuyper, Jonathan, Heike Schroeder, and Björn-Ola. Linnér. 2018. The Evolution of the UNFCCC. *Annual Review of Environment and Resources* 43 (1): 343–368. https://doi.org/10.1146/annurev-environ-102017-030119.

Lawrence, Peter, and Daryl Wong. 2017. Soft Law in the Paris Climate Agreement: Strength or Weakness? *Review of European, Comparative & International Environmental Law* 26 (3): 276–286. https://doi.org/10.1111/reel.12210.

Le Billon, Philippe, Païvi Lujala, Devyani Singh, Vance Culbert, and Berit Kristoffersen. 'Fossil Fuels, Climate Change, and the COVID-19 Crisis: Pathways for a Just and Green Post-Pandemic Recovery'. *Climate Policy* 21, no. 10 (26 November 2021): 1347–56. https://doi.org/10.1080/14693062.2021.1965524.

Loureiro, Maria L., and Justus Lotade. 'Do Fair Trade and Eco-Labels in Coffee Wake up the Consumer Conscience?' *Ecological Economics* 53, no. 1 (1 April 2005): 129–38. https://doi.org/10.1016/j.ecolecon.2004.11.002.

Maji, Ibrahim Kabiru. 'Impact of Clean Energy and Inclusive Development on CO2 Emissions in Sub-Saharan Africa'. *Journal of Cleaner Production* 240 (10 December 2019): 118186. https://doi.org/10.1016/j.jclepro.2019.118186.

Makomere, Reuben, and Kennedy Liti Mbeva. 'Squaring the Circle: Development Prospects Within the Paris Agreement'. *Carbon & Climate Law Review* 12, no. 1 (2018): 31–40. https://doi.org/10.21552/cclr/2018/1/7.

Mangeni, Francis, and Calestous Juma. *Emergent Africa. Evolution of Regional Economic Integration*. Terra Alta, WV: Headline Books, 2019.

Mountford, Helen, and Mauricio Cárdenas. 'How to Reach Net Zero'. Project Syndicate, 20 July 2021. https://www.project-syndicate.org/commentary/five-ways-to-reach-net-zero-emissions-by-mid-century-by-helen-mountford-and-mauricio-cardenas-2021-07.

Mutezo, G., and J. Mulopo. 'A Review of Africa's Transition from Fossil Fuels to Renewable Energy Using Circular Economy Principles'. *Renewable and Sustainable Energy Reviews* 137 (1 March 2021): 110609. https://doi.org/10.1016/j.rser.2020.110609.

Nemet, Gregory F. *How Solar Energy Became Cheap: A Model for Low-Carbon Innovation*. London: Routledge, 2019. https://doi.org/10.4324/978036 7136604.

Neslen, Arthur. 'Catholic Church to Make Record Divestment from Fossil Fuels'. *The Guardian*, 3 October 2017, sec. Environment. https://www.the guardian.com/environment/2017/oct/03/catholic-church-to-make-record-divestment-from-fossil-fuels.

Noussan, Michel, Pier Paolo Raimondi, Rossana Scita, and Manfred Hafner. 'The Role of Green and Blue Hydrogen in the Energy Transition—A Technological and Geopolitical Perspective'. *Sustainability* 13, no. 1 (January 2021): 298. https://doi.org/10.3390/su13010298.

Ockwell, David, and Rob Byrne. 'Improving Technology Transfer through National Systems of Innovation: Climate Relevant Innovation-System Builders (CRIBs)'. *Climate Policy* 16, no. 7 (2 October 2016): 836–54. https://doi.org/10.1080/14693062.2015.1052958.

Oertzen, Detlof von. 'Issues, Challenges and Opportunities to Develop Green Hydrogen in Namibia'. Windhoek, Namibia: Konrad Adenauer Stiftung, October 2021.

Oldekop, Johan A., Rory Horner, David Hulme, Roshan Adhikari, Bina Agarwal, Matthew Alford, Oliver Bakewell, et al. 'COVID-19 and the Case for Global Development'. *World Development* 134 (1 October 2020): 105044. https://doi.org/10.1016/j.worlddev.2020.105044.

Oshionebo, Evaristus. 'Sovereign Wealth Funds in Developing Countries: A Case Study of the Ghana Petroleum Funds'. *Journal of Energy & Natural Resources Law* 36, no. 1 (2 January 2018): 33–59. https://doi.org/10.1080/026 46811.2017.1329120.

Ouedraogo, Nadia S. 'Opportunities, Barriers and Issues with Renewable Energy Development in Africa: A Comprehensible Review'. *Current Sustainable/Renewable Energy Reports* 6, no. 2 (1 June 2019): 52–60. https://doi.org/10.1007/s40518-019-00130-7.

Pahle, Michael, Dallas Burtraw, Christian Flachsland, Nina Kelsey, Eric Biber, Jonas Meckling, Ottmar Edenhofer, and John Zysman. October 2018. Sequencing to Ratchet up Climate Policy Stringency. *Nature Climate Change* 8 (10): 861–867. https://doi.org/10.1038/s41558-018-0287-6.

Paul, T V. 'Globalization, Deglobalization and Reglobalization: Adapting Liberal International Order'. *International Affairs* 97, no. 5 (1 September 2021): 1599–1620. https://doi.org/10.1093/ia/iiab072.

Pauw, Pieter, Davide Cassanmagnano, Kennedy Mbeva, Jonas Hein, Alejandro Guarin, Clara Brandi, Thomas Bock, et al. *NDC Explorer*. Bonn, Germany and Nairobi, Kenya: German Development Institute / Deutsches Institut für Entwicklungspolitik (DIE), and African Centre for Technology Studies (ACTS), 2016. http://klimalog.die-gdi.de/ndc/.

Pihl, Erik, Eva Alfredsson, Magnus Bengtsson, Kathryn J. Bowen, Vanesa Cástan Broto, Kuei Tien Chou, Helen Cleugh, et al. 'Ten New Insights in Climate Science 2020—A Horizon Scan'. *Global Sustainability* 4 (ed 2021). https://doi.org/10.1017/sus.2021.2.

Pistelli, Lapo. 'Addressing Africa's Energy Dilemma'. In *The Geopolitics of the Global Energy Transition*, edited by Manfred Hafner and Simone Tagliapietra, 151–74. Lecture Notes in Energy. Cham: Springer International Publishing, 2020. https://doi.org/10.1007/978-3-030-39066-2_7.

Rampa, Francesco, Sanoussi Bilal, and Elizabeth Sidiropoulos. 'Leveraging South–South Cooperation for Africa's Development'. *South African Journal of International Affairs* 19, no. 2 (1 August 2012): 247–69. https://doi.org/10.1080/10220461.2012.709400.

Rimmer, Matthew. 'Investing in the Future: Norway, Climate Change, and Fossil Fuel Divestment'. SSRN Scholarly Paper. Rochester, NY: Social Science Research Network, 2016. https://papers.ssrn.com/abstract=2770844.

Rogelj, Joeri, Oliver Geden, Annette Cowie, and Andy Reisinger. March 2021. Net-Zero Emissions Targets Are Vague: Three Ways to Fix. *Nature* 591 (7850): 365–368. https://doi.org/10.1038/d41586-021-00662-3.

Röser, Frauke, Oscar Widerberg, Niklas Höhne, and Thomas Day. 'Ambition in the Making: Analysing the Preparation and Implementation Process of the Nationally Determined Contributions under the Paris Agreement'. *Climate Policy* 20, no. 4 (20 April 2020): 415–29. https://doi.org/10.1080/146 93062.2019.1708697.

Seck, Gondia Sokhna, Emmanuel Hache, and Charlène Barnet. 'Potential Bottleneck in the Energy Transition: The Case of Cobalt in an Accelerating Electro-Mobility World'. *Resources Policy* 75 (1 March 2022): 102516. https://doi.org/10.1016/j.resourpol.2021.102516.

Soest, Heleen L. van, Michel G. J. den Elzen, and Detlef P. van Vuuren. 'Net-Zero Emission Targets for Major Emitting Countries Consistent with the Paris Agreement'. *Nature Communications* 12, no. 1 (9 April 2021): 2140. https://doi.org/10.1038/s41467-021-22294-x.

Sokona, Youba, and Fatma Denton. 'Climate Change Impacts: Can Africa Cope with the Challenges?' *Climate Policy* 1, no. 1 (1 January 2001): 117–23. https://doi.org/10.3763/cpol.2001.0110.

Spittler, Nathalie, Brynhildur Davidsdottir, Ehsan Shafiei, and Arnaud Diemer. 'Implications of Renewable Resource Dynamics for Energy System Planning: The Case of Geothermal and Hydropower in Kenya'. *Energy Policy* 150 (1 March 2021): 111985. https://doi.org/10.1016/j.enpol.2020.111985.

'The Path to Net Zero by 2050 Is Narrow and Challenging'. *Emerald Expert Briefings* oxan-db, no. oxan-db (1 January 2021). https://doi.org/10.1108/OXAN-DB263035.

Thomas, Adelle, and Emily Theokritoff. November 2021. Debt-for-Climate Swaps for Small Islands. *Nature Climate Change* 11 (11): 889–891. https://doi.org/10.1038/s41558-021-01194-4.

Tienhaara, Kyla. July2018. Regulatory Chill in a Warming World: The Threat to Climate Policy Posed by Investor-State Dispute Settlement. *Transnational Environmental Law* 7 (2): 229–250. https://doi.org/10.1017/S2047102517000309.

Tienhaara, Kyla, and Christian Downie. 'Risky Business? The Energy Charter Treaty, Renewable Energy, and Investor-State Disputes'. *Global Governance: A Review of Multilateralism and International Organizations* 24, no. 3 (12 September 2018): 451–71. https://doi.org/10.1163/19426720-02403009.

Trollip, Hilton, Bryce McCall, and Chris Bataille. 'How Green Primary Iron Production in South Africa Could Help Global Decarbonization'. *Climate Policy* 0, no. 0 (13 January 2022): 1–12. https://doi.org/10.1080/14693062.2021.2024123.

Turunen, Linda Lisa Maria, and Minna Halme. 'Communicating Actionable Sustainability Information to Consumers: The Shades of Green Instrument for Fashion'. *Journal of Cleaner Production* 297 (15 May 2021): 126605. https://doi.org/10.1016/j.jclepro.2021.126605.

UNCTAD. 'A European Union Carbon Border Adjustment Mechanism: Implications for Developing Countries'. Geneva, Switzerland: United Nations Conference on Trade and Development., 2021. https://unctad.org/system/files/official-document/osginf2021d2_en.pdf.

Van de Graaf, Thijs, Indra Overland, Daniel Scholten, and Kirsten Westphal. 'The New Oil? The Geopolitics and International Governance of Hydrogen'. *Energy Research & Social Science* 70 (1 December 2020): 101667. https://doi.org/10.1016/j.erss.2020.101667.

Voigt, Christina. 2016. The Compliance and Implementation Mechanism of the Paris Agreement. *Review of European, Comparative & International Environmental Law* 25 (2): 161–173. https://doi.org/10.1111/reel.12155.

Volz, Ulrich, Shamshad Akhtar, Kevin P Gallagher, Stephany Griffith-Jones, Jörg Haas, and Moritz Kraemer. 'Debt Relief for a Green and Inclusive Recovery: Securing Private-Sector Participation and Creating Policy Space for Sustainable Development'. Berlin, London, and Boston, MA: Heinrich Böll Stiftung; Boston University Global Development Policy Center; Centre for Sustainable

Finance SOAS University of London, June 2021. https://eprints.soas.ac.uk/35254/1/DRGR%20Report%202021.pdf.

Werksman, Jacob. 'Compliance and the Use of Trade Measures'. In *Promoting Compliance in an Evolving Climate Regime*, edited by Jutta Brunnée, Lavanya Rajamani, and Meinhard Doelle, 262–85. Cambridge: Cambridge University Press, 2011. https://doi.org/10.1017/CBO9780511979286.017.

Williams, Ollie. 'Zambia's Default Fuels Fears of African "debt Tsunami" as Covid Impact Bites'. *The Guardian*, 25 November 2020, sec. Global development. https://www.theguardian.com/global-development/2020/nov/25/zambias-default-fuels-fears-of-african-debt-tsunami-as-covid-impact-bites.

Winkler, Harald, Emily Tyler, Samantha Keen, and Andrew Marquard. 'Just Transition Transaction in South Africa: An Innovative Way to Finance Accelerated Phase out of Coal and Fund Social Justice'. *Journal of Sustainable Finance & Investment* 0, no. 0 (3 September 2021): 1–24. https://doi.org/10.1080/20430795.2021.1972678.

Zhang, Yiping, and Olaf Weber. January 2022. Investors' Moral and Financial Concerns—Ethical and Financial Divestment in the Fossil Fuel Industry. *Sustainability* 14 (4): 1952. https://doi.org/10.3390/su14041952.

CHAPTER 8

Governing Complexity

The Nobel Laureate Physicist Murray Gell-Mann famously said that "in the twenty-first century, the most important kind of mind will be the synthesizing mind".[1] Thus, if the international climate regime is characterised by complexity, dynamism and irreversible evolution, then governing complexity would be the most appropriate policy approach. Scholarly and policy approaches to governing complex and dynamic systems also allow for creativity, as changing systems open up new opportunities for innovative governance. Such an approach will be critical to Africa's engagement in international climate cooperation.

This chapter argues that a 'Governing Complexity' approach is the most appropriate for Africa's engagement in international climate cooperation. In the first part of the chapter, various cognitive approaches to perceiving and managing complexity are examined, with a focus on decision-making. Such an examination is a stark departure from the conventional approach which is based on the static equilibrium notions that Africa will still continue playing a marginal role in greenhouse gas emissions reductions, while also expecting resource transfers especially from the global North. Instead, the chapter argues that the rapidly evolving international climate change regime not only presents strategic challenges, but also novel opportunities that can be harnessed to contribute to both ambitious climate action and the broader goals

© The Author(s), under exclusive license to Springer Nature Switzerland AG 2023
K. Mbeva et al., *Africa's Right to Development in a Climate-Constrained World*, Contemporary African Political Economy,
https://doi.org/10.1007/978-3-031-22887-2_8

227

of sustainable development. Moreover, a cognitive policy approach that embraces and appreciates complexity and dynamism would allow for the development of longer-term climate policies that would also be adaptive to the changing circumstances.

In other words, the chapter argues that as the international climate regime irreversibly evolves into greater complexity, policy makers will have to act as what has been termed as *complex designers* in order to engage effectively.[2] To ground the argument for a cognitive approach based on governing complexity, the second part of the chapter draws on concrete projects implemented, and insights accrued, by the authors. The illustrations will try to outline the key components of the complex system, how they depart from conventional understanding, and how they reflect 'governing complexity'. The chapter concludes that complexity thinking is not alien to regional cooperation and governance in Africa. In economic affairs, for instance, complexity has been a key feature of regional integration, as characterised by the various overlapping regional institutions in the continent.[3] What the chapter emphasises is the need for a similar approach to be applied to climate policy, where the issue of a just transition is accorded the status of utmost policy priority.

8.1 COMPLEXITY AND DECISION-MAKING

Complexity has been a key feature of the scholarly debate on the design and operation of international regimes.[4] Given their broad definition, international regimes open several avenues for governing issue areas. As scholars have long understood, regimes encompass a wide array of governance arrangements, from norms to principles to rules and regulations. Social science and policy research has therefore substantially engaged with complex systems, drawing from the natural sciences.

8.1.1 *The Regime Complex for Climate Change*

In the climate domain, scholars have characterised the emergence of a 'regime complex for climate change'.[5] The regime complex for climate change includes various institutions, actors, principles and norms that address climate change. But as the preceding chapter has shown, the regime has been growing more complex over time, and will most likely continue evolving into greater complexity. Such a trend is in tandem with the broader growing complexity of multilateral environmental regimes. As a novel study that examined the evolution of MEAs over several decades showed, the MEAs were becoming more interconnected and were thus creating a complex and dynamic structure.[6]

Complexity in the social sciences and policy studies has often focused on the structural level, examining the key characteristics of complex and dynamic systems. Moreover, such studies have also explored the emergent principles of such systems.[7] Self-organisation has been a central feature of scholarly focus, where complex systems are viewed as reducing the scope of agents, a clear departure from the rationalistic approach that is more deterministic. In her Nobel Prize-winning research on governing commons, Eleanor Ostrom showed how decentralisation can lead to more effective governance systems.[8] It is this insight from Ostrom that forms the basis of polycentric governance, including on climate change.[9]

8.1.2   *Bounded Rationality*

While complexity studies have yielded important insights into governing complex systems, a major criticism has been the excessive emphasis on structural features and the diminution, if not exclusion, of actors. In a quest to bring back the role and significance of actors in governing complex systems, scholars have taken various approaches.[10]

Scholarship on decision-making were undertaken in psychology studies, and they were premised on the notion of full rationality.[11] That is, the studies assumed that decision-making is based on conditions where actors had sufficient information to make calculated decisions. Some scholars talked of the 'synthesising mind', as well as notions of 'multiple intelligences'.[12] Full rationality also underpinned the core of economic studies and international relations.[13]

However, subsequent studies in psychology showed that human beings make decisions without the full repertoire of pertinent information. In other words, human beings make decisions based on bounded rationality.[14] Initially controversial, the bounded rationality hypothesis was tested and confirmed through laboratory and other experimental studies. Bounded rationality took off in psychology, was adopted in economic theory, and finally embraced by policy diffusion scholarship. In international affairs, bounded rationality has been applied to explain the behaviour of key decision-makers, such as state leaders, in high-stakes situations such as international security crises.[15]

8.1.3 Complex Designers

Scholarship on decision-making amidst uncertainty has generated a productive research agenda.[16] But it has yet to fully engage with complex and dynamic systems that are constantly evolving. Given the excessive focus on the self-organisation of complex adaptive systems, the role of actors, especially decision-makers, has been peripheral to complexity studies.

To address this gap, a novel study introduced the notion of *complex designers*.[17] Simply defined, complex designers are "actors who seek to design and redesign institutions within complex adaptive systems."[18] Complex designers, are guided by three key emergent principles, namely "flexible structures, balanced content and adaptive management processes".[19] By combining the concept of complex designers and the emergent principles that guide their decision-making, the role of actors in engaging with complex adaptive systems is rehabilitated. It also provides a framework for policy analysis, especially in governing complexity.

Applied to the African policy context, the concept of complex designers allows us to explore how policy makers in the continent can creatively and effectively deal with the dynamic and complex international climate change regime. Such an approach would of course be broadly guided by the three emergent principles as aforementioned.

Complexity, evolution and uncertainty have been the key features of the policy landscape in Africa. It has been long recognised that an effective policy approach in Africa is one that embraces the complexity and dynamism of the policy landscape. In their pioneering article critiquing the dominant reductionist approach to policy-making in Africa, Juma and Clark noted that,

> [A] major problem with contemporary policy analysis is that it has difficulty coming to terms with complex economic change. This in turn is probably influenced by a view of socioeconomic systems that still harks back to the classical mechanics of the nineteenth century and a relatively stable world in which social action could reasonably be informed by disinterested scientific research of a traditional kind. [A] more realistic approach [in Africa] would recognize the evolutionary nature of modern socioeconomic systems and base policy interventions accordingly. In particular, there is a need to see 'policy' as a process of complex change requiring innovative institutional contexts and novel managerial capabilities.[20]

Moreover, Juma and Clark argue that the use of metaphors is important in thinking and discussing policy research and analysis in Africa. They identify the key policy metaphors as: a mechanistic world view of society as a machine (which they deem as prevalent but inappropriate); from linear to nonlinear processes; policy as arguments; policy as social experiments; and policy as interactive learning.[21] We follow Juma and Clark's approach in analysing and proposing how African policy makers can govern the complexity of the international climate regime. After all, the complex designers' concept is suitable for analysing the international climate change regime.[22]

8.2 Climate Policy Landscape in Africa

Does the climate policy landscape in Africa resemble a complex adaptive system? To answer this question, we first have to examine the kinds of climate policies in Africa, and the trend in their adoption over time. Such an analysis would show whether climate policy has been perceived as a discrete or cross-cutting policy issue. Figure 8.1 shows the temporal trends in the adoption of climate policies in Africa.

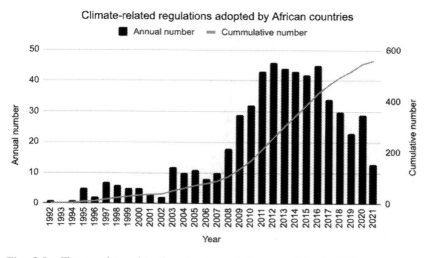

Fig. 8.1 Temporal trend in the adoption of climate policies in African countries (*Data source* GLOBE Database)

It is apparent from Fig. 8.1 that there has been a rapid adoption of climate policies in Africa, especially at the beginning of the twenty-first century. In the decade from 2005 and 2015, there appears to be a rapid adoption of climate policies in the continent. This might be due to the momentum at the multilateral level from the crisis of the Copenhagen Accord to the landmark adoption of the Paris Agreement in 2015.[23] In total, about six hundred climate policies have been adopted across all African countries. That is an incredible number of climate policies governing a single issue area—climate change.

But is the adoption of climate policies uniform across African countries. As Fig. 8.2 shows, only a handful of African countries account for a disproportionate number of the climate policies. There is therefore a significant variation in the adoption of climate policies in Africa.

The significant geographical variation in the adoption of climate policies in Africa indicates that some countries have adopted more climate policies than others. In some ways, this may be an indication of the variation in vulnerability, priorities and capability of dealing with climate change. More important, however, is that each country in Africa has

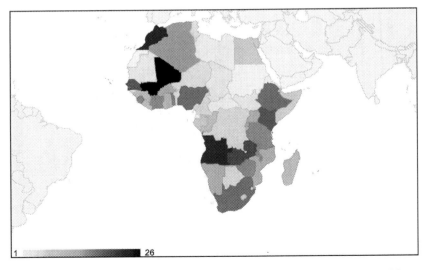

Fig. 8.2 Geographical trend in the adoption of climate policies in African countries (*Data source* GLOBE Database)

adopted at least one climate policy. Also crucial to note is that although African countries often coordinate their positions and bargain together in multilateral climate change negotiations under the UNFCCC, there are nationally contingent circumstances that shape the climate policies of individual countries.

Almost all African countries have adopted long-term climate change commitments. As Fig. 8.3 shows, these targets range from the years 2030 to 2050, with some of the targets not having an end date. What this trend indicates is that African countries have committed themselves to a structural transformation based on ambitious climate reduction targets, in line with the concept of the Great Climate Transformation. Delivering on these commitments will thus pose a major policy challenge, one that will require creative policy-making. That is, African policy makers would have to fully embrace the role of *complex designers*.

8.3 CONSOLIDATED LESSONS

As much as we have argued for a 'Governing Complexity' approach to climate policy in Africa, and the need for African policy makers to assume the role of complex designers, there are already initiatives in the continent that embody these insights. In this section, we draw on insights from the initiatives, most of which we have implemented as African scholars and policy analysts, to illustrate what governing complexity looks like in practice. In doing so, we seek to use the examples to not only ground the preceding discussion in the chapter, but to also stimulate and catalyse further research along similar lines. We identify the following lessons as the most pertinent in governing complexity in climate policy in Africa: transformation and uncertainty; institutional innovation; building endogenous capacity; co-generation of policy evidence base; dynamic transnational partnerships; continuous experimentation and learning; and strategic geopolitical engagement. All the lessons embody the emergent principles that guide complex designers—flexible structures, balanced content and adaptive management processes.[25] Each of the consolidated lessons and its attendant themes are examined in turn below.

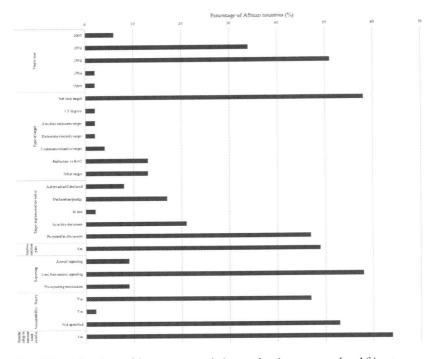

Fig. 8.3 Adoption of long-term emission reduction targets by African countries. Overall, almost all African countries (50) have a long-term emission reduction target (*Data source* Net Zero Tracker[24])

8.3.1 Transformation and Uncertainty

Given the nature of the transnational sustainability challenges across the globe, there have been calls for transformative change. In this formulation, changes should not only be undertaken to discrete challenges or policy domains, but to the entire social system.[26] A common refrain of activists, for instance, is the need for "systems change, not climate change". System change, in this instance, is the abolition of capitalism and replacing it with socialism.[27] But while the clamour for transformation for sustainability is widely accepted, at least in its generic form, the particularities are very much contested. In particular, there are competing views on the nature of the transformation, the pathways of transformation, as well as the drivers (actors) of the transformation. Uncertainty also pervades these calls for transformation.[28]

In partnership with institutions and organisations from various parts of the world, the Pathways to Sustainability Project, expelled these themes. Based at the STEPS Centre of the University of Sussex, the project examines how various contexts shape the pathways to sustainability. In Africa, the project involved critically analysing the so-called transformation brought about by the coupling of mobile phone platforms and solar energy systems. A synthesis and summary of the overall project have been published in two books titled *The Politics of Uncertainty Challenges of Transformation*, and *Transformative Pathways to Sustainability Learning Across Disciplines, Cultures and Contexts.*[29]

Using the concept of 'Transformative Labs (T-Labs)', the projects under the Pathways to Sustainability projects examined whether the profiled projects really were transformative.[30] Projects were implemented across nine countries in the Global South. In Africa, as has been mentioned, the transformative potential of mobile-based payment systems coupled with solar energy systems was examined. Specifically, the M-KOPA product, the most prominent product embodied the socio-technical approach, was critically analysed.

Mobile payment systems have transformed banking and the broader socio-economic system in Africa. Pioneered by the M-PESA platform, mobile-based payment systems are ubiquitous in Africa. Moreover, the transformative impacts of the mobile-based payment systems have been well documented.[31] By combining such systems with a credit system and using it as a basis for selling solar energy systems to especially low-income communities, the M-KOPA product promised to deliver the twin benefits of accessibility through cheap credit and the promotion of the uptake of renewable energy products.[32] The focus of the research was, therefore, to analyse whether M-KOPA was indeed leading to transformation towards sustainability.

Based on multi-stakeholder T-Lab workshops, which included developers and users of the M-KOPA product, we asked participants to identify whether they considered the product transformation. We also asked the participants what their understanding of transformation for sustainability entailed. We also conducted detailed surveys with key actors, including policy makers, product developers, product users, civil society organisations and others. The main finding from the M-KOPA project was that even though the product's formulation promised transformation towards sustainability, the various stakeholders had varying opinions of whether this was the case. Part of the divergence in the opinions of the stakeholders was due to the varying emphasis on dimensions of sustainability. While the product developers focused on the financial benefits and flexibility of the product, the users sometimes felt that the products were too expensive in the long run. Policy makers were more interested in the socio-economic impacts of the product, especially on poverty alleviation, while researchers were more interested in whether the business model could be scaled to solve the more complex systemic challenge of sustainable energy access in the country as well as socio-economic transformation. In all, the views on transformation towards sustainability were varied and nuanced, thus underscoring the complexity of the issue.[33]

Even though the M-KOPA example focuses on a small geographical scale, insights from the project are instructive at the continental scale. As Chapter 3 demonstrated, reconciling socio-economic development with climate policy is a major challenge. Since mobile-payment systems in particular, and digital technologies in general, have been touted as one of the major innovations that have significant transformational potential across the continent, it follows that leveraging them to pursue sustainability policy objectives including on climate change would also generate such transformative impacts.[34] Yet as the M-KOPA project has shown, such a linear approach does not necessarily lead to desired transformation. Addressing the nuances and complexities that surround such innovations is more important. Such insights are applicable to other innovations deemed to lead to socio-economic and sustainability transformations.

8.3.2   *Institutional Innovation*

Institutions are a key feature of governance. Institutions have been central to regional and continental cooperation in Africa. At the apex of continental cooperation is the African Union (AU). Initially conceived as the main institution to promote cooperation amongst post-colonial independent African states, the Organization for African Unity (OAU), as it was originally called, provided the forum for decolonisation. Moreover, the OAU had been envisioned as the headquarters of what would be the federation of African states, as envisioned by the pan-Africanist and Ghana's first president, Kwameh Nkrumah. Eventually, Nkrumah's dream of a United States of Africa did not materialise, and decolonisation remained as the OAU's chief mandate.[35]

Upon achieving the decolonisation goal with the independence of Namibia in 1990, the OAU was revamped to the AU in 2002. The new mandate of the AU would be to promote continental economic cooperation, pursuant to the Africa Economic Cooperation Treaty (also known as the Abuja Treaty) of 1990. Through the transformation of the OAU to the AU, it is evident that African countries could repurpose institutions to address different challenges.[36] It is within this context that the AU was mandated by African states to promote cooperation on climate change.

One way that African countries have used the AU to foster climate policy is through the coordination of national positions in the lead up to the annual climate change negotiations under the UNFCCC. Coordination at national level has been undertaken through the African Ministerial Conference on the Environment (AMCEN), which was established in 1985 to 'provide advocacy for environmental protection in Africa; to ensure that basic human needs are met adequately and in a sustainable manner; facilitate social and economic development; and to ensure that agricultural activities and practises meet the food security needs of the region.'[37]

At the technical level, and through delegation from AMCEN, African countries negotiate at the UNFCCC through the African Group of Negotiators (AGN). Established in 1995, the AGN includes senior government officials as well as members of the civil society, private sector and others, who comprise the official national delegations. The AGN defines itself as

[T]he technical body of the three-tier African negotiating structure that engages in the technical negotiations during the Conferences of the Parties and the intersessional negotiations. The AGN prepares and drafts text and common positions, guided by decisions and key messages from Committee of African Heads of State and Government on Climate Change (CAHOSCC), and the African Ministerial Conference on Environment and Natural Resources (AMCEN), and prepares text for adoption by Ministers during the COPs

Another important institution established by African Countries to support climate policy is the African Centre for Climate Policy (ACPC). The ACPC

[I]s a hub for knowledge generation on climate change in Africa. It addresses the need for greatly improved climate information for Africa and strengthening the use of such information for decision making, by improving analytical capacity, knowledge management and dissemination activities. The ACPC is an integral part of the Climate for Development in Africa (ClimDev-Africa) programme, which is a joint initiative of the African Union Commission(AUC), the United Nations Economic Commission for Africa (UNECA) and the African Development Bank (AfDB). ClimDev-Africa has been mandated at regional meetings of African Heads of State and Government, as well as by Africa's Ministers of Finance, Ministers of Planning and Ministers of Environment. The ACPC has three broad activity areas around which its current work programme is arranged. These are: Knowledge generation, sharing and networking that consist of research, knowledge management and peer learning, and outreach activities; Advocacy and consensus building; and Advisory services and technical cooperation, which comprise capacity mobilization, capacity building and technical assistance.[38]

In addition to the aforementioned institutions, the African Development Bank (AfDB) has also been an important locus for continental climate coordination in Africa. Under the AfDB, there are several institutional arrangements to address climate change. A crucial one is the AfDB Climate Change Fund, whose mandate is to mobilise and finance climate change projects and initiatives in Africa.[39]

African countries have also been coordinating their climate change efforts at the sub-regional level, in particular through Regional Economic Communities (RECs). Through the East African Community (EAC) REC, for instance, partner countries have established a Climate Change Unit and attendant regional climate policies. Another REC, the Southern Africa Development Community (SADC) has established the Climate Change Mitigation and Adaptation programme. In a sign of increasing institutional complexity, the EAC, SADC and another REC—the Common Market for East and Southern Africa (COMESA)—have also launched a joint called "The African Solution" under an approach termed as the "Tripartite Programme on Climate Change Adaptation and Mitigation."[40]

While it is clear from the foregoing that African countries have established a suite of institutions to coordinate their climate policies and diplomacy at the continental level, there is a major gap in the research dimension—with the exception of the ACPC. Although there are many research organisations that deal with climate policy in Africa, including with continental mandates, their modes of operation are highly localised to a few high-profile countries. A major gap therefore exists between innovative research and public policy on climate change. The gap is exacerbated by sub-regional contexts and nuances that get overlooked in generalisations of the African condition.

To address this research gap, policy research networks including the Africa Research and Impact Network (ARIN) have also emerged. Designed as a platform, ARIN "brings together a network of scholars across Africa who have been undertaking research in various fields including natural resource management, climate change, agriculture, forestry, energy, water, trade, gender and cities to leverage their knowledge and experiences in helping research and donor organisations understand and pursue impact pathways. The team includes both top level researchers and technocrats."[41] Instead of the secretariat being the central institutional feature, ARIN has a network of young African scholars, practitioners and policy makers from various parts of Africa, under the ARIN Fellowship. Moreover, ARIN also has sub-regional focal points from the four geographical regions in Africa, thus emphasising the sub-regional contexts of the continent. While still in its formative phase, ARIN has implemented innovative projects including the innovative Bilingual NDC Finance Fellowship, which is described in detail in the next section. While ARIN does not capture the full gamut of continental climate policy research, it presents a viable model of institutional innovation in Africa in the research and policy domains.

8.3.3 Building and Enhancing Endogenous Capacity

In Chapter 5 on dynamic differentiation, we critiqued and highlighted the limitations arising from an overreliance on multilateral transfers of means of implementation—finance, technology and capacity—as the main mechanism of building and enhancing capability in the continent. Instead, we emphasised the need for building and enhancing endogenous capacity to tackle climate policy and ensure a just transition for the continent.

We have engaged in various projects which have sought to build the endogenous capability of African countries to mobilise resources to effectively address climate change. As we noted earlier in the book, some scholars have argued for the need to re-examine some long-standing concepts and critically evaluate their relevance. One such concept is "technology transfer", which is the lynchpin of efforts to mobilise resources from the global North to the South. But re-examination of these concepts presupposes that the conditions for which they were developed no longer exist. This is true for technology transfer.[42]

It has been argued that in the age of exponential innovation, technological abundance, the concept of "technology transfer", at least as originally envisioned, is no longer fit for purpose.[43] Technology transfer has been a key feature of Multilateral Environmental Agreements (MEAs) including on climate change. In most formulations, industrialised countries, given their greater capability and responsibility to address environmental challenges, have often been expected, if not obligated, to transfer technology to emerging countries. Developed under the "derived development" programme that characterised the post-war world, technology transfer has persisted over the decades. Its continued relevance was also bolstered by the clamour of developing countries for a more equitable international order, especially through the New International Economic Order (NIEO).[44]

Conceptually, technology transfer is premised on the Cartesian notion of static equilibrium and dichotomy, which has underpinned the failed bifurcated approach to multilateral climate change cooperation. To engage with the more dynamic and complex international climate change regime, the endogenous capability of developing countries becomes more important than the nominal transfer of resources from the global North to South. "Technology acquisition" and "absorptive capacity" have been identified as suitable alternatives to "technology transfer" at least in the long run.[45]

Premised on the concepts of technology acquisition and absorptive capacity, and in collaboration with the University of Sussex, we implemented the Climate Relevant Innovation Systems-builders (CRIBS) project. Specifically, the project examined how the CRIBS could be leveraged to implement the Nationally Determined Contributions (NDCs) submitted by African countries. With a focus on building the domestic capacity to absorb and domesticate climate technologies, we worked with key policy makers from various East African countries as well as key stakeholders such as the private sector and international development partners.[46]

By flipping the primary responsibility from industrialised countries transferring technologies to recipient (African) countries strengthening their domestic capacity to absorb the climate technologies from a greater geographical variety, the CRIBS projects found the latter approach more viable. That African countries had only attracted less than three per cent (3%) of Clean Development Mechanism (CDM) financing under the Kyoto Protocol—with the bulk of the finances going to South Africa—revealed the limits of technology transfer.[47] Amongst the policy makers in the CRIBS project, there are those who advocated for national-level approaches to building capability, while others favoured sectoral approaches. What was commonly agreed, however, was a paradigm shift away from technology transfer and towards technology acquisition and strengthening the attendant absorptive capacity.[48]

Accessing climate finance has also been a major challenge for African countries. Under the UNFCCC and its derivative legal instruments, several climate finance mechanisms have been established. The most prominent is the Green Climate Fund (GCF), which was conceived as the main multilateral mechanism through which climate finance would be mobilised and disbursed. Studies have, however, shown that developing countries, especially those with limited capacity, have struggled to access climate funds. Challenges in accessing the funds arise from the high transaction costs due to the complex bureaucratic nature of accessing the climate funds. For some African countries, it costs more to access the funds vis-à-vis the eventual disbursed funds.

Building and enhancing the technical capacity of African countries to navigate the complex climate finance mechanisms is critical to accessing the funds. Moreover, there is a need to diversify the sources of funding, as NDCs submitted by African as well as other developing countries have revealed. In partnership with the Frankfurt School of Finance, and with support from the Canadian International Development Research Centre (IDRC), we implemented the Bilingual NDC Finance Fellowship project. The project sought to build the capacity of African policy makers, practitioners and scholars to understand and access the various kinds of finance to support the implementation of their countries' NDCs. Overall, the project has trained about two hundred Fellows, who after graduating were encouraged to implement their project ideas. By broadening the understanding and capability of accessing various kinds of climate finance, it is hoped the project has also built the capacity of African researchers, practitioners and policy makers to mobilise resources to support the implementation of their respective countries' NDCs.[49]

8.3.4 Dynamic Transnational Partnerships

Scholarly and policy debates on international climate policy often draw distinctions between the global North and South. While there is some relevance to such an approach, there is much more synergy in practice. In terms of research, there is much scope for collaboration especially between researchers in both the global North and South. After all, climate change is a global common good, but its manifestation is differentiated.

In seeking to address some of the policy challenges in Africa, we have worked closely with various institutions and organisations from across the world. To understand the dynamics of transformations for sustainability, we collaborated with several organisations from the world over under the aegis of a consortium called the Social, Technological and Environmental Pathways to Sustainability (STEPS) Centre's 'Pathways to Sustainability: Knowledge, Politics and Power' project. Through the STEPS Centre, we implemented projects ranging from socio-technical transitions in renewable energy to the politics of knowledge production.

As part of the Pathways project, exchange visits with consortium members allowed for the sharing of lessons and experiences from various parts of the world. In one such exchange, researchers from Kenya and China visited each other's country. Researchers from Kenya shared their experiences on convening transformation labs (T-Labs) examining mobile-based payment systems for solar, while the Chinese researchers shared their experiences in implementing a project examining the dynamics of green economy transformations.[50]

Within a broader context, the Pathways project also convened workshops where all the various regional hubs shared lessons on implementing T-Labs in their respective countries. What was interesting about the workshop sessions was that participants could broaden and deepen their knowledge on the dynamics of sustainability transformations in various countries and regions. Expanding the knowledge base through such initiatives holds much promise, as it allows mutually beneficial learning. Insights from the Pathways project have been compiled into an edited book volume.[51]

Other dynamic partnerships that we have engaged in have also generated novel findings on emergent climate policy issues. In a project designed as a comparative study, we collaborated with various partners to examine the dynamics of transnational, subnational and non-state climate action in the global South, focusing on the case studies of Kenya and

India.[52] The "ClimateSouth" project was novel in that it explored an under-theorised area of climate action in the global South. Much scholarly attention and work on this topic has been in the global North. Comparing India and Kenya opened up opportunities for better understanding the promise and challenges of transnational climate governance.

Beyond generating interesting research findings, the ClimateSouth project also benefited the transnational, sub- and non-state actors that were engaged through the project. In a survey of small and medium enterprises (SMEs), which form the bulk of economic actors in both Kenya and India, most of the survey respondents noted that they had not paid much attention to the need to institutionalise climate change in their business activities. Engagement in the project thus drew their interest in adopting climate policies. For the sub-state actors, their interest was on how they could engage more effectively in transnational climate governance. Overall, the project brought together the innovative trends of transnational climate governance with transnational, non- and sub-state actors in Africa.

8.3.5 Strategic Geopolitical Engagement

Some African policy makers have demonstrated keen understanding of geopolitical changes and they have responded accordingly. Through various geopolitical partnerships, these policy makers have engaged in initiatives that have departed from the undue reliance on multilateral climate change negotiations, within the broader context of the just transition.

The rise of China to the status of a great power is arguably the most significant geopolitical development of the twenty-first century.[53] China's rise marked the advent of multipolarity hence the onset of great power politics.[54] Sino-African relations have been a key element of China's rise and the resultant great power politics. In Africa, China's growing strategic engagement has challenged the hegemony of former colonial powers from the West.[55] As outlined in Chapter 4 of this book on the changing geopolitical environment, China's rise has significantly changed the dynamics of international climate cooperation. China's rise as a technological superpower has also transformed the dynamics underpinning technology transfer, thus raising the salience of South-South cooperation forum.[56]

Sino-African cooperation has mostly been undertaken under the auspices of the Forum for China-Africa Cooperation (FOCAC). Traditionally, FOCAC has focused on conventional economic development issues, especially infrastructure. But recently, the scope of cooperation has broadened to include cooperation on sustainability issues.[57] At the FOCAC summit held in Dakar, Senegal, cooperation on climate change was elevated to a top policy priority. As a result, a high-level declaration on climate change was adopted, highlighting the political importance of the topic.[58] A unique feature of Sino-African cooperation is that the relationship is not characterised by a previous colonial relation. In contrast, the relationship is largely based on solidarity within the broader context of South-South cooperation. China's establishment and capitalisation of a South-South Climate Fund is further evidence of the deepening South-South cooperation, of which Africa is a crucial member.[59]

Related, many African countries are also members of the International Solar Alliance (ISA). The ISA was established by India to promote solar technology in developing countries. As an emerging power, the ISA provides an important platform for India to establish its geopolitical credentials.[60] But the ISA also directly addresses some of the key energy needs of African countries. Moreover, the ISA not only includes the transfer of technology, but also the requisite technical knowledge and capacity. The engagement of African countries in the ISA indicates that they are leveraging the array of institutions to pursue their climate policies.

Particular African countries have also engaged in innovative geopolitical partnerships. As outlined in Chapter 4 on geopolitical dynamics, South Africa has engaged in such geopolitical initiatives. Prigogine noted that the bifurcation leads to the development of novel dissipative structure, which opens windows for innovation. Likewise, South Africa has taken advantage of the advent of multipolarity and also leveraged its significant diplomatic capacity to launch the innovative strategic initiatives on the just transition. In partnership with France, Germany, UK, US and EU, South Africa launched the 'International Just Energy Transition Partnership'. The project seeks to mobilise about US$ 8.5 billion to finance South Africa's just transition, with a focus on its electricity grid.[61] While South Africa is an outlier in Africa, given its significant diplomatic capability, the strategic initiative indicates a viable model of geopolitical engagement that goes beyond the multilateral focus on support for implementation of climate policies.

8.3.6 *Experimentation and Learning*

In the broader policy context, policy experimentation and learning will be critical to securing a just transition in Africa. What is encouraging is that African countries have significant experience in experimenting with novel policy and institutional arrangements. In addition, learning has been a critical component of Africa's policy processes. It is in the economic realm, especially in regional economic integration through trade policy, that African countries have truly demonstrated the political and diplomatic initiative in addressing development challenges.[62]

As complex designers, Africa's policy makers should continue placing experimentation and learning at the heart of institutional and policy development. Already, the establishment of the continental and sub-regional institutions indicates experimentation and learning. But what is needed is closing the divide between scholars and policy makers. Policy makers are often wont to maintaining the status quo, while scholars are often characterised as utopians whose ideas have little or no connection to reality. Bridging the academic and policy divide thus would be critical to effectively engaging with the international climate regime especially as complex designers.[63] Projects such as the Future of Climate Cooperation, which seek to catalyse engagements between policy makers and researchers on the emerging and long-run climate policy issues, could serve as an inspirational model.[64]

8.4   CONCLUSION

If the international climate regime is characterised by complexity, dynamism and irreversible evolution, then a 'governing complexity' approach would be the most suitable. Such an approach would entail decision-making that would foster effective engagement with the international climate regime. Policy makers and other key actors would need to assume the role of complex designers. As complex designers, the actors would be guided by the emergent principles of flexibility, balanced content and adaptive management practices.

Drawing on concrete examples of initiatives implemented by the authors as well as other actors, including African governments, the chapter has demonstrated the feasibility of the complex designers approach. It has been shown that, already, African governments have creatively responded to some of the climate policy challenges by establishing novel institutional and policy arrangements. Moreover, it has also been shown how African researchers can also contribute to generating the pertinent knowledge not only on the changing nature of the climate change problem, but also how to effectively address the urgent policy challenges. While the nature of the emerging climate policy issues is to some degree indeterminate, what is certain is the need for African policy makers and other actors to fully assume their role as complex designers. Doing so would open up novel avenues for securing a just transition for Africa, especially in the long run.

NOTES

1. Howard Gardner, *A Synthesizing Mind: A Memoir from the Creator of Multiple Intelligences Theory* (Cambridge: MIT Press, 2020), 187.
2. Anthea Roberts and Taylor St John, 'Complex Designers and Emergent Design: Reforming the Investment Treaty System', *American Journal of International Law* 116, no. 1 (January 2022): 96–149, https://doi.org/10.1017/ajil.2021.57.
3. Francis Mangeni and Calestous Juma, *Emergent Africa: Evolution of Regional Economic Integration* (Terra Alta, WV: Headline Books, 2019), chap. 1.
4. e.g. see Laura Gómez-Mera, 'International Regime Complexity', Oxford Research Encyclopedia of International Studies, 31 August 2021, https://doi.org/10.1093/acrefore/9780190846626.013.648; Karen J. Alter and Sophie Meunier, 'The Politics of International Regime Complexity', *Perspectives on Politics* 7, no. 1 (March 2009): 13–24, https://doi.org/10.1017/S1537592709090033; Daniel W. Drezner, 'The Power and Peril of International Regime Complexity', *Perspectives on Politics* 7, no. 1 (March 2009): 65–70, https://doi.org/10.1017/S153759270909010; Benjamin Faude and Felix Große-Kreul, 'Let's Justify! How Regime Complexes Enhance the Normative Legitimacy of Global Governance', *International Studies Quarterly* 64, no. 2 (1 June 2020): 431–39, https://doi.org/10.1093/isq/sqaa024; Robert Keohane and David Victor, 'The Regime Complex for Climate Change', *Perspectives on Politics* 9, no. 1 (March 2011): 7–23, https://doi.org/10.1017/S1537592710004068.
5. Keohane and Victor, 'The Regime Complex for Climate Change'.
6. Rakhyun E. Kim, 'The Emergent Network Structure of the Multilateral Environmental Agreement System', *Global Environmental Change* 23, no. 5 (October 2013): 980–91, https://doi.org/10.1016/j.gloenvcha.2013.07.006.

7. Nigel Gilbert and Seth Bullock, 'Complexity at the Social Science Interface', *Complexity* 19, no. 6 (2014): 1–4, https://doi.org/10.1002/cplx. 21550; Robert Geyer and Paul Cairney, eds., *Handbook on Complexity and Public Policy*, First, Handbooks of Research on Policy (Cheltenham, UK and Northampton, MA: Edward Elgar, 2015), https://www.elgaro nline.com/view/9781782549512.xml.
8. Elinor Ostrom, *Governing the Commons: The Evolution of Institutions for Collective Action* (Cambridge, United Kingdom: Cambridge University Press, 1990).
9. Andrew J. Jordan et al., 'Emergence of Polycentric Climate Governance and Its Future Prospects', *Nature Climate Change* 5, no. 11 (November 2015): 977–82, https://doi.org/10.1038/nclimate2725; Elinor Ostrom, *A Polycentric Approach for Coping with Climate Change*, Policy Research Working Papers (The World Bank, 2009), https://doi.org/10.1596/ 1813-9450-5095; Andrew Jordan et al., 'Governing Climate Change Polycentrically', in *Governing Climate Change: Polycentricity in Action?* ed. Andrew Jordan et al. (Cambridge: Cambridge University Press, 2018), 3–26, https://doi.org/10.1017/9781108284646.002.
10. Roberts and John, 'Complex Designers and Emergent Design', 111.
11. Herbert A. Simon, 'Decision Making: Rational, Nonrational, and Irrational', *Educational Administration Quarterly* 29, no. 3 (1 August 1993): 392–411, https://doi.org/10.1177/0013161X93029003009; Alfred R. Mele and Piers Rawling, *The Oxford Handbook of Rationality* (Oxford: Oxford University Press, 2004); Thomas Sturm, 'The "Rationality Wars" in Psychology: Where They Are and Where They Could Go', *Inquiry* 55, no. 1 (1 February 2012): 66–81, https://doi.org/10.1080/0020174X. 2012.643628.
12. Gardner, *A Synthesizing Mind*; Howard E. Gardner, *Intelligence Reframed: Multiple Intelligences for the 21st Century* (London: Hachette UK, 2000).
13. David Dequech, 'Bounded Rationality, Institutions, and Uncertainty', *Journal of Economic Issues* 35, no. 4 (1 December 2001): 911–29, https://doi.org/10.1080/00213624.2001.11506420; Duncan Snidal, 'Rational Choice and International Relations', in *Handbook of International Relations*, ed. Walter Carlsnaes, Thomas Risse, and Beth Simmons (London: Sage Publications Ltd, 2002), 73–94, https://doi.org/10. 4135/9781848608290; Stephen M. Walt, 'Rigor or Rigor Mortis? Rational Choice and Security Studies', *International Security* 23, no. 4 (1 April 1999): 5–48, https://doi.org/10.1162/isec.23.4.5.
14. Herbert A. Simon, 'Bounded Rationality', in *Utility and Probability*, ed. John Eatwell, Murray Milgate, and Peter Newman, *The New Palgrave* (London: Palgrave Macmillan UK, 1990), 15–18, https://doi.org/10. 1007/978-1-349-20568-4_5; Simon.

15. Robert Jervis, *Perception and Misperception in International Politics: New Edition* (Princeton, NJ: Princeton University Press, 1976).
16. Dequech, 'Bounded Rationality, Institutions, and Uncertainty'.
17. Roberts and John, 'Complex Designers and Emergent Design'.
18. Roberts and John, 96.
19. Roberts and John, 96.
20. Calestous Juma and Norman Clark, 'Policy Research in Sub-Saharan Africa: An Exploration', *Public Administration and Development* 15, no. 2 (1995): 121.
21. Juma and Clark, 'Policy Research in Sub-Saharan Africa'.
22. Roberts and John, 'Complex Designers and Emergent Design', 148.
23. Jeffrey McGee and Jens Steffek, 'The Copenhagen Turn in Global Climate Governance and the Contentious History of Differentiation in International Law', *Journal of Environmental Law* 28, no. 1 (1 March 2016): 37–63, https://doi.org/10.1093/jel/eqw003; Robert Falkner, 'The Paris Agreement and the New Logic of International Climate Politics', *International Affairs* 92, no. 5 (1 September 2016): 1107–25, https://doi.org/10.1111/1468-2346.12708; Thomas Hale, 'Catalytic Cooperation', *Global Environmental Politics* 20, no. 4 (1 November 2020): 73–98, https://doi.org/10.1162/glep_a_00561.
24. Thomas Hale et al., 'Net Zero Tracker' (Oxford, UK: Energy and Climate Intelligence Unit, Data-Driven EnviroLab, NewClimate Institute, Oxford Net Zero, 2021), https://zerotracker.net/.
25. Roberts and John, 'Complex Designers and Emergent Design', 96.
26. William E. Rees, 'Achieving Sustainability: Reform or Transformation?' *Journal of Planning Literature* 9, no. 4 (1 May 1995): 343–61, https://doi.org/10.1177/088541229500900402; Carl Folke et al., 'Resilience Thinking: Integrating Resilience, Adaptability and Transformability', *Ecology and Society* 15, no. 4 (15 November 2010), https://doi.org/10.5751/ES-03610-150420.
27. Sheila M. Cannon, 'Climate Strikes: Greta Thunberg Calls for "System Change Not Climate Change"—Here's What That Could Look like', The Conversation, 15 March 2019, http://theconversation.com/climate-strikes-greta-thunberg-calls-for-system-change-not-climate-change-heres-what-that-could-look-like-112891; Christopher Todd Beer, '"Systems Change Not Climate Change": Support for a Radical Shift Away from Capitalism at Mainstream U.S. Climate Change Protest Events', *The Sociological Quarterly* 63, no. 1 (30 November 2020): 1–24, https://doi.org/10.1080/00380253.2020.1842141.
28. Andy Stirling, 'Risk, Uncertainty and Precaution: Some Instrumental Implications from the Social Sciences', in *Negotiating Environmental Change: New Perspectives from Social Science*, ed. F. Berkhout, Melissa

Leach, and Ian Scoones (Cheltenham, UK: Edward Elgar Publishing, 2003).

29. Ian Scoones and Andy Stirling, *The Politics of Uncertainty: Challenges of Transformation* (London: Routledge, 2020), https://doi.org/10.4324/9781003023845; Pathways Network, *Transformative Pathways to Sustainability: Learning Across Disciplines, Cultures and Contexts* (London: Routledge, 2021), https://doi.org/10.4324/9780429331930.

30. Laura Pereira et al., 'Transformative Spaces in the Making: Key Lessons from Nine Cases in the Global South', *Sustainability Science* 15, no. 1 (1 January 2020): 161–78, https://doi.org/10.1007/s11625-019-00749-x.

31. Simplice A. Asongu, Nicholas Biekpe, and Danny Cassimon, 'Understanding the Greater Diffusion of Mobile Money Innovations in Africa', *Telecommunications Policy* 44, no. 8 (1 September 2020): 102,000, https://doi.org/10.1016/j.telpol.2020.102000; Wenxiu (Vince) Nan, Xiaolin (Christina) Zhu, and M. Lynne Markus, 'What We Know and Don't Know About the Socioeconomic Impacts of Mobile Money in Sub-Saharan Africa: A Systematic Literature Review', *The Electronic Journal of Information Systems in Developing Countries* 87, no. 2 (2021): e12155, https://doi.org/10.1002/isd2.12155.

32. Charu Rastogi, 'M-Kopa Solar: Lighting up the Dark Continent', *South Asian Journal of Business and Management Cases* 7, no. 2 (1 December 2018): 93–103, https://doi.org/10.1177/2277977918774648.

33. Victoria Chengo and Kennedy Mbeva, 'How Transformative Are Mobile Payments for Solar Home Systems in Kenya?', STEPS Centre, 28 September 2018, https://steps-centre.org/blog/how-transformative-is-kenyas-mobile-payment-system-for-solar-home-systems/.

34. Bitange Ndemo and Tim Weiss, 'Making Sense of Africa's Emerging Digital Transformation and Its Many Futures', *Africa Journal of Management* 3, no. 3–4 (2 October 2017): 328–47, https://doi.org/10.1080/23322373.2017.1400260; Tawfik Jelassi and Francisco J. Martínez-López, 'Digital Business Transformation in Silicon Savannah: How M-PESA Changed Safaricom (Kenya)', in *Strategies for E-Business: Concepts and Cases on Value Creation and Digital Business Transformation*, ed. Tawfik Jelassi and Francisco J. Martínez-López, Classroom Companion: Business (Cham: Springer International Publishing, 2020), 633–58, https://doi.org/10.1007/978-3-030-48950-2_23; M. Lynne Markus and Wenxiu (Vince) Nan, 'Theorizing the Connections between Digital Innovations and Societal Transformation: Learning from the Case of M-Pesa in Kenya', *Handbook of Digital Innovation*, 14 July 2020, https://www.elgaronline.com/view/edcoll/9781788119979/9781788119979.00013.xml; Korbla P. Puplampu, Kobena T. Hanson, and Peter Arthur, 'Disruptive Technologies, Innovation and Transformation in Africa: The Present and Future', in *Disruptive Technologies, Innovation and*

Development in Africa, ed. Peter Arthur, Kobena T. Hanson, and Korbla P. Puplampu, International Political Economy Series (Cham: Springer International Publishing, 2020), 3–13, https://doi.org/10.1007/978-3-030-40647-9_1.

35. Alfred W. Chanda, 'The Organization of African Unity: An Appraisal', *Zambia Law Journal* 21–24 (1989): 1; Victor Osaro Edo and Michael Abiodun Olanrewaju, 'An Assessment of the Transformation of the Organization of African Unity (O.A.U) to the African Union (A.U), 1963–2007', *Journal of the Historical Society of Nigeria* 21 (2012): 41–69.

36. Corinne A. A. Packer and Donald Rukare, 'The New African Union and Its Constitutive Act', *American Journal of International Law* 96, no. 2 (April 2002): 365–79, https://doi.org/10.2307/2693932.

37. UNEP, 'About AMCEN', UNEP—UN Environment Programme, 31 October 2019, http://www.unep.org/regions/africa/african-ministerial-conference-environment/about-amcen.

38. ACPC, 'The African Climate Policy Centre (ACPC) | ClimDev-Africa', 2022, https://www.climdev-africa.org/afrian-climate-policy-center.

39. African Development Bank, 'Africa Climate Change Fund', Text, African Development Bank—Building Today, a Better Africa Tomorrow (African Development Bank Group, 16 April 2019), https://www.afdb.org/en/topics-and-sectors/initiatives-partnerships/africa-climate-change-fund; Maarten Van Aalst, Molly Hellmuth, and Daniele Ponzi, 'Working Paper 89—Come Rain or Shine—Integrating Climate Risk Management into African Development Bank Operations', Working Paper Series (African Development Bank, 9 December 2007), https://ideas.repec.org/p/adb/adbwps/224.html.

40. SADC, 'Southern African Development Community: Programme on Climate Change Adaptation and Mitigation in Eastern and Southern Africa (COMESA-EAC-SADC)', 2012, https://www.sadc.int/sadc-secretariat/directorates/office-deputy-executive-secretary-regional-integration/food-agriculture-natural-resources/tripartite-programme-climate-change-adaptation-and-mitigatio/.

41. ARIN, 'About Us—Africa Research & Impact Network', 2022, https://www.arin-africa.org/about-us/.

42. Calestous Juma, 'Complexity, Innovation, and Development: Schumpeter Revisited', *Policy and Complex Systems* 1, no. 1 (2014): 4–21, https://doi.org/10.18278/jpcs.1.1.1: ; Calestous Juma, 'Exponential Innovation and Human Rights: Implications for Science and Technology Diplomacy', SSRN Scholarly Paper (Rochester, NY: Social Science Research Network, 27 February 2018), https://papers.ssrn.com/abstract=3131243.

43. Juma, 'Exponential Innovation and Human Rights'; Juma, 'Complexity, Innovation, and Development: Schumpeter Revisited'.

44. Juma, 'Complexity, Innovation, and Development: Schumpeter Revisited'.

45. Juma, 'Exponential Innovation and Human Rights', 17.
46. David Ockwell et al., 'Making Climate Finance Work for Africa: Using NDCs to Leverage Climate Relevant Innovation System Builders (CRIBS)', Policy Brief (Nairobi, Kenya: African Centre for Technology Studies (ACTS); Steps Africa, April 2017), https://media.africaportal.org/documents/CRIBS-Training-brief-2.pdf.
47. David Ockwell and Rob Byrne, 'Improving Technology Transfer through National Systems of Innovation: Climate Relevant Innovation-System Builders (CRIBs)', *Climate Policy* 16, no. 7 (2 October 2016): 844, https://doi.org/10.1080/14693062.2015.1052958.
48. Ockwell and Byrne, 'Improving Technology Transfer through National Systems of Innovation'.
49. FS, 'The NDC Financing Fellowship Programme (NDC-FFP)' (Frankfurt School of Finance and Management, 2022), https://www.frankfurt-school.de/idrc/ndcffp.
50. Nathan Oxley, 'Sharing Insights across Continents: Africa Sustainability Hub Researcher Visits China Hub', STEPS Centre, 1 December 2016, https://steps-centre.org/news/sharing-insights-across-continents-africa-sustainability-hub-researcher-visits-china-hub/.
51. Pathways Network, *Transformative Pathways to Sustainability*.
52. Thomas Hale et al., 'Global Performance & Delivery in the Global South. Preliminary Findings of the ClimateSouth Project for the Global Climate Action Summit', GCAS Brief, Cooperative Climate Action (Oxford, UK: Global Economic Governance Programme, 10 September 2018), https://www.geg.ox.ac.uk/publication/cooperative-climate-action-global-performance-delivery-global-south.
53. Henry Kissinger, *On China* (London: Penguin, 2012); Rush Doshi, *The Long Game: China's Grand Strategy to Displace American Order* (Oxford University Press, 2021).
54. John J. Mearsheimer, *The Tragedy of Great Power Politics* (New York: W. W. Norton & Company, 2001).
55. Lina Benabdallah, *Shaping the Future of Power: Knowledge Production and Network-Building in China-Africa Relations* (Ann Arbor: University of Michigan Press, 2020).
56. Giles Mohan and May Tan-Mullins, 'The Geopolitics of South–South Infrastructure Development: Chinese-Financed Energy Projects in the Global South', *Urban Studies* 56, no. 7 (1 May 2019): 1368–85, https://doi.org/10.1177/0042098018794351; Anthea Roberts, Henrique Choer Moraes, and Victor Ferguson, 'Toward a Geoeconomic Order in International Trade and Investment', *Journal of International Economic Law* 22, no. 4 (20 December 2019): 655–76, https://doi.org/10.1093/jiel/jgz036.

57. Ian Taylor, *The Forum on China- Africa Cooperation (FOCAC)* (London: Routledge, 2010), https://doi.org/10.4324/9780203835005.
58. MFA, 'Declaration on China-Africa Cooperation on Combating Climate Change', 2 December 2021, https://www.fmprc.gov.cn/mfa_eng/wjdt_665385/2649_665393/202112/t20211203_10461772.html.
59. Martin Khor, 'China's Boost to South-South Cooperation', *South Bulletin* 90 (16 May 2016), https://www.southcentre.int/question/chinas-boost-to-south-south-cooperation.
60. ISA, 'International Solar Alliance', n.d, https://isolaralliance.org/about/background.
61. EC, 'Just Energy Transition Partnership with South Africa', Press Release, European Commission, 2 November 2021, https://ec.europa.eu/commission/presscorner/detail/en/IP_21_5768.
62. Mangeni and Juma, *Emergent Africa. Evolution of Regional Economic Integration*, pt. II.
63. Juma, 'Complexity, Innovation, and Development: Schumpeter Revisited', 106–8.
64. Thomas Hale, Jason Anderson, and Andrew Higham, 'The Future of the Climate Regime: What Is Needed 2020–2050?' (Oxford, UK: Blavatnik School of Government, Mission2020, ClimateWorks Foundation, 2020).

REFERENCES

Aalst, Maarten Van, Molly Hellmuth, and Daniele Ponzi. 'Working Paper 89—Come Rain or Shine—Integrating Climate Risk Management into African Development Bank Operations'. Working Paper Series. African Development Bank, 9 December 2007. https://ideas.repec.org/p/adb/adbwps/224.html.

ACPC. 'The African Climate Policy Centre (ACPC) | ClimDev-Africa', 2022. https://www.climdev-africa.org/afrian-climate-policy-center.

Alter, Karen J., and Sophie Meunier. 'The Politics of International Regime Complexity'. *Perspectives on Politics* 7, no. 1 (March 2009): 13–24. https://doi.org/10.1017/S1537592709090033.

ARIN. 'About Us—Africa Research & Impact Network', 2022. https://www.arin-africa.org/about-us/.

Asongu, Simplice A., Nicholas Biekpe, and Danny Cassimon. 'Understanding the Greater Diffusion of Mobile Money Innovations in Africa'. *Telecommunications Policy* 44, no. 8 (1 September 2020): 102000. https://doi.org/10.1016/j.telpol.2020.102000.

Bank, African Development. 'Africa Climate Change Fund'. Text. African Development Bank—Building Today, a Better Africa Tomorrow. African Development Bank Group, 16 April 2019. https://www.afdb.org/en/topics-and-sectors/initiatives-partnerships/africa-climate-change-fund.

Beer, Christopher Todd. '"Systems Change Not Climate Change": Support for a Radical Shift Away from Capitalism at Mainstream U.S. Climate Change Protest Events'. *The Sociological Quarterly* 63, no. 1 (30 November 2020): 1–24. https://doi.org/10.1080/00380253.2020.1842141.

Benabdallah, Lina. *Shaping the Future of Power: Knowledge Production and Network-Building in China-Africa Relations*. Ann Arbor: University of Michigan Press, 2020.

Cannon, Sheila M. 'Climate Strikes: Greta Thunberg Calls for "System Change Not Climate Change"—Here's What That Could Look Like'. The Conversation, 15 March 2019. http://theconversation.com/climate-strikes-greta-thunberg-calls-for-system-change-not-climate-change-heres-what-that-could-look-like-112891.

Chanda, Alfred W. 'The Organization of African Unity: An Appraisal'. *Zambia Law Journal* 21–24 (1989): 1–29.

Chengo, Victoria, and Kennedy Mbeva. 'How Transformative Are Mobile Payments for Solar Home Systems in Kenya?' STEPS Centre, 28 September 2018. https://steps-centre.org/blog/how-transformative-is-kenyas-mobile-payment-system-for-solar-home-systems/.

Dequech, David. 'Bounded Rationality, Institutions, and Uncertainty'. *Journal of Economic Issues* 35, no. 4 (1 December 2001): 911–29. https://doi.org/10.1080/00213624.2001.11506420.

Doshi, Rush. *The Long Game: China's Grand Strategy to Displace American Order*. Oxford: Oxford University Press, 2021.

Drezner, Daniel W. 'The Power and Peril of International Regime Complexity'. *Perspectives on Politics* 7, no. 1 (March 2009): 65–70. https://doi.org/10.1017/S1537592709090100.

EC. 'Just Energy Transition Partnership with South Africa'. Press Release. European Commission, 2 November 2021. https://ec.europa.eu/commission/presscorner/detail/en/IP_21_5768.

Edo, Victor Osaro, and Michael Abiodun Olanrewaju. 'An Assessment of the Transformation of the Organization of African Unity (O.A.U) to the African Union (A.U), 1963–2007'. *Journal of the Historical Society of Nigeria* 21 (2012): 41–69.

Falkner, Robert. 'The Paris Agreement and the New Logic of International Climate Politics'. *International Affairs* 92, no. 5 (1 September 2016): 1107–25. https://doi.org/10.1111/1468-2346.12708.

Faude, Benjamin, and Felix Große-Kreul. 'Let's Justify! How Regime Complexes Enhance the Normative Legitimacy of Global Governance'. *International Studies Quarterly* 64, no. 2 (1 June 2020): 431–39. https://doi.org/10.1093/isq/sqaa024.

Folke, Carl, Stephen Carpenter, Brian Walker, Marten Scheffer, Terry Chapin, and Johan Rockström. 'Resilience Thinking: Integrating Resilience, Adaptability and Transformability'. *Ecology and Society* 15, no. 4 (15 November 2010). https://doi.org/10.5751/ES-03610-150420.

FS. 'The NDC Financing Fellowship Programme (NDC-FFP)'. Frankfurt School of Finance and Management, 2022. https://www.frankfurt-school.de/idrc/ndcffp.

Gardner, Howard E. *Intelligence Reframed: Multiple Intelligences for the 21st Century*. London: Hachette UK, 2000.

————. *A Synthesizing Mind: A Memoir from the Creator of Multiple Intelligences Theory*. Cambridge: MIT Press, 2020.

Geyer, Robert, and Paul Cairney, eds. *Handbook on Complexity and Public Policy*. First. Handbooks of Research on Policy. Cheltenham, UK and Northampton, MA: Edward Elgar, 2015. https://www.elgaronline.com/view/9781782549512.xml.

Gilbert, Nigel, and Seth Bullock. 'Complexity at the Social Science Interface'. *Complexity* 19, no. 6 (2014): 1–4. https://doi.org/10.1002/cplx.21550.

Gómez-Mera, Laura. 'International Regime Complexity'. Oxford Research Encyclopedia of International Studies, 31 August 2021. https://doi.org/10.1093/acrefore/9780190846626.013.648.

Hale, Thomas. 'Catalytic Cooperation'. *Global Environmental Politics* 20, no. 4 (1 November 2020): 73–98. https://doi.org/10.1162/glep_a_00561.

Hale, Thomas, Jason Anderson, and Andrew Higham. 'The Future of the Climate Regime: What Is Needed 2020–2050?' Oxford, UK: Blavatnik School of Government, Mission2020, ClimateWorks Foundation, 2020.

Hale, Thomas, Sander Chan, Kennedy Mbeva, Manish Shrivastava, Jacopo Bencini, Victoria Chengo, Ganesh Gorti, et al. 'Global Performance & Delivery in the Global South. Preliminary Findings of the ClimateSouth Project for the Global Climate Action Summit'. GCAS Brief. Cooperative Climate Action. Oxford, UK: Global Economic Governance Programme, 10 September 2018. https://www.geg.ox.ac.uk/publication/cooperative-climate-action-global-performance-delivery-global-south.

Hale, Thomas, Takeshi Kuramochi, John Lang, Brendan Mapes, Steve Smith, Ria Aiyer, Richard Black, et al. 'Net Zero Tracker'. Oxford, UK: Energy and Climate Intelligence Unit, Data-Driven EnviroLab, NewClimate Institute, Oxford Net Zero, 2021. https://zerotracker.net/.

ISA. 'International Solar Alliance', n.d. https://isolaralliance.org/about/background.

Jelassi, Tawfik, and Francisco J. Martínez-López. 'Digital Business Transformation in Silicon Savannah: How M-PESA Changed Safaricom (Kenya)'. In *Strategies for E-Business: Concepts and Cases on Value Creation and Digital*

Business Transformation, edited by Tawfik Jelassi and Francisco J. Martínez-López, 633–58. Classroom Companion: Business. Cham: Springer International Publishing, 2020. https://doi.org/10.1007/978-3-030-48950-2_23.

Jervis, Robert. *Perception and Misperception in International Politics: New Edition.* Princeton, NJ: Princeton University Press, 1976.

Jordan, Andrew J., Dave Huitema, Mikael Hildén, Harro van Asselt, Tim J. Rayner, Jonas J. Schoenefeld, Jale Tosun, Johanna Forster, and Elin L. Boasson. 'Emergence of Polycentric Climate Governance and Its Future Prospects'. *Nature Climate Change* 5, no. 11 (November 2015): 977–82. https://doi.org/10.1038/nclimate2725.

Jordan, Andrew, Dave Huitema, Jonas Schoenefeld, Harro van Asselt, and Johanna Forster. 'Governing Climate Change Polycentrically'. In *Governing Climate Change: Polycentricity in Action?* edited by Andrew Jordan, Dave Huitema, Harro van Asselt, and Johanna Forster, 3–26. Cambridge: Cambridge University Press, 2018. https://doi.org/10.1017/978110828 4646.002.

Juma, Calestous. 'Complexity, Innovation, and Development: Schumpeter Revisited'. *Policy and Complex Systems* 1, no. 1 (2014): 4–21. https://doi.org/10.18278/jpcs.1.1.1.

———. 'Exponential Innovation and Human Rights: Implications for Science and Technology Diplomacy'. SSRN Scholarly Paper. Rochester, NY: Social Science Research Network, 27 February 2018. https://papers.ssrn.com/abstract=3131243.

Juma, Calestous, and Norman Clark. 'Policy Research in Sub-Saharan Africa: An Exploration'. *Public Administration and Development* 15, no. 2 (1995): 121–37.

Keohane, Robert, and David Victor. 'The Regime Complex for Climate Change'. *Perspectives on Politics* 9, no. 1 (March 2011): 7–23. https://doi.org/10.1017/S1537592710004068.

Khor, Martin. 'China's Boost to South-South Cooperation'. *South Bulletin* 90 (16 May 2016). https://www.southcentre.int/question/chinas-boost-to-south-south-cooperation/.

Kim, Rakhyun E. 'The Emergent Network Structure of the Multilateral Environmental Agreement System'. *Global Environmental Change* 23, no. 5 (October 2013): 980–91. https://doi.org/10.1016/j.gloenvcha.2013.07.006.

Kissinger, Henry. *On China*. London: Penguin, 2012.

Mangeni, Francis, and Calestous Juma. *Emergent Africa: Evolution of Regional Economic Integration*. Terra Alta, WV: Headline Books, 2019.

Markus, M. Lynne, and Wenxiu (Vince) Nan. 'Theorizing the Connections between Digital Innovations and Societal Transformation: Learning from the Case of M-Pesa in Kenya'. *Handbook of Digital Innovation*, 14 July

2020. https://www.elgaronline.com/view/edcoll/9781788119979/978178 8119979.00013.xml.

McGee, Jeffrey, and Jens Steffek. 'The Copenhagen Turn in Global Climate Governance and the Contentious History of Differentiation in International Law'. *Journal of Environmental Law* 28, no. 1 (1 March 2016): 37–63. https://doi.org/10.1093/jel/eqw003.

Mearsheimer, John J. *The Tragedy of Great Power Politics*. New York: W. W. Norton & Company, 2001.

Mele, Alfred R., and Piers Rawling. *The Oxford Handbook of Rationality*. Oxford: Oxford University Press, 2004.

MFA. 'Declaration on China-Africa Cooperation on Combating Climate Change', 2 December 2021. https://www.fmprc.gov.cn/mfa_eng/wjdt_6 65385/2649_665393/202112/t20211203_10461772.html.

Mohan, Giles, and May Tan-Mullins. 'The Geopolitics of South–South Infrastructure Development: Chinese-Financed Energy Projects in the Global South'. *Urban Studies* 56, no. 7 (1 May 2019): 1368–85. https://doi.org/ 10.1177/0042098018794351.

Nan, Wenxiu (Vince), Xiaolin (Christina) Zhu, and M. Lynne Markus. 'What We Know and Don't Know About the Socioeconomic Impacts of Mobile Money in Sub-Saharan Africa: A Systematic Literature Review'. *The Electronic Journal of Information Systems in Developing Countries* 87, no. 2 (2021): e12155. https://doi.org/10.1002/isd2.12155.

Ndemo, Bitange, and Tim Weiss. 'Making Sense of Africa's Emerging Digital Transformation and Its Many Futures'. *Africa Journal of Management* 3, no. 3–4 (2 October 2017): 328–47. https://doi.org/10.1080/23322373.2017. 1400260.

Ockwell, David, and Rob Byrne. 'Improving Technology Transfer through National Systems of Innovation: Climate Relevant Innovation-System Builders (CRIBs)'. *Climate Policy* 16, no. 7 (2 October 2016): 836–54. https://doi. org/10.1080/14693062.2015.1052958.

Ockwell, David, Rob Byrne, Joanes Atela, Kennedy Mbeva, and Reuben Makomere. 'Making Climate Finance Work for Africa: Using NDCs to Leverage Climate Relevant Innovation System Builders (CRIBS)'. Policy Brief. Nairobi, Kenya: African Centre for Technology Studies (ACTS); Steps Africa, April 2017. https://media.africaportal.org/documents/CRIBS-Training-brief-2.pdf.

Ostrom, Elinor. *Governing the Commons: The Evolution of Institutions for Collective Action*. Cambridge, United Kingdom: Cambridge University Press, 1990.

———. *A Polycentric Approach for Coping With Climate Change*. Policy Research Working Papers. The World Bank, 2009. https://doi.org/10.1596/1813-9450-5095.

Oxley, Nathan. 'Sharing Insights Across Continents: Africa Sustainability Hub Researcher Visits China Hub'. STEPS Centre, 1 December 2016. https://steps-centre.org/news/sharing-insights-across-continents-africa-sustainability-hub-researcher-visits-china-hub/.

Packer, Corinne A. A., and Donald Rukare. 'The New African Union and Its Constitutive Act'. *American Journal of International Law* 96, no. 2 (April 2002): 365–79. https://doi.org/10.2307/2693932.

Pathways Network. *Transformative Pathways to Sustainability: Learning Across Disciplines, Cultures and Contexts*. London: Routledge, 2021. https://doi.org/10.4324/9780429331930.

Pereira, Laura, Niki Frantzeskaki, Aniek Hebinck, Lakshmi Charli-Joseph, Scott Drimie, Michelle Dyer, Hallie Eakin, et al. 'Transformative Spaces in the Making: Key Lessons from Nine Cases in the Global South'. *Sustainability Science* 15, no. 1 (1 January 2020): 161–78. https://doi.org/10.1007/s11625-019-00749-x.

Puplampu, Korbla P., Kobena T. Hanson, and Peter Arthur. 'Disruptive Technologies, Innovation and Transformation in Africa: The Present and Future'. In *Disruptive Technologies, Innovation and Development in Africa*, edited by Peter Arthur, Kobena T. Hanson, and Korbla P. Puplampu, 3–13. International Political Economy Series. Cham: Springer International Publishing, 2020. https://doi.org/10.1007/978-3-030-40647-9_1.

Rastogi, Charu. 'M-Kopa Solar: Lighting up the Dark Continent'. *South Asian Journal of Business and Management Cases* 7, no. 2 (1 December 2018): 93–103. https://doi.org/10.1177/2277977918774648.

Rees, William E. 'Achieving Sustainability: Reform or Transformation?' *Journal of Planning Literature* 9, no. 4 (1 May 1995): 343–61. https://doi.org/10.1177/088541229500900402.

Roberts, Anthea, and Taylor St John. 'Complex Designers and Emergent Design: Reforming the Investment Treaty System'. *American Journal of International Law* 116, no. 1 (January 2022): 96–149. https://doi.org/10.1017/ajil.2021.57.

Roberts, Anthea, Henrique Choer Moraes, and Victor Ferguson. 'Toward a Geoeconomic Order in International Trade and Investment'. *Journal of International Economic Law* 22, no. 4 (20 December 2019): 655–76. https://doi.org/10.1093/jiel/jgz036.

SADC. 'Southern African Development Community: Programme on Climate Change Adaptation and Mitigation in Eastern and Southern Africa (COMESA-EAC-SADC)', 2012. https://www.sadc.int/sadc-secretariat/directorates/office-deputy-executive-secretary-regional-integration/food-agriculture-natural-resources/tripartite-programme-climate-change-adaptation-and-mitigatio/.

Scoones, Ian, and Andy Stirling. *The Politics of Uncertainty: Challenges of Transformation*. London: Routledge, 2020. https://doi.org/10.4324/978100302 3845.

Simon, Herbert A. 'Bounded Rationality'. In *Utility and Probability*, edited by John Eatwell, Murray Milgate, and Peter Newman, 15–18. *The New Palgrave*. London: Palgrave Macmillan UK, 1990. https://doi.org/10.1007/978-1-349-20568-4_5.

———. 'Decision Making: Rational, Nonrational, and Irrational'. *Educational Administration Quarterly* 29, no. 3 (1 August 1993): 392–411. https://doi.org/10.1177/0013161X93029003009.

Snidal, Duncan. 'Rational Choice and International Relations'. In *Handbook of International Relations*, edited by Walter Carlsnaes, Thomas Risse, and Beth Simmons, 73–94. London: Sage Publications Ltd, 2002. https://doi.org/10.4135/9781848608290.

Stirling, Andy. 'Risk, Uncertainty and Precaution: Some Instrumental Implications from the Social Sciences'. In *Negotiating Environmental Change: New Perspectives from Social Science*, edited by F. Berkhout, Melissa Leach, and Ian Scoones, 33–76. Cheltenham, UK: Edward Elgar Publishing, 2003.

Sturm, Thomas. 'The "Rationality Wars" in Psychology: Where They Are and Where They Could Go'. *Inquiry* 55, no. 1 (1 February 2012): 66–81. https://doi.org/10.1080/0020174X.2012.643628.

Taylor, Ian. *The Forum on China- Africa Cooperation (FOCAC)*. London: Routledge, 2010. https://doi.org/10.4324/9780203835005.

UNEP. 'About AMCEN'. UNEP—UN Environment Programme, 31 October 2019. http://www.unep.org/regions/africa/african-ministerial-conference-environment/about-amcen.

Walt, Stephen M. 'Rigor or Rigor Mortis? Rational Choice and Security Studies'. *International Security* 23, no. 4 (1 April 1999): 5–48. https://doi.org/10.1162/isec.23.4.5.

CHAPTER 9

Conclusion

Africa finds itself at a crossroads. On the one hand, the continent is expected to experience rapid economic transformation, as indicated by the adoption of the landmark Africa Continental Free Trade Agreement (AfCFTA). After centuries of exploitation and underdevelopment, African countries are keen to utilise their abundant natural resources, including increasingly large fossil fuel reserves, to develop their economies. However, they have also committed to significantly reduce their emissions over time, in line with the Paris Agreement on Climate Change. Even though the rhetoric of realising both climate and development policy objectives has been clear, reconciling these two policy objectives is emerging as a major challenge in practice and will continue to be so especially in the coming decades.

As the preceding chapters in the book have demonstrated, reconciling development and climate policy objectives would require adoption of a different conceptual vantage point that will allow African countries to effectively navigate the evolution of both the global climate and continental developmental policy. That is, African countries will have to find a way of balancing the impetus of radically reducing their emissions, while also developing the industrial base necessary for economic development. Such an approach would enable Africa to contribute to the global climate effort, while also ensuring that the continent realises its

---

© The Author(s), under exclusive license to Springer Nature Switzerland AG 2023

K. Mbeva et al., *Africa's Right to Development in a Climate-Constrained World*, Contemporary African Political Economy, https://doi.org/10.1007/978-3-031-22887-2_9

259

development policy objectives. Going forward, we propose three key recommendations.

First, we suggest the establishment of a research programme on long-run international climate cooperation, from an African perspective. Research programmes are important in organising scholarly inquiry, especially on salient policy issues, at least in the Lakatosian sense.[1] The research programme would be based on assumptions that better reflect the dynamics of the Great Climate Transformation.

As an example, the research programme could be predicted on the core assumption that a Just Transition in Africa needs to be endogenously secured; multilateral appeals such as through the traditional notions of reparative transfer of resources to African countries would only form part of a bigger picture. In doing so, the concept of a Just Transition would be recast from a primarily normative to a strategic one. After all, it is well documented that Africa has only accrued nominal benefits from multilateral appeals for support. Consider the fact that African countries accounted for less than three (3) per cent of Clean Development Mechanism (CDM) funding under the Kyoto Protocol, with South Africa accounting for a disproportionate share.[2]

In a broader sense, the proposed research programme would be a derivative of a long-standing but underdeveloped policy research agenda in Africa where "there is a need to see 'policy' as a process of complex change requiring innovative institutional contexts and novel managerial capabilities".[3] It is hoped that this book has contributed to this research effort.

Second, and as a policy recommendation, we suggest the establishment of an institutional and policy framework to govern Just Climate Transition in Africa. At the institutional level, we suggest the establishment of an 'African Union High Level Panel on a Just Transition'. The high-level panel would function akin to similar orans of the AU, offering a forum for policy coordination at the continental level. Moreover, the high-level panel would also consolidate the other disparate initiatives related to climate change policy. Members of the AU high-level panel could include policy makers, scholars, civil society, marginalised groups and the private sector, among others.

A key objective of the AU high-level panel on a just transition would be to develop a continental policy mechanism. The policy might would be adopted in lieu of the conventional net zero policy framework, and it would include a clear articulation of the 'just' dimension of the transition.

The policy would engage with both the strategic risks and opportunities posed by the Great Climate Transformation. Moreover, the policy would align with the timeline of the continent's landmark policy blueprint—the AU Agenda 2063. Serving as a continental coordination policy, the policy could be devolved to the sub-regional, national and even sub-national levels.

In the long run, the Great Climate Transformation will be the defining feature of global cooperation in the coming decades. Creative policy-making and attendant supporting research will be central to Africa realising a just transition in particular, and its broader development policy objectives in general. A proactive rather than a reactive scholarly and policy approach would be key. Already, Africa has shown that it can conclude projects of significant political and policy complexity and ambition in record time, as the adoption of the AfCFTA demonstrated.[4] Similar momentum could be harnessed to secure the Just Transition. As the old adage goes, the future belongs to those who prepare for it today.

NOTES

1. Imre Lakatos, 'Falsification and the Methodology of Scientific Research Programmes', in *Can Theories be Refuted? Essays on the Duhem-Quine Thesis*, ed. Sandra G. Harding (Dordrecht: Springer Netherlands, 1976), 205–59, https://doi.org/10.1007/978-94-010-1863-0_14.
2. David Ockwell and Rob Byrne, 'Improving Technology Transfer through National Systems of Innovation: Climate Relevant Innovation-System Builders (CRIBs)', *Climate Policy* 16, no. 7 (2 October 2016): 844, https://doi.org/10.1080/14693062.2015.1052958.
3. Calestous Juma and Norman Clark, 'Policy Research in Sub-Saharan Africa: An Exploration', *Public Administration and Development* 15, no. 2 (1995): 121.
4. Francis Mangeni and Calestous Juma, *Emergent Africa. Evolution of Regional Economic Integration* (Terra Alta, WV: Headline Books, 2019).

REFERENCES

Juma, Calestous, and Norman Clark. 1995. Policy Research in Sub-Saharan Africa: An Exploration. *Public Administration and Development* 15, no. 2: 121–137.

Lakatos, Imre. 'Falsification and the Methodology of Scientific Research Programmes'. In *Can Theories be Refuted? Essays on the Duhem-Quine Thesis*, edited by Sandra G. Harding, 205–59. Dordrecht: Springer Netherlands, 1976. https://doi.org/10.1007/978-94-010-1863-0_14.

Mangeni, Francis, and Calestous Juma. 2019. *Emergent Africa: Evolution of Regional Economic Integration*. Terra Alta, WV: Headline Books.

Ockwell, David, and Rob Byrne. 'Improving Technology Transfer through National Systems of Innovation: Climate Relevant Innovation-System Builders (CRIBs)'. *Climate Policy* 16, no. 7 (2 October 2016): 836–54. https://doi.org/10.1080/14693062.2015.1052958.

REFERENCES

Aalst, Maarten Van, Molly Hellmuth, and Daniele Ponzi. 'Working Paper 89—Come Rain or Shine—Integrating Climate Risk Management into African Development Bank Operations'. Working Paper Series. African Development Bank, 9 December 2007. https://ideas.repec.org/p/adb/adbwps/224.html.

ACPC. 'The African Climate Policy Centre (ACPC) | ClimDev-Africa', 2022. https://www.climdev-africa.org/afrian-climate-policy-center.

Adede, Andronico O. 'International Environmental Law from Stockholm to Rio: An Overview of Past Lessons and Future Challenges'. *Journal of Environmental Law and Policy* 22 (1992): 88.

Adimo, Aggrey Ochieng, John Bosco Njoroge, Leaven Claessens, and Leonard S. Wamocho. 'Land Use and Climate Change Adaptation Strategies in Kenya'. *Mitigation and Adaptation Strategies for Global Change* 17, no. 2 (1 February 2012): 153–71. https://doi.org/10.1007/s11027-011-9318-6.

Aemro, Yohannes Biru, Pedro Moura, and Aníbal T. de Almeida. 'Inefficient Cooking Systems a Challenge for Sustainable Development: A Case of Rural Areas of Sub-Saharan Africa'. *Environment, Development and Sustainability* 23, no. 10 (1 October 2021): 14697–721. https://doi.org/10.1007/s10668-021-01266-7.

'African Youth Initiative on Climate Change (AYICC) | Devex'. Accessed 27 September 2021. https://www.devex.com/organizations/african-youth-initiative-on-climate-change-ayicc-101004.

Agarwala, A.N. *The Economics of Underdevelopment*. Oxford: Oxford University Press, 1961.

© The Editor(s) (if applicable) and The Author(s), under exclusive license to Springer Nature Switzerland AG 2023
K. Mbeva et al., *Africa's Right to Development in a Climate-Constrained World*, Contemporary African Political Economy,
https://doi.org/10.1007/978-3-031-22887-2

264 REFERENCES

Agozino, Biko. 'Reparative Justice: The Final Stage of Decolonization'. *Punishment & Society* 23, no. 5 (1 December 2021): 613–30. https://doi.org/10.1177/14624745211024342.

Aklin, Michaël, and Matto Mildenberger. 'Prisoners of the Wrong Dilemma: Why Distributive Conflict, Not Collective Action, Characterizes the Politics of Climate Change'. *Global Environmental Politics* 20, no. 4 (1 November 2020): 4–27. https://doi.org/10.1162/glep_a_00578.

Allan, Jen Iris, Charles B. Roger, Thomas N. Hale, Steven Bernstein, Yves Tiberghien, and Richard Balme. 'Making the Paris Agreement: Historical Processes and the Drivers of Institutional Design'. *Political Studies*, 6 October 2021, 00323217211049294. https://doi.org/10.1177/00323217211049294.

Allen, Peter, and Ilya Prigogine. 'The Challenge of Complexity'. In *Self-Organization and Dissipative Structures: Applications in the Physical and Social Sciences*, edited by William Schieve and Peter Allen. Austin: University of Texas Press, 2021. https://doi.org/10.7560/703544.

Allison, Graham. 'The New Spheres of Influence: Sharing the Globe With Other Great Powers'. *Foreign Affairs*, 19 October 2021. https://www.foreignaffairs.com/articles/united-states/2020-02-10/new-spheres-influence.

Alter, Karen J., and Sophie Meunier. 'The Politics of International Regime Complexity'. *Perspectives on Politics* 7, no. 1 (March 2009): 13–24. https://doi.org/10.1017/S1537592709090033.

Andonova, Liliana B., Michele M. Betsill, and Harriet Bulkeley. 'Transnational Climate Governance.' *Global Environmental Politics* 9, no. 2 (May 2009): 52–73.

Andonova, Liliana B., Thomas Hale, and Charles B. Roger. 'National Policy and Transnational Governance of Climate Change: Substitutes or Complements?' *International Studies Quarterly* 61, no. 2 (1 June 2017): 253–68. https://doi.org/10.1093/isq/sqx014.

ARIN. 'About Us—Africa Research & Impact Network', 2022. https://www.arin-africa.org/about-us/.

Asongu, Simplice A., Nicholas Biekpe, and Danny Cassimon. 'Understanding the Greater Diffusion of Mobile Money Innovations in Africa'. *Telecommunications Policy* 44, no. 8 (1 September 2020): 102000. https://doi.org/10.1016/j.telpol.2020.102000.

Asselt, Harro van. 'The Prospects of Trade and Climate Disputes before the WTO'. SSRN Scholarly Paper. Rochester, NY: Social Science Research Network, 2020. https://doi.org/10.2139/ssrn.3658327.

Atela, Joanes Odiwuor, Claire Hellen Quinn, Albert A. Arhin, Lalisa Duguma, and Kennedy Liti Mbeva. 'Exploring the Agency of Africa in Climate Change

Negotiations: The Case of REDD+'. *International Environmental Agreements: Politics, Law and Economics* 17, no. 4 (1 August 2017): 463–82. https://doi.org/10.1007/s10784-016-9329-6.

AU. 'African Leaders Push for Adequate Financial and Technical Support to Address Climate Change Challenges in the Lead up to COP27. | African Union'. African Union, 6 February 2022. https://au.int/es/node/41467.

AU. 'African Union Green Recovery Action Plan 2021–2027'. Addis Ababa, Ethiopia: African Union, 2021. https://au.int/sites/default/files/newsev ents/workingdocuments/40567-wd-AU_Green_Recovery_Action_Plan_E NGLISH.pdf.

AU. 'Agenda 2063: The Africa We Want (Popular Version)'. Addis Ababa, Ethiopia: African Union Commission, 2015. https://au.int/sites/default/ files/documents/36204-doc-agenda2063_popular_version_en.pdf.

———. 'Agreement Establishing the African Continental Free Trade Area', 2018. https://au.int/sites/default/files/treaties/36437-treaty-consolidated_ text_on_cfta_-_en.pdf.

———. 'Meeting of the Committee of African Heads of State and Government on Climate Change (CAHOSCC) | African Union'. African Union, 9 February 2019. https://au.int/en/newsevents/20190209/meeting-commit tee-african-heads-state-and-government-climate-change-cahoscc.

———. 'Draft Africa Climate Change Strategy (2020–2030)'. Addis Ababa, Ethiopia: African Union, 2020. https://www.uneca.org/sites/default/files/ ACPC/Africa-climate-change-strategy/AU%20CC%20Strategy%20REV-28-12-2020%20EN.pdf.

Audet, René. 'Climate Justice and Bargaining Coalitions: A Discourse Analysis'. *International Environmental Agreements: Politics, Law and Economics* 13, no. 3 (1 September 2013): 369–86. https://doi.org/10.1007/s10784-012-9195-9.

Ayompe, Lacour M., Steven J. Davis, and Benis N. Egoh. 'Trends and Drivers of African Fossil Fuel CO2 Emissions 1990–2017'. *Environmental Research Letters* 15, no. 12 (December 2020): 124039. https://doi.org/10.1088/1748-9326/abc64f.

Ayres, Alyssa. *Our Time Has Come: How India Is Making Its Place in the World.* Oxford and New York: Oxford University Press, 2018.

Bäckstrand, Karin, Jonathan W. Kuyper, Björn-Ola Linnér, and Eva Lövbrand. 'Non-State Actors in Global Climate Governance: From Copenhagen to Paris and Beyond'. *Environmental Politics* 26, no. 4 (4 July 2017): 561–79. https://doi.org/10.1080/09644016.2017.1327485.

Bank, African Development. 'Africa Climate Change Fund'. Text. African Development Bank—Building Today, a Better Africa Tomorrow. African Development Bank Group, 16 April 2019. https://www.afdb.org/en/topics-and-sec tors/initiatives-partnerships/africa-climate-change-fund.

266 REFERENCES

Barnett, Michael N. 'Bringing in the New World Order: Liberalism, Legitimacy, and the United Nations'. Edited by Boutros Boutros-Ghali, Commission on Global Governance, Gareth Evans, and Report of the Independent Working Group on the Future of the United Nations. *World Politics* 49, no. 4 (1997): 526–51.

Barnsley, Ingrid. 'Dealing with Change: Australia, Canada and the Kyoto Protocol to the Framework Convention on Climate Change'. *The Round Table* 95, no. 385 (1 July 2006): 399–410. https://doi.org/10.1080/003 58530600748358.

BBC News. 'Kenya Halts Lamu Coal Power Project at World Heritage Site', 26 June 2019, sec. Africa. https://www.bbc.com/news/world-africa-48771519.

Beer, Christopher Todd. '"Systems Change Not Climate Change": Support for a Radical Shift Away from Capitalism at Mainstream U.S. Climate Change Protest Events'. *The Sociological Quarterly* 63, no. 1 (30 November 2020): 1–24. https://doi.org/10.1080/00380253.2020.1842141.

Bell, Stephen, and Andrew Hindmoor. 'Governance Without Government? The Case of the Forest Stewardship Council'. *Public Administration* 90, no. 1 (2012): 144–59. https://doi.org/10.1111/j.1467-9299.2011.01954.x.

Benabdallah, Lina. *Shaping the Future of Power: Knowledge Production and Network-Building in China-Africa Relations.* Ann Arbor: University of Michigan Press, 2020.

Berlin, Isaiah. *The Hedgehog and The Fox: An Essay on Tolstoy's View of History.* London: Hachette UK, 2011.

Bernard, Florence, Peter A. Minang, Bryan Adkins, and Jeremy T. Freund. 'REDD+ Projects and National-Level Readiness Processes: A Case Study from Kenya'. *Climate Policy* 14, no. 6 (2 November 2014): 788–800. https://doi.org/10.1080/14693062.2014.905440.

Bhagwati, Jagdish N., ed. 'The New International Economic Order: The North-South Debate'. *MIT Bicentennial Studies (USA)*, 1977. https://agris.fao.org/agris-search/search.do?recordID=US8003918.

Birkbeck, Carolyn Deere. 'How Can the WTO and Its Ministerial Conference in 2021 be Used to Support Climate Action?' *One Earth* 4, no. 5 (21 May 2021): 595–98. https://doi.org/10.1016/j.oneear.2021.05.001.

Bjørn, Anders, Shannon Lloyd, and Damon Matthews. 'From the Paris Agreement to Corporate Climate Commitments: Evaluation of Seven Methods for Setting "Science-Based" Emission Targets'. *Environmental Research Letters*, 2021. https://doi.org/10.1088/1748-9326/abe57b.

Bodansky, Daniel. 'The History of the Global Climate Change Regime'. *International Relations and Global Climate Change* 23, no. 23 (2001): 23–40.

———. 'Legal Form of a New Climate Agreement: Avenues and Options'. *Center for Climate and Energy Solutions* (blog), 15 April

2009. https://www.c2es.org/document/legal-form-of-a-new-climate-agreem ent-avenues-and-options/.

———. 'The Copenhagen Climate Change Conference: A Postmortem'. *American Journal of International Law* 104, no. 2 (April 2010): 230–40. https://doi.org/10.5305/amerjintelaw.104.2.0230.

———. 'A Tale of Two Architectures: The Once and Future U.N. Climate Change Regime'. *Climate Change and Environmental Hazards Related to Shipping: An International Legal Framework*, 1 January 2013, 35–51. https://doi.org/10.1163/9789004244955_005.

———. 'The Legal Character of the Paris Agreement'. *Review of European, Comparative & International Environmental Law* 25, no. 2 (2016): 142–50. https://doi.org/10.1111/reel.12154.

———. 'The Paris Climate Change Agreement: A New Hope?' *American Journal of International Law* 110, no. 2 (April 2016): 288–319. https://doi.org/10.5305/amerjintelaw.110.2.0288.

Bodansky, Daniel, and Lavanya Rajamani. 'The Evolution and Governance Architecture of the United Nations Climate Change Regime'. In *Global Climate Policy: Actors, Concepts, and Enduring Challenges*, edited by Urs Luterbacher and Detlef F. Sprinz. Camdridge: MIT Press, 2018.

Bodansky, Daniel, and Lavanya Rajamani. 'The Issues That Never Die'. *Carbon & Climate Law Review* 12, no. 3 (2018): 184–90. https://doi.org/10.21552/cclr/2018/3/4.

Böhringer, Christoph. 'The Kyoto Protocol: A Review and Perspectives'. *Oxford Review of Economic Policy* 19, no. 3 (1 September 2003): 451–66. https://doi.org/10.1093/oxrep/19.3.451.

Böhringer, Christoph, and Carsten Vogt. 'The Dismantling of a Breakthrough: The Kyoto Protocol as Symbolic Policy'. *European Journal of Political Economy* 20, no. 3 (1 September 2004): 597–617. https://doi.org/10.1016/j.ejpoleco.2004.02.004.

Boulle, Michael. 'The Hazy Rise of Coal in Kenya: The Actors, Interests, and Discursive Contradictions Shaping Kenya's Electricity Future'. *Energy Research & Social Science* 56 (1 October 2019): 101205. https://doi.org/10.1016/j.erss.2019.05.015.

Bowman, Megan, and Stephen Minas. 'Resilience through Interlinkage: The Green Climate Fund and Climate Finance Governance'. *Climate Policy* 19, no. 3 (16 March 2019): 342–53. https://doi.org/10.1080/14693062.2018.1513358.

Brown, William, and Sophie Harman. 'African Agency in International Politics', 2013. https://doi.org/10.4324/9780203526071-6.

Brundtland, Gru, Mansour Khalid, Susanna Agnelli, Sali Al-Athel, Bernard Chidzero, Lamina Fadika, Volker Hauff, Istvan Lang, Ma Shijun, and

Margarita Morino de Botero. 'Our Common Future ('Brundtland Report')', 1987.

Brunnée, Jutta, and Charlotte Streck. 'The UNFCCC as a Negotiation Forum: Towards Common but More Differentiated Responsibilities'. *Climate Policy* 13, no. 5 (1 September 2013): 589–607. https://doi.org/10.1080/146 93062.2013.822661.

Bulkeley, Harriet, Liliana B. Andonova, Michele M. Betsill, Daniel Compagnon, Thomas Hale, Matthew J. Hoffmann, Peter Newell, Matthew Paterson, Charles Roger, and Stacy D. Van Deveer. *Transnational Climate Change Governance*. Cambridge: Cambridge University Press, 2014. https://doi.org/10.1017/CBO9781107706033.

Burgis, Tom. *The Looting Machine: Warlords, Tycoons, Smugglers, and the Systematic Theft of Africa's Wealth*. UK: William Collins, 2015.

CA. '1.5°C National Pathway Explorer'. Climate Analytics, 2022. https://1p5 ndc-pathways.climateanalytics.org/.

Campbell, Horace. 'China in Africa: Challenging US Global Hegemony'. *Third World Quarterly* 29, no. 1 (1 February 2008): 89–105. https://doi.org/10.1080/01436590701726517.

Cannon, Sheila M. 'Climate Strikes: Greta Thunberg Calls for "System Change Not Climate Change"—Here's What That Could Look like'. The Conversation, 15 March 2019. http://theconversation.com/climate-strikes-greta-thunberg-calls-for-system-change-not-climate-change-heres-what-that-could-look-like-112891.

CARI, 2022. 'Data: Chinese Investment in Africa'. China Africa Research Initiative, 2022. http://www.sais-cari.org/chinese-investment-in-africa.

Carmody, Doctor Padraig. *The Rise of the BRICS in Africa: The Geopolitics of South-South Relations*. London: Zed Books Ltd., 2013.

Carrington, Damian. 'World's Biggest Sovereign Wealth Fund Dumps Dozens of Coal Companies'. *The Guardian*, 5 February 2015, sec. Environment. https://www.theguardian.com/environment/2015/feb/05/worlds-biggest-sovereign-wealth-fund-dumps-dozens-of-coal-companies.

———. '"Hypocrisy": 90% of UK-Africa Summit's Energy Deals Were in Fossil Fuels'. *The Guardian*, 24 January 2020, sec. Environment. https://www.theguardian.com/environment/2020/jan/24/90-pe-cent-uk-africa-energy-deals-fossil-fuels.

Castelier, Sebastian. 'Gulf States' Quest to Find "New Oil" Turns to Hydrogen—Al-Monitor: The Pulse of the Middle East'. *Al-Monitor*, 15 February 2021. https://www.al-monitor.com/originals/2021/02/gulf-sta tes-quest-new-oil-hydrogen-green-energy-solar-wind.html.

Chan, Nicholas. '"Special Circumstances" and the Politics of Climate Vulnerability: African Agency in the UN Climate Change Negotiations'. *Africa Spectrum*, 24 June 2021. https://doi.org/10.1177/0002039721991151.

————. 'The Paris Agreement as Analogy in Global Environmental Politics'. *Global Environmental Politics*, 20 September 2021, 1–8. https://doi.org/10.1162/glep_a_00622.

————. '"Special Circumstances" and the Politics of Climate Vulnerability: African Agency in the UN Climate Change Negotiations'. *Africa Spectrum* 56, no. 3 (1 December 2021): 314–32. https://doi.org/10.1177/000203 9721991151.

Chan, Sander, Clara Brandi, and Steffen Bauer. 'Aligning Transnational Climate Action with International Climate Governance: The Road from Paris'. *Review of European, Comparative & International Environmental Law* 25, no. 2 (2016): 238–47. https://doi.org/10.1111/reel.12168.

Chan, Sander, Idil Boran, Harro van Asselt, Paula Ellinger, Miriam Garcia, Thomas Hale, Lukas Hermwille, et al. 'Climate Ambition and Sustainable Development for a New Decade: A Catalytic Framework'. *Global Policy* 12, no. 3 (2021): 245–59. https://doi.org/10.1111/1758-5899.12932.

Chan, Sander, Idil Boran, Harro van Asselt, Gabriela Iacobuta, Navam Niles, Katharine Rietig, Michelle Scobie, et al. 'Promises and Risks of Nonstate Action in Climate and Sustainability Governance'. *Wiley Interdisciplinary Reviews: Climate Change* 10, no. 3 (2019): e572. https://doi.org/10.1002/wcc.572.

Chan, Sander, Friederike Eichhorn, Frank Biermann, and Aron Teunissen. 'A Momentum for Change? Systemic Effects and Catalytic Impacts of Transnational Climate Action'. *Earth System Governance* 9 (1 September 2021): 100119. https://doi.org/10.1016/j.esg.2021.100119.

Chan, Sander, Paula Ellinger, and Oscar Widerberg. 'Exploring National and Regional Orchestration of Non-State Action for a <1.5 °C World'. *International Environmental Agreements: Politics, Law and Economics* 18, no. 1 (1 February 2018): 135–52. https://doi.org/10.1007/s10784-018-9384-2.

Chan, Sander, Robert Falkner, Matthew Goldberg, and Harro van Asselt. 'Effective and Geographically Balanced? An Output-Based Assessment of Non-State Climate Actions'. *Climate Policy* 18, no. 1 (2 January 2018): 24–35. https://doi.org/10.1080/14693062.2016.1248343.

Chan, Sander, Harro van Asselt, Thomas Hale, Kenneth W. Abbott, Marianne Beisheim, Matthew Hoffmann, Brendan Guy, et al. 'Reinvigorating International Climate Policy: A Comprehensive Framework for Effective Nonstate Action'. *Global Policy* 6, no. 4 (2015): 466–73. https://doi.org/10.1111/1758-5899.12294.

Chanda, Alfred W. 'The Organization of African Unity: An Appraisal'. *Zambia Law Journal* 21–24 (1989): 1–29.

Chengo, Victoria, and Kennedy Mbeva. 'How Transformative Are Mobile Payments for Solar Home Systems in Kenya?' STEPS Centre, 28

September 2018. https://steps-centre.org/blog/how-transformative-is-ken yas-mobile-payment-system-for-solar-home-systems/.

———. 'Briefing: Africa and the Paris Climate Change Agreement'. *African Affairs* 115, no. 459 (1 April 2016): 359–68. https://doi.org/10.1093/afraf/adw005.

Chin-Yee, Simon, Tobias Dan Nielsen, and Lau Øfjord Blaxekjær. 'One Voice, One Africa: The African Group of Negotiators'. In *Coalitions in the Climate Change Negotiations*. London: Routledge, 2020.

Chirambo, Dumisani. 'Towards the Achievement of SDG 7 in Sub-Saharan Africa: Creating Synergies between Power Africa, Sustainable Energy for All and Climate Finance in-Order to Achieve Universal Energy Access before 2030'. *Renewable and Sustainable Energy Reviews* 94 (1 October 2018): 600–608. https://doi.org/10.1016/j.rser.2018.06.025.

Christoff, Peter. 'Post-Kyoto? Post-Bush? Towards an Effective "Climate Coalition of the Willing"'. *International Affairs* 82, no. 5 (1 September 2006): 831–60. https://doi.org/10.1111/j.1468-2346.2006.00574.x.

Chu, Wai-Li. 'Cold War and Decolonisation'. In *Hong Kong History: Themes in Global Perspective*, edited by Man-Kong Wong and Chi-Man Kwong, 83–113. Hong Kong Studies Reader Series. Singapore: Springer, 2022. https://doi.org/10.1007/978-981-16-2806-1_4.

Ciplet, David, and J. Timmons Roberts. 'Splintering South: Ecologically Unequal Exchange Theory in a Fragmented Global Climate'. *Journal of World-Systems Research* 23, no. 2 (11 August 2017): 372–98. https://doi.org/10.5195/jwsr.2017.669.

Ciplet, David, J. Timmons Roberts, and Mizan Khan. 'The Politics of International Climate Adaptation Funding: Justice and Divisions in the Greenhouse'. *Global Environmental Politics* 13, no. 1 (18 December 2012): 49–68. https://doi.org/10.1162/GLEP_a_00153.

Clapham, Christopher. *Africa and the International System: The Politics of State Survival*. Cambridge Studies in International Relations: 50. Cambridge: Cambridge University Press, 1996. https://ezp.lib.unimelb.edu.au/login?url=https://search.ebscohost.com/login.aspx?direct=true&db=cat00006a&AN=melb.b2195139&site=eds-live&scope=site.

Clark, Norman, and Calestous Juma. *Long-Run Economics: An Evolutionary Approach to Economic Growth*. London and New York: Pinter Publisher, 1987.

Cock, Jacklyn. 'Resistance to Coal Inequalities and the Possibilities of a Just Transition in South Africa'. *Development Southern Africa* 36, no. 6 (2 November 2019): 860–73. https://doi.org/10.1080/0376835X.2019.1660859.

CoG. '7th Annual Devolution Conference 2021'. Maarifa Centre | Council of Governors, 23 November 2021. https://maarifa.cog.go.ke/221/7th-annual-devolution-conference-2021/.

Council of the European Union. 'Presidency Conclusions—Brussels, 22 and 23 March 2005—IV. Climate Change, 7619/1/05 REV 1 CONCL 1'. Brussels: European Council, 2005. http://www.consilium.europa.eu/uedocs/cms_data/docs/pressdata/en/ec/84335.pdf.

Cox, Robert W. 'Social Forces, States and World Orders: Beyond International Relations Theory'. *Millennium* 10, no. 2 (1 June 1981): 126–55. https://doi.org/10.1177/03058298810100020501.

Crowley, Kate. 'Is Australia Faking It? The Kyoto Protocol and the Greenhouse Policy Challenge'. *Global Environmental Politics* 7, no. 4 (1 November 2007): 118–39. https://doi.org/10.1162/glep.2007.7.4.118.

Dal Maso, Mirko, Karen Holm Olsen, Yan Dong, Mathilde Brix Pedersen, and Michael Zwicky Hauschild. 'Sustainable Development Impacts of Nationally Determined Contributions: Assessing the Case of Mini-Grids in Kenya'. *Climate Policy* 20, no. 7 (8 August 2020): 815–31. https://doi.org/10.1080/14693062.2019.1644987.

Darwin, John. *Britain and Decolonisation: The Retreat from Empire in the Post-War World*. Basingstoke: Macmillan International Higher Education, 1988.

Das, Kasturi, Harro van Asselt, Susanne Droege, and Michael A. Mehling. 'Towards a Trade Regime That Works for the Paris Agreement'. *Economic and Political Weekly* 54, no. 50 (5 June 2015): 7–8.

Deborah Brautigam. 'A Critical Look at Chinese "Debt-Trap Diplomacy": The Rise of a Meme'. *Area Development and Policy* 5, no. 1 (2020): 1–14.

Deleuil, Thomas. 'The Common But Differentiated Responsibilities Principle: Changes in Continuity after the Durban Conference of the Parties'. *Review of European Community & International Environmental Law* 21, no. 3 (2012): 271–81. https://doi.org/10.1111/j.1467-9388.2012.00758.x.

Depledge, Joanna, and Farhana Yamin. 'The Global Climate-Change Regime: A Defence'. In *The Economics and Politics of Climate Change*, edited by Dieter Helm and Cameron Hepburn. Oxford: Oxford University Press, 2009. https://doi.org/10.1093/acprof:osobl/9780199573288.003.0021.

Dequech, David. 'Bounded Rationality, Institutions, and Uncertainty'. *Journal of Economic Issues* 35, no. 4 (1 December 2001): 911–29. https://doi.org/10.1080/00213624.2001.11506420.

Deshmukh, R., A. Mileva, and G. C. Wu. 'Renewable Energy Alternatives to Mega Hydropower: A Case Study of Inga 3 for Southern Africa'. *Environmental Research Letters* 13, no. 6 (June 2018): 064020. https://doi.org/10.1088/1748-9326/aabf60.

Devarajan, Shantayanan, Indermit S Gill, and Kenan Karakülah. 'Debt, Growth and Stability in Africa: Speculative Calculations and Policy Responses †'. *Journal of African Economies* 30, no. Supplement_1 (8 November 2021): 74–102. https://doi.org/10.1093/jae/ejab022.

Di Gregorio, Monica, Kate Massarella, Heike Schroeder, Maria Brockhaus, and Thuy Thu Pham. 'Building Authority and Legitimacy in Transnational Climate Change Governance: Evidence from the Governors' Climate and Forests Task Force'. *Global Environmental Change* 64 (1 September 2020): 102126. https://doi.org/10.1016/j.gloenvcha.2020.102126.

Dibley, Arjuna, Thom Wetzer, and Cameron Hepburn. 'National COVID Debts: Climate Change Imperils Countries' Ability to Repay'. *Nature* 592, no. 7853 (April 2021): 184–87. https://doi.org/10.1038/d41586-021-00871-w.

Donelli, Federico. 'The Ankara Consensus: The Significance of Turkey's Engagement in Sub-Saharan Africa'. *Global Change, Peace & Security* 30, no. 1 (2 January 2018): 57–76. https://doi.org/10.1080/14781158.2018.1438384.

Doshi, Rush. *The Long Game: China's Grand Strategy to Displace American Order*. Oxford: Oxford University Press, 2021.

Drezner, Daniel W. 'The Power and Peril of International Regime Complexity'. *Perspectives on Politics* 7, no. 1 (March 2009): 65–70. https://doi.org/10.1017/S1537592709090100.

Dubash, Navroz K. 'Copenhagen: Climate of Mistrust'. *Economic and Political Weekly* 44, no. 52 (2009): 8–11.

Dubash, Navroz K., ed. *India in a Warming World: Integrating Climate Change and Development*. Oxford and New York: Oxford University Press, 2019.

Dunn, Kevin C. 'Introduction: Africa and International Relations Theory'. In *Africa's Challenge to International Relations Theory*, edited by Kevin C. Dunn and Timothy M. Shaw, 1–8. International Political Economy Series. London: Palgrave Macmillan UK, 2001. https://doi.org/10.1057/9780333977538_1.

E3G. '"Global Gateway": The EU Green Deal Goes Global'. E3G, 1 December 2021. https://www.e3g.org/news/global-gateway-eu-green-deal-goes-global/.

EAC. 'East African Climate Change Policy'. Arusha, Tanzania: East African Community Secretariat, 2011. http://repository.eac.int/bitstream/handle/11671/538/EAC%20Climate%20Change%20Policy_April%202011.pdf?sequence=1&isAllowed=y.

———. 'East African Community Climate Change Master Plan 2011–2031'. Arusha, Tanzania: East African Community Secretariat, 2011. https://www.meteorwanda.gov.rw/fileadmin/Template/Policies/EAC_Climate_Change_Master_Plan.pdf.

Early, Catherine. 'The EU Can Expect Heavy Pushback on Its Carbon Border Tax'. *China Dialogue* (blog), 1 September 2020. https://chinadialogue.net/en/business/eu-can-expect-heavy-pushback-carbon-border-tax/.

EC. 'Just Energy Transition Partnership with South Africa'. Press Release. European Commission, 2 November 2021. https://ec.europa.eu/commission/presscorner/detail/en/IP_21_5768.

REFERENCES 273

Eckersley, Robyn. 'Ambushed: The Kyoto Protocol, the Bush Administration's Climate Policy and the Erosion of Legitimacy'. *International Politics* 44, no. 2 (1 March 2007): 306–24. https://doi.org/10.1057/palgrave.ip.8800190.

———. 'The Politics of Carbon Leakage and the Fairness of Border Measures'. *Ethics & International Affairs* 24, no. 4 (ed 2010): 367–93. https://doi.org/10.1111/j.1747-7093.2010.00277.x.

———. 'Moving Forward in the Climate Negotiations: Multilateralism or Minilateralism?' *Global Environmental Politics* 12, no. 2 (20 March 2012): 24–42. https://doi.org/10.1162/GLEP_a_00107.

Economist. 'Africa's Population Will Double by 2050'. *The Economist*, 26 March 2020. https://www.economist.com/special-report/2020/03/26/africas-population-will-double-by-2050.

Edmonds, J., and S. Smith. 'The Technology of Two Degrees'. In *Avoiding Dangerous Climate Change*, edited by H. J. Schellenhuber, W. Cramer, N. Nakicenovic, T. Wrigley, and G. Yohe. Cambridge: Cambridge University Press, 2006.

Edo, Victor Osaro, and Michael Abiodun Olanrewaju. 'An Assessment of the Transformation of the Organization of African Unity (O.A.U) to the African Union (A.U), 1963–2007'. *Journal of the Historical Society of Nigeria* 21 (2012): 41–69.

Emmelin, Lars. 'The Stockholm Conferences'. *Ambio* 1, no. 4 (1972): 135–40.

Essers, Dennis, Danny Cassimon, and Martin Prowse. 'Debt-for-Climate Swaps: Killing Two Birds with One Stone?' *Global Environmental Change* 71 (1 November 2021): 102407. https://doi.org/10.1016/j.gloenvcha.2021.102407.

EurActiv. 'African Countries Deem EU Carbon Border Levy "Protectionist"'. *ECEEE*, 25 March 2021. https://www.eceee.org/all-news/news/african-countries-deem-eu-carbon-border-levy-protectionist/.

Evans, Stuart, Michael A. Mehling, Robert A. Ritz, and Paul Sammon. 'Border Carbon Adjustments and Industrial Competitiveness in a European Green Deal'. *Climate Policy* 21, no. 3 (16 March 2021): 307–17. https://doi.org/10.1080/14693062.2020.1856637.

Falkner, Robert, and Barry Buzan, eds. *Great Powers, Climate Change, and Global Environmental Responsibilities*. Oxford and New York: Oxford University Press, 2022.

Falkner, Robert. 'American Hegemony and the Global Environment'. *International Studies Review* 7, no. 4 (1 December 2005): 585–99. https://doi.org/10.1111/j.1468-2486.2005.00534.x.

———. 'The Paris Agreement and the New Logic of International Climate Politics'. *International Affairs* 92, no. 5 (1 September 2016): 1107–25. https://doi.org/10.1111/1468-2346.12708.

Farooki, Masuma, and Raphael Kaplinsky. *The Impact of China on Global Commodity Prices: The Global Reshaping of the Resource Sector*. London: Routledge, 2013.

Faude, Benjamin, and Felix Große-Kreul. 'Let's Justify! How Regime Complexes Enhance the Normative Legitimacy of Global Governance'. *International Studies Quarterly* 64, no. 2 (1 June 2020): 431–39. https://doi.org/10.1093/isq/sqaa024.

Faudot, Adrien. 'The Keynes Plan and Bretton Woods Debates: The Early Radical Criticisms by Balogh, Schumacher and Kalecki'. *Cambridge Journal of Economics* 45, no. 4 (1 July 2021): 751–70. https://doi.org/10.1093/cje/beab018.

Fisher, Jonathan. 'Reproducing Remoteness? States, Internationals and the Co-Constitution of Aid "Bunkerization" in the East African Periphery'. Knowledge and Expertise in International Interventions, 2018. https://doi.org/10.4324/9781351241458-6.

Flammer, Caroline, Michael W. Toffel, and Kala Viswanathan. 'Shareholder Activism and Firms' Voluntary Disclosure of Climate Change Risks'. *Strategic Management Journal* 42, no. 10 (2021): 1850–79. https://doi.org/10.1002/smj.3313.

Folke, Carl, Stephen Carpenter, Brian Walker, Marten Scheffer, Terry Chapin, and Johan Rockström. 'Resilience Thinking: Integrating Resilience, Adaptability and Transformability'. *Ecology and Society* 15, no. 4 (15 November 2010). https://doi.org/10.5751/ES-03610-150420.

French, Howard W. *Born in Blackness: Africa, Africans, and the Making of the Modern World, 1471 to the Second World War*. New York: Liveright Publishing Corporation, 2021.

Frey, Christopher. 'Mega-Regional Trade Agreements and Post-2015 Climate Protection: Bridging the Gap'. *Journal for European Environmental & Planning Law* 12, no. 3–4 (8 December 2015): 264–85. https://doi.org/10.1163/18760104-01204003.

Friedman, Lisa. 'Democrats Propose a Border Tax Based on Countries' Greenhouse Gas Emissions'. *The New York Times*, 19 July 2021, sec. Climate. https://www.nytimes.com/2021/07/19/climate/democrats-border-carbon-tax.html.

FS. 'The NDC Financing Fellowship Programme (NDC-FFP)'. Frankfurt School of Finance and Management, 2022. https://www.frankfurt-school.de/idrc/ndcffp.

Fukuyama, Francis. 'The End of History?' *The National Interest*, no. 16 (1989): 3–18.

Gannon, Kate Elizabeth, Florence Crick, Joanes Atela, and Declan Conway. 'What Role for Multi-Stakeholder Partnerships in Adaptation to Climate Change? Experiences from Private Sector Adaptation in Kenya'. *Climate Risk*

Management 32 (1 January 2021): 100319. https://doi.org/10.1016/j.crm.2021.100319.

Gardner, Howard E. *Intelligence Reframed: Multiple Intelligences for the 21st Century.* London: Hachette UK, 2000.

———. *A Synthesizing Mind: A Memoir from the Creator of Multiple Intelligences Theory.* Cambridge: MIT Press, 2020.

Getachew, Adom. *Worldmaking After Empire: The Rise and Fall of Self-Determination.* Princeton, NJ: Princeton University Press, 2020.

Geyer, Robert, and Paul Cairney, eds. *Handbook on Complexity and Public Policy.* First. Handbooks of Research on Policy. Cheltenham, UK and Northampton, MA: Edward Elgar, 2015. https://www.elgaronline.com/view/9781782549512.xml.

Ghosh, Arunabha, and Kanika Chawla. 'The Role of International Solar Alliance in Advancing the Energy Transition in Asia'. In *Renewable Energy Transition in Asia: Policies, Markets and Emerging Issues,* edited by Nandakumar Janardhanan and Vaibhav Chaturvedi, 63–87. Singapore: Springer, 2021. https://doi.org/10.1007/978-981-15-8905-8_4.

Gilbert, Nigel, and Seth Bullock. 'Complexity at the Social Science Interface'. *Complexity* 19, no. 6 (2014): 1–4. https://doi.org/10.1002/cplx.21550.

Glansdorff, Paul, and Ilya Prigogine. *Thermodynamic Theory of Structure, Stability and Fluctuations.* Vol. 306. New York: Wiley-Interscience, 1971.

Gleeson, Margaret. 'International Energy Agency Calls Time on New Fossil Fuels'. *Green Left Weekly,* no. 1311 (n.d.): 10. https://doi.org/10.3316/informit.849458544850871.

GoK. 'Kenya: Second National Communication to the United Nations Framework Convention on Climate Change'. Government of Kenya, 2015. https://unfccc.int/sites/default/files/resource/Kennc2.pdf.

———. 'Kenya's Updated Nationally Determined Contribution (NDC)'. Government of Kenya, 2020. https://www4.unfccc.int/sites/ndcstaging/PublishedDocuments/Kenya%20First/Kenya%27s%20First%20%20NDC%20(updated%20version).pdf.

Goldgeier, James M., and Michael McFaul. 'A Tale of Two Worlds: Core and Periphery in the Post-Cold War Era'. *International Organization* 46, no. 2 (1992): 467–91. https://doi.org/10.1017/S0020818300027788.

GoM. 'The Public Finance Management Act Regulations, 2015 Arrangement of Regulations | Climate Change'. Government of Makueni County, 2015. https://www.makueni.go.ke/site/files/2018/11/Makueni-County-Climate-Change-Fund-Regulations-2015.pdf.

Gomes, Joana. 'Von Der Leyen Calls for African Green Deal'. EURACTIV, 23 April 2021. https://www.euractiv.com/section/energy-environment/news/von-der-leyen-calls-for-african-green-deal/.

Gómez-Mera, Laura. 'International Regime Complexity'. Oxford Research Encyclopedia of International Studies, 31 August 2021. https://doi.org/10.1093/acrefore/9780190846626.013.648.

Grady-Benson, Jessica, and Brinda Sarathy. 'Fossil Fuel Divestment in US Higher Education: Student-Led Organising for Climate Justice'. *Local Environment* 21, no. 6 (2 June 2016): 661–81. https://doi.org/10.1080/13549839.2015.1009825.

Gray, Kevin, and Barry K. Gills. 'South–South Cooperation and the Rise of the Global South'. *Third World Quarterly* 37, no. 4 (2 April 2016): 557–74. https://doi.org/10.1080/01436597.2015.1128817.

Green, Jessica F. *Rethinking Private Authority: Agents and Entrepreneurs in Global Environmental Governance*. Illustrated edition. Princeton: Princeton University Press, 2013.

Green, Fergus. 'Anti-Fossil Fuel Norms'. *Climatic Change* 150, no. 1 (1 September 2018): 103–16. https://doi.org/10.1007/s10584-017-2134-6.

Grieco, Joseph, Robert Powell, and Duncan Snidal. 'The Relative-Gains Problem for International Cooperation'. *The American Political Science Review* 87, no. 3 (1993): 727–43. https://doi.org/10.2307/2938747.

Grimm, Sven. 'Sustainability in China-Africa Relations—"Greening" FOCAC'. *African East-Asian Affairs* 71 (18 June 2013). https://doi.org/10.7552/71-0-81.

Grundig, Frank. 'Patterns of International Cooperation and the Explanatory Power of Relative Gains: An Analysis of Cooperation on Global Climate Change, Ozone Depletion, and International Trade'. *International Studies Quarterly* 50, no. 4 (1 December 2006): 781–801. https://doi.org/10.1111/j.1468-2478.2006.00425.x.

Gunningham, Neil. 'Review Essay: Divestment, Nonstate Governance, and Climate Change'. *Law & Policy* 39, no. 4 (2017): 309–24. https://doi.org/10.1111/lapo.12085.

Güntay, Vahit. '(Is) African Spring in Chinese Foreign Policy (?)'. *Asia Europe Journal* 19, no. 3 (1 September 2021): 275–90. https://doi.org/10.1007/s10308-021-00602-w.

Gusev, Alexander. 'Evolution of Russian Climate Policy: From the Kyoto Protocol to the Paris Agreement'. *L'Europe En Formation* 380, no. 2 (2016): 39–52.

Hafner, Manfred, Simone Tagliapietra, and Lucia de Strasser. 'Prospects for Renewable Energy in Africa'. In *Energy in Africa: Challenges and Opportunities*, edited by Manfred Hafner, Simone Tagliapietra, and Lucia de Strasser, 47–75. SpringerBriefs in Energy. Cham: Springer International Publishing, 2018. https://doi.org/10.1007/978-3-319-92219-5_3.

Hale, Thomas N. 'The Role of Sub-State and Non-State Actors in International Climate Processes'. Research Paper. London, UK: The Royal Institute of

International Affairs (Chatham House), 2018. https://www.chathamhouse.org/sites/default/files/publications/research/2018-11-28-non-state-sctors-climate-synthesis-hale-final.pdf.

Hale, Thomas. '"All Hands on Deck": The Paris Agreement and Nonstate Climate Action'. *Global Environmental Politics* 16, no. 3 (15 July 2016): 12–22. https://doi.org/10.1162/GLEP_a_00362.

———. 'Catalytic Cooperation'. *Global Environmental Politics* 20, no. 4 (1 November 2020): 73–98. https://doi.org/10.1162/glep_a_00561.

———. 'Transnational Actors and Transnational Governance in Global Environmental Politics'. *Annual Review of Political Science* 23, no. 1 (2020): null. https://doi.org/10.1146/annurev-polisci-050718-032644.

———. 'Governing Net Zero: The Conveyor Belt'. Policy Memo. Oxford, UK: Blavatnik School of Government, 2021. https://www.bsg.ox.ac.uk/sites/default/files/2021-11/2021-11%20Hale%20Net%20Zero%20Policy%20Memo.pdf.

Hale, Thomas, Jason Anderson, and Andrew Higham. 'The Future of the Climate Regime: What Is Needed 2020–2050?' Oxford, UK: Blavatnik School of Government, Mission2020, ClimateWorks Foundation, 2020.

Hale, Thomas, Sander Chan, Kennedy Mbeva, Manish Shrivastava, Jacopo Bencini, Victoria Chengo, Ganesh Gorti, et al. 'Global Performance & Delivery in the Global South. Preliminary Findings of the ClimateSouth Project for the Global Climate Action Summit'. GCAS Brief. Cooperative Climate Action. Oxford, UK: Global Economic Governance Programme, 10 September 2018. https://www.geg.ox.ac.uk/publication/cooperative-climate-action-global-performance-delivery-global-south.

Hale, Thomas, David Held, and Kevin Young. *Gridlock: Why Global Cooperation Is Failing When We Need It Most.* Cambridge, UK and Malden, USA: Polity Press, 2013.

Hale, Thomas, Chuyu Liu, and Johannes Urpelainen. 'Belt and Road Decision-Making in China and Recipient Countries: How and to What Extent Does Sustainability Matter?' Oxford, UK: Blavatnik School of Government, Initiative for Sustainable Energy Policy (ISEP), and ClimateWorks Foundation, 24 April 2020.

Hale, Thomas, and Charles Roger. 'Orchestration and Transnational Climate Governance'. *The Review of International Organizations* 9, no. 1 (2014): 59–82.

Hale, Thomas, Takeshi Kuramochi, John Lang, Brendan Mapes, Steve Smith, Ria Aiyer, Richard Black, et al. 'Net Zero Tracker'. Oxford, UK: Energy and Climate Intelligence Unit, Data-Driven EnviroLab, NewClimate Institute, Oxford Net Zero, 2021. https://zerotracker.net/.

278 REFERENCES

Han, Xiao, and Michael Webber. 'From Chinese Dam Building in Africa to the Belt and Road Initiative: Assembling Infrastructure Projects and Their Linkages'. *Political Geography* 77 (1 March 2020): 102102. https://doi.org/10.1016/j.polgeo.2019.102102.

Handl, Günther. 'Declaration of the United Nations Conference on the Human Environment—Main Page'. United Nations, 1972. https://legal.un.org/avl/ha/dunche/dunche.html.

Haq, Mahbub ul. *The Poverty Curtain: Choices for the Third World*. New York: Columbia University Press, 1976.

Hardin, Russell. *Collective Action*. New York: Routledge, 1982.

Harstad, Bård. 'Pledge-and-Review Bargaining'. SSRN Scholarly Paper. Rochester, NY: Social Science Research Network, 2018. https://doi.org/10.2139/ssrn.3338622.

Hart, Jeffrey A. *The New International Economic Order: Conflict and Cooperation in North-South Economic Relations, 1974–77*. London: Springer, 1983.

Hecht, Susanna, and Alexander Cockburn. 'Rhetoric and Reality in Rio'. *Nation* 254, no. 24 (1992): 848–53.

Held, David, and Charles Roger. 'Three Models of Global Climate Governance: From Kyoto to Paris and Beyond'. *Global Policy* 9, no. 4 (2018): 527–37. https://doi.org/10.1111/1758-5899.12617.

Helm, Dieter. 'The Kyoto Approach Has Failed'. *Nature* 491, no. 7426 (November 2012): 663–65. https://doi.org/10.1038/491663a.

Hepburn, Cameron, Brian O'Callaghan, Nicholas Stern, Joseph Stiglitz, and Dimitri Zenghelis. 'Will COVID-19 Fiscal Recovery Packages Accelerate or Retard Progress on Climate Change?' *Oxford Review of Economic Policy* 36, no. 1 (28 September 2020): S359–81. https://doi.org/10.1093/oxrep/graa015.

Hirpa, Feyera A., Ellen Dyer, Rob Hope, Daniel O. Olago, and Simon J. Dadson. 'Finding Sustainable Water Futures in Data-Sparse Regions under Climate Change: Insights from the Turkwel River Basin, Kenya'. *Journal of Hydrology: Regional Studies* 19 (1 October 2018): 124–35. https://doi.org/10.1016/j.ejrh.2018.08.005.

Höhne, Niklas, Matthew J. Gidden, Michel den Elzen, Frederic Hans, Claire Fyson, Andreas Geiges, M. Louise Jeffery, et al. 'Wave of Net Zero Emission Targets Opens Window to Meeting the Paris Agreement'. *Nature Climate Change*, 16 September 2021, 1–3. https://doi.org/10.1038/s41558-021-01142-2.

Hood, Christina, and Carly Soo. 'Accounting for Mitigation Targets in Nationally Determined Contributions under the Paris Agreement', 2017. https://www.oecd-ilibrary.org/content/paper/63937a2b-en.

Hovi, John, and Tora Skodvin, eds. 'Climate Governance and the Paris Agreement'. *Politics and Governance* 4, no. 3 (2016).

Hovi, Jon, Tora Skodvin, and Steinar Andresen. 'The Persistence of the Kyoto Protocol: Why Other Annex I Countries Move on Without the United States'. *Global Environmental Politics* 3, no. 4 (1 November 2003): 1–23. https://doi.org/10.1162/152638003322757907.

Hsu, Angel, John Brandt, Oscar Widerberg, Sander Chan, and Amy Weinfurter. 'Exploring Links between National Climate Strategies and Non-State and Subnational Climate Action in Nationally Determined Contributions (NDCs)'. *Climate Policy* 20, no. 4 (20 April 2020): 443–57. https://doi.org/10.1080/14693062.2019.1624252.

Hunt, Chelsie, and Olaf Weber. 'Fossil Fuel Divestment Strategies: Financial and Carbon-Related Consequences'. *Organization & Environment* 32, no. 1 (1 March 2019): 41–61. https://doi.org/10.1177/1086026618773985.

Hwang, Jung-Ah, Youkyoung Park, and Yeonbae Kim. 'Why Do Consumers Respond to Eco-Labels? The Case of Korea'. *SpringerPlus* 5, no. 1 (4 November 2016): 1915. https://doi.org/10.1186/s40064-016-3550-1.

IISD. 'ENB Report | Global Pact for the Environment OEWG-3 | 20–22 May 2019 | Nairobi, Kenya | IISD Reporting Services'. *Earth Negotiations Bulletin (ENB)*, 22 May 2019. http://enb.iisd.org/vol35/enb3503e.html.

Ikenberry, G. John. 'America's Liberal Hegemony'. *Current History; Philadelphia*, January 1999.

ISA. 'International Solar Alliance', n.d. https://isolaralliance.org/about/background.

Jarso, James Farole. 'The East African Community and the Climate Change Agenda: An Inventory of the Progress, Hurdles, and Prospects'. *Sustainable Development Law & Policy* 12 (2011): 19.

Jelassi, Tawfik, and Francisco J. Martínez-López. 'Digital Business Transformation in Silicon Savannah: How M-PESA Changed Safaricom (Kenya)'. In *Strategies for E-Business: Concepts and Cases on Value Creation and Digital Business Transformation*, edited by Tawfik Jelassi and Francisco J. Martínez-López, 633–58. Classroom Companion: Business. Cham: Springer International Publishing, 2020. https://doi.org/10.1007/978-3-030-48950-2_23.

Jervis, Robert. *Perception and Misperception in International Politics: New Edition*. Princeton, NJ: Princeton University Press, 1976.

Ji, Zou, and Fu Sha. 'The Challenges of the Post-COP21 Regime: Interpreting CBDR in the INDC Context'. *International Environmental Agreements: Politics, Law and Economics* 15, no. 4 (1 November 2015): 421–30. https://doi.org/10.1007/s10784-015-9303-8.

Jiboku, Peace A., and Kelly Omosat Osifo. 'Monitoring Democratic Governance: Modus Operandi of NEPAD's African Peer Review Mechanism'. *Journal of African Union Studies* 10, no. 2 (August 2021): 27–50. https://doi.org/10.31920/2050-4306/2021/10n2a2.

Jordan, Andrew J., Dave Huitema, Mikael Hildén, Harro van Asselt, Tim J. Rayner, Jonas J. Schoenefeld, Jale Tosun, Johanna Forster, and Elin L. Boasson. 'Emergence of Polycentric Climate Governance and Its Future Prospects'. *Nature Climate Change* 5, no. 11 (November 2015): 977–82. https://doi.org/10.1038/nclimate2725.

Jordan, Andrew, Dave Huitema, Jonas Schoenefeld, Harro van Asselt, and Johanna Forster. 'Governing Climate Change Polycentrically'. In *Governing Climate Change: Polycentricity in Action?* edited by Andrew Jordan, Dave Huitema, Harro van Asselt, and Johanna Forster, 3–26. Cambridge: Cambridge University Press, 2018. https://doi.org/10.1017/978110828 4646.002.

Joseph L. Love. 'Raul Prebisch and the Origins of the Doctrine of Unequal Exchange'. *Latin American Research Review* 15, no. 3 (1980): 45–72.

Juma, Calestous. 'Complexity, Innovation, and Development: Schumpeter Revisited'. *Policy and Complex Systems* 1, no. 1 (2014): 4–21. https://doi.org/10.18278/jpcs.1.1.1.

———. 'Exponential Innovation and Human Rights: Implications for Science and Technology Diplomacy'. SSRN Scholarly Paper. Rochester, NY: Social Science Research Network, 27 February 2018. https://papers.ssrn.com/abstract=3131243.

Juma, Calestous, and Norman Clark. 'Policy Research in Sub-Saharan Africa: An Exploration'. *Public Administration and Development* 15, no. 2 (1995): 121–37.

Kabubo-Mariara, Jane, and Fredrick K. Karanja. 'The Economic Impact of Climate Change on Kenyan Crop Agriculture: A Ricardian Approach'. *Global and Planetary Change* 57, no. 3 (1 June 2007): 319–30. https://doi.org/10.1016/j.gloplacha.2007.01.002.

Kalantzakos, Sophia. 'The Race for Critical Minerals in an Era of Geopolitical Realignments'. *The International Spectator* 55, no. 3 (2 July 2020): 1–16. https://doi.org/10.1080/03932729.2020.1786926.

Kanie, Norichika, and Frank Biermann. *Governing Through Goals: Sustainable Development Goals as Governance Innovation*. Cambridge, MA: MIT Press, 2017.

Kay, A. David, and Eugene B. Skolnikoff. 'World Eco-Crisis', 1972.

Kazungu, Kalume. 'Kenya: Lamu County Puts Coal-Fired Power Plant On Hold'. *Daily Nation*, 9 August 2016. http://allafrica.com/stories/201608100091.html.

Kemp, Luke. 'Bypassing the "Ratification Straitjacket": Reviewing US Legal Participation in a Climate Agreement'. *Climate Policy* 16, no. 8 (16 November 2016): 1011–28. https://doi.org/10.1080/14693062.2015.1061472.

———. 'US-Proofing the Paris Climate Agreement'. *Climate Policy* 17, no. 1 (2 January 2017): 86–101. https://doi.org/10.1080/14693062.2016.117 6007.

———. 'Better Out than in'. *Nature Climate Change* 7 (22 May 2017): 458.

———. 'Limiting the Climate Impact of the Trump Administration'. *Palgrave Communications* 3, no. 1 (31 October 2017): 9. https://doi.org/10.1057/s41599-017-0003-6.

Kempe, Ronald Hope. 'Climate Change and Poverty in Africa'. *International Journal of Sustainable Development & World Ecology* 16, no. 6 (2009): 451–61. https://doi.org/10.1080/13504500903354424.

Keohane, Robert O. 'The Theory of Hegemonic Stability and Changes in International Economic Regimes, 1967–1977'. In *Change in the International System*. London: Routledge, 1980.

———. *After Hegemony: Cooperation and Discord in the World Political Economy*. Princeton: Princeton University Press, 1984. http://www.jstor.org/stable/j.ctt7sq9s.

Keohane, Robert O., and Michael Oppenheimer. 'Paris: Beyond the Climate Dead End through Pledge and Review?' *Politics and Governance* 4, no. 3 (8 September 2016): 142–51. https://doi.org/10.17645/pag.v4i3.634.

Keohane, Robert, and David Victor. 'The Regime Complex for Climate Change'. *Perspectives on Politics* 9, no. 1 (March 2011): 7–23. https://doi.org/10.1017/S1537592710004068.

Khor, Martin. 'China's Boost to South-South Cooperation'. *South Bulletin* 90 (16 May 2016). https://www.southcentre.int/question/chinas-boost-to-south-south-cooperation/.

Kidunduhu, Noreen. 'Energy Transition in Africa: Context, Barriers and Strategies'. In *Energy Transitions and the Future of the African Energy Sector: Law, Policy and Governance*, edited by Victoria R. Nalule, 73–111. Cham: Springer International Publishing, 2021. https://doi.org/10.1007/978-3-030-56849-8_3.

Kim, Rakhyun E. 'The Emergent Network Structure of the Multilateral Environmental Agreement System'. *Global Environmental Change* 23, no. 5 (October 2013): 980–91. https://doi.org/10.1016/j.gloenvcha.2013.07.006.

Kim, Rakhyun E., and Brendan Mackey. 'International Environmental Law as a Complex Adaptive System'. *International Environmental Agreements: Politics, Law and Economics* 14, no. 1 (1 March 2014): 5–24. https://doi.org/10.1007/s10784-013-9225-2.

Kim, Margret J., and Robert E. Jones. 'China: Climate Change Superpower and the Clean Technology Revolution'. *Natural Resources & Environment* 22, no. 3 (2008): 9–13.

282 REFERENCES

Kindleberger, Charles P., and Ford International Professor of Economics Charles P. Kindleberger. *The World in Depression, 1929–1939: Revised and Enlarged Edition*. Berkeley: University of California Press, 1973.

King, Edward. 'Africa's "Buyer's Remorse" over Paris Climate Deal'. Climate Home, 3 November 2016. http://www.climatechangenews.com/2016/11/03/africas-buyers-remorse-over-paris-climate-deal/.

Kissinger, Henry. *Nuclear Weapons and Foreign Policy*. Boulder, CO: Westview Press, 1957.

———. *On China*. London: Penguin, 2012.

Klenk, Nicole, and Katie Meehan. 'Climate Change and Transdisciplinary Science: Problematizing the Integration Imperative'. *Environmental Science & Policy* 54 (1 December 2015): 160–67. https://doi.org/10.1016/j.envsci.2015.05.017.

Kogo, Benjamin Kipkemboi, Lalit Kumar, and Richard Koech. 'Climate Change and Variability in Kenya: A Review of Impacts on Agriculture and Food Security'. *Environment, Development and Sustainability* 23, no. 1 (1 January 2021): 23–43. https://doi.org/10.1007/s10668-020-00589-1.

Kombe, Emmanuel Yeri, and Joseph Muguthu. 'Geothermal Energy Development in East Africa: Barriers and Strategies'. *Journal of Energy Research and Reviews*, 2019, 1–6. https://doi.org/10.9734/jenrr/2019/v2i129722.

Kornprobst, Markus, and T. V. Paul. 'Globalization, Deglobalization and the Liberal International Order'. *International Affairs* 97, no. 5 (1 September 2021): 1305–16. https://doi.org/10.1093/ia/iiab120.

Krauthammer, Charles. 'The Unipolar Moment'. *Foreign Affairs* 70, no. 1 (1990): 23–33. https://doi.org/10.2307/20044692.

Kuyper, Jonathan, Heike Schroeder, and Björn-Ola Linnér. 'The Evolution of the UNFCCC'. *Annual Review of Environment and Resources* 43, no. 1 (2018): 343–68. https://doi.org/10.1146/annurev-environ-102017-030119.

Lakatos, Imre. 'Falsification and the Methodology of Scientific Research Programmes'. In *Can Theories be Refuted? Essays on the Duhem-Quine Thesis*, edited by Sandra G. Harding, 205–59. Dordrecht: Springer Netherlands, 1976. https://doi.org/10.1007/978-94-010-1863-0_14.

Landry, David. 'Under a Money Tree? Comparing the Determinants of Western and Chinese Development Finance Flows to Africa'. *Oxford Development Studies* 49, no. 2 (3 April 2021): 149–68. https://doi.org/10.1080/13600818.2020.1865901.

Larmer, Miles. 'Leslie James, George Padmore and Decolonisation from Below: Pan-Africanism, the Cold War and the End of Empire'. *Journal of Contemporary History* 53, no. 2 (1 April 2018): 462–64. https://doi.org/10.1177/0022009417749502m.

Lavelle, Kathryn. 'Moving in from the Periphery: Africa and the Study of International Political Economy'. *Review of International Political Economy* 12, no. 2 (2005): 364–79. https://doi.org/10.1080/09692290500105946.

Lawrence, Peter, and Daryl Wong. 'Soft Law in the Paris Climate Agreement: Strength or Weakness?' *Review of European, Comparative & International Environmental Law* 26, no. 3 (2017): 276–86. https://doi.org/10.1111/reel.12210.

Lee, Christopher J. 'At the Rendezvous of Decolonization'. *Interventions* 11, no. 1 (1 March 2009): 81–93. https://doi.org/10.1080/13698010902752806.

Le Billon, Philippe, Païvi Lujala, Devyani Singh, Vance Culbert, and Berit Kristoffersen. 'Fossil Fuels, Climate Change, and the COVID-19 Crisis: Pathways for a Just and Green Post-Pandemic Recovery'. *Climate Policy* 21, no. 10 (26 November 2021): 1347–56. https://doi.org/10.1080/14693062.2021.1965524.

Lélé, Sharachchandra M. 'Sustainable Development: A Critical Review'. *World Development* 19, no. 6 (1991): 607–21. https://doi.org/10.1016/0305-750X(91)90197-P.

Lisowski, Michael. 'Playing the Two-Level Game: Us President Bush's Decision to Repudiate the Kyoto Protocol'. *Environmental Politics* 11, no. 4 (1 December 2002): 101–19. https://doi.org/10.1080/714000641.

Loureiro, Maria L., and Justus Lotade. 'Do Fair Trade and Eco-Labels in Coffee Wake up the Consumer Conscience?' *Ecological Economics* 53, no. 1 (1 April 2005): 129–38. https://doi.org/10.1016/j.ecolecon.2004.11.002.

MacLean, Lauren M., and Jennifer N. Brass. 'Foreign Aid, NGOs and the Private Sector: New Forms of Hybridity in Renewable Energy Provision in Kenya and Uganda'. *Africa Today* 62, no. 1 (2015): 57–82. https://doi.org/10.2979/africatoday.62.1.57.

Mahmood Mamdani. 'Historicizing Power and Responses to Power: Indirect Rule and Its Reform'. *Social Research*, 1999, 859–86.

Maji, Ibrahim Kabiru. 'Impact of Clean Energy and Inclusive Development on CO2 Emissions in Sub-Saharan Africa'. *Journal of Cleaner Production* 240 (10 December 2019): 118186. https://doi.org/10.1016/j.jclepro.2019.118186.

Makarov, Igor. 'Climate Change Policies and Resource Abundance: The Case of Russia'. *Handbook of Sustainable Politics and Economics of Natural Resources*, 10 December 2021. https://www.elgaronline.com/view/edcoll/9781789908763/9781789908763.00017.xml.

Makomere, Reuben, and Kennedy Liti Mbeva. 'Squaring the Circle: Development Prospects Within the Paris Agreement'. *Carbon & Climate Law Review* 12, no. 1 (2018): 31–40. https://doi.org/10.21552/cclr/2018/1/7.

Maneschi, Andrea. *Comparative Advantage in International Trade: A Historical Perspective*. Edward Elgar Publishing, 1998.

Mangeni, Francis, and Calestous Juma. *Emergent Africa. Evolution of Regional Economic Integration.* Terra Alta, WV: Headline Books, 2019.

Markus, M. Lynne, and Wenxiu (Vince) Nan. 'Theorizing the Connections between Digital Innovations and Societal Transformation: Learning from the Case of M-Pesa in Kenya'. *Handbook of Digital Innovation*, 14 July 2020. https://www.elgaronline.com/view/edcoll/9781788119979/9781788119979.00013.xml.

Marx, Axel, and Dieter Cuypers. 'Forest Certification as a Global Environmental Governance Tool: What Is the Macro-Effectiveness of the Forest Stewardship Council?' *Regulation & Governance* 4, no. 4 (2010): 408–34. https://doi.org/10.1111/j.1748-5991.2010.01088.x.

Mazrui, Ali. 'Tanzaphilia'. *Transition* 6, no. 31 (1967): 20–26. https://doi.org/10.2307/2934403.

Mbaku, John Mukum. 'Constitutional Coups as a Threat to Democratic Governance in Africa'. *International Comparative, Policy & Ethics Law Review* 2 (2018): 77.

Mbeva, Kennedy, and Reuben Makomere. 'The End of Affirmative Multilateralism?' SSRN Scholarly Paper. Rochester, NY: Social Science Research Network, 7 May 2021. https://doi.org/10.2139/ssrn.3841282.

Mbeva, Kennedy, and Pieter Pauw. 'Self-Differentiation of Countries' Responsibilities. Addressing Climate Change through Intended Nationally Determined Contributions'. Discussion Paper. Bonn, Germany: German Development Institute/Deutsches Institut für Entwicklungspolitik (DIE), 2016. https://www.die-gdi.de/uploads/media/DP_4.2016.pdf.

McGee, Jeffrey, and Jens Steffek. 'The Copenhagen Turn in Global Climate Governance and the Contentious History of Differentiation in International Law'. *Journal of Environmental Law* 28, no. 1 (1 March 2016): 37–63. https://doi.org/10.1093/jel/eqw003.

Mearsheimer, John J. *The Tragedy of Great Power Politics.* New York: W. W. Norton, 2001.

———. 'Bound to Fail: The Rise and Fall of the Liberal International Order'. *International Security* 43, no. 4 (1 April 2019): 7–50. https://doi.org/10.1162/isec_a_00342.

———. 'The Inevitable Rivalry: America, China, and the Tragedy of Great-Power Politics'. *Foreign Affairs* 100, no. 48 (2021): 48–58.

Mehling, Michael A., Harro van Asselt, Kasturi Das, Susanne Droege, and Cleo Verkuijl. 'Designing Border Carbon Adjustments for Enhanced Climate Action'. *American Journal of International Law* 113, no. 3 (July 2019): 433–81. https://doi.org/10.1017/ajil.2019.22.

Méjean, Aurélie, Franck Lecocq, and Yacob Mulugetta. 'Equity, Burden Sharing and Development Pathways: Reframing International Climate Negotiations'. *International Environmental Agreements: Politics, Law and Economics* 15, no. 4 (1 November 2015): 387–402. https://doi.org/10.1007/s10784-015-9302-9.

Mele, Alfred R., and Piers Rawling. *The Oxford Handbook of Rationality*. Oxford: Oxford University Press, 2004.

Meyer, Lukas H., and Dominic Roser. 'Distributive Justice and Climate Change. The Allocation of Emission Rights'. *Analyse & Kritik* 28, no. 2 (2016): 223–49. https://doi.org/10.1515/auk-2006-0207.

MFA. 'Declaration on China-Africa Cooperation on Combating Climate Change', 2 December 2021. https://www.fmprc.gov.cn/mfa_eng/wjdt_6 65385/2649_665393/202112/t20211203_10461772.html.

———. 'Dakar Declaration of the Eighth Ministerial Conference of the Forum on China-Africa Cooperation', 3 December 2021. https://www.fmprc.gov.cn/mfa_eng/wjdt_665385/2649_665393/202112/t20211203_10461779.html.

Milkoreit, Manjana. 'The Paris Agreement on Climate Change—Made in USA?' *Perspectives on Politics* 17, no. 4 (December 2019): 1019–37. https://doi.org/10.1017/S1537592719000951.

Miller, Marian A. *The Third World in Global Environmental Politics*. Boulder, CO: Lynne Rienner Publishers, 1995.

Mohan, Giles, and May Tan-Mullins. 'The Geopolitics of South–South Infrastructure Development: Chinese-Financed Energy Projects in the Global South'. *Urban Studies* 56, no. 7 (1 May 2019): 1368–85. https://doi.org/10.1177/0042098018794351.

Morseletto, Piero, Frank Biermann, and Philipp Pattberg. 'Governing by Targets: Reductio Ad Unum and Evolution of the Two-Degree Climate Target'. *International Environmental Agreements: Politics, Law and Economics* 17, no. 5 (1 October 2017): 655–76. https://doi.org/10.1007/s10784-016-9336-7.

Moss, Todd, and Morgan Bazilian. 'Signalling, Governance, and Goals: Reorienting the United States Power Africa Initiative'. *Energy Research & Social Science* 39 (1 May 2018): 74–77. https://doi.org/10.1016/j.erss.2017.11.001.

Mountford, Helen, and Mauricio Cárdenas. 'How to Reach Net Zero'. Project Syndicate, 20 July 2021. https://www.project-syndicate.org/commentary/five-ways-to-reach-net-zero-emissions-by-mid-century-by-helen-mountford-and-mauricio-cardenas-2021-07.

Moyo, Dambisa. 'Why Foreign Aid Is Hurting Africa'. *Wall Street Journal*, 22 March 2009, sec. World News. https://www.wsj.com/articles/SB1237588 95999200083.

———. *Dead Aid: Why Aid Is Not Working and How There Is a Better Way for Africa*. Reprint edition. Farrar, Straus and Giroux, 2010.

Mutezo, G., and J. Mulopo. 'A Review of Africa's Transition from Fossil Fuels to Renewable Energy Using Circular Economy Principles'. *Renewable and*

Sustainable Energy Reviews 137 (1 March 2021): 110609. https://doi.org/10.1016/j.rser.2020.110609.

Naeku, Meissy Janet. 'Climate Change Governance: An Analysis of the Climate Change Legal Regime in Kenya'. *Environmental Law Review* 22, no. 3 (1 September 2020): 170–83. https://doi.org/10.1177/1461452920958398.

Naess, Lars Otto, Peter Newell, Andrew Newsham, Jon Phillips, Julian Quan, and Thomas Tanner. 'Climate Policy Meets National Development Contexts: Insights from Kenya and Mozambique'. *Global Environmental Change* 35 (1 November 2015): 534–44. https://doi.org/10.1016/j.gloenvcha.2015.08.015.

Najam, Adil. 'Developing Countries and Global Environmental Governance: From Contestation to Participation to Engagement'. *International Environmental Agreements: Politics, Law and Economics* 5, no. 3 (1 September 2005): 303–21. https://doi.org/10.1007/s10784-005-3807-6.

Najam, Adil, Saleemul Huq, and Youba Sokona. 'Climate Negotiations beyond Kyoto: Developing Countries Concerns and Interests'. *Climate Policy* 3, no. 3 (1 January 2003): 221–31. https://doi.org/10.3763/cpol.2003.0329.

Nalule, Victoria R. 'Transitioning to a Low Carbon Economy: Is Africa Ready to Bid Farewell to Fossil Fuels?' In *The Palgrave Handbook of Managing Fossil Fuels and Energy Transitions*, edited by Geoffrey Wood and Keith Baker, 261–86. Cham: Springer International Publishing, 2020. https://doi.org/10.1007/978-3-030-28076-5_10.

Nan, Wenxiu (Vince), Xiaolin (Christina) Zhu, and M. Lynne Markus. 'What We Know and Don't Know about the Socioeconomic Impacts of Mobile Money in Sub-Saharan Africa: A Systematic Literature Review'. *The Electronic Journal of Information Systems In Developing Countries* 87, no. 2 (2021): e12155. https://doi.org/10.1002/isd2.12155.

Napoli, Christopher. 'Understanding Kyoto's Failure'. *SAIS Review of International Affairs* 32, no. 2 (2012): 183–96.

Ndemo, Bitange, and Tim Weiss. 'Making Sense of Africa's Emerging Digital Transformation and Its Many Futures'. *Africa Journal of Management* 3, no. 3–4 (2 October 2017): 328–47. https://doi.org/10.1080/23322373.2017.1400260.

Ndlovu-Gatsheni, Sabelo J. 'Decoloniality in Africa: A Continuing Search for a New World Order'. *The Australasian Review of African Studies* 36, no. 2 (2015): 22–50. https://doi.org/10.3316/informit.640531150387614.

Nemet, Gregory F. *How Solar Energy Became Cheap: A Model for Low-Carbon Innovation*. London: Routledge, 2019. https://doi.org/10.4324/9780367136604.

Neslen, Arthur. 'Catholic Church to Make Record Divestment from Fossil Fuels'. *The Guardian*, 3 October 2017, sec. Environment. https://www.the guardian.com/environment/2017/oct/03/catholic-church-to-make-record-divestment-from-fossil-fuels.

Newell, Peter, and Harriet Bulkeley. 'Landscape for Change? International Climate Policy and Energy Transitions: Evidence from Sub-Saharan Africa'. *Climate Policy* 17, no. 5 (2017): 650–63. https://doi.org/10.1080/146 93062.2016.1173003.

Newell, Peter, Jon Phillips, Ana Pueyo, Edith Kirumba, Nicolas Ozor, and Kevin Urama. 'The Political Economy of Low Carbon Energy in Kenya'. *IDS Working Papers* 2014, no. 445 (2014): 1–38. https://doi.org/10.1111/j. 2040-0209.2014.00445.x.

Ngigi, Samuel, and Doreen Busolo. 'Devolution in Kenya: The Good, the Bad and the Ugly'. *Public Policy and Administration Research* 9, no. 6 (2019), 9–21.

Njoroge, Joseph M., Beate M.W. Ratter, and Lucy Atieno. 'Climate Change Policy-Making Process in Kenya: Deliberative Inclusionary Processes in Play'. *International Journal of Climate Change Strategies and Management* 9, no. 4 (1 January 2017): 535–54. https://doi.org/10.1108/IJCCSM-10-2016-0154.

Nkrumah, Kwame. *Neo-Colonialism: The Last Stage of Imperialism*. London: Panaf, 1974.

Nordhaus, William, and Joseph Boyer. 'Requiem for Kyoto: An Economic Analysis of the Kyoto Protocol'. *The Energy Journal* 20 (1999): 93–130.

Noussan, Michel, Pier Paolo Raimondi, Rossana Scita, and Manfred Hafner. 'The Role of Green and Blue Hydrogen in the Energy Transition—A Technological and Geopolitical Perspective'. *Sustainability* 13, no. 1 (January 2021): 298. https://doi.org/10.3390/su13010298.

NSE. 'Nairobi Securities Exchange ESG Disclosure Guidance Manual'. Nairobi Securities Exchange, 30 July 2021. https://sseinitiative.org/wp-content/upl oads/2021/12/NSE-ESG-Disclosures-Guidance.pdf.

Nyabola, Nanjala. 'Cashing in on Coal: Kenya's Unnecessary Power Plant'. *World Policy Journal* 34, no. 3 (2017): 69–75.

Nye, Joseph S., and Robert O. Keohane. 'Transnational Relations and World Politics: An Introduction'. *International Organization* 25, no. 3 (1971): 329–49.

Nyong, Anthony. 'Climate Change Impacts in the Developing World: Implications for Sustainable Development'. *Climate Change and Global Poverty: A Billion Lives in the Balance*, 43–64. Washington, DC: Brookings Institution Press, 2009.

O'Brien, Karen, Siri Eriksen, Lynn Nygaard, and Ane Schjolden. 'Why Different Interpretations of Vulnerability Matter in Climate Change Discourses'.

Climate Policy 7, no. 1 (1 January 2007): 73–88. https://doi.org/10.1080/14693062.2007.9685639.

O'Sullivan, Meghan, Indra Overland, and David Sandalow. 'The Geopolitics of Renewable Energy'. Working Paper. New York, NY; and Cambridge, MA: Center on Global Energy Policy, Columbia University|SIPA; and The Geopolitics of Energy Project, Belfer Center for Science and International Affairs, Harvard Kennedy School, 2017. https://www.belfercenter.org/sites/default/files/files/publication/Geopolitics%20Renewables%20-%20final%20report%206.26.17.pdf.

Obama, Barack. 'The Irreversible Momentum of Clean Energy'. *Science* 355, no. 6321 (13 January 2017). https://doi.org/10.1126/science.aam6284.

Ockwell, David, and Rob Byrne. 'Improving Technology Transfer through National Systems of Innovation: Climate Relevant Innovation-System Builders (CRIBs)'. *Climate Policy* 16, no. 7 (2 October 2016): 836–54. https://doi.org/10.1080/14693062.2015.1052958.

Ockwell, David, Rob Byrne, Joanes Atela, Kennedy Mbeva, and Reuben Makomere. 'Making Climate Finance Work for Africa: Using NDCs to Leverage Climate Relevant Innovation System Builders (CRIBS)'. Policy Brief. Nairobi, Kenya: African Centre for Technology Studies (ACTS); Steps Africa, April 2017. https://media.africaportal.org/documents/CRIBS-Training-brief-2.pdf.

Oertzen, Detlof von. 'Issues, Challenges and Opportunities to Develop Green Hydrogen in Namibia'. Windhoek, Namibia: Konrad Adenauer Stiftung, October 2021.

Okereke, Chukwumerije. 'Climate Justice and the International Regime'. *WIREs Climate Change* 1, no. 3 (2010): 462–74. https://doi.org/10.1002/wcc.52.

———. 'North-South Inequity and Global Environmental Governance'. In *Routledge Handbook of Global Sustainability Governance*. London: Routledge, 2019.

Oldekop, Johan A., Rory Horner, David Hulme, Roshan Adhikari, Bina Agarwal, Matthew Alford, Oliver Bakewell, et al. 'COVID-19 and the Case for Global Development'. *World Development* 134 (1 October 2020): 105044. https://doi.org/10.1016/j.worlddev.2020.105044.

Olson, Mancur. *The Logic of Collective Action. Public Goods and the Theory of Groups*. Cambridge, MA: Harvard University Press, 1965.

Oshionebo, Evaristus. 'Sovereign Wealth Funds in Developing Countries: A Case Study of the Ghana Petroleum Funds'. *Journal of Energy & Natural Resources Law* 36, no. 1 (2 January 2018): 33–59. https://doi.org/10.1080/02646811.2017.1329120.

Osofsky, Hari M. 'The Complexities of Multipolar Approaches to Climate Change: Lessons from Litigation and Local Action'. *Proceedings of the ASIL*

Annual Meeting 107 (ed 2013): 73–75. https://doi.org/10.5305/procan nmeetasil.107.0073.

Ostrom, Elinor. *Governing the Commons: The Evolution of Institutions for Collective Action*. Cambridge, United Kingdom: Cambridge University Press, 1990.

———. *A Polycentric Approach for Coping With Climate Change*. Policy Research Working Papers. The World Bank, 2009. https://doi.org/10.1596/1813-9450-5095.

Ouedraogo, Nadia S. 'Opportunities, Barriers and Issues with Renewable Energy Development in Africa: A Comprehensible Review'. *Current Sustainable/Renewable Energy Reports* 6, no. 2 (1 June 2019): 52–60. https://doi.org/10.1007/s40518-019-00130-7.

Owino, Ochieng Willis, Oludhe Christopher, Dulo Simeon, and Olaka Lydia. 'An Analytical Assessment of Climate Change Trends and Their Impacts on Hydropower in Sondu Miriu River Basin, Kenya'. *African Journal of Environmental Science and Technology* 15, no. 12 (31 December 2021): 519–28. https://doi.org/10.5897/AJEST2021.3064.

Oxley, Nathan. 'Sharing Insights Across Continents: Africa Sustainability Hub Researcher Visits China Hub'. STEPS Centre, 1 December 2016. https://steps-centre.org/news/sharing-insights-across-continents-africa-sustainability-hub-researcher-visits-china-hub/.

Packer, Corinne A. A., and Donald Rukare. 'The New African Union and Its Constitutive Act'. *American Journal of International Law* 96, no. 2 (April 2002): 365–79. https://doi.org/10.2307/2693932.

Paglia, Eric. 'The Swedish Initiative and the 1972 Stockholm Conference: The Decisive Role of Science Diplomacy in the Emergence of Global Environmental Governance'. *Humanities and Social Sciences Communications* 8, no. 1 (5 January 2021): 1–10. https://doi.org/10.1057/s41599-020-00681-x.

Pahle, Michael, Dallas Burtraw, Christian Flachsland, Nina Kelsey, Eric Biber, Jonas Meckling, Ottmar Edenhofer, and John Zysman. 'Sequencing to Ratchet up Climate Policy Stringency'. *Nature Climate Change* 8, no. 10 (October 2018): 861–67. https://doi.org/10.1038/s41558-018-0287-6.

Parker, Charles F., and Christer Karlsson. 'The UN Climate Change Negotiations and the Role of the United States: Assessing American Leadership from Copenhagen to Paris'. *Environmental Politics* 27, no. 3 (4 May 2018): 519–40. https://doi.org/10.1080/09644016.2018.1442388.

Pathways Network. *Transformative Pathways to Sustainability: Learning Across Disciplines, Cultures and Contexts*. London: Routledge, 2021. https://doi.org/10.4324/9780429331930

Pattberg, Philipp. 'What Role for Private Rule-Making in Global Environmental Governance? Analysing the Forest Stewardship Council (FSC)'. *International*

Environmental Agreements: Politics, Law and Economics 5, no. 2 (1 June 2005): 175–89. https://doi.org/10.1007/s10784-005-0951-y.

Paul, T. V. 'Globalization, Deglobalization and Reglobalization: Adapting Liberal International Order'. *International Affairs* 97, no. 5 (1 September 2021): 1599–1620. https://doi.org/10.1093/ia/iiab072.

Pauw, Pieter, Steffen Bauer, Carmen Richerzhagen, Clara Brandi, and Hannah Schmole. 'Different Perspectives on Differentiated Responsibilities. A State-of-the-Art Review of the Notion of Common But Differentiated Responsibilities in International Negotiations'. Discussion Paper. Bonn, Germany: German Development Institute/Deutsches Institut für Entwicklungspolitik (DIE), 2014. https://www.die-gdi.de/uploads/media/DP_6.2014.pdf.

Pauw, Pieter, Davide Cassanmagnano, Kennedy Mbeva, Jonas Hein, Alejandro Guarin, Clara Brandi, Thomas Bock, et al. *NDC Explorer*. Bonn, Germany and Nairobi, Kenya: German Development Institute/Deutsches Institut für Entwicklungspolitik (DIE), and African Centre for Technology Studies (ACTS), 2016. http://klimalog.die-gdi.de/ndc/.

Pauw, P., Richard J. T. Klein, Kennedy Mbeva, Adis Dzebo, Davide Cassanmagnago, and Anna Rudloff. 'Beyond Headline Mitigation Numbers: We Need More Transparent and Comparable NDCs to Achieve the Paris Agreement on Climate Change'. *Climatic Change* 147, no. 1 (1 March 2018): 23–29. https://doi.org/10.1007/s10584-017-2122-x.

Pauw, Pieter, Kennedy Mbeva, and Harro van Asselt. 'Subtle Differentiation of Countries' Responsibilities under the Paris Agreement'. *Palgrave Communications* 5, no. 1 (30 July 2019): 1–7. https://doi.org/10.1057/s41599-019-0298-6.

Pauw, W., P. Castro, J. Pickering, and S. Bhasin. 'Conditional Nationally Determined Contributions in the Paris Agreement: Foothold for Equity or Achilles Heel?' *Climate Policy* 20, no. 4 (20 April 2020): 468–84. https://doi.org/10.1080/14693062.2019.1635874.

Pereira, Laura, Niki Frantzeskaki, Aniek Hebinck, Lakshmi Charli-Joseph, Scott Drimie, Michelle Dyer, Hallie Eakin, et al. 'Transformative Spaces in the Making: Key Lessons from Nine Cases in the Global South'. *Sustainability Science* 15, no. 1 (1 January 2020): 161–78. https://doi.org/10.1007/s11625-019-00749-x.

Pettenger, Mary E. *The Social Construction of Climate Change: Power, Knowledge, Norms, Discourses*. Aldershot: Ashgate Publishing, Ltd., 2013.

Pickering, Jonathan, Jeffrey S. McGee, Tim Stephens, and Sylvia I. Karlsson-Vinkhuyzen. 'The Impact of the US Retreat from the Paris Agreement: Kyoto Revisited?' *Climate Policy* 18 (18 December 2017): 818–27. https://doi.org/10.1080/14693062.2017.1412934.

REFERENCES 291

Piero Morseletto, Frank Biermann, and Philipp Pattberg. 'Governing by Targets: Reductio Ad Unum and Evolution of the Two-Degree Climate Target'. *International Environmental Agreements: Politics, Law and Economics* 17, no. 5 (1 October 2017): 655–76. https://doi.org/10.1007/s10784-016-9336-7.

Pihl, Erik, Eva Alfredsson, Magnus Bengtsson, Kathryn J. Bowen, Vanesa Cástan Broto, Kuei Tien Chou, Helen Cleugh, et al. 'Ten New Insights in Climate Science 2020—A Horizon Scan'. *Global Sustainability* 4 (ed 2021). https://doi.org/10.1017/sus.2021.2.

Pistelli, Lapo. 'Addressing Africa's Energy Dilemma'. In *The Geopolitics of the Global Energy Transition*, edited by Manfred Hafner and Simone Tagliapietra, 151–74. Lecture Notes in Energy. Cham: Springer International Publishing, 2020. https://doi.org/10.1007/978-3-030-39066-2_7.

Prebisch, Raúl. 'The Economic Development of Latin America and Its Principal Problems', 27 April 1950. https://repositorio.cepal.org/handle/11362/29973.

Pont, Yann Robiou du, M. Louise Jeffery, Johannes Gütschow, Joeri Rogelj, Peter Christoff, and Malte Meinshausen. 'Equitable Mitigation to Achieve the Paris Agreement Goals'. *Nature Climate Change* 7, no. 1 (January 2017): 38–43. https://doi.org/10.1038/nclimate3186.

Presidency. 'Speech by H.E. President Uhuru Kenyatta C.G.H. During the Official Opening of the 7TH Annual Devolution Conference in Makueni County on 24th November, 2021 | The Presidency'. Office of the President of Kenya, 24 November 2021. https://www.president.go.ke/2021/11/24/speech-by-h-e-president-uhuru-kenyatta-c-g-h-during-the-official-opening-of-the-7th-annual-devolution-conference-in-makueni-county-on-24th-november-2021/.

President George W. Bush. 'Text of a Letter from the President to Senators Hagel, Helms, Craig, and Roberts', 13 March 2001. https://georgewbush-whitehouse.archives.gov/news/releases/2001/03/20010314.html.

Prigogine, Ilya. 'Order through Fluctuation: Self-Organization and Social System'. In *Evolution and Consciousness: Human Systems in Transition*, edited by Erich Jantsch, 93–130. Reading, MA: Addison-Wesley, 1976.

———. 'Time, Structure, and Fluctuations'. *Science* 201, no. 4358 (1978): 777–85. https://doi.org/10.1126/science.201.4358.777

———. *From Being to Becoming Time and Complexity in the Physical Sciences /Ilya Prigogine*. New York: W.H. Freeman, 1980.

Prigogine, Ilya, and Isabelle Stengers. *The End of Certainty*. New York: Simon and Schuster, 1997.

Prins, Gwyn, and Steve Rayner. 'Time to Ditch Kyoto'. *Nature* 449, no. 7165 (25 October 2007): 973–75. https://doi.org/10.1038/449973a.

REFERENCES

Pueyo, Ana, and Pedro Linares. 'Renewable Technology Transfer to Developing Countries: One Size Does Not Fit All'. *IDS Working Papers* 2012, no. 412 (2012): 1–39. https://doi.org/10.1111/j.2040-0209.2012.00412.x.

Puplampu, Korbla P., Kobena T. Hanson, and Peter Arthur. 'Disruptive Technologies, Innovation and Transformation in Africa: The Present and Future'. In *Disruptive Technologies, Innovation and Development in Africa*, edited by Peter Arthur, Kobena T. Hanson, and Korbla P. Puplampu, 3–13. International Political Economy Series. Cham: Springer International Publishing, 2020. https://doi.org/10.1007/978-3-030-40647-9_1.

Rajamani, Lavanya. *Differential Treatment in International Environmental Law*. Oxford Monographs in International Law. Oxford and New York: Oxford University Press, 2006.

———. 'The Reach and Limits of the Principle of Common But Differentiated Responsibilities and Respective Capabilities in the Climate Change Regime'. In *Handbook of Climate Change and India*. London: Routledge, 2011. https://doi.org/10.4324/9780203153284.ch8.

———. 'The Durban Platform for Enhanced Action and the Future of the Climate Regime'. *International & Comparative Law Quarterly* 61, no. 2 (April 2012): 501–18. https://doi.org/10.1017/S0020589312000085.

———. 'Negotiating the 2015 Climate Agreement: Issues Relating to Legal Form and Nature'. Research Paper. Cape Town, South Africa: Mitigation Action Plans & Scenarios, 2015. https://cprindia.org/sites/default/files/Paper_Negotiating-the-2015-Climate-Agreement_Rajamani.pdf.

———. 'The Principle of Common but Differentiated Responsibilities and Respective Capabilities in the International Climate Change Regime'. In *Research Handbook on Climate Disaster Law*, edited by Rosemary Lyster and Robert Verchick, 46–60. Cheltenham, UK and Northampton, MA: Edward Elgar, 2018. https://www.elgaronline.com/view/edcoll/9781786430021/9781786430021.00009.xml.

Rampa, Francesco, Sanoussi Bilal, and Elizabeth Sidiropoulos. 'Leveraging South–South Cooperation for Africa's Development'. *South African Journal of International Affairs* 19, no. 2 (1 August 2012): 247–69. https://doi.org/10.1080/10220461.2012.709400.

Rastogi, Charu. 'M-Kopa Solar: Lighting up the Dark Continent'. *South Asian Journal of Business and Management Cases* 7, no. 2 (1 December 2018): 93–103. https://doi.org/10.1177/2277977918774648.

Rayner, Steve, and Gwyn Prins. 'The Wrong Trousers: Radically Rethinking Climate Policy'. Other Working Paper. Oxford, UK: James Martin Institute for Science and Civilization, University of Oxford and the MacKinder Centre for the Study of Long-Wave Events, London School of Economics, 2007. http://www.sbs.ox.ac.uk/centres/insis/Documents/TheWrongTrousers.pdf.

Rees, William E. 'Achieving Sustainability: Reform or Transformation?' *Journal of Planning Literature* 9, no. 4 (1 May 1995): 343–61. https://doi.org/10.1177/088541229500900402.

Report of Experts Convened by the Secretary General of the United Nations Conference on the Human Environment. 'Environment and Development: The Founex Report on Development and Environment'. Founex: Carnegie Endowment for International Peace, 1972.

Riddell, J. Barry. 'Things Fall Apart Again: Structural Adjustment Programmes in Sub-Saharan Africa'. *The Journal of Modern African Studies* 30, no. 1 (1992): 53–68.

Ridder, Marjolein de. *The Geopolitics of Mineral Resources for Renewable Energy Technologies*. The Hague: Centre for Strategic Studies, 2013.

Rimmer, Matthew. 'Investing in the Future: Norway, Climate Change, and Fossil Fuel Divestment'. SSRN Scholarly Paper. Rochester, NY: Social Science Research Network, 2016. https://papers.ssrn.com/abstract=2770844.

Ritchie, Hannah, and David S. Reay. 'Delivering the Two Degree Global Climate Change Target Using a Flexible Ratchet Framework'. *Climate Policy* 17, no. 8 (17 November 2017): 1031–45. https://doi.org/10.1080/14693062.2016.1222260.

Roberts, Anthea, and Taylor St John. 'Complex Designers and Emergent Design: Reforming the Investment Treaty System'. *American Journal of International Law* 116, no. 1 (January 2022): 96–149. https://doi.org/10.1017/ajil.2021.57.

Roberts, Anthea, Henrique Choer Moraes, and Victor Ferguson. 'Toward a Geoeconomic Order in International Trade and Investment'. *Journal of International Economic Law* 22, no. 4 (20 December 2019): 655–76. https://doi.org/10.1093/jiel/jgz036.

Roberts, J. Timmons, Martin Stadelmann, and Saleemul Huq. 'Copenhagen's Climate Finance Promise: Six Key Questions'. Briefing. London, UK: International Institute for Environment and Development (IIED), 2010. https://www.osti.gov/etdeweb/servlets/purl/22041098.

———. 'Multipolarity and the New World (Dis)Order: US Hegemonic Decline and the Fragmentation of the Global Climate Regime'. *Global Environmental Change*, Symposium on Social Theory and the Environment in the New World (dis)Order, 21, no. 3 (1 August 2011): 776–84. https://doi.org/10.1016/j.gloenvcha.2011.03.017.

Rodney, Walter. *How Europe Underdeveloped Africa*. Revised edition. Washington, DC: Howard Univ Press, 1981.

Rogelj, Joeri, Michel den Elzen, Niklas Höhne, Taryn Fransen, Hanna Fekete, Harald Winkler, Roberto Schaeffer, Fu Sha, Keywan Riahi, and Malte Meinshausen. 'Paris Agreement Climate Proposals Need a Boost to Keep Warming

Well Below 2 °C'. *Nature* 534, no. 7609 (30 June 2016): 631–39. https://doi.org/10.1038/nature18307.

Rogelj, Joeri, Oliver Geden, Annette Cowie, and Andy Reisinger. 'Net-Zero Emissions Targets Are Vague: Three Ways to Fix'. *Nature* 591, no. 7850 (March 2021): 365–68. https://doi.org/10.1038/d41586-021-00662-3.

Roger, Charles, and Satishkumar Belliethathan. 'Africa in the Global Climate Change Negotiations'. *International Environmental Agreements: Politics, Law and Economics* 16, no. 1 (1 February 2016): 91–108. https://doi.org/10.1007/s10784-014-9244-7.

Rosen, Amanda M. 'The Wrong Solution at the Right Time: The Failure of the Kyoto Protocol on Climate Change'. *Politics & Policy* 43, no. 1 (2015): 30–58. https://doi.org/10.1111/polp.12105.

Röser, Frauke, Oscar Widerberg, Niklas Höhne, and Thomas Day. 'Ambition in the Making: Analysing the Preparation and Implementation Process of the Nationally Determined Contributions under the Paris Agreement'. *Climate Policy* 20, no. 4 (20 April 2020): 415–29. https://doi.org/10.1080/14693062.2019.1708697.

Round, Jeffery I., and Matthew Odedokun. 'Aid Effort and Its Determinants'. *International Review of Economics & Finance* 13, no. 3 (1 January 2004): 293–309. https://doi.org/10.1016/j.iref.2003.11.006.

SADC. 'Southern African Development Community: Programme on Climate Change Adaptation and Mitigation in Eastern and Southern Africa (COMESA-EAC-SADC)', 2012. https://www.sadc.int/sadc-secretariat/directorates/office-deputy-executive-secretary-regional-integration/food-agriculture-natural-resources/tripartite-programme-climate-change-adaptation-and-mitigatio/.

Sanger, David E. 'Bush Will Continue to Oppose Kyoto Pact on Global Warming'. *The New York Times*, 12 June 2001, sec. World. https://www.nytimes.com/2001/06/12/world/bush-will-continue-to-oppose-kyoto-pact-on-global-warming.html.

Sauer, Natalie. 'Mozambique "Faces Climate Debt Trap" as Cyclone Kenneth Follows Idai'. *Climate Home News*, 26 April 2019. https://www.climatechangenews.com/2019/04/26/mozambique-faces-climate-debt-trap-cyclone-kenneth-follows-idai/.

Sauvant, Karl P., and Hajo Hasenpflug. *The New International Economic Order: Confrontation or Cooperation between North and South?* London: Routledge, 2019.

Savvidou, Georgia, Aaron Atteridge, Kulthoum Omari-Motsumi, and Christopher H. Trisos. 'Quantifying International Public Finance for Climate Change Adaptation in Africa'. *Climate Policy* 21, no. 8 (14 September 2021): 1020–36. https://doi.org/10.1080/14693062.2021.1978053.

REFERENCES 295

Schelling, Thomas C. *Micromotives and Macrobehavior*. New York: W. W. Norton, 1978.

Scoones, Ian, and Andy Stirling. *The Politics of Uncertainty: Challenges of Transformation*. London: Routledge, 2020. https://doi.org/10.4324/9781003023845.

Seck, Gondia Sokhna, Emmanuel Hache, and Charlène Barnet. 'Potential Bottleneck in the Energy Transition: The Case of Cobalt in an Accelerating Electro-Mobility World'. *Resources Policy* 75 (1 March 2022): 102516. https://doi.org/10.1016/j.resourpol.2021.102516.

Shackleton, Sheona E., and Charlie M. Shackleton. 'Linking Poverty, HIV/AIDS and Climate Change to Human and Ecosystem Vulnerability in Southern Africa: Consequences for Livelihoods and Sustainable Ecosystem Management'. *International Journal of Sustainable Development & World Ecology* 19, no. 3 (2012): 275–86. https://doi.org/10.1080/13504509.2011.641039.

Sheng, Li, and Dmitri Felix do Nascimento. *The Belt and Road Initiative in South–South Cooperation: The Impact on World Trade and Geopolitics*. Cham: Springer Nature, 2021.

Simon, Herbert A. 'Bounded Rationality'. In *Utility and Probability*, edited by John Eatwell, Murray Milgate, and Peter Newman, 15–18. *The New Palgrave*. London: Palgrave Macmillan UK, 1990. https://doi.org/10.1007/978-1-349-20568-4_5.

———. 'Decision Making: Rational, Nonrational, and Irrational'. *Educational Administration Quarterly* 29, no. 3 (1 August 1993): 392–411. https://doi.org/10.1177/0013161X93029003009.

Skidelsky, Robert. 'Keynes, Globalisation and the Bretton Woods Institutions in the Light of Changing Ideas About Markets'. *World Economics* 6, no. 1 (2005): 15–30.

Snidal, Duncan. 'The Limits of Hegemonic Stability Theory'. *International Organization* 39, no. 4 (ed 1985): 579–614. https://doi.org/10.1017/S002081830002703X.

———. 'Rational Choice and International Relations'. In *Handbook of International Relations*, edited by Walter Carlsnaes, Thomas Risse, and Beth Simmons, 73–94. London: Sage Publications Ltd, 2002. https://doi.org/10.4135/9781848608290.

Sokona, Youba, and Fatma Denton. 'Climate Change Impacts: Can Africa Cope with the Challenges?' *Climate Policy* 1, no. 1 (1 January 2001): 117–23. https://doi.org/10.3763/cpol.2001.0110.

Soulé, Folashadé. '"Africa+1" Summit Diplomacy and the "New Scramble" Narrative: Recentering African Agency'. *African Affairs* 119, no. 477 (1 October 2020): 633–46. https://doi.org/10.1093/afraf/adaa015.

Spittler, Nathalie, Brynhildur Davidsdottir, Ehsan Shafiei, and Arnaud Diemer. 'Implications of Renewable Resource Dynamics for Energy System Planning:

The Case of Geothermal and Hydropower in Kenya'. *Energy Policy* 150 (1 March 2021): 111985. https://doi.org/10.1016/j.enpol.2020.111985.

Springer, Cecilia Han. 'China's Withdrawal from Overseas Coal in Context'. *World Development Perspectives* 25 (1 March 2022): 100397. https://doi.org/10.1016/j.wdp.2022.100397.

Stadelmann, Martin, J. Timmons Roberts, and Axel Michaelowa. 'New and Additional to What? Assessing Options for Baselines to Assess Climate Finance Pledges'. *Climate and Development* 3, no. 3 (2011): 175–92. https://doi.org/10.1080/17565529.2011.599550.

Staff. 'Canada Pulls out of Kyoto Protocol'. *The Guardian*, 13 December 2011, sec. Environment. https://www.theguardian.com/environment/2011/dec/13/canada-pulls-out-kyoto-protocol.

Stalley, Phillip. 'Norms from the Periphery: Tracing the Rise of the Common But Differentiated Principle in International Environmental Politics'. *Cambridge Review of International Affairs* 31, no. 2 (4 March 2018): 141–61. https://doi.org/10.1080/09557571.2018.1481824.

Stiglitz, Joseph. *Globalization and Its Discontents*. New York: W. W. Norton, 2002.

Stirling, Andy. 'Risk, Uncertainty and Precaution: Some Instrumental Implications from the Social Sciences'. In *Negotiating Environmental Change: New Perspectives from Social Science*, edited by F. Berkhout, Melissa Leach, and Ian Scoones, 33–76. Cheltenham, UK: Edward Elgar Publishing, 2003.

Stokes, Leah Cardamore. *Short Circuiting Policy: Interest Groups and the Battle Over Clean Energy and Climate Policy in the American States*. Oxford: Oxford University Press, 2020.

Stone, Christopher D. 'Common But Differentiated Responsibilities in International Law'. *American Journal of International Law* 98, no. 2 (April 2004): 276–301. https://doi.org/10.2307/3176729.

Sturm, Thomas. 'The "Rationality Wars" in Psychology: Where They Are and Where They Could Go'. *Inquiry* 55, no. 1 (1 February 2012): 66–81. https://doi.org/10.1080/0020174X.2012.643628.

Sun, Yixian. 'China Will No Longer Build Overseas Coal Power Plants—What Energy Projects Will It Invest in Instead?' The Conversation, 28 September 2021. http://theconversation.com/china-will-no-longer-build-overseas-coal-power-plants-what-energy-projects-will-it-invest-in-instead-168614.

Taylor, Ian. *The Forum on China—Africa Cooperation (FOCAC)*. London: Routledge, 2010. https://doi.org/10.4324/9780203835005.

Teevan, Chloe, Luca Barana, Daniele Fattibene, Daniela Iacobuta, Silke Weinlich, and Steffen Bauer. 'A New Multilateralism for the Post-COVID World: What Role for the EU-Africa Partnership?' N. Bonn: European think Tanks Group, 2021. https://ettg.eu/wp-content/uploads/2021/04/ETTG_new_multilateralism_post-Covid-April_2021_final.pdf.

The Economist. 'Africa's Population Will Double by 2050 |', March 2020. https://www.economist.com/special-report/2020/03/26/africas-pop ulation-will-double-by-2050.

'The Path to Net Zero by 2050 Is Narrow and Challenging'. *Emerald Expert Briefings* oxan-db, no. oxan-db (1 January 2021). https://doi.org/10.1108/ OXAN-DB263035.

Thomas, Adelle, and Emily Theokritoff. 'Debt-for-Climate Swaps for Small Islands'. *Nature Climate Change* 11, no. 11 (November 2021): 889–91. https://doi.org/10.1038/s41558-021-01194-4.

Tienhaara, Kyla. 'Regulatory Chill in a Warming World: The Threat to Climate Policy Posed by Investor-State Dispute Settlement'. *Transnational Environmental Law* 7, no. 2 (July 2018): 229–50. https://doi.org/10.1017/S20 47102517000309.

Tienhaara, Kyla, and Christian Downie. 'Risky Business? The Energy Charter Treaty, Renewable Energy, and Investor-State Disputes'. *Global Governance: A Review of Multilateralism and International Organizations* 24, no. 3 (12 September 2018): 451–71. https://doi.org/10.1163/19426720-02403009.

Trollip, Hilton, Bryce McCall, and Chris Bataille. 'How Green Primary Iron Production in South Africa Could Help Global Decarbonization'. *Climate Policy* 22, no. 2 (13 January 2022): 236–247. https://doi.org/10.1080/ 14693062.2021.2024123.

Turunen, Linda Lisa Maria, and Minna Halme. 'Communicating Actionable Sustainability Information to Consumers: The Shades of Green Instrument for Fashion'. *Journal of Cleaner Production* 297 (15 May 2021): 126605. https://doi.org/10.1016/j.jclepro.2021.126605.

UN. 'Agenda 21'. Rio de Janeiro: United Nations, 1992. https://sustainabled evelopment.un.org/content/documents/Agenda21.pdf.

UN. 'Declaration of the United Nations Conference on the Human Environment'. United Nations, 1972. https://legal.un.org/avl/ha/dunche/dunche. html.

———. 'Hague Declaration on the Environment*'. *International Legal Materials* 28, no. 5 (September 1989): 1308–10. https://doi.org/10.1017/S00 20782900022750.

———. 'Protection of Global Climate for Present and Future Generations of Mankind': UN, 17 January 1991. http://digitallibrary.un.org/record/ 196769.

———. 'Rio Declaration on Environment and Development'. Rio de Janeiro: United Nations General Assembly, 1992. https://www.un.org/en/develo pment/desa/population/migration/generalassembly/docs/globalcompact/ A_CONF.151_26_Vol.I_Declaration.pdf.

—. 'United Nations Conference on Environment and Development (UNCED), Earth Summit'. Rio de Janeiro, 1992. https://sustainabledevelopment.un.org/milestones/unced.

UNCED. 'Agenda 21'. Rio de Janeiro: United Nations, 1992. https://sustainabledevelopment.un.org/outcomedocuments/agenda21.

UNCTAD. 'Nairobi Securities Exchange Joins United Nations Sustainable Stock Exchanges Initiative | UNCTAD'. UNCTAD | Prosperity for All, 10 March 2015. https://unctad.org/news/nairobi-securities-exchange-joins-united-nations-sustainable-stock-exchanges-initiative.

—. 'A European Union Carbon Border Adjustment Mechanism: Implications for Developing Countries'. Geneva, Switzerland: United Nations Conference on Trade and Development, 2021. https://unctad.org/system/files/official-document/osginf2021d2_en.pdf.

UNDP, and GoK. 'Private Sector Engagement and Coordination Framework for the Implementation of the National Climate Change Action Plan in Kenya'. New York and Nairobi: United Nations Development Program (UNDP); Government of Kenya, April 2019. https://www1.undp.org/content/dam/LECB/docs/pubs-reports/undp-ndcsp-kenya-private-sector-framework-final.pdf.

UNEP. 'In Defence of the Earth. The Basic Texts on Environment: Founex. Stockholm. Cocoyoc'. Executive Series. Nairobi, Kenya: United Nations Environment Programme, 1981.

—. 'Press Backgrounder: A Brief History of the Climate Change Convention'. Bonn, Germany: Information Unit for Conventions, United Nations Environment Programme, 1997. https://unfccc.int/cop3/fccc/info/backgrod.htm#:~:text=The%20Berlin%20Mandate%20calls%20on,new%20commitments%20for%20developing%20countries.

—. 'About AMCEN'. UNEP—UN Environment Programme, 31 October 2019. http://www.unep.org/regions/africa/african-ministerial-conference-environment/about-amcen.

UNFCCC. 'Decision-/CP.20. Lima Call for Climate Action'. United Nations Framework Convention on Climate Change (UNFCCC), 2014. https://unfccc.int/files/meetings/lima_dec_2014/application/pdf/auv_cop20_lima_call_for_climate_action.pdf.

—. *Paris Agreement on Climate Change*. New York: United Nations, 2015. https://unfccc.int/sites/default/files/english_paris_agreement.pdf.

—. 'GCAP UNFCCC—Home Page'. Global Climate Action—NAZCA, 2022. https://climateaction.unfccc.int/.

UNGA. 'UN Conference on Environment and Development': New York: United Nations, 22 March 1990. http://digitallibrary.un.org/record/82555.

Urpelainen, Johannes, and Thijs Van de Graaf. 'United States Non-Cooperation and the Paris Agreement'. *Climate Policy* 18, no. 7 (9 August 2018): 839–51. https://doi.org/10.1080/14693062.2017.1406843.

USGOV. 'Text of a Letter from the President'. Washington, DC: The White House, 13 March 2001. https://georgewbush-whitehouse.archives.gov/news/releases/2001/03/20010314.html.

———. 'FACT SHEET: President Biden and G7 Leaders Launch Build Back Better World (B3W) Partnership'. The White House, 12 June 2021. https://www.whitehouse.gov/briefing-room/statements-releases/2021/06/12/fact-sheet-president-biden-and-g7-leaders-launch-build-back-better-world-b3w-partnership/.

Vakulchuk, Roman, Indra Overland, and Daniel Scholten. 'Renewable Energy and Geopolitics: A Review'. *Renewable and Sustainable Energy Reviews* 122 (1 April 2020): 109547. https://doi.org/10.1016/j.rser.2019.109547.

Van de Graaf, Thijs, Indra Overland, Daniel Scholten, and Kirsten Westphal. 'The New Oil? The Geopolitics and International Governance of Hydrogen'. *Energy Research & Social Science* 70 (1 December 2020): 101667. https://doi.org/10.1016/j.erss.2020.101667.

van Soest, Heleen L., Michel G. J. den Elzen, and Detlef P. van Vuuren. 'Net-Zero Emission Targets for Major Emitting Countries Consistent with the Paris Agreement'. *Nature Communications* 12, no. 1 (9 April 2021): 2140. https://doi.org/10.1038/s41467-021-22294-x.

Vellinga, Pier, and Robert Swart. 'The Greenhouse Marathon: A Proposal for Global Strategy'. *Climatic Change; (Netherlands)* 18, no. 1 (1 January 1991). https://doi.org/10.1007/BF00142501.

Vernengo, Matías. 'The Consolidation of Dollar Hegemony After the Collapse of Bretton Woods: Bringing Power Back in'. *Review of Political Economy* 33, no. 4 (2 October 2021): 529–51. https://doi.org/10.1080/09538259.2021.1950966.

Victor, David G. 'International Agreements and the Struggle to Tame Carbon'. In *Global Climate Change*, edited by James N. Griffin, 204–40. Bush Series in the Economics of Public Policy. Cheltenham, UK and Northampton, MA: Edward Elgar Publishing, 2003.

Voigt, Christina. 'The Compliance and Implementation Mechanism of the Paris Agreement'. *Review of European, Comparative & International Environmental Law* 25, no. 2 (2016): 161–73. https://doi.org/10.1111/reel.12155.

Voigt, Christina, and Felipe Ferreira. '"Dynamic Differentiation": The Principles of CBDR-RC, Progression and Highest Possible Ambition in the Paris Agreement'. *Transnational Environmental Law* 5, no. 2 (October 2016): 285–303. https://doi.org/10.1017/S2047102516000212.

Volz, Ulrich, Shamshad Akhtar, Kevin P. Gallagher, Stephany Griffith-Jones, Jörg Haas, and Moritz Kraemer. 'Debt Relief for a Green and Inclusive Recovery: Securing Private-Sector Participation and Creating Policy Space for Sustainable Development'. Berlin, London, and Boston, MA: Heinrich Böll Stiftung; Boston University Global Development Policy Center; Centre for Sustainable Finance SOAS University of London, June 2021. https://eprints.soas.ac.uk/35254/1/DRGR%20Report%202021.pdf.

Walt, Stephen M. 'Rigor or Rigor Mortis? Rational Choice and Security Studies'. *International Security* 23, no. 4 (1 April 1999): 5–48. https://doi.org/10.1162/isec.23.4.5.

Waltz, Kenneth N. 'The Stability of a Bipolar World'. *Daedalus* 93, no. 3 (1964): 881–909.

Wambua, Clarice. 'The Kenya Climate Change Act 2016: Emerging Lessons From a Pioneer Law'. *Carbon & Climate Law Review* 13, no. 4 (2019): 257–69. https://doi.org/10.21552/cclr/2019/4/6.

Watts, Jonathan. 'China Pledge to Stop Funding Coal Projects "Buys Time for Emissions Target"'. *The Guardian*, 22 September 2021, sec. World news. https://www.theguardian.com/world/2021/sep/22/china-pledge-to-stop-funding-coal-projects-buys-time-for-emissions-target.

Webb, Michael C., and Stephen D. Krasner. 'Hegemonic Stability Theory: An Empirical Assessment'. *Review of International Studies* 15, no. 2 (1989): 183–98.

Welch, Claude E. 'Emerging Patterns of Civil-Military Relations in Africa: Radical Coups d'Etat and Political Stability'. In *African Security Issues: Sovereignty, Stability, and Solidarity*. London: Routledge, 1984.

Werksman, Jacob. 'Compliance and the Use of Trade Measures'. In *Promoting Compliance in an Evolving Climate Regime*, edited by Jutta Brunnée, Lavanya Rajamani, and Meinhard Doelle, 262–85. Cambridge: Cambridge University Press, 2011. https://doi.org/10.1017/CBO9780511979286.017.

White, Robin C. A. 'A New International Economic Order'. *International & Comparative Law Quarterly* 24, no. 3 (1975): 542–52. https://doi.org/10.1093/iclqaj/24.3.542.

Williams, Ollie. 'Zambia's Default Fuels Fears of African "Debt Tsunami" as Covid Impact Bites'. *The Guardian*, 25 November 2020, sec. Global Development. https://www.theguardian.com/global-development/2020/nov/25/zambias-default-fuels-fears-of-african-debt-tsunami-as-covid-impact-bites.

Winkler, Harald, Anya Boyd, Marta Torres Gunfaus, and Stefan Raubenheimer. 'Reconsidering Development by Reflecting on Climate Change'. *International Environmental Agreements: Politics, Law and Economics* 15, no. 4 (1 November 2015): 369–85. https://doi.org/10.1007/s10784-015-9304-7.

Winkler, Harald, Emily Tyler, Samantha Keen, and Andrew Marquard. 'Just Transition Transaction in South Africa: An Innovative Way to Finance Accelerated Phase out of Coal and Fund Social Justice'. *Journal of Sustainable Finance & Investment* (3 September 2021): 1–24. https://doi.org/10.1080/20430795.2021.1972678.

Xolisa, Ngwadla. 'Equitable Access to Sustainable Development: Relevance to Negotiations and Actions on Climate Change'. Cape Town, South Africa: Mitigation Action Plan & Scenarios (MAPS), 2013. http://www.mapsprogramme.org/wp-content/uploads/EASD-Relevance-to-negotiations_Paper.pdf.

Zhang, Yiping, and Olaf Weber. 'Investors' Moral and Financial Concerns—Ethical and Financial Divestment in the Fossil Fuel Industry'. *Sustainability* 14, no. 4 (January 2022): 1952. https://doi.org/10.3390/su14041952.

Zimm, Caroline, and Nebojsa Nakicenovic. 'What Are the Implications of the Paris Agreement for Inequality?' *Climate Policy* 20, no. 4 (20 April 2020): 458–67. https://doi.org/10.1080/14693062.2019.1581048.

INDEX

A

Abuja Treaty, 237

Access to sustainable development (EASD), 58

Africa+1 Initiatives, 105

Africa Continental Free Trade Agreement (AFCFTA), 1, 8, 65, 195, 202, 259, 261

African countries, 1–3, 5, 7, 8, 14, 16, 26, 30, 31, 47–49, 51, 52, 56, 65–67, 86, 87, 89, 93, 98–105, 127, 128, 131, 141–148, 159–161, 172, 175, 176, 189–194, 196–198, 200–205, 232, 233, 237–241, 244, 245, 259, 260

African Development Bank (AfDB), 203, 214, 238, 250

African Group of Negotiators (AGN), 87, 99, 100, 237

African Ministerial Conference on the Environment (AMCEN), 237

African Union (AU), 1, 190, 203, 206, 209–211, 214, 236, 237, 260, 261

Africa Research and Impact Network (ARIN), 239, 250

Annex I countries, 18, 19, 23, 93–95, 97, 147

Asia Pacific Partnership on Clean Development and Climate, 59, 137

B

Belt and Road Initiative (BRI), 25, 102–104

Berlin Mandate, 58, 73, 135, 151

Brundtland report, 56, 133, 149, 150

Build Back Better World (B3W), 25, 104

© The Editor(s) (if applicable) and The Author(s), under exclusive license to Springer Nature Switzerland AG 2023
K. Mbeva et al., *Africa's Right to Development in a Climate-Constrained World*, Contemporary African Political Economy,
https://doi.org/10.1007/978-3-031-22887-2

304 INDEX

C

Carbon Border Adjustment Mechanism (CBAM), 104, 194, 195, 201
Carbon dioxide emissions, 29
Chad, 3, 22, 192
China, 7, 18, 21, 23–25, 58, 59, 64, 65, 85–88, 95, 97, 98, 100–103, 130, 137, 193, 205, 242–244
Clean Development Mechanisms (CDM), 59, 103, 201, 241, 260
Climate Change Law of 2017, 162
Climate-debt swaps, 198
Climate for Development in Africa (ClimDev-Africa), 238
Climate governance, 59–62, 67, 134–137, 139, 160–163, 169, 170, 172, 175, 176
Climate Relevant Innovation Systems-builders (CRIBS) project, 240, 241
ClimateSouth project, 163, 178, 243
Coal power, 102, 196
Cocoyoc Declaration, 52, 56
Cold War, 23, 88, 89, 92, 129
Common but Differentiated Responsibility (CBDR), 25, 27, 58, 60, 61, 67, 92, 128, 129, 132, 136, 138–140, 144
Common Market for East and Southern Africa (COMESA), 64, 65, 238
Côte d'Ivoire, 55
COVID-19 pandemic, 190, 197–199

D

Decarbonisation, 105, 199–202
Democratic Republic of Congo, 100
Department for International Development (DFID), 171
Developing countries, 2, 4, 6, 7, 13, 14, 16–18, 21–27, 47, 49, 50, 52, 54–58, 60, 61, 66, 67, 86–88, 90–94, 98, 99, 101–104, 106, 127–137, 139–142, 147, 164, 172, 175, 191, 194, 205, 240, 241, 244
Development, 1–3, 6–8, 13, 14, 16, 20, 21, 23–25, 27–31, 47–59, 62, 64–66, 68, 87, 89, 90, 93, 94, 101, 103, 104, 127, 129, 131–134, 137, 141, 144, 146, 160, 163, 167, 171, 174, 189, 193, 195, 196, 198, 200, 202–205, 228, 236, 237, 240, 243–245, 259–261
Divestment movement, 192, 193
Durban Platform, 24, 26

E

Economic Community of West African States (ECOWAS), 64
Energy efficiency targets, 165
Environmental governance, 21, 49, 52, 55, 56, 61, 68, 132–136, 160
EU-Africa Green New Deal, 103
European Union (EU), 24, 25, 62, 63, 86, 87, 100, 103, 104, 137, 194, 244

F

Forest Stewardship Council (FSC), 160
Forum for China-Africa Cooperation (FOCAC), 101, 102, 205, 244
Fossil fuels, 7, 29, 67, 93–95, 102, 144, 192, 193, 195–197, 201–204, 259
Founex Report, 52–56, 61, 62
French, Howard, 85, 106

G

Gell-Mann, Murray, 227
Geopolitics, 85–87, 105
Getachew, Adom, 89, 107, 108
Global Compact for the Environment, 27, 67
Global Gateway initiative, 25, 104
'Governing Complexity' approach, 5, 7, 227, 233, 245
Great Climate Transformation, 2, 3, 5–8, 13–17, 19, 20, 24, 25, 28–31, 48, 67, 127, 130, 260, 261
Green Climate Fund (GCF), 28, 241
Greenhouse gas, 2, 17, 26, 28, 58, 59, 62, 87, 93, 97, 129, 135, 137, 170, 195, 200, 227

I

Industrialised countries, 2, 4, 13, 14, 17, 18, 21–26, 28, 47, 49, 50, 54, 58, 61, 66, 72, 88, 90–93, 127–129, 131–133, 135, 136, 140, 142, 191, 196, 202, 205, 240
Institute for Development Studies, Sussex University, viii
Intended Nationally Determined Contributions (INDCs), 61, 138
Intergovernmental Panel on Climate Change (IPCC), 57, 98, 134, 135
International Climate Change Taskforce, 62
International Development Research Centre (IDRC), 241
International Energy Agency (IEA), 193, 196
International Monetary Fund (IMF), 198
International Solar Alliance (ISA), 103, 244, 252

J

Juma, Calestous, 9, 10, 70, 76, 108, 211, 213, 215, 230, 231, 246, 248, 250–252, 261

K

Kenya Association of Manufacturing (KAM), 166, 167
Kenyan Counties, 167
Kenya Private Sector Alliance (KEPSA), 166, 167
Kyoto Protocol, 2, 3, 7, 17–21, 23–26, 58–60, 86, 94–97, 103, 130, 135–140, 147, 161, 201, 241, 260

L

Land-use mitigation targets, 170
Least developed countries (LDCs), 3, 26, 27, 103, 104, 139
Lima-Paris Action Agenda (LPAA), 29

M

Macrosystems, 6, 15
Mazrui, Ali, 8
Millennium Development Goals (MDGS), 27
M-KOPA project, 235, 236
Mobile-based payment systems, 235, 242
Montreal Protocol, 134, 136
Multilateral climate regime, 2, 4, 7, 17, 31, 48, 56, 85, 87, 95, 99, 128–130, 142, 147, 205
Multilateral environmental agreements (MEAs), 91, 92, 129, 229, 240

N

Najam, Adil, 21, 35, 36, 39, 49, 52, 69–72, 109, 148–150

306 INDEX

Namibia, 63, 201, 212, 237
Nationally determined contribution
(NDCs), 22, 26, 31, 48, 59–61,
66, 128, 130, 131, 139–144,
146, 148, 163, 172, 175, 191,
192, 197, 198, 202, 240, 241,
251
Neoliberal institutionalist theory, 18
New International Economic Order
(NIEO), 52, 90, 129, 240
New Partnership for Africa's
Development (NEPAD), 203
Newtonian-Cartesian static
equilibrium, 240
Nkrumah, Kwameh, 115, 236
Non-aligned movement (NAM), 89
Non-Governmental Organisations
(NGOs), 28, 171
Non-state actors (NSAs), 21, 28, 29,
148, 159–161, 163, 165, 166,
175, 176, 195, 243
Non-state Zone for Climate Action
(NAZCA), 161, 175, 176

O

Olsonian logic of cooperation, 17–19,
92, 94, 129–131
Olsonian logic of international
cooperation, 17
Organization for African Unity
(OAU), 63, 236, 237
Ostrom, Eleanor, 229, 247

P

Paris Agreement on Climate Change,
1, 20, 24, 26, 28, 75, 98, 191,
259
Pathways to Sustainability Project,
235
Prebisch, Raúl, 50

Preferential Trade Agreements
(PTAs), 4, 51
President Obama, Barack, 24, 96, 112
Prigogine, Ilya, 6, 14, 15, 17, 20, 32,
33, 107, 144, 211, 244

R

Renewable energy, 100, 102, 144,
165, 169, 170, 199, 200, 203,
235, 242
Rio Conference, 92, 131, 134
Rio Earth Summit, 56, 60

S

Second World War, 13, 85, 88, 89,
91, 129
Sino-African cooperation, 244
Small and Medium Enterprises
(SMEs), 163–165, 243
Snidal, Duncan, 19, 34, 108, 111,
112, 130, 149, 247
Social, Technological and
Environmental Pathways to
Sustainability (STEPS), 235, 242
South Africa, 35, 59, 64, 73, 103,
105, 201, 202, 241, 244, 260
South-South Cooperation, 7, 30, 101,
243, 244
Sovereign wealth funds (SWFs), 192,
201
Sustainable development, 1–3, 5–8,
16, 21, 22, 28, 48–50, 56, 131,
144, 146, 164, 172, 174, 192,
228
Sustainable Development Goals
(SDGs), 27, 174

T

Target-setting, 164, 165, 170

INDEX 307

Technology transfer, 5, 7, 49, 88, 130, 205, 240, 241, 243
Toronto Conference on Changing the Atmosphere, 57, 134
Tripartite Free Trade Agreement, 65

U

UN Centre for Science and Technology for Development, 90
UN Commission for Science and Technology for Development, 90
UN Fund on Science and Technology for Development, 90
UN institutions, 90
Union of Soviet Socialist Republics (USSR), 88, 89
United Nations Conference on Environment and Development (UNCED), 56, 58, 131, 134, 135, 149
United Nations Conference on the Human Environment (UNCHE), 52, 54, 55, 92, 132, 134
United Nations Development Program (UNDP), 90, 180

United Nations Environment Programme (UNEP), 135, 151, 171, 250
United Nations Framework Convention on Climate Change (UNFCC), 2, 4, 16–18, 20, 21, 23, 25, 27–29, 58–60, 62, 75, 86, 87, 92, 94, 96, 100, 135–138, 140, 147, 150, 152, 161, 176, 179, 191, 204, 233, 237, 241
United States (US), 18, 21, 23–25, 28, 58–60, 64, 65, 85–89, 92, 94–100, 104, 105, 129, 136–138, 194, 244
US B3W, 25, 104
US President Bush, George, 24, 59, 94–96, 137

W

World Climate Conference, 57, 134
World Commission on Environment and Development (WCED), 56, 133
World Trade Organization (WTO), 4, 51, 193, 204